DANTON

DANTON

A BIOGRAPHY
by Robert Christophe

TRANSLATED FROM THE FRENCH

by Peter Green

DOUBLEDAY & COMPANY, INC.
GARDEN CITY, NEW YORK
1967

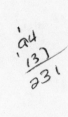

Contents

Prologue

IN THE MIDDLE OF the nineteenth century the most respected citizen of the little French town of Noirt was an incredibly wrinkled old lady named Louise Dupin. Rumor had it that Madame Dupin had been a great and famous beauty in her youth and that she had been the wife of a great man of the Revolution. But the respect in which she was held by her fellow citizens was, with Gallic practicality, based upon more recent accomplishments, and the good Noirtais were careful to greet her as "Madame la Baronne" (for these were the palmy days of the Second Empire) or as "Madame la Préfète"—the Governor's lady.

Louise, Baroness Dupin, had known and lived through—to take them in reverse chronological order—such diverse events as the establishment of Napoleon III on the throne of France, the Second Republic, the 1848 Revolution, the July Monarchy of Louis-Philippe and the June Days, the Empire and the Consulate, 18 Brumaire, the Directory, 9 Thermidor, the Revolution, and, lastly, the final years of Louis XVI and Marie-Antoinette. What memories she had to draw upon in the evening, by the fireside, when her grandchildren demanded: "Grandmother, tell us about . . . ," "Grandmama, tell us the story of . . ."

Then the ancient baroness, widow of the Governor of Les Deux-Sèvres, would collect the fleeting scraps of the past that lingered still in her mind. She could tell the story of Napoleon's first appearance at Noirt, in August of 1808, en route from

Bordeaux to Paris. Josephine was with him, and the imperial couple had slept—a few hours only, for the Corsican was always in a hurry—in Madame Dupin's own bedroom. Or Louise could look back still further, to Paris before the Empire. Born in the capital at a time when Marie-Antoinette still was playing at being a shepherdess, she could recall her departure for Noirt in 1800. Her husband had just been appointed Governor of the *département* of Les Deux-Sèvres, and had been charged by First Consul Bonaparte with the pacification of the Vendée.

Louise had been married to Claude Dupin since 1796, and she was twenty-two at the time of the move to Noirt. Yet, though her venture into matrimony was fairly precocious—she was but eighteen at the time—it could not be regarded entirely as a first plunge. The youthful Madame Dupin (née Gély) had been married before.

Louise hardly ever mentioned her first husband. Barely sixteen when she married him in 1793 at the height of the Terror, how could the old lady be expected to remember him in 1856? She had loved him, beyond a doubt, but for a few brief months only. Now, in the twilight of her life, the memory of the episode had become blurred. Yet she could recall clearly enough her drawing room in the rue des Cordeliers, and herself wearing a satin dress and posing for the famous painter Boilly. The First Republic's most fashionable artist was recording for posterity the features of Madame Danton, as Louise was then called.

And then Germinal came; the attack by Robespierre and his supporters; Danton's arrest; the Revolutionary Tribunal; the scaffold. And Louise Danton, still only sixteen, found herself Danton's widow. It is hardly to be wondered at that, after two solitary years, she changed the whole pattern of her life; or that, four years later, she was only too glad to turn a deaf ear to the clamor of Paris.

Time passed. The imperial epoch came and went. In 1815 the Governor of Les Deux-Sèvres was removed from office by the reinstated Bourbons and returned to live in the capital. After the political temperature of the times had had time to subside, Dupin was appointed by Louis XVIII to a senior judgeship. He died on November 11, 1828.

Widowed for the second time, Louise once more abandoned

the city of her birth. The tranquillity of provincial life was more to her liking than the bustle of Paris; besides, the city had only grim associations for her, while Noirt was a place of friends. So she returned to Les Deux-Sèvres, where she lived for another twenty-eight years.

Since July of 1856 the remains of Louise Dupin have reposed in the cemetery at Noirt; but when the gravestone was laid over that frail body it did not succeed in shutting out the echoes of Georges Danton's extraordinary life. "You must never speak to me of *him*," Claude Dupin had commanded his young wife. But historians, those enemies of human privacy, have little by little uncovered the secrets that Louise knew. Every decade, indeed almost every year, new material emerges from the obscurity to which collectors, private families, and lawyers have relegated it. Such material, some old and some hitherto unpublished, is the source on which the author has drawn for the present work.

CHAPTER I

The Café du Parnasse

EVERY PARISIAN KNOWS the rue de l'Arbre-Sec and the rue de la Monnaie. They run from the Seine in the direction of Les Halles and form a block which contains, among other things, one of the large La Samaritaine chain stores and the main entrance to the Pont-Neuf Métro station.

In the time of Louis XVI these same two streets enclosed, on the same site, a pair of houses which were to be among the victims of the demolition workers of the nineteenth century. The ground floor of one of them was a restaurant, the Café du Parnasse. But despite this official name, which appeared in letters of wrought iron on the sign, its clientele always referred to the place as the Café de l'École. The reason, it seems clear, was because it looked out on the Quai de l'École, known today as the Quai du Louvre.

The café possessed no outside terrace. From its windows one had a view of the Seine, and of the Pont-Neuf, and of a curious monument no longer in existence—an edifice erected on piles and attached to the bridge, which housed a pumping apparatus. This pump was lowered into the river, sucked up water from it, and distributed it to the neighborhood. It was known, appropriately enough, as La Samaritaine ("the Samaritan"), a nickname taken from a gilded lead statue beside it representing Jesus and the woman of Samaria at Jacob's well. A little farther off one could see the equestrian statue of Le Vert-Galant, and—if one turned one's head to the left—the houses on the Place Dauphine and along the Quai des Morfondus (today the Quai de l'Horloge), and, finally, the towers of the Law Courts, the Palais de Justice.

To get from the Law Courts to the Café du Parnasse (or Café de l'École) took no more than five or six minutes on foot. Was this the reason why its clientele consisted largely of judges and lawyers? Partly, perhaps; but there was another cause. Though the proprietor often helped out his waiters, taking orders himself with a napkin over one arm, he was no ordinary innkeeper. As an Inspector of Tax Concessions (that is, an officially appointed examiner of taxes levied), Sieur Charpentier not only served drinks, he also served the State.

He served drinks to customers who arrived wearing the cocked hat or the magistrate's cap of office. The State he served by checking the accounts of the "tax farmers." These latter had nothing to do with agriculture. They were civil servants who had bought their appointments (just as M. Charpentier himself had done) and who were responsible for collecting taxes and delivering the money to the Treasury—after each took his own slice. M. Charpentier's business was mainly to see that this slice did not get too large. Whenever he discovered any such exaggeration in a tax farmer's books, the government paid Charpentier a fixed percentage of the amount involved. In good and bad years alike, the income this brought him was never less than 3000 *livres*—which meant that Charpentier continued to draw his commission when the taxpayer was protesting most bitterly at the assessments, poor relief, salt tax, and tithes he found himself required to pay. And since protests sometimes led to legal actions (which very often rebounded to the discomfort of the plaintiff) François-Jérôme Charpentier could combine his two businesses and talk over these suits with his customers— the lawyers who, in court robes or town dress, would drop in to taste his wines, drink his cider, or flirt, very discreetly, with his wife. The fact that M. Charpentier managed successfully to handle two so strikingly different jobs was of no surprise to anybody. The eighteenth century was rich in anomalies of this sort. At Châlons, for instance, we find a certain Maître Failly who was both a magistrate and a wine merchant; and in Paris there was a M. Robert who ran a grocer's shop in the intervals of teaching common law.

Mme. Charpentier presided over the till. Her maiden name had been Angélique Soldini, and she was Italian by origin, a dark-skinned woman who much resembled the models used by the Florentine painters. Though she was always smiling and eager to please, she commanded respect. Elegantly dressed, she was responsible for the supervision both of the waiters and of the servants' hall. When her husband was away attending to his duties as a tax-farming inspector, Angélique used to welcome the customers on his behalf.

The atmosphere in the Café de l'École was conditioned by its distinguished proprietors and customers. Ladies' hands were kissed there, and people talked in subdued voices. Gaming was rare, apart from dominos and the occasional hand of lotto—the latter a game of chance that would lead grumblers to quote a couple of quatrains by the Comte de Ségur:

> Though lotto may not please all views
> It will, no doubt, be long in fashion;
> 'Tis every trifler's best excuse,
> And every wit's new relaxation.

> This truly philosophic game
> Is our great social leveler-down:
> The tyranny of self-esteem
> To lotto now must yield its crown.

It was very rarely that a burst of loud argument would be heard at the marble-topped tables. Even when the talk turned to politics, restraint was observed. Yet the monarchy was guttering down to its end, and a host of new ideas, launched by the *philosophes,* were causing ferment everywhere. The returning veterans of the American War of Independence fanned this flame. Surrounded by incompetent Ministers, the King floundered on, never deviating from a routine which by now was giving serious cause for alarm. After Joly de Fleury and d'Ormesson, Louis XVI had sent for Calonne. Finding the Treasury on its last legs, Calonne decided to float a loan; he was of the opinion that the best way to attract investors was by a shopwindow display of nonexistent wealth. "People only lend to the rich" was one of his favorite remarks. By showering largesse abroad, however, he merely aggravated the deficit, and by increasing direct taxation he became the target for public abuse. And as this Minister was encouraging the Court—the Queen in particular—to feign conspicuous affluence, he unintentionally focused and intensified resentment against "the Austrian woman." There was a broadsheet ballad, sold under the counter, which put the following lines into the mouth of Marie-Antoinette:

> It's not Calonne himself I love
> But all the gold he throws about.
> The only time I turn to *him*
> Is when my cash is running out.
> So does my girl friend, and afterward we
> Have a good laugh at him, quietly—
> Quietly, quietly, quietly.

One evening in 1784 M. Charpentier saw a customer come in who was unfamiliar to him: a giant of a man with a somewhat ugly face, his skin still scarred by the ravages of smallpox. This was Danton. He looked in his mid-thirties but was in fact only twenty-five. His dress was respectable, but no more than respectable. He wore the long double-breasted tail coat that was the uniform of the bourgeoisie, a waistcoat with vertical red stripes, gray breeches, white stockings, and buckle shoes. He had on a wig, but it was unpowdered, and affected a short pigtail done up with a ribbon. His plain white linen cravat looked very unassuming beside that of the landlord, a splendid muslin affair trimmed with lace.

The newcomer observed one or two acquaintances among the clientele, and nodded to them discreetly. Another of those legal fellows, M. Charpentier thought to himself. Though Danton's physical appearance hardly suggested the office boy, the simplicity of his attire nevertheless (to the proprietor's way of thinking) identified him as a clerk whose business it was to run menial errands for some advocate in chambers.

Angélique's husband was only half wrong. Georges Danton did, in fact, run errands for Maître Vinot, a parliamentary lawyer. But he also "covered the courts" for him. Every morning he set out from his employer's chambers in the Île Saint-Louis to take various notes and cases into town. Afterward he would go on to the Law Courts and keep an eye on M. Vinot's interests there, acting as the lawyer's representative and drawing up legal documents on his behalf as long as the courts were in session. The young clerk could muster scant enthusiasm for his relationship with these smooth-talking lawyers. He was built more like an athlete, and felt a need for the kind of action which legal pettifoggery—especially at such a subordinate level —could hardly begin to satisfy.

M. Charpentier saw him again, more than once, in the Café de l'École. As the weeks and months went by, Danton was to become one of his most regular customers. Over a glass of wine one tends to become talkative, and little by little the Charpentiers got to know the newcomer. Georges-Jacques Danton had been born at Arcis-sur-Aube on October 26, 1759, the son of a local bailiff's court clerk. His mother, whose maiden name was Camus, already had four daughters when her son appeared in the world. When Abbé Leflon, the parish priest, baptized the infant lying in the arms of its godfather and godmother—Uncle Georges Camus and a young lady, Mlle. Papillon—he could scarcely have realized that, by giving his blessing to the newborn child, he was ushering in one of the most fateful chapters in all French history.

As was customary, the whole family attended the ceremony. There were two attorneys and a sheriff's officer from Troyes; a postmaster—that is, the official in charge of a relay post for horses; a joiner, several farmers, and a merchant, all with their decent if somewhat countrified wives. Finally, there were two priests: Father Nicolas Danton, *curé* of Allemanche, and Father Pierre Danton, *curé* of Saint-Lyé. All the Dantons were distinguished by their height and girth, their cool impudence, and their capacity to drive a hard bargain. Georges was built in the family mold and had inherited all his ancestral characteristics. One anecdote will suffice to illustrate his impudence. When he arrived in Paris, at the age of twenty-one, he sought an interview with Maître Vinot.

"What can you do?" the lawyer asked him. No doubt the young man's reply left him unsatisfied, because he said, finally: "Do you write a fair hand? I'll take you on as a clerk."

With ill-concealed fury Danton replied: "Do you think I came here to *copy letters?*"

M. Vinot concealed his amusement. This applicant's self-confidence appealed to him. He took the young man on to do his donkey work and to substitute for him in the Law Courts. His effrontery had earned him the customary bed and board such posts carried at the time—not to mention an occupation which would bring him into touch with every eminent lawyer in Paris. But the satisfaction this gave him did not last for long. He found the art of public debate more to his taste than legal minutiae—but in order to indulge his taste for oratory he would have first to qualify for an attorney's gown. The young Danton was ambitious, and spent the larger part of his free time studying law. He possessed enough intelligence to tackle the subject on his own, without a teacher. When he was a boarder at the college in Troyes, had he not learned Latin, Italian, and English without any trouble? Indeed, he now spoke them fluently.

It was, in fact, his knowledge of Italian which gave him a pull with the Charpentiers—who had many connections among the lawyers frequenting the Café du Parnasse. Mme. Charpentier, having been born on the far side of the Alps, was only too pleased to chatter away in her mother tongue with this young bullnecked clerk. It gave her a quite childish delight to answer his *"Buon giorno, Signora!"* Then the sly devil would ask her, with a wink so ironic that it removed the least suspicion of concupiscence: *"E in casa il Signor Charpentier?"* And she would enter into the game and reply: *"No, il Signore è uscito."* Then the conversation would begin in earnest, enlivened by sparkling flashes of southern wit and verve. It was all, quite clearly, on a most honorable level; Danton was only making use of his hostess to further his ambitions, and in any case respected her too much to make any advances. Besides, she was a good deal older than he was. If he made a show of paying court to this still youthful-looking and desirable woman, she probably thought he was merely indulging in the mild, witty style of flirtation so fashionable at this period. Had he not addressed playful verses to Maître Vinot's wife? With Angélique—no, *Angelica*—Charpentier he discussed Tasso, Ariosto, or Dante. He possessed a prodigious memory and would recite her whole cantos of *Orlando Furioso* or the *Inferno*. Often the customers would gather around and listen while he declaimed. His powerful personality turned naturally to the gestures and eloquence of the public platform. Rounds of applause would ring out; when Danton's warm, slightly theatrical voice began to speak, the normal silence of the Café de l'École was broken. And there must have been many who thought: He's got the makings of an orator—or a mountebank.

The Charpentiers' children would sometimes be present on these occasions. There was the elder son, Victor, whose wife had considerable talent as a painter; his young brother Antoine-François, who was studying jurisprudence with the intention of becoming a notary; and the daughter, Antoinette-Gabrielle, who as yet seldom appeared in the café. Very soon, however, she would begin helping her mother to look after the till and organize the staff. It was then that Danton was to strike up a friendship with her and feel the first stirrings of love.

But as yet the young clerk had no idea of the turn his feelings would take. As he told his listeners the story of his childhood he spoke in his usual jovial manner: his eyes glinted mischievously as he sketched the perils and hazards of his early years. Arcis-sur-Aube, the town where he was born, had less than three thousand inhabitants. It lies on the road from Châlons-sur-Marne to Troyes, and is built along a meandering river that flows at the foot of a wooded hillside. The district is known as *la Champagne pouilleuse*—the barren region of Champagne. At this period it was extremely poor; it was not until much later that it would reap the benefits of agricultural technology.

To his new friends Danton spoke of the chalky, pine-clad slopes, of the flat plainland where rye and buckwheat struggled to survive in the thin soil. In the midst of this pampas-like scene Arcis stood, an oasis of greenery that reminded the young clerk of his exploits in the meadow-flanked River Aube. He was an intrepid swimmer (the fact that few of his contemporaries could swim at all probably boosted his reputation); at the age of twelve he had caught pneumonia and very nearly died of it. He was an unruly child, always running off where his mother could not keep an eye on him. When he was out in the pastures he would sometimes suck the milk from the cows' udders. One evening a bull set on him, and split his lips with a blow from its horn. Determined to get his revenge, the boy came back three days later and tried to settle matters with the beast. He emerged from the lists with a broken nose. On another occasion he was trampled on by a herd of pigs. These encounters left scars that lasted all his life. His face was also pitted with the remains of innumerable smallpox scars. He would never be anything but ugly. The famous Mme. Roland was to describe him, in her *Memoirs*, as "repulsive and hideous." But Manon exaggerated. Since she could feel nothing for this muscular giant, she was always inclined to emphasize his shortcomings. When one looked at him in silence, he might have seemed rather terrifying. But the moment he opened his mouth, that extraordinary charm began to work, and Danton seemed almost handsome.

So, at any rate, he appeared to Gabrielle, the landlord's daughter. When they first met, she found this stentorian lawyer's clerk alarming. When she knew him better, the adolescent girl came to feel an emotion for him that she did not analyze. A childhood friend of Danton's, Alexandre de Saint-Albin, was afterward to write about these two young people: "She admired his wit, which most people found too sharp; she admired his spirit, which most people felt was too ardent and impulsive; and the voice which seemed to most people loud and frightening *she found gentle*." It must be admitted that Danton knew how to moderate it sometimes.

It was not always his exploits as an unruly urchin with which he regaled his listeners at the Parnasse. He would also often tell stories about his studious and independent boyhood. Then his eyes would gleam under that powerful forehead, and the light in them would hold his audience spellbound. From the lips which that Arcis bull's horn had split and scarred, the Charpentiers heard, in the end, the whole tale of his unhappy childhood and adolescence. He was not three years old when his father passed away, at forty, leaving four small daughters, a boy, and a pregnant wife. (In her grief the poor woman produced a still-born child.) Her brother, M. Camus the joiner, and her various brothers-in-law, the priests, the lawyers, and the sheriff's officer, all helped the young widow to manage her inheritance, which was tied up in houses and land. Georges was turned over to a governess but preferred to play truant. His elder sisters were more amenable to reason but very little better behaved. Exhausted by the noisy and unruly household for which she was responsible, Mme. Danton finally resolved to start life over again. In 1770 she married an Arcis merchant called Recordain, a widower with one child to bring up. But if she hoped to find happiness in this new union she was doomed to disappointment. No doubt Jean Recordain proved himself an excellent husband. No doubt he bestowed every affection on his stepdaughters and his stepson. But he made his wife pregnant on four occasions, and every time the child died while still a baby. He also attempted to market a device for spinning cotton—this was before Richard Lenoir had imported the mule jenny from England—and, as things turned out, this crazy enterprise ruined him.

Meanwhile he enrolled little Georges, now aged ten, in the local preparatory school. Here was another setback. The boy showed no more liking for mathematics than he did for history or geography. On the other hand, he seemed to take naturally to Latin. This slight penchant was enough (in his stepfather's mind at any rate) to decide the boy's future. Georges would be a priest. It was the obvious choice. In October of 1773, Georges was sent away to the minor seminary at Troyes.

Every morning the Lazarists who ran the seminary would take their boarders to the college of the Oratorians. Here Georges Danton picked up Latin without any difficulty. It turned out that he had a natural linguistic gift, so he learned English and Italian as well. The rest of the curriculum he found less interesting; he much preferred the clandestine card games he played with the four companions who were to remain his friends, colleagues, and collaborators when the name of Danton had been crowned with glory and blood. They were the future Minister Jules Paré; Edme Courtois, later to become a Deputy; Louis Béon, a "conforming" priest; and Alexandre de Saint-Albin, whom Barras employed as his private secretary, and who edited the great stateman's *Memoirs* for publication.

Through the two last-named, Béon and Saint-Albin, history was to learn one or two of their fellow pupil's schoolboy pranks.

Both devoted scant space to his early years, but what they did put down was full of racy detail. "The Republican," as he was already nicknamed at the seminary, could not stomach the school's religious atmosphere. The endless ringing of bells drove him crazy. "They'll be ringing for my funeral in the end," he grumbled. After desperate entreaties to his stepfather, he was allowed to move into the *pension* run by a teacher named M. Richard. Here, in this secular institution (its pupils also attended the Oratorians' classes), Danton could breathe more freely. The result of the move was unexpected. Not content with keeping up his high standards in Latin and English and Italian, the onetime dunce in all other subjects proceeded to sweep the board with them, too.

His constant readiness to be up in arms against injustice meant that the masters had their work cut out to deal with him. Every day he met his friends from the seminary in class. One morning, during the rhetoric period, Paré did not know the work he had been assigned. The master, one Father Béranger, wanted to rap him on the fingertips, a punishment traditionally reserved for the senior class. The smaller culprits were given a good spanking. At the age of sixteen, Paré rebelled against such a penalty. He refused to place his hands in the proper position, fingertips touching, to receive the strokes of the ruler. It did too much damage, he said, morally as well as physically. The master flew into a rage and insisted that the culprit submit to authority. But Danton sprang to his friend's defense. As though speaking in a debate, he launched an impassioned plea against corporal punishment, whether inflicted at school or in the army or as an instrument of law. The thunderous voice that was later to astonish the world now rang out for the first time before a captive audience. This unlooked-for counsel won his case: the Rector forbade Father Béranger to punish his pupil in that way. Danton had found his vocation; he would be the champion of the weak and the oppressed. Meanwhile he acquired a quite staggering reputation throughout the college.

He took advantage of this to play one very cool trick indeed. During that year (1775) the Cathedral of Rheims was preparing to welcome Louis XVI for his coronation. Here was a fine essay subject, which the French master duly gave his pupils. On

June 11, the day after this task had been set, Danton was missing from his class. The Rector thought he must be ill in bed at M. Richard's *pension,* while M. Richard himself thought he had left for college as he did every morning. In actual fact, he was rattling along toward Rheims. Greatly daring, he had decided to observe the ceremony as an eyewitness in order to write a better account of it; he preferred direct observation to the more or less distorting eye of fancy. Where, we may wonder, did he get the money for his seat in the coach? The journey was one of twenty-eight leagues (or seventy miles) at a rate of thirteen sous a league. Rousselin de Saint-Albin, who is the source for this story, believes that his friend borrowed the eighteen francs off some of his classmates.

But at any rate he reached Rheims. He watched, we are told, "all the ceremonies." Though he had no invitation, he nevertheless managed to worm his way into the Cathedral and get glimpses of the officiating clergy, the young King, his dazzling Queen, and the Court. He heard Louis XVI, hand resting on the Gospel, swear "to rule according to law and for the welfare of the nation." All this enchanted the young student. Unfortunately he also heard the sovereign, in compliance with a barbarous custom, extend his oath to include "the extermination of heretics." This threat he found utterly disgusting.

The rest of Saint-Albin's narrative—his return to Troyes, the cheers of his comrades, the brilliant quality of his essay, M. Richard and the Rector's joint threats to send him back home to his family as a punishment—all this sounds highly exaggerated. How could a sixteen-year-old schoolboy, even if he was a head higher than most adults, have got past the barriers and mingled with the elegant crowd of invited guests? Yet if we can trust Louis Béon, who confirms Saint-Albin's account, the story is true enough. It may be implausible in detail, but it is certainly characteristic. At sixteen the future Minister was already "a person of audacity."

Did the hero of this youthful outburst tell the story to the Charpentiers—in Italian to the landlord-*cum*-tax-inspector's wife, and with half hints and gallant smiles to their daughter Gabrielle? Everything suggests that he did. This native of Champagne had the true southerner's gift of gab.

In 1786, at the time when he was becoming a regular
customer at the Café de l'École, Danton lived not very far away,
in the rue de la Tixanderie. Twenty-seven years old now, he
was no longer a lawyer's clerk, but a parliamentary advocate.

To understand this rise in his circumstances, we must glance
back first to the time when—still a pupil of the Oratorians—he
was finishing his classical studies at Troyes; and then watch him
going the rounds of three relatives (also in Troyes) who were
either attorneys or sheriff's officers. In their service he assimilated
a good deal about the practice of law. But these studies had not
culminated in the award of any diploma.

During this period the average expectation of life was thirty,
a fact which produced a maturity in the young that we no
longer know. Like all his contemporaries, the young office clerk
was an adult in every way. When he had barely attained his
majority he gave evidence of what to us would be an astonishing
sophistication. On coming into his father's estate at the age of
twenty-one, he proceeded to put it at his stepfather's disposal—
under certain conditions. M. Recordain was on the verge of
bankruptcy. His attempts to perfect an industrial spinner for so
brittle and difficult a fiber as cotton were eating up his own
resources and making inroads into his wife's fortune as well.
Danton went through his books, checked the extent of his
liabilities, and provided him both with capital and sound legal
advice. "Before taking a long journey," he said, "one should
always set one's affairs in order."

The long journey in question was to Paris. Danton was
suffocating in Troyes. Twenty-five thousand inhabitants, a few
textile factories, an ancient château, and a warren of poor
houses jammed behind medieval city walls—this hardly added
up to the stage which a devouringly ambitious man required to
give his talents full rein. Not knowing the capital, Danton was
determined to set forth and conquer it. But before doing so he
went all around the district, sometimes on foot, sometimes by
horse, making his adieus to every member of the family. However widely scattered they might be, their young and inde-
pendent-minded relative sought them out and kissed them
good-by. One might really have thought he was emigrating to
America. This round of visits is rather touching; it shows, too,

how much the slowness of transport in those days could isolate people from one another within a comparatively small area.

Uncle Nicolas, the *curé* of Barberey, had previously urged Recordain to put his stepson in the seminary. When the young man called to take his leave before making that "long journey," did the priest, one wonders, upbraid him for abandoning an ecclesiastical career? And what about Marie-Cécile, Danton's sister, whom he visited at the Convent of the Annunciation, where she was a novice? Were her prayers added to her uncle's regrets? We cannot tell. But Danton's second sister, now engaged to a merchant named Pierre Menuel, approved of this independent-spirited brother, whose ambitions everyone else found so terrifying. As for Mme. Recordain, Danton's mother, her attitude toward this son of hers was rather like that of a hen that, having hatched a duckling, now watches it plunge into the pond. She shed some tears when Danton kissed her good-by.

But it was time for him to be gone now: a kiss for the two youngest sisters, a handshake for his stepfather and stepbrother, and then—his pockets nearly empty, because most of his capital had been invested in the Recordain spinner—Danton marched off, with very little luggage, to await the Paris coach. Having opted for civil rather than canon law, he was now setting forth on the road that, in a bare thirteen years, would carry him to the heights of glory—and condemn him to the most ignominious death. During those thirteen years he was to cram enough living for several lifetimes.

The fare on the stagecoach, as we have already had occasion to note, was thirteen sous a league. But the carrier was a friend of the family and let Danton travel free. The coachman whipped up his horses, and Danton watched the unfamiliar countryside unroll before his eyes. There were relay changes at Sézanne, Ferté-Gaucher, Coulommiers, and Lagny. The ponderous vehicle took a whole day to travel the forty leagues between Arcis and the capital.

At last they arrived. The streets of this modern Babylon were dark and narrow, and fitfully lit by swaying lanterns suspended at intervals from overhead wires. There were no sidewalks: this particular luxury was only invented during the

Empire, by a civil engineer named Dillon. The cobbled surface sloped gently from the houses on either side down to the middle, where an open gutter carried domestic sewage away on a tide of brown and filthy water.

When he emerged from the Cour des Messageries on the rue Notre-Dame-des-Victoires (the present site of the Treasury Department, Seine Division) Georges Danton stopped to ask his way of the passers-by. At Troyes he had been advised to seek lodging in the Black Horse Inn, rue Geoffroy-l'Asnier. The landlord, M. Layron, was from Champagne himself and made special terms for his fellow countrymen—besides giving them sound advice while they settled in; there were many crooks in this great sprawling octopus of a city and new arrivals had to be on their guard against being conned. So now Danton was on his way to the Black Horse Inn, and its host M. Layron.

He stopped a workman and asked for the Church of Saint-Gervais. The rue Geoffroy-l'Asnier, he had been told, lay within its parish boundaries. After several wrong turns he eventually found it. Carrying his bag, he strode across the Place de Grève, skirted the houses clustering around the City Hall, and finally came out on the Place Saint-Gervais. There was the church, dedicated to the martyr of Milan. Once more he stopped and asked the way. He was now on the edge of Le Marais, in a district where luxury marched hand in hand with squalor, and slum dwellings proliferated beside the most magnificent town houses. It was quite dark. He passed the rue François-Miron, the rue des Barres, and the rue du Grenier-sur-l'Eau. At last he found the rue Geoffroy-l'Asnier. There were two splendid-looking houses, the Hôtel d'Aumont and the Hôtel de Luxembourg. And, on the other side of the street—hardly more than an alleyway in fact—down toward the river, Danton made out the sign of the Black Horse.

The following day, thanks to a letter of recommendation from his uncle (one of the two lawyers in Troyes) the young man up from Arcis was taken on by Maître Vinot, at his chambers in the rue Saint-Louis-en-l'Île. His job of deviling at the Law Courts must have taught him a good deal more about the complex machinery of justice than he could have picked up back home in Troyes. There were so vast a number of separate jurisdictions that merely to remember them all took some doing: provostries, bailiwicks, seneschals' courts, the High Court of Parliament, courts of inquiry, the Chambre de la Tournelle, commercial courts, the Court of Forestage, the Chancery Division, the King's Bench, the Châtelet—all these were among the tribunals of royal justice. Add the seignorial manor courts and those of the ecclesiastical authorities, and one realizes what energy was required to keep swimming from one to another.

Here, in the Paris Parliament and the great ministries, there were more active, fermenting brains to be found than anywhere else; here, too, the forces of development and reaction engaged in single combat at every level. It was a world to which the young lawyer's clerk very soon acclimatized himself. If his intelligence caused a certain amount of jealousy, his cheerful manner made him some good friends. In 1782 his former classmate Paré arrived, and they were soon on the old intimate footing once more. Saint-Albin, Béon, and Courtois did not join them till later.

When he was not occupied with his professional duties, Danton read voraciously, taking no notes but remembering everything. Law, history, and literature formed the staple diet of his leisure hours. He spent much time with the Charpentiers—with Mme. Charpentier in particular—in order to improve his spoken Italian; and with Gabrielle, too, drawn by her innocent adolescent charms. She made a change from his other feminine acquaintances, the sort of girl whom his charged and passionate nature drove him to seek out. "I must have women," he was to declare later, in an attempt to excuse his infidelities.

Very often he would give himself over to the pleasures of fencing, and the intoxicating delight of a dip in the river. He used to swim in the Seine, wearing a pair of linen drawers. When he plunged into the water—rare prowess in those days—a crowd of idlers would always gather to watch him. There is a "historical anecdote" told about him in this connection, the truth of which cannot be verified. He is supposed to have remarked, on clambering out of the water not far from the Bastille: "I find that great fortress a most offensive and irksome eyesore. Shall we ever see it pulled down? When the day comes, I wouldn't mind taking a pick to it myself."

A "hot and cold" chill, caught as the result of taking a bath immediately after an energetic fencing match, brought him very nearly to death's door. Confined to bed for several weeks—still with Maître Vinot, who provided accommodation for his staff—Danton spent his period of convalescence tearing through Montesquieu, Voltaire, Rousseau, Buffon, and Beccaria; reading Shakespeare, Milton, Dante, and Ariosto in the original; and putting a fine edge on his Latin. As though it were the merest game, his prodigious memory stored all this knowledge safely away in the recesses of his brain.

When he was back on his feet again, he decided it was essential for him to obtain some sort of diploma. Without a degree he could not be called to the bar. His employer was fond of him: this towering, ugly young man had a charm that everyone found it hard to resist. Although dismayed at the prospect of losing his assistant, Maître Vinot nevertheless gave him a good tip, which was that he should go and obtain his legal diploma at Rheims. The examiners, he said, were far less exacting than their Parisian counterparts. Quite a few lawyers, destined by Providence to become famous in after years, owed their right to plead in court to these easygoing gentlemen. It was even alleged that they had bought their diplomas. One who benefited from this practice was Brissot, the famous Girondist, who wrote in his *Memoirs:* "The accommodating nature of the University of Rheims was legendary. This was where Lanthenas, Roland, and Danton all went to obtain their degrees." And he went on to quote the following passage from a letter by Roland, written in 1770: "I arrived in Rheims on July 30, and duly enrolled myself as a member of the University on the 31st. At the same time I received a reading course, studied day and night, took an examination on Civil Law and Canon Law on August 3, was admitted to the bachelor's degree, received another reading course that day, was examined again on the 5th, and granted my diploma before I left." Seven days residence was all that was required to obtain a degree.

It was a wise recommendation, and Danton followed it. By October of 1784 he could write the words "Attorney at Law" beneath his name. But what aberrant quirk made "The Republican," bow to the vanities of his time and sign himself

"d'Anton?" Democrat he may have been, but he was much
attached to that apostrophe.

On the other hand, the first case he conducted was that of a
herdsman who brought suit against his local *seigneur*. The court
record of this case was subsequently lost in a fire, and we know
nothing about it except the verdict, which Saint-Albin mentions
in his brief *Memoirs*. Maître d'Anton accepted the countryman's
brief, and although the Bench was packed with the gentry, this
fledgling attorney won his case. Thanks to him, a commoner of
the humblest sort triumphed over a member of the feudal
aristocracy.

Were there other cases during this period—less spectacular,
perhaps, but equally noteworthy—which marked Danton out as
a coming man? When Mme. Roland comes to describe this
part of his life, she refers to "the starveling lawyer, with more
debts than briefs." The fire that destroyed the library of the
Law Courts has made it impossible for us to confirm or contradict the "Girondine's" spiteful judgment. But can that judgment be regarded as impartial? Mme. Roland detested Danton.
Need one add that she wrote her *Memoirs* in prison—or, indeed,
that it was Danton's political decisions which were responsible
for her incarceration? The poor creature felt herself done for,
condemned, inevitably, to the guillotine; perhaps that is enough
to explain why she wrote as she did.

The rue de la Tixanderie, where Danton lodged after he left
Maître Vinot's chambers, was to disappear during the nineteenth century. It was a narrow street that stretched in a long
curve across the space (today a section of the rue de Rivoli)
which separates the City Hall from the bazaar which bears its
name. The old City Hall had been built in 1533 and was
burned down by rioters in 1871. It was far smaller than the
present building, occupying no more than a quarter of its ground
plan; and the Place de Grève, the ancestor of the modern Place
de l'Hôtel de Ville, was only a third the size of its successor. A
whole network of back streets and alleys ran into it. One of
these, the rue du Mouton, linked the square and the rue de la
Tixanderie. The building in which Danton lodged stood op-

posite. From his windows he could look down the rue du Mouton and see the antique sculptures of the City Hall.

By the rue du Mouton it was less than a minute's walk to the Place de Grève. Here the Sanson brothers, those master executioners, would frequently hang and behead criminals, or rack them alive on the wheel.

On the same floor of the building in which Danton had his apartment, there lived a girl from his part of the country whose acquaintance he had previously made in Troyes, while staying with one of his lawyer-uncles. Her name was Mlle. Françoise-Julie Duhauttoir. Now Danton met her again in the capital, where she rented a pied-à-terre in the rue de la Tixanderie. A legacy from her parents had left her relatively wealthy, and she spent half each year in Troyes, half in Paris. While in Troyes she attended, with some efficiency, to her property. In Paris, where she was less well known and did not run such a risk of stirring up gossip, she had a discreetly good time. Danton did not install himself next door to her for nothing. For some while now he had been paying her frequent visits. When he gave her advice on how to manage her inheritance, did he ask nothing in return apart from his legal fee?

A few steps from their house (where the rear façade of the City Hall stands today) stood the Church of Saint-Jean-en-Grève. In accordance with the law of the day, the *curé* also acted as registrar of births and deaths for his entire parish. One day in March of 1783 Mlle. Duhauttoir appeared before him to announce the birth—on February 23—of a boy called Jean-Louis, by "some person unknown." Was Danton responsible for this event? We shall have another look at this mystery later, when the sequence of events has provided us with one or two indispensable details.

But Danton's intrigue—whether genuine or supposititious—with Françoise-Julie did not stop him paying flirtatious court to Gabrielle, the virtuous daughter of M. Charpentier. Though she was by no means a complete simpleton, he felt there was a purity about her—and in their relationship—which flattered his lower-middle-class soul. By now Mlle. Charpentier was helping her mother at the cash desk. Every evening, when he left the Law Courts, Danton would drop in for supper at the Quai de l'École. Since he had a good square meal at midday in a cheap chophouse, he contented himself, about six o'clock in the evening, with a cup of milky coffee and some bread and butter. As he consumed this frugal repast, he would chat with his colleagues, and with the Charpentiers—father, mother, and, especially, daughter.

As dark-complexioned as her Italian mother, a fresh, healthy girl (though a little on the plump side), Gabrielle moved among the customers with a graceful bearing that won her smiles from everyone. Her modesty and reserve commanded respect. People joked with her, but they did not amuse themselves at her expense. In any case her father would never have allowed it. When he went off on one of his tax-inspection trips, his wife or son would automatically replace him as guardian watchdog. Gabrielle's virtue was well protected.

The portrait of Gabrielle attributed to David shows a girl with serious eyes, a generous, curving mouth, full cheeks, and the ghost of a double chin. On her head she has the sober bonnet worn by any middle-class woman with no desire to ape the fashions of the nobility. Around her neck, secured by a black silk bodice, she has a muslin scarf, through which the very smallest triangle of skin is just visible. Mlle. Charpentier, it is clear, was not the kind of girl to lead a man on.

There is no known portrait of Danton in existence from this period. The picture painted by Greuze we can ignore. It shows us a mildly effeminate Adonis, with features of rare distinction, a pair of fine sensuous lips, and a throat too generously denuded of the famous Dantonesque bullneck. This Danton bears no conceivable resemblance to the descriptions of those who knew and wrote about him—and even less to the sketches by David, or the anonymous charcoal-and-pastel portrait now in the museum at Troyes, which is beyond a doubt the best likeness of Danton to have survived. Though time has blurred its lines, the scar left under Danton's lower lip by the bull's horn at Arcis is still clearly visible. The man portrayed here is far from good-looking. There can be no more than five or six years between the time Danton modeled for Greuze and the period when other artists painted him. Can anyone change so much in so short a period? If not, one of two things must be true: either the traditional belief that Greuze's sitter was Danton is mistaken or else Greuze was determined to flatter his client. There is no trace in his treatment of the face which Manon Roland found so "repulsive and hideous."

When his evening meal was over, the young lawyer would talk for hours with the Charpentier family and his fellow customers. Sometimes he would leave them early for a visit to the theater—but more often to go home, where he would be joined by his former classmates who had now followed him to Paris. Françoise Duhauttoir was the only woman present at these meetings. But then was she not—like Louis Béon, Courtois, Saint-Albin, and Jules Paré—a native of Troyes? Béon had by now been ordained as a priest. Another, rather older priest used to join them from time to time—none other than that Father Béranger who had wanted to punish Paré in college, and who was now a close friend of the group. These, together with a few new acquaintances picked up in the capital, formed Danton's permanent audience. By now he felt the zest for battle surging up in him. They would discuss such topics as philosophy, law, or public finance, and often the discussion went on till well after midnight.

When the guests had departed, did Danton join Françoise in her apartment? It does not appear so. On the contrary: though Mlle. Duhauttoir may well have solaced his leisure hours when he was working for Maître Vinot, it looks as though the relationship was now strictly platonic. Better still, either deliberately or by accident Danton was to play a part in bringing about his friend's marriage. One day he introduced her to Maître Huet de Paisy, a lawyer and Counsel to the King's Bench and the two fell in love with each other. First as lover and mistress, and later as husband and wife, Maître Huet de Paisy and Mlle. Duhauttoir—partly through the fact of their marriage, partly by a most odd combination of circumstances—helped to bring about Danton's own marriage to Gabrielle Charpentier.

Danton had no great hopes—for the immediate future, at any rate—that such a match was within his reach. To maintain a domestic establishment required the kind of situation he did not at present possess. According to Mme. Roland, he was getting nowhere in his career, and the modest meals he ate would seem to confirm her statement. Anxious to get on in the world and widen the circle of his acquaintances, he began knocking at various doors which opened without any trouble—that of Free-masonry, for instance.

This mysterious organization, exclusively philanthropic in its aims, was based on, and inspired by, the tenets of Christian morality. Imported from England, it did not rank as heretical, and a man still imbued with Catholicism—as Danton was at the time of his affiliation—could find some satisfaction for his humanitarian urges in belonging to it. This was why, about 1786, he "saw the light" in the Reverend Lodge of the Nine Sisters. He was regarded as possessing the "talent and qualifications" needed to do so.

The mysteries of the Lodge were celebrated in a house on the rue du Pot-de-Fer. A famous astronomer, Joseph de Lalande, held the grade of Venerable in this Lodge, and various other savants figured among the Masters and Companions: Lacépède, Condorcet, Bailly, Guillotin, and others. There were well-known artists, such as Hubert Robert, Joseph Vernet, and Greuze (the "Adonis portrait" of Danton dates from this period). There was a famous sculptor, Houdon, and several successful writers: Choderlos de Laclos (the author of *Les Liaisons Dangereuses*), Florian the fabulist, Chamfort the moral essayist, and the poet Parny. There was a lawyer later called upon, by a quirk of Providence, to defend the King: this was Raymond de Sèze. There was a parliamentary Judge of Appeal, Duval d'Éprémesnil; a prince, Msgr. de Rohan; a duke, M. de la Rochefoucauld; and a marquis, M. de Beaumont.

Among the Apprentices, the lowest grade of the Order, Danton found three of his colleagues from the Law Courts: Maître Camille Desmoulins, whose inflammatory speeches were to lead the mob on to storm the Bastille; Maître Pétion de Villeneuve, who later brought back the King from Varennes; and Maître Brissot, also known as de Warville, who became one of the leading Girondists. Besides these he made the acquaintance of Mirabeau, already a well-known figure in Paris; Rabaud-Saint-Étienne, who was to press for freedom of worship at the

meeting of the States-General; Dom Gerle, who made his mark
on the occasion of the Tennis Court Oath, and the Abbé Sieyès,
who was to compose that incendiary pamphlet beginning:
"What is the Third Estate? Nothing. What should it be? Everything . . ."

The Grand Master, the supreme Head of the Order, was
none other than His Royal Highness the Duke of Orléans,
cousin to Louis XVI, First Prince of the Blood, and—para-
doxically—one of the régime's most severe critics.

In fact the entire Revolution was contained, in embryo, in the
Lodge of the Nine Sisters. Danton, "The Republican," could not
have failed to acquire, from such company, the stamp that
afterward made him "The Man of August 10."

It is very unlikely that he would have described his initiation
to the proprietor of the Café de l'École, or given any details of
the investiture ceremony either to Gabrielle or her mother—
such as the swords of the Brethren pricking the thighs and
calves of the neophyte as he lay on the ground, prostrate and
blindfolded, while the Venerable Master pronounced the ritual
formula of initiation over him; or the white apron, with set
square and compasses embroidered on it in gold, which was
tied around his waist; or, finally, the "steel arch" of swords
under which he must pass, humble and happy, after his affiliation. The mysteries of a secret society are not to be divulged,
even to the woman one loves. Danton had "seen the light," but
the pleasures of that illumination he had perforce to keep to
himself.

But there were other pleasures involved—not least the new
acquaintances which the Lodge brought him. Among these was
a Brother who did not, on the face of it, seem likely to play much
part in Danton's career as a lawyer. This was an obscure
general named Dumouriez, a funny little man who turned up in
the rue du Pot-de-Fer wearing the civilian dress of an ordinary
bourgeois. Little known, despite the twenty-two wounds that had
earned him a pension, he had more of a reputation for espionage
than for strategical skill. Louis XV had employed him as a
secret agent, sending him on missions to Corsica, Prussia, and
Poland. While passing through Hanover, Dumouriez had made
the acquaintance of a German Freemason, the Duke of Bruns-

wick, a most illustrious pawn on the military chessboard. Their
Masonic connections brought about a friendship between them.
When Danton established his own close relationship with
Dumouriez—a man twenty years older than he—it could not
have occurred to him that the general's connection with the
Duke might, in the long run, further his, Danton's, political
designs. Dumouriez had done a spell in the Bastille after falling
out with some member of the aristocracy, and emerged from
prison an angry and embittered man. His favorite doctrine
henceforward was the equality under the law, for taxation, and
before God, of all men. He brought an incisive mind to the
discussions that took place in the Lodge, and Danton sensed
that he was capable of flattering and cajoling a crowd into
doing just what he wanted. Dumouriez, similarly, divined the
same potential qualities in this new initiate.

Both Dumouriez and Danton were frequent visitors at the
house of one Armand-Gaston Camus, who shared their views
and was being drawn toward a demagogue's career as a consequence. But Camus had not, like them, "seen the light." The
Freemasons had rejected him. His name, incidentally, was the
same as that of Danton's mother before her marriage. It is possible that they were related. At all events, either their distant
kinship or the coincidence of name seems to have drawn the
two men together. Besides, they were both parliamentary lawyers.
Since he was the older by some sixteen years, Camus used to give
the young Danton much advice. Danton accepted the advice but
did not follow it. What he most liked about Camus was his
incessantly proclaimed love of the people. What he found most
irritating was his devoutness. Every day Camus would lose himself in the contemplation of a great wooden crucifix that hung in
his room: he spent hours at a time thus employed. But Maître
Camus was accredited legal representative to the Clergy of
France, to the Elector of Trèves, and to the German principality
of Salm-Salm; thus he, like Dumouriez, had solid and useful
connections beyond the Rhine, though of a rather different nature. He certainly did not know the Duke of Brunswick. Destiny
plays some odd tricks. It would be hard to find three men more
diverse in age, temperament, or beliefs than Dumouriez, Danton,

and Camus. Yet later they were to form a close coalition to save the country when Brunswick attacked it. The crisis once past, they fell out among themselves.

But all this still lay in the future, and none of the protagonists could have foreseen it. Dumouriez commanded the garrison at Cherbourg, and only came up to Paris to preach his egalitarian principles in the Lodge of the Nine Sisters. Camus spent his time in the Law Courts, handling briefs for the servants of the Church. As for Danton, he was willing to take on practically anyone. Posterity has preserved no record of these minor cases. Mme. Roland, when describing this period in her *Memoirs*, was to present Danton as a needy advocate, always on the lookout for clients. For once the beautiful but spiteful Egeria of the Gironde commands our belief. Danton was finding it difficult to make both ends meet in Paris. His childhood companions—now, like him, transplanted to the capital—were afterward to portray him as an impecunious young man, taking his midday meal in a cheap cookshop with the significant name of Hôtel de la Modestie. In the evening he would make do with his milky coffee and bread and jam at the Café de l'École. Here he could also spend some time with Gabrielle, which consoled him for his frugal diet.

He laid siege to the young girl with some subtlety. His courtship, though discreet enough and always conducted in the presence of Gabrielle's parents or her brother, was kept up steadily and did not give the family any grounds for supposing that Danton was merely in search of an *affaire*. What drove Danton was the unadmitted desire for a good bourgeois marriage—a fairly wealthy match, too, and (what may be counted an extenuating circumstance) one that would bring love into his life and allow him fine fun and games in bed. To win the daughter, Danton billed and cooed in Italian with her mother. He talked shop to Antoine-François, now a notary's clerk waiting till he could purchase a practice of his own, and discussed politics, from time to time, with M. Charpentier himself. The latter saw very well that Gabrielle was not indifferent to her aspiring suitor. He was sorry in a way, because the young man was so ugly; but what point was in struggling against the course of true love? An infatuated girl no longer sees any fault in the man of her choice.

Had one the right to be more demanding than the party principally concerned? Gabrielle did not, as yet, dare to reveal her delectable secret, and the café proprietor could sense a demand for his daughter's hand looming up on the horizon. He therefore made inquiries among his customers concerning young Danton's morals, integrity, and future prospects. It was clear enough that the fledgling lawyer was not rolling in money. But with some assistance he might obtain a very profitable appointment. Indeed, Danton himself was as well placed as anyone to know what offices were for sale. (This is where Mlle. Duhauttoir and her new lover Maître Huet de Paisy come into the picture.) So M. Charpentier made up his own mind, privately; and when Danton put on his white gloves and came calling with a formal request for Gabrielle's hand, he found his prospective in-laws quite willing to accept his suit. Now Gabrielle was his fiancée, and he had the right to press those scarred lips of his upon her pure and virginal brow.

CHAPTER II

The Mysterious Affair of Danton's First Marriage

AT THE TIME when Danton made his declaration of love—March of 1787—French finances were going through a very sticky period. Ever since February 22, an Assembly of Notables had been doing its best to save the economy from collapse. This body, convened by Calonne, met in the château of Versailles and insisted on inspecting all public accounts. As a result of their inquiries they demanded the removal of the Royal Treasurer. His place was taken by a member of the Assembly of Notables itself, Archbishop Loménie de Brienne, who obtained the tax demands that his colleagues had refused to his predecessor.

This news caused much public grumbling, and those members of the aristocracy who supported the popular movement actively encouraged such complaints. The Marquis de la Fayette, who had enjoyed great popularity ever since his return from America, talked about a new meeting of the States-General. These two words aroused no very clear memory among the general public; they vaguely recalled something that had happened in the far distant past, a bloody crisis the nation had passed through during the Renaissance. All the same, they were enough to cause serious alarm among nobility and commons alike.

In the Café du Parnasse, M. Charpentier and his clientele discussed the crisis. Though Danton was acutely concerned by this turn of events, no one would have guessed it from his behavior; but then he had other things to think about. M. Charpentier had told him, in effect, that he must get himself a profitable situation; it was only on this condition that he, M. Charpentier, would approve the marriage. So Danton was trying to secure himself—on the best possible terms, though with what money? —a position as Counsel to the King's Bench.

An ancient custom, the so-called Sale of Offices, effectively prevented any poor man from obtaining an important post. In order to hold such a position, the applicant was required to purchase it. Colonels not only commanded their regiments; they owned them. The *fermiers généraux,* thanks to this same usage, owned the exclusive right of levying direct taxes, while ordinary tax farmers had the privilege of collecting all indirect dues. M. Charpentier had purchased his right to inspect some of their companies. All financial administration, even the Mint itself, operated similarly on a contractual basis.

In the sphere of justice everything was for sale: the offices of attorneys, notaries, and bailiffs, even a seat on the magistrates' bench. The very executioners acquired their business and good will, as it were, on a strictly commercial basis. Only parliamentary attorneys—positions which brought little profit to young and relatively unknown men—could enter the legal profession without dipping into their purse beforehand. On the other hand, those lawyers who obtained the office of Counsel to the King's Bench were obliged to pay for it, and it was just such a post that Danton was anxious to acquire.

Despite his title, a King's Counsel did not give advice to the sovereign. He and his fellows rendered justice in the sovereign's name, dealing with cases that involved either two Ministries of State or else the Crown and some private person or persons. There were seven such Conciliar Courts in existence: the so-called Upper Chamber, which derived its name from the fact that it sat on the main floor of the Law Courts, and which in ways foreshadowed the modern Council of State; the Court of Dispatch, which dealt primarily with administrative litigation; the Court of Excise, which specialized in cases relating to tax farming and general levies; the Court of Commerce, more or less the direct ancestor of the modern Commercial Tribunal; the quaintly named Court of Conscience which settled conflicting claims over ecclesiastical benefices; the special court to deal with cases involving "the so-called reformed religion"; and lastly the

Court of Civil Parties, the function of which it would take too long to explain here in any detail.

These various jurisdictions demanded a fluctuating number of judges; and there was a regular body of seventy lawyers who handled all the cases which came before them. The good will for such a Counsel's office cost more or less according to the wealth and importance of the incumbent's clientele.

Danton knew one of them—Maître Huet de Paisy, Françoise's new lover. Indeed, he had introduced Maître Huet to his fellow tenant and compatriot, and they had been so taken with each other that they were now thinking of putting their relationship on a regular footing. Meanwhile they had settled down like any properly married couple in the rue de la Tixanderie: they occupied not only Mlle. Duhauttoir's apartment, but Danton's, too, which he had vacated for their benefit. He himself had moved into new lodgings down the rue des Mauvaises-Paroles, a few yards from the Quai de l'École and the home of his future in-laws (they slept over the café).

Since Maître Huet de Paisy wanted to resign his position as Counsel to the King's Bench, it was quite natural that he should offer Danton the chance of taking it over. Danton accepted, subject to his raising the necessary sum through a series of loans.

The contract was signed before Maître Dosfant, a notary with offices in the rue de l'Arbre-Sec: Antoine Charpentier, Gabrielle's brother, was one of his clerks. By this agreement, dated March 29, 1787, Maître Huet de Paisy undertook to have Maître Georges d'Anton admitted as a member of the College of Advocates to the Court of the King's Bench; to make over to him the "substance" of his office for 10,000 *livres*, and the clientele for 68,000. Danton was to pay over this total of 78,000 *livres* in the following manner: 56,000 on signature, 10,000 after his enrollment in the College, and 12,000 four years later, on March 29, 1791.

Since he could lay hands on only 5000 *livres* of his own, where on earth was he to find the remaining 73,000? This was where Françoise Duhauttoir's friendship proved useful. The vendor's new mistress advanced the purchaser a sum of 36,000 *livres*—a purchaser who was certainly her close friend, even if

one cannot say with certainty that he was her ex-lover or the
father of her child. Scarcely was this money out of Françoise's
purse before it returned there, albeit by a somewhat indirect
route, since Danton turned it over to Huet de Paisy, the lender's
lover.

There remained another 37,000 *livres* to find. Danton borrowed 15,000 from his future father-in-law (who was to waive
his claim on the debt after the marriage contract was signed),
and 10,000 from a certain M. Lhuillier, Household Comptroller
to the Court, this sum to be repaid by 1792, on the security of
his office as Counsel. As for the remaining 12,000 *livres,* payable
at the end of four years, those various uncles and aunts back
in Troyes were so fond of their nephew that they agreed to go
bail on his behalf for the full amount.

All this seems honest and straightforward enough—even
though when Huet de Paisy married Mlle. Duhauttoir, three
years later, he was to accept as his own that mysteriously sired
child, born before he had even made the acquaintance of its
unwed mother. Is it conceivable that this declaration of paternity had been promised to Danton in advance? And if so, does
such a promise explain why Danton had to pay 78,000 *livres* for
an office which Huet de Paisy had picked up himself, thirteen
years previously, for a mere 30,000? In any case, in 1787 he
made a clear profit of 48,000 *livres* on his transaction with
Danton—a profit all the more questionable in that the position
brought its new incumbent, during the whole course of his professional career, no more than twenty-two cases. There had been
something very close to fraudulence in the vendor's approach
to the purchaser; and the purchaser knew it.

He also knew that Huet de Paisy had not paid a lump sum
of 30,000 *livres* to the previous holder of the office, one Beyres de
Castanède. Far from it: Huet had, in fact, undertaken to pay
Beyres de Castanède an annual rent of 1500 *livres* in perpetuity.
Furthermore, since 1774, the year in which this contract was
drawn up, he had not paid one penny of this rental, not even
the interest on the loan.

During the thirteen years since then, Beyres de Castanède had
died. His heirs and creditors, on learning that Huet de Paisy
was turning the office over to Danton, lodged an appeal against

the payments that the latter had agreed to make to the vendor. There were eight of these gentlemen, and they appointed an attorney, Maître Mel de Saint-Céran, to make representations to Danton on their behalf. This attorney informed Danton that he was liable for thirteen years' back payments on the dues which Huet de Paisy owed to Castanède's heirs and assigns.

Danton agreed to everything. He undertook to pay 78,000 *livres* for a position that was worth no more than 30,000. He undertook to repay, at a future date, 36,000 *livres* that had been lent him by Françoise, and which—as a result of Huet's crafty dealing—would in fact go straight back into her funds again. He undertook to settle the outstanding interest on thirteen years' unpaid rental of 1500 *livres per annum* (which Huet had never taken steps to meet), plus the accumulated rental itself, to the attorney acting for Castanède's heirs. In order to marry, he was mortgaging his entire future, and he showed no apparent qualms or hesitation about plunging into this horrific financial quagmire.

From these facts two conclusions can be drawn: first, that he was besotted with Gabrielle Charpentier and determined to marry her at all costs; and secondly, that he could refuse Mlle. Duhauttoir nothing, since he was purchasing his situation— on quite abominable terms—from the new lover and fiancé of the girl who had given birth to a child "by some person unknown."

M. Charpentier must have been aware of these bewildering complications, which gave a fairly strong presumptive hint as to the identity of the father. His son Antoine, Danton's future brother-in-law, worked as a clerk with Maître Dosfant, who was the café proprietor's notary. Even if he did not draw up the act of sale and Gabrielle's marriage contract in person, Antoine could hardly have been unaware of their general terms—especially since he was shortly to buy up his employer's practice, and later had to put pressure on Danton to honor his obligations. Gabrielle, whom time showed to be an intelligent girl, must have known what these obligations were. She adored Danton and had doubtless persuaded her father, mother, and brothers to sanction this shaky structure as the foundation for her own happiness. It seems to me impossible that M. Charpentier, as an

Inspector of Tax Concessions, would have agreed to let his daughter become involved in such complex legal quibbling unless Gabrielle had threatened to do something desperate if her family proved obdurate. Love, as we know, is blind. Gabrielle could see nothing: neither the debts that held their joint future in mortgage, nor the significance of Françoise Duhauttoir, nor the existence of that child by some person unknown.

The rue des Mauvaises-Paroles, where Danton lived after his move, disappeared during the nineteenth century to make way for the rue de Rivoli. It linked the rue des Bourdonnais to the rue des Lavandières Sainte-Opportune. In these narrow streets, close to Les Halles, farmyard poultry wandered about quite freely, and passers-by were likely to be charged by stray pigs. These creatures sometimes attacked children in order to steal their bread and butter—and they were apt to wolf the hand as well as the bread it held. A police report of 1791 makes a reference to "the number of children crippled or maimed by these voracious beasts."

Such inconveniences of the district did not bother Danton. As a child had he not joined battle with a bull? In the rue des Mauvaises-Paroles he was only ten minutes away from his fiancée, and for him nothing else mattered. When she moved into his apartment Gabrielle would be the happiest of wives—or so at least he told himself he would make her. But he gave scarcely any thought to furnishing his rooms well; he did not possess the means.

On June 5 or 6, 1787, he made his way to the Cour des Messageries, rue Notre-Dame des Victoires. The coaches from Troyes and Arcis were bringing in his relations, who had come to the capital to be present at his wedding. Danton first of all welcomed his mother, Mme. Recordain, who descended from the coach with her stepson and a cousin of hers, a Dr. Papillon. Mother and son embraced each other joyfully. The next day other vehicles arrived bringing men, women, children, a couple of priests—in fact, almost the entire Danton clan.

Mme. Recordain was now sixty-seven. Her portrait, painted by Laneuville and on display in the museum at Troyes, shows us a little old lady with wrinkled skin, a humorous mouth, and big, rather cow-like eyes, in unexpected contrast to her high forehead—the latter normally a sign of intelligence. On her head is a meticulously goffered white lace bonnet, with a blue ribbon. Around her neck, almost as though supporting the flesh it rests on, is a narrow band of black velvet.

While in Paris Mme. Recordain lodged with her son. There is no record of where the rest of the family found accommodation.

On June 9 there was all the fuss and ceremony of signing the contract in Maître Dosfant's office. With the assistance of a colleague named Leville, the notary read out the clauses to the engaged couple, in the presence of their various parents, brothers, sisters, uncles, aunts, and cousins. Also among the witnesses were Maître Vinot and his wife, who had come to bestow the honor of their presence on Maître Vinot's former clerk. The lawyer's wife was visibly moved. Perhaps she remembered the verses Danton had addressed to her when he was working for her husband.

Maître Dosfant gave precise details concerning the prospects of either party. They had agreed to have all property in common on marriage. The notary then enumerated the goods that each would contribute in the first instance. First Danton: on his side he brought his office as advocate, with a titular value of 78,000 *livres*, together with lands at Arcis, being part of his family inheritance, which were valued at 12,000 *livres*. Gabrielle, for her part, brought a dowry of 18,000 *livres*, 15,000 of which had been paid over the previous March, at the time of the agreement signed with Huet de Paisy; plus 2000 *livres* belonging to her in her own right, and consisting of her personal savings. There were also various minor items such as jewelry, watches, and "wardrobe"—that is, personal wearing apparel. But Papa Charpentier, who knew all about his son-in-law's confused financial position, had insisted on guarantees to secure his daughter's future. The contract specifically stated that Mme. Danton-Charpentier should not be held liable for any debts or mortgages that her husband had contracted before their marriage; and, further, that the said husband was to settle on his wife a stipulated jointure of 800 *livres per annum*, the capital, 16,000 *livres*, being entailed to the couple's children. One more financial obligation for Danton; his marriage might fill his heart with joy, but it left his pockets nearly empty. Still, he was twenty-eight and Gabrielle twenty-four, and the heart of eager youth always makes light of the future. So the bridegroom put his signature to this contract, styling himself "d'Anton."

The choir of Saint-Germain-l'Auxerrois sang for him on June 14. Gabrielle, blushing, walked down the aisle on her father's arm, her white lace veil floating around her. Georges-Jacques, holding himself very erect, looked even taller and stronger than usual. It was a colossal figure of a man whom Mme. Recordain —dwarfed beside her son—now led to the altar.

The Café de l'École was closed for the day and became the scene of a dinner and ball for about a hundred invited guests. It would be interesting to know whether Maître Huet de Paisy and his fiancée were among those present. Unfortunately, history does not tell us.

CHAPTER III

Maître d'Anton, Counsel to the King's Bench

THE YOUNG MARRIED PAIR moved into Danton's apartment in
the rue des Mauvaises-Paroles. His honeymoon did not put other
problems out of his mind. In a month's time the College of
Counsels to the King's Bench would receive him with elaborate ceremony. The member-elect was required to deliver a
speech in Latin, according to the rules governing this august and
learned assembly. Such a stipulation was no trouble to Danton,
whose mastery of Latin was perfect. But there was another ancient tradition which laid down that the subject on which the
neophyte had to discourse should not be revealed to him before
the ceremony.

What would his particular theme be? This remained a mystery—and all the more disturbing a mystery in that Danton, as
he knew very well, did not enjoy a good reputation among his
future colleagues. His loud voice and outspoken audacity dis-
pleased them. Suppose they were to set a trap for him? Suppose
the subject of his address had some kind of political implication?
If the candidate did not obtain the votes of his peers, the arrangement with Huet de Paisy and his associates would lack any
concrete result.

The great day dawned at last. Maître d'Anton, in cap and
gown, entered the hall reserved for Counsels to the King's
Bench. The President of the Bar rose and said to him, in Latin:
"Pray address us on the moral and political situation of our
country as it affects the administration of justice."

Here was a trap indeed, the very one which Danton had

feared. At this moment Parliament was still refusing to ratify the
edicts dealing with the new taxes that the Assembly of Notables
had imposed. As a result the topic laid down for Danton was a
double-edged weapon. The parliamentarians were, it is true, in
furious opposition to the executive branch, but this did not make
them any the less a privileged class themselves, much attached to
the special benefits granted them by the monarchy. How was
Danton to play a double game in his discussion of the problem?
And how could he develop the theme straight off the cuff, without any preparation? He turned around, looking rather pale, and
murmured to his sponsor, Huet de Paisy, and his friends Rousselin de Saint-Albin and Jules Paré, who had accompanied him:
"They want to make me walk the razor's edge."

But any alarm he may have felt vanished in a few seconds.
A man of his stamp is not so easily flustered. He had to flatter
the College of Advocates, win the sympathy of his new confreres,
without forfeiting in any degree his reputation for frankness, or
prejudicing his integrity by the least hint of gross toadyism. It
took him very little time to decide his line of approach. Then the
lion advanced into the arena. Danton rose, cap in hand. The
audience stared curiously at this giant of a man whose ugliness
was already legendary, and who was plainly not in the least
disconcerted by the sixty-nine pairs of eyes now trained on him.

What did he actually say to them? Since no trace of the
speech has survived, we can only rely on Saint-Albin, who gives
a brief summary of it. For Danton this was an occasion to take
up a public stand. He called on the nobles and the clergy to
make certain sacrifices. The people were hungry: their position
must be understood. In the duel between Parliament and the
King, the speaker could see nothing but a quarrel involving two
privileged classes, with no possible advantage for more humble
folk. For a long time now the latter had been muttering; in the
end, they would revolt. France would live through some fearful
times. And Danton closed on a great prophetic peroration: "Woe
to those who provoke revolutions, woe to those who make
them!"

His words shook the hall. The Counsels to the King's Bench
were not used to hearing such indictments of the régime. Older
members shook their heads, frowning, though the younger ones

displayed more signs of comprehension. The former, their Latin perhaps a little rusty with age, asked Danton to produce a written version of his address so they could study it at their leisure. The second group tried to soothe their ruffled feathers and explain to these old buffers just what the suspect words actually meant. Danton, relying on his prodigious memory, offered to repeat the entire speech there and then. This produced protestations from one group and loud approval from the other. But in the end all differences were settled, and the new member was admitted without further formalities.

His wife and his mother-in-law kissed him, Charpentier and Huet de Paisy offered him their congratulations: here he was, established in a position far more remunerative—on the face of it—than his previous job. Did he plead frequently, and in cases of some importance? He did not. Emile Bos's researches in 1881 on "The Conciliar Advocates" do not allow Maître d'Anton more than three cases between 1787 and 1791. Yet his friend Courtois was still able to say, in August of the latter year: "There are at this very moment something like twelve million[!] or more briefs held over in his office, which his reputation and talent have brought him in." Many years afterward, in 1910, André Fribourg published a critical edition of Danton's speeches. According to this author, the Counsel to the King's Bench pleaded twenty-one cases. My own research suggests that the figure should be twenty-two. Which view are we to believe? In any case, can twenty-two cases be held to represent "twelve million" cases, even in the eighteenth century? Everything depends on their importance, on the wealth or the nobility of the parties involved.

In the earlier cases the element of nobility is beyond question. Danton was retained by M. de Barentin, President of the Board of Excise, and on behalf of the four sons of the Vicomte de Langlade du Chayla de Montgros. He continued to affect the apostrophe in his name, doubtless in order to attract this flattering clientele. As far as his practice was concerned, he remained "Maître d'Anton." He used no other signature, and Brissot could write, during the clash between Girondists and Montagnards: "It would be a pleasant jest to see us arraigned by the

Republican Danton, who not two years ago was calling himself
M. d'Anton."

It would, indeed, have been impossible for M. d'Anton to
prove his nobility by adducing—as he did for the Vicomte mentioned above—twenty-three relevant documents in evidence. Nor
could he have written on his own behalf remarks such as the
following, taken from the draft statement composed for the sons
of this aristocrat (whose rank some opponent had challenged):
"The hand of the Vicomte du Chayla, member of the Order of
Chivalry, impressed on several of the documents in evidence adduced by the supplicants, will not have pointed out in vain that
they owe their being to the same source from which he is sprung,
since *His Majesty* will find no flaw in the attestation of this
noble warrior, whose name already stands hallowed by history,
which has passed down to posterity the valor with which a du
Chayla helped to rout that redoubtable enemy force at whose
hands the fortunes of *His Majesty's august forebear* long hung in
the balance on the field of Fontenoy."

For a man who was to denounce all "tyrants and their lack-
eys" from the platforms of various revolutionary clubs, this "august forebear" of "His Majesty" smells too much of the courtier. But the advocate of those days had only one aim in view:
to win his case. And as for Danton's style . . . ! We shall have
further occasion to observe that this brilliant orator was a very
mediocre writer.

In a case somewhat similar to that of the du Chayla brothers,
that of the Marquis de la Devèze, Danton was to declare that
"nobility is the most precious of possessions." He was to change
his tune a few years later, when political developments had
rendered hereditary titles the worst sort of stigma.

During 1787, meanwhile, the situation continued to deterio-
rate. In August the King signed a general decree, over his own
seal, against Parliament as a whole. Since this body still refused
to ratify the new tax measures, the King ordained its banishment
to Troyes. This removal of the highest officers of the realm was
not carried through without incident. Seditious broadsheets appeared, pasted up on walls. Faced with the hostility of the people, who threatened to oppose this forced exodus, the govern-

ment placed Paris under martial law. Troops began to patrol the streets.

In September another incident took place which drew large crowds—this time on the Seine—and produced a fresh case for Danton to handle. Demolition workers set about removing the Pont-au-Change. The shanties which ever since the Middle Ages had crowded this bridge from side to side now vanished in clouds of dust. To demolish the bridge meant the expropriation of its inhabitants. One of them, a tailor named Sansac, received from the municipal authorities an indemnity of 33,500 *livres.* Since he himself estimated his loss at 42,000, he briefed Maître d'Anton to take charge of his interests. The case was heard on December 7, and—for the first time—Danton lost.

Meanwhile Parliament had come back from Troyes. Louis XVI lifted his interdict in the belief that the members of that ancient assembly, having been made contrite by their exile, would prove more amenable in the future. The King was mistaken, however; next year Parliament refused to ratify two further edicts, one extending civil rights to Protestants, the other authorizing a loan of 420 millions.

On October 24, M. Charpentier sold his café business: this was four months after his daughter's wedding. No doubt the Inspector of Tax Concessions felt that the wife of a Counsel to the King's Bench should not have a father who was a café proprietor. He sold Le Parnasse for 41,200 *livres,* to a man named Pascal Maulu. With this money he purchased a house and garden at Fontenay-sous-Bois, and settled down there with his wife.

Their daughter visited them there frequently: Fontenay was an easily accessible suburb. Mme. d'Anton had become very elegant—*noblesse oblige* in more senses than one—and made a great impression on the local residents. In the end they came to call her "la belle Gabrielle," and their mayor gave her name to a new thoroughfare in Fontenay. (This Avenue de la Belle-Gabrielle is still in existence, though popular tradition attributes its title to a memory of Henri IV's mistress.) At the same time, Mme. d'Anton began to develop a certain telltale plumpness. The child was born at the rue des Mauvaises-Paroles in April of 1788. The young father picked up his son in clumsy hands, astonished that so large a man could have produced so tiny a baby. The child squalled, and Danton rocked it in an unsuccessful effort to quiet it. But he was also delighted: the new arrival was obviously going to have his father's powerful voice.

M. de Barentin, the President of the Board of Excise, had been—as we observed above—the new Counsel's first client. On that occasion there had been a conflict between two different tribunals. Certain forges situated at Conches, in Normandy, and forming part of a family inheritance, had been sold by the heirs of one René de Capelles. The creditors, who objected to this sale, demanded that the Châtelet—the court which had criminal jurisdiction over the Paris region—should take cognizance of the matter. The opposing party wanted the case to be tried by the bailiff's court in Conches. Danton was briefed by M. de Barentin, pleaded the case before the Court of Dispatch, and succeeded in having the case referred to the Châtelet.

As a result of this victory the President of the Board of Excise developed a high opinion of Danton's professional abilities, so much so that he retained the young man to take care of all his interests. Admitted to Barentin's confidence, Danton became something very like his intimate friend. During their discussions Gabrielle's husband would talk politics with his client. The latter, struck by Danton's original ideas, one day introduced him to Archbishop Loménie de Brienne, the Minister of Finance. Barentin thought that since both men were from Champagne, they ought to get on fairly easily. The prelate was born in Brienne (his château is still standing there), a small town just over sixteen miles from Arcis, with a military school that was afterward to acquire fame from Napoleon's having studied there.

Danton drew up a scheme of social and economic renovation for his illustrious compatriot's benefit. He incorporated in this project much of the introductory discourse he had delivered before the College of Advocates. It was vital that the King should stop this running battle with Parliament. Let him convince its members—with rather more subtle arguments than a ukase of provincial exile—of the pressing need for his reforms. Finally, let both the nobility and the clergy, who had a share in the payment of taxes that hit the Third Estate hardest, forego some part of their privileges. The acceptance of such a program would allow the King to work in peace. The commons would then be satisfied with his conduct and stop threatening to wreck all normal institutions. The executive itself would become the leader and instrument of national renovation.

Unluckily for Louis XVI and for France, Loménie de Brienne did not carry this project any further.

"The fool!" Danton cried when he told this story to Gabrielle. "He can't see that he's digging the monarchy's grave!"

Throughout all this the new Advocate was forever preoccupied with making money, paying off his debts, and keeping his wife happy: to this end he undertook a varied collection of cases. After the nobles who had been his first clients, a much humbler collection of people now filled his consulting room. The months passed; he acepted cases from farmers, merchants, goldbeaters, a shoelace manufacturer, a journeyman tailor, and an innkeeper.

Was this change a deliberate one, in accordance with his political ideas? We cannot tell. But toward the summer of 1788, a year after his marriage, he began to drop that carefully assumed apostrophe of his. On several deeds his name appears as plain "Maître Danton." On others he continued to ennoble himself.

He could not know that a hundred and fifty years later a telephone exchange area in Paris would bear his name—an area, moreover, on the Left Bank, whereas he now lived on the Right —nor that in the middle of it there would stand his statue, executed by a sculptor with the fatefully appropriate name of . . . Paris. It stands near the Odéon Métro station, in the middle of a sidewalk on the Boulevard Saint-Germain, at the end of the rue de l'École-de-Médecine. Erect, one arm outstretched, this is Danton for all eternity, thunderous and brazen.

The reason the City Council, in 1894, decided to erect the statue at this particular point is a very simple one. In fact, Danton *did* live here, on the Left Bank of the Seine, after leaving the rue des Mauvaises-Paroles. Gabrielle was tired of living so close to Les Halles. Farmyard animals cluttering up the street, pigs attacking small children, the smell of rotting vegetables—all these inconveniences drove the young couple to move. Besides, Danton's in-laws no longer lived on the Quai de l'École, but at Fontenay-sous-Bois. Since there was no longer any familial reason for staying in the neighborhood, the Dantons decided to move. Gabrielle set about looking for an apartment.

There was a certain M. Gély, a parliamentary usher and former regular customer at the Café du Parnasse, who lived with his wife and daughter in a house in the rue des Cordeliers. (The street is known today as the rue de l'École-de-Médecine, and the opening up of the Boulevard Saint-Germain in 1876 destroyed a good half of it.) The building in which the Gély family lived in 1788 was No. 24, which formed part of the section now lost. There was an apartment to rent underneath theirs. Mme. Gély told Gabrielle's parents about it, and Gabrielle herself went to have a look. She liked the place on sight. Danton went over it as well, and an agreement was soon drawn up with the landlord. The front door of the house opened at the exact spot where Danton's statue stands today. Its area was at the end of a cul-de-sac where numerous small shopkeepers had their booths.

Above the central archway there were five floors of good solid dressed stone, with an apartment on each floor. Danton and his family moved in on May 12, occupying the main-floor apartment directly above the mezzanine landing. This contained six principal rooms, plus kitchen, pantry, and the usual offices. The main drawing room, Danton's study, and the master bedroom looked out on the rue des Cordeliers. The other rooms, including the dining room, had windows that opened over the Cour de Commerce. There was a private staircase leading down to the mezzanine, where the servants' quarters were. Gabrielle took on two domestics, a chambermaid and a cook.

The modest nature of the furnishings—at least during the early part of their stay there—and the credit terms which Danton obtained from those who supplied them make it clear that despite the size of the apartment and the employment of domestic staff, the Advocate and his wife were far from well off. Among their notary's papers one interesting detail turns up. A year after they had moved in—on August 22, 1789, to be precise —Danton was still living on extended credit. He signed two agreements with one Louis Froyer, a maker of carpets and tapestries with a shop "under the small arcade of Les Halles," for a total sum of 3316 *livres,* payable in two installments: the first fell due in January of 1794, the second in January of 1796. The appointment which Huet had sold him was certainly not proving lucrative.

By doing her own shopping (in order to avoid loss through "housemaid's tricks") Gabrielle came to know all the local shop-keepers. When she wanted shoes repaired, for instance, she went to the cobbler whose shop stood right beneath her window. His name was Simon. When Danton became a Minister, it was Si-mon who guarded the little Dauphin in the Tower of the Tem-ple. And for her meat Gabrielle went to a butcher called Legendre, a man of herculean build, with a crimson complexion and strangler's hands. The popular vote was to make this Legendre a colleague of Danton's in the Convention.

Indeed, the entire area was thick with people whom the Rev-olution later raised from obscurity to prominence. When Gabri-elle leaned out of her dining-room window, she could look straight down into the Cour du Commerce and hear the noise of a printing press clanking away beneath her. This machine stood in a modest workshop and was operated by a man named Guillaume Brune. Twenty years later Napoleon was to create him Marshal of France. A little farther on, at the point where the Cour de Rouen joined the Cour du Commerce, lived an aristo-crat who abhorred the principle of aristocracy. The wealthy Marquis de Saint-Huruge could not forgive a régime which, thanks to the use of *lettres de cachet,* had allowed his wife—a comedienne of bourgeois stock—to remain locked up in the asy-lum of Charenton for three years. When the Revolution finally broke out, M. de Saint-Huruge gave vent to his rancor by as-suming the garb of a market porter, the title of Generalissimo of the *Sans-Culottes,* and the voice and manner of a popular demagogue.

Stanislas Fréron, another unknown whom the Revolution brought to fame and honor, lived only a hundred yards from Danton, in the rue du Théâtre-Français, now the rue de l'Odéon. Here he edited a periodical entitled *L'Année Littéraire*, until the time came when he was called to publish *L'Orateur du Peuple*. Not far away, in the rue des Deux-Portes-Saint-André, dwelt a twenty-eight-year-old medical student who much preferred the public platform to the dissecting room. His name was Chaumette, and he was to become a Public Prosecutor under the Commune. In the rue Monsieur-de-Prince there was a poet who scraped a lean living by his pen. Though all Paris was singing his famous refrain *"Il pleut, il pleut, bergère"* ("It's raining, shepherdess"), this man, Fabre d'Églantine, led the most indigent existence. In the rue de Tournon there lodged a Luxembourg *émigrée,* a woman called Théroigne de Méricourt, who astonished her neighbors by her slightly common beauty, the originality of her costume, and the somewhat unedifying manner in which she spent her leisure hours. Later she was to immortalize her name for posterity by taking part in the attack on the Tuileries—and by killing the journalist Suleau, an act for which she afterward received a public whipping on the Terrasse des Feuillants. Near to her lived one M. Pache, who worked in the Ministry of Marine until—thanks to the special Providence which looks after revolutionaries—he rose to become a Minister himself, and Mayor of Paris.

To cut a long story short—the list could be prolonged for pages on end—we can say, without exaggeration, that this district contained all the gunpowder that was to explode when destiny thrust a blazing torch into it. Dulaure, in the rue du Théâtre-Français; Anacharsis Clootz, in the rue Jacob; Lakanal, in the rue du Bac; the Abbé Grégoire, in the rue du Colombier; Hanriot, in the rue de la Clef; Manuel, in the rue Serpente; Buzot, on the Quai Malaquais; François Robert, in the rue de Condé; Sergent, in the rue des Poitevins; Momoro, in the rue de la Harpe; Fournier the American; Vincent; Ronsin; Jourdeuil—all these individuals whom Providence held ready in one *quartier* of Paris never doubted, from the moment they first set eyes on the fellow unknown who was called Danton, that they would rise up with him to overthrow the régime as soon as two final anonymous figures, Desmoulins and Marat, joined them in this seedbed of the future.

Did Danton in fact know Marat and Desmoulins at this period? In the case of Marat, the answer must be negative. When Danton moved to the rue des Cordeliers, this Swiss-German doctor, of Italian ancestry, had not yet Gallicized his name by the addition of a final *t*. He had lived in Switzerland, where he was born, and afterward in France, Spain, and England. At the present he was domiciled in Paris, leading a squalid and miserable existence, no one is quite sure exactly where. He wrote to Frederick II, the King of Prussia, "that land where freedom, forever persecuted, has taken refuge," offering his services. Reminding Frederick that Neuchâtel belonged to the monarchy, Dr. *Mara* came out boldly in favor of Prussian nationalism. But Frederick made no reply, and Marat duly classed him among the "tyrants" whom it would be necessary, sooner or later, to cast down in the dust. Danton knew nothing of all this; he only learned it later, when Marat became his neighbor.

Camille Desmoulins, on the other hand, Danton had known since he was called to the bar. Morover, they often met at the Lodge of the Nine Sisters. The two lawyers got on well with each other—perhaps because they formed so striking a contrast. Where Danton was physically forceful, eloquent, and relatively moderate in his views, Camille Desmoulins was a puny, stammering figure who yet possessed a far sharper and more incisive mind. The one was equipped to use a bludgeon, the other a rapier. Danton found it easier to speak than to write, whereas Desmoulins had a talent for pamphleteering but began to stammer the moment he opened his mouth. Except, that is, when he was pleading a case. In this he was like all stutterers, who invariably find singing their easiest mode of self-expression. He was, perhaps, a little crazy. He spurned fees, forgot to collect them from his clients, and lived from hand to mouth with the cheerful indifference of a professional beggar. In affairs of the heart he was even more unstable: he had fallen desperately in love with a woman well into her forties, Mme. Duplessis by name, the wife of a senior clerk in the Treasury. To this respectable middle-class lady—pretty still, but decidedly mature—Camille paid assiduous court. One day he sent her the following execrable quatrain:

Happy who can from near at hand admire
Your charms, and needs no distant quizzing glass;
Why should not *I* to this delight aspire?—
A temple door stands wide, and all may pass.

After being pestered by such attentions for some time, this
attractive person had him in and gave him a good talking-to.
Really, she told him, it was high time he stopped such childish
games. She was much older than he was: he must watch out or
people might start laughing at him. During this discussion a third
person came in: Mme. Duplessis's sixteen-year-old daughter. The
results were catastrophic. Desmoulins's perilous passion for the
mother turned into equally violent adoration of young Lucile.
This new love left him sleepless. He declared himself. But Duplessis *père* rejected the claims of so inconsiderable a suitor. Desmoulins took Danton into his confidence, and the latter was full
of good advice. What Camille should do, he said, was to go on
playing the gallant with Madame—strictly on a platonic level.
This would raise him in her esteem, and finally she would persuade her husband to let him marry Lucile. After all, Danton reminded him, the same maneuver had worked very well with
Mme. Charpentier when he, Danton, wanted to marry Gabrielle.

Desmoulins followed this somewhat dangerous recommendation to the letter. Unfortunately, Mme. Duplessis guessed his
motives. Though not in the least eager to succumb to the illicit
embraces of so harum-scarum a character, she began (for very
natural, if not wholly admirable, reasons) to feel somewhat jealous of her daughter. The result was that for a long time she
remained resolutely opposed to the marriage.

To top everything else, Lucile did not find Camille particularly attractive. His pointed features, long thin hands, and yel-
lowish complexion gave him a singular resemblance to a heron,
or wader. He floundered hopelessly in conversation. It was only
at the Law Courts, in the feverish excitement of pleading a case,
that he managed to unlock his tongue: the same facility that
he afterward used to drive the mob against the Bastille. But in a
drawing room the poor fellow was put out of countenance the
moment anyone asked him a question. How could Lucile Duplessis possibly become involved with such a clown—especially

when both her father and her mother were both dead against the
relationship?

Yet the clown had one thing in his favor: he was intelligent.
He had brains and to spare. Otherwise Danton would certainly
not have bothered to include him in his circle. And though she
mocked his stutter by nicknaming him "Monsieur Hon-Hon,"
the charming Lucile also succumbed in the end. She promised
him her hand, always subject to family approval. Though now
besieged by two young lunatics instead of one, M. and Mme.
Duplessis continued to withhold their consent to the match for
another three years.

Camille often came round for a meal with the Dantons, and
sometimes he brought Lucile with him. A friendship sprang up
between her and Gabrielle. The latter was twenty-five, Lucile
only seventeen, and the younger girl tended to follow where
Gabrielle led. Danton and his wife became, in effect, the young
couple's friendly mentors. They in turn envied the Dantons' domestic happiness, and helped look after their small baby. Around
the dinner table their conversation invariably turned to politics.
Parliament was continuing its opposition to the executive; the
executive was employing every weapon at its disposal to fight
back. Finally, irked by constant parliamentary criticism, the executive prepared a *coup d'état* to neutralize its critics. The government was determined to substitute for the parliamentary system a plenary court and a group of *grands bailliages*. An edict
decreeing the change was actually signed by the King. But one
member, Duval d'Éprémesnil, obtained a copy of this ordinance
by bribery before it was officially published. He read it out in
public session, interspersing the text with his own indignant comments. Two other members, Fréteau de Saint-Just and Sabatier
de Cabre, joined him in his protest. Louis XVI gave immediate
orders to deal with the situation. In full public assembly the
officers of the watch appeared, and, amid general uproar, arrested the three members.

The first of them, Duval d'Éprémesnil, Danton, and Desmoulins met less often at the Law Courts than in the Lodge of
the Nine Sisters. Discussing the incident among themselves, they
approved of his action and regretted the fate that had befallen

him. D'Éprémesnil was seized by the police on May 5, 1788, bundled into a closed carriage, and driven to Cannes, where he remained incarcerated in the fortress on the Île Sainte-Marguerite till September 24.

Shortly after the arrest, the King proclaimed a "vacation" for the provincial Assemblies. Furious at this virtual proscription, they swung solidly into line behind the Paris Parliament. Trouble broke out immediately in Brittany and the Dauphiné. Despite the government's ban, the states of the southeast decided to meet in September at the Château de Vizille, near Grenoble. Since he was powerless to stop this movement, Loménie de Brienne decided to canalize it. The meeting of the States-General, which had been planned for 1792, was now brought forward to May 1, 1789. But the march of events had handled him too roughly, and he resigned his portfolio in favor of Necker, having first proclaimed a state of bankruptcy.

Bankruptcy: a terrible word, more dangerous than any underground mine. The State ceased its payments, and all France trembled. Gold and silver were hoarded, the cost of living soared, bakers shut up shop.

M. de Barentin was offered a seat in Necker's Cabinet, as Minister of Justice. He remembered the reconstruction plan that had been drafted by his attorney, and subsequently shelved by the Minister to whom it was submitted, Loménie de Brienne. Fearing that its author might be tempted to waste his knowledge in the ranks of the opposition, Barentin offered him the post of Secretary to the Chancellery. Though flattered, Danton refused. He was nervous of being tagged with so compromising a label. Besides, he felt, very strongly, that in rejecting his advice the executive had let slip its one hope of self-preservation. Now it was already too late: the first secret rumblings of the revolutionary storm could be heard. "Can't you see the avalanche coming?" he asked the Minister of Justice.

The preliminary symptoms of that avalanche were already shaking Paris. Necker's recall provoked simultaneous delight and alarm. The letters we have from the period give a very clear picture of this ambiguous feeling. One of them, written from Paris on August 30, 1788, to a notary in Châlons, shows us the populace screaming "Long live the King," throwing squibs and fireworks in the public gardens, and forcing the inhabitants of the Place Dauphine, "under pain of having all their glass stoned out," to put lights in every window. Meanwhile the police "put mounted patrols and foot patrols around the Pont-Neuf and the adjacent streets, and cordoned off the Place Dauphine with the Switzers and the French Guard"; the mob shouted insults at the latter, calling them "good-for-nothings and miserable clods."

"These gentlemen," the letter-writer continues, "were incensed by such words, and presently set about the rabble with their bayonets and the butts of their muskets: the result was plainly murder, a most abominable massacre. . . ." It also brought out some three thousand men, armed with sticks, knives, and pistols, from the two suburbs of Saint-Marcel and Saint-Antoine. There were scuffles all over Paris in which people were killed and wounded.

Faced with the "avalanche" that Danton had predicted, the new Minister of Justice renewed his offer. "Come in with me," he begged Danton. "Accept the post of Secretary General to the Chancellery." But once more the offer was declined. This refusal, and the reasons Danton gave for it, merely strengthened the resolve of his friends. Who, in fact, were they now, apart from Camille Desmoulins?

To begin with there was Jules Paré, Danton's former classmate from Troyes, who had become his old comrade's Chief Clerk and now lived in the same area, in the rue du Paon. Next, there was a lawyer called M. de la Croix, a Norman by birth. Sensing the wind of change that was beginning to blow, he changed his name first to Delacroix, then to plain Lacroix. Later this Lacroix was to become a leading lieutenant of the man who was his colleague in 1788. A frequent visitor to Lacroix was Danton's neighbor, Fabre d'Églantine, a playwright, actor, and poet, a man now approaching forty, constantly broke and always sponging on friends or relatives.

François Robert and his wife were also among Gabrielle's most regular guests. Robert was twenty-eight, a lecturer in law at the Société Philosophique. At the same time, this somewhat eccentric jurist ran a grocery store with a special line in colonial foodstuffs; it was his own property. His young wife, whose

maiden name had been de Kéralio, acted simultaneously as his
secretary and his shop assistant. In this way, although highly
educated and of very good family, she proclaimed her pro-
gressive, reformist beliefs. The Revolution was to take this impassioned, quixotic, likable couple and make them the founders
of the *Mercure National.*

Another regular guest in the Dantons' house was their
neighbor Guillaume Brune, the jobbing printer from the Cour
du Commerce. In 1788 there was nothing of the soldier about
this future Marshal of France. He had worked his way up from
typesetter to foreman, till at last he owned his own little business.
Before he turned to working for the political press, he had made
a living from setting up commercial documents. In his spare
time he devoted himself to literature. He had published a work
entitled *A Picturesque and Sentimental Journey into Divers
Western Provinces of France;* the bravura eloquence of this
essay must have stirred the reader to laughter and tears in
about equal proportions. When the Revolution broke out, Brune
was to become Danton's bodyguard. The latter referred to him
as "my Patagonian," because of his vast height. So, at least,
Barras was to assert in his *Memoirs.* But since their real author
and editor was none other than Rousselin de Saint-Albin, Barras's
secretary and the childhood friend of Danton, we have no reason
to doubt the veracity of this anecdote.

So the regular circle around Danton and his wife consisted of
Desmoulins and his clandestine fiancée, Guillaume Brune,
Rousselin de Saint-Albin, and Jules Paré. Infrequently, though
at least on several known occasions, they would be joined by M.
de Barentin and Duval d'Éprémesnil. It is strange to think of
the various fates to which these men and women were destined.
By the main door or the back stairs, they entered the turmoil of
politics and revolution; they knew glory, wealth, love, and
sudden death. Whirled away in the maelstrom of events, they
could no longer turn back, even had they wished to do so. It
was the most distinguished of them who had declared, in his
speech before the College of Advocates: "Woe to those who
provoke revolutions, woe to those who make them!"

CHAPTER IV

True Elector, False Captain

A CENTURY EARLIER, La Fontaine had written two lines which people would do well to ponder in any time of trouble:

> We must conclude that Providence
> Knows, better than we do, what we need.

What did the men who dreamed of "the great smash-up" really need in 1788? A national disaster of some kind, that would cause widespread devastation, thus bringing nerves near breaking point and driving the populace to commit excesses. This catastrophe, this scourge was obligingly supplied by Providence in the form of an appallingly hard winter.

The Seine froze as far as Le Havre, the Loire to Nantes, and every canal in the kingdom iced up. The barges were immobilized, frozen solid, and grain and cheese rotted in their holds. A similar fate befell carts and wagons on the snowbound roads. When the snow melted, glazed frost took its place. Since workshops were not getting any raw materials, they began to lay off their craftsmen. In several areas there was a real threat of famine. The cost of living soared up by leaps and bounds. In Paris the price of a four-pound loaf rose from eight to fifteen sous. Soon there was a nation-wide emergency. Certain speculators, convinced that prices would continue to rise, refused to sell the foodstuffs they had in their warehouses. Liberal pamphleteers attacked these practices. Others of a more strictly political bent accused the Court of shielding those who thus set out to starve the people. In actual fact, the royal family knew of the country's plight only through the lying reports their courtiers provided.

The Duke of Orléans, on the other hand, was much better informed as to the miserable plight of the poor. This royal cousin and First Prince of the Blood did not live in the fatuous isolation which prevailed at Versailles. Living in Paris, where he occupied the Palais-Royal, he could mingle with the crowds and was well aware of their needs. An interesting mixture of genuine charity and undoubted ambition, he lent his support to the popular cause in the secret hope of one day attaining power. On December 20, 1788, he announced, via the press, his decision to distribute a thousand pounds of bread daily to the poor people of Saint-Eustache, to defray the lying-in expenses of pregnant women, to forego the tithes that he levied on grain harvested from his estates, and, finally, to abolish the restrictive game laws in all his preserves. During a period of famine this generous move could not fail to have considerable effect. Till then only the nobility had possessed the right to hunt game. By throwing open his domains to any common hunter—not to mention poachers—Philippe d'Orléans was making a genuinely revolutionary innovation.

He was already unpopular enough at Court, and this step did nothing to improve matters. At Versailles it was felt that his generosity was not nearly so ardent as his ambition. In Paris, on the other hand, he was generally admired and referred to as a great patriot. The term "patriot" emanated from the Masonic Lodges, of which the Duke was Grand Master, and where Desmoulins, Danton, and their friends remained very small fry.

But this word "patriot" did not carry the meaning we give to it today. The division of the country into various provinces, all with different customs, individual Parliaments, strictly enforced customs barriers, and, sometimes, quite separate languages meant that each province was a country in miniature, behind which the larger State tended to be forgotten. Though the word "patriot" existed as early as the sixteenth century, it was only beginning to come into popular usage in 1788. People really adopted it—and with what abuse of meaning!—only when provincial divisions had been replaced by those of the *départements,* and devotion to the monarchy by affection for *la patrie.*

Prior to this transformation, no one was surprised to see French generals in command of foreign armies, or officers from various countries abroad winning high rank and honors in the French armed services. This was the way it had been for centuries. During the Franco-Spanish War of 1658, the Great Condé commanded the Spanish forces, while Turenne—who was not a Frenchman—commanded those of France. On other occasions we find a Duke of Saxe-Weimar leading French troops against his own country, while a Swiss in the service of Sweden, Jean-Louis d'Erlach, switched his allegiance to France and rose to obtain a Marshal's baton. Other Marshals of France include Schomberg, a German, and Rantzau, who was Danish. To come down nearer the period under discussion, we can take one last example: Baron Luckner, a Bavarian who held a colonelcy from the King of Prussia and was a general under Louis XVI before finally receiving his baton as Marshal of France in 1791— from the revolutionary leaders.

The ordinary soldiers, the rank and file, would hire themselves out to any prince who paid them. These mercenaries were not defending their fatherland: they were exercising a profession. Often they found themselves fighting against their own kind, and unspoken agreements existed by which they were allowed to spare their friends, cousins, or brothers when they came face to face with them, by accident, on the field of battle.

Thus under the Ancien Régime the word *patrie* ("fatherland") evoked no associations except for a more or less determined opposition to the traditions of the monarchy. We can now see why the label of "patriot" which the Freemasons stuck on the Duke of Orléans earned him, at one and the same time, the distrust of the Court, the admiration of the bourgeoisie, and the fanatical devotion of the masses.

Paris was divided up into twenty-one *quartiers*, the population of which varied so considerably that it was impossible for each of them—at least with any semblance of equity—to elect a Deputy of the Third Estate as delegate to the States-General. A new ordinance of April 17, 1789, redivided the capital into sixty new districts. These electoral divisions corresponded, roughly speaking, to the Parisian parish boundaries. Out of a total population of 700,000, no more than 40,000 were owners of landed property, and paid the "contribution of a silver mark" which gave them the right to vote. Nor were they at liberty to designate their own representatives to the States-General. Split up into as many Primary Assemblies as there were voting districts, these 40,000 enfranchised persons were required to nominate 407 grand electors. The latter, in turn, had the task of electing the twenty Deputies allowed, by law, to the people of Paris. The notion of universal suffrage, we see, had not yet begun to exercise people's minds.

As an owner of property at Arcis (and of a Counsel's office) Danton was included among the 40,000 primary electors. His too-lazy friend Desmoulins, though a parliamentary attorney, did not have a sufficient income in 1789 to belong to this category. His rancor was as great as that of the proletariat: both felt that they had been denied a voice in consultations of national importance simply on a basis of cash. As for women, it never occurred to anyone that *they* should be summoned to the voting booths.

In the same District des Cordeliers where Danton occupied a large apartment (even though it was furnished on credit) Desmoulins kept shifting from hotel to hotel, the degree of comfort varying in accordance with the current state of his finances. On the morning of April 21, while Danton was on his way to the Couvent des Cordeliers (the church of which was being utilized as a polling station), Camille went off to vent his wrath on the other side of the river, in the gardens of the Palais-Royal. The Duke of Orléans, who owned this verdurous oasis, left it open for any malcontent who cared to come there. Danton, on the other hand, marched into the sanctuary of Les Cordeliers with all the self-satisfaction of a dyed-in-the-wool bourgeois.

Under the vaulting of the old sixteenth-century church the electors of the district strolled to and fro. A municipal clerk, ensconced behind a table, handed out two printed forms to each of them in turn. They were required to write, on one form, their full names, addresses, and occupations; and on the other, the names of the ten grand electors who, as chosen by them, would then participate (if elected) in the task of designating the twenty Paris Deputies.

Naturally, such a novel procedure provoked discussion. When their electoral duties were concluded, the voters did not go home. They stayed in the church, moving from one group to another to press home their various points of view. Sometimes they would get up on a chair and express them to the entire gathering. Their function was not restricted to choosing the electors of the twenty Paris Deputies. They still had the task of formulating various demands and complaints and submitting them in tabulated form—the so-called *Cahiers de Doléances*—to the States-General.

Denied the right to vote because they did not pay sufficient taxes, the common people were seething with well-justified indignation. But it was a completely false rumor that drove them over the edge. Word went around that a certain M. Réveillon, a papermaker from the Faubourg Saint-Antoine, had declared on his way to the polling station: "The workers can manage perfectly well on fifteen sous a day! I have some under me who make twenty, and they go around with watches in their fobs—very soon they'll be better off than I am!"

Apocryphal or not, this story went around Paris like wildfire. It reached the Dantons, who—despite their lively interest in public affairs—paid scant attention to it: they had other things to worry about. Their son, who was now just over a year old, had succumbed to an illness which the family doctor could do nothing to cure. The poor child went into a swift decline and died on April 24. The funeral took place two days later. Gabrielle was heartbroken. Being an extremely devout woman, she went to seek consolation in a religious atmosphere. Her husband, on the contrary, inveighed noisily against Providence. He accompanied Gabrielle as far as the church door but would not cross the threshold with her. His ugliness intensified by anger, he strode away, staring straight in front of him, pacing the streets and mingling with the various groups that were all excitedly discussing the supposed remarks of the factory owner from the Faubourg Saint-Antoine.

On the 27th, three days after the death of Danton's child, some hotheaded demonstrators besieged the manufacturer's pri-

vate residence. Driven off by a strong police detachment, they
turned their wrath on the owner of a saltpeter refinery, M.
Henriot—though he, in fact, had sacrificed part of his fortune
to keep his personnel fed. Troops were brought in, but it took a
couple of days to get the rioting under control. More than a
hundred corpses were found lying in the streets afterward.

The feverish atmosphere in the capital had not yet subsided
when the States-General opened at Versailles. The first session,
on May 5, took place without the Third Estate Deputies from
Paris. The slowness of the voting procedure, the moral pressure
exerted around the polling booths (which reduced the 40,000
primary electors to a mere 11,706)—all these obstacles combined
to prevent the twenty Parisians elected from appearing in the
Assembly before May 23.

Among them there were very few people destined to achieve
fame. All the same, they included M. Bailly, member both of the
Academy of Sciences and the French Academy; Dr. Guillotin,
whose name needs no introduction; and the Abbé Sieyès, author
of the famous pamphlet on the Third Estate referred to before.
("What is the Third Estate? Nothing. What should it be?
Everything . . .") Danton knew these three men well: he used
to meet them at the Lodge of the Nine Sisters.

Two more of his friends were included among the Deputies:
Maître Camus, the lawyer who bore Mme. Recordain's maiden
name, and Maître Dosfant, who had drawn up Danton's marriage contract and employed Gabrielle's brother Antoine as his
clerk.

Danton might have put forward his own candidature. Did he
consider doing so? It would seem improbable. If he wanted to
make a living and pay off his debts, it was better, surely, to stick
to his legal practice rather than go off and live in a rented room
at Versailles. The eighteen *livres* that a Deputy received as an
allowance for each session would hardly have begun to fill the
financial gulf which his love match had opened up under his
feet. In order to act as the people's representative, he would
have had to leave Paris and let his cases gather dust there. Such
an ambition called for the kind of resources he did not possess.

Nevertheless, he was able to follow all the deliberations of the
Assembly, thanks to a rash of new broadsheets and the various

rumors that traveled back from Versailles. Since June, Mirabeau had been publishing the *Journal des États Généraux;* Gorsas, the *Courrier de Versailles à Paris;* Barère, *Le Point du Jour;* and Brissot, *Le Patriote Français.* Reading these kept Parisians abreast of fresh events. It was through them that they learned of the Tennis Court Oath, Mirabeau's famous apostrophe to the Marquis of Dreux-Brézé, and the transformation of the States-General into a National Constituent Assembly.

The whole population took an impassioned interest in these happenings. In the gardens of the Palais-Royal people discussed them with frenzied excitement. Built by the Duke of Orléans some years previously, the buildings that surrounded (and still surround) the vast and verdant enclosure ringed it with a circle of shops and restaurants. It served, at one and the same time, as a meeting place for persons of fashion, the main public square of Paris, a central stage for every kind of tub-thumper, and an open-air cloister where thinkers could stroll about and exchange ideas.

The crowds surged to and fro beneath the trees. Respectable women and ladies of easy virtue jostled each other outside the shopwindows, admiring the dresses and jewelry and finely bound books on display. There was much pushing in the crowded entrance of the Caveau—a café still in existence today, the one survivor from this period; there were arguments over tables on the sidewalk outside La Grotte Flamande, renowned for its beer; there was the Café des Italiens, with its vast and globular Dutch stove that attracted customers in chilly weather; and the Café de Chartres, where the young Duke of that name, Philippe d'Orléans's elder brother, had his portrait on view; and lastly the Café de Foy, where they sold the *eau-de-vie d'Andaye* that connoisseurs went into ecstasies over.

But what a bear garden the Café de Foy was! This was where the Patriotic Society of the Palais-Royal held its meetings—outside in the open air, with orators standing on chairs, sometimes on tables, unless they were put off stride by a rainstorm. The fieriest speakers were men like Saint-Giniès, Loustalot, Harivel, and Collard. But the real organizers of the group were Danton, the Marquis de Saint-Huruge, and Camille

Desmoulins. The last-named wrote to his father, who lived in Guise: "The Palais-Royal is the home of patriotism."

When, quite by chance, the Duke of Orléans appeared on one of his balconies, he was given a great ovation. At least one statue was made of him during his lifetime: he figured in the waxwork exhibition of Christophe Curtius, which was on display in the Hôtel d'Aligre, only a couple of doors down from the Prince's residence. Beside the noble liberal, Curtius had placed a smiling wax representation of Necker: a fair juxtaposition. Necker and the Duke of Orléans were the two most popular figures in 1789, with General de La Fayette trailing a little behind them—despite the fact that he had been one of those responsible for the calling of the States-General. Compared to these leading actors, Danton was, as yet, the merest supernumerary.

When wolves are hungry, they come down from the forests. So, now, were there armed bands roaming everywhere in France. Sometimes hundreds strong, they plundered farms and warehouses, not hesitating to kill the occasional peasant who dared to defend himself against their depredations.

By the end of June these tattered hordes had reached the outskirts of Paris. Among the bourgeoisie the word "brigands" passed from mouth to mouth. They called on the King to protect them, and Louis XVI threw a cordon of troops all around the city. Something like thirty thousand men took up defensive positions at various strategic points. Their officers were told to maintain law and order, protect grain convoys making for the capital, and stop the brigands from doing likewise. But despite their vigilance, between fifteen and eighteen thousand of these unfortunates got through the cordon, some on their own, others in groups; whereupon the civic authorities, in order to keep this formidable body of unemployed persons occupied, opened a weird collection of workshops in Montmartre, and employed them there at twenty sous a day. But in the evening they would descend from their rustic hillside and mingle with the crowds in the Palais-Royal gardens. Here they applauded the speeches of Saint-Huruge and Camille Desmoulins and Danton, and of a newcomer, one Dr. Marat.

On being informed of this popular unrest and agitation, Louis XVI ordered his troops to quit the barricades, march back into Paris, and pitch camp on the Champ-de-Mars. Numerous regiments set up their tents there, together with some battalions of Swiss and German mercenaries—not to mention the four thousand soldiers of the French Guard, whose reputation for bravery and honor was no more than a memory. The members of this corps had the right to pursue a second occupation apart from their military service: most of them seem to have gone in for procuring.

After June 23 this riffraff began to show signs of insubordination. In a tactless and clumsy speech Louis XVI had made it known that he would continue to refuse senior rank to commoners. When the French Guard heard about this, they showed their displeasure in no uncertain fashion. In order to nip a potential mutiny in the bud, the authorities arrested the ringleaders. There were about a dozen of them; they were promptly locked up in the Prison de l'Abbaye.

When the crowds outside the Palais-Royal heard of their incarceration, they rioted, spurred on by the Marquis de Saint-Huruge and Loustalot (the latter was a journalist). The Duke of Orléans's locksmith distributed pikes to several hundreds of men, who then set off, shouting for the release of the imprisoned soldiers. When they reached the Abbaye, they forced the gates, to the somewhat surprising battle cry of "Long Live the King!," and carried the French Guard back shoulder high to the Palais-Royal.

Since the situation was rapidly getting out of hand, Louis XVI decided to dismiss Necker, whom he regarded as too soft for the job. On July 11 he told him to go back to his native Switzerland, and summoned M. de Breteuil to take over the government.

The next day Camille Desmoulins got up on a table outside the Café de Foy and before a frantically excited audience (already worked up enough by the sultry heat) proceeded to deliver his famous harangue: "Citizens! I have just returned from Versailles. There is not a moment to lose. M. Necker has been dismissed! This dismissal will sound the tocsin for a St. Bartholomew's Eve massacre of patriots! Tonight all the Swiss and German battalions will move from the Champ-de-Mars to cut our throats. We have only one recourse left—to take up arms!"

These words produced the most tremendous effect. Fear of the brigands, who were looting shops and burning tollhouses, was reinforced by fear of the troops, who might drive out the brigands, but might also destroy the nation's aspirations while they were at it.

Desmoulins's speech turned the capital into an inferno. There was brawling everywhere: skirmishes between the troops and the people, convents invaded on the pretense of looking for hidden arms, apartments forced open by lunatic, witless crowds. The sorcerer's apprentice had got his wish: now he was famous, and believed that Lucile would love him all the more because of it.

In order to quell this serious agitation, the municipal authorities ordered the formation of a "bourgeois militia" of 42,000 men. For a city of 700,000 inhabitants the figure was hardly excessive. Each electoral district was required to furnish a battalion. Churches sounded the tocsin to summon volunteers to every district headquarters. At the same time, clerks hurried around the streets ringing hand bells. If any inhabitant showed curiosity, they explained the reason for the noise they were making.

Warned by all this activity, Danton hurried out. Just as he left his apartment he met his fellow tenant M. Gély. Together they went down to the Church of the Couvent des Cordeliers (a Franciscan monastery). Danton, always so calm as a Counsel in the Law Courts, felt himself catching the mood of public excitement. A few days before, outside the Palais-Royal, someone had seen him get up on a table and harangue the crowd. Now he did the same thing again in the sanctuary of the monastery. His colleague Lavaux was astounded to hear him shouting: "Citizens! Let us arm ourselves—let us arm ourselves to repel the 15,000 brigands assembled in Montmartre, and the 30,000 military who are ready to descend on Paris, to loot the city and slaughter its inhabitants!"

At the sound of his voice, many neighbors volunteered for the Bataillon des Cordeliers. He himself enrolled, and so did his friend Paré, as well as M. Gély. But Maître Lavaux, on the other hand, told him quite bluntly: "I have just come back from Montmartre. I saw nothing there except workmen, quarrymen, and masons going about their ordinary business—"

"You don't understand what's going on, do you?" Danton cut in. "The sovereign people is rising against despotism. Be one of us. The monarchy is finished, your position is lost anyway. Use your head—"

Lavaux said: "I see nothing in this so-called movement except a common insurrection that will lead you, and those like you, to the gallows."

But Danton paid no attention to his colleague and continued his stump speech. The civilians who enlisted were now joined by a number of soldiers. The French Guard, in fact, were deserting their regiment *en masse* and transferring to the militia. Almost all the districts accepted them—partly because they were afraid of them, but also because they brought their arms and ammunition with them. These were two commodities which the civic authorities could not supply to the bourgeoisie. Besides, the French Guard's bearskins would add a nice touch to the picture, it was felt: they might give the militia a slightly more martial air.

Danton's eloquence worked wonders. The Bataillon des Cordeliers soon numbered 571 men. But the orator, to his great surprise, was not given command of it. The rank and file preferred a certain M. Crèvecoeur, who had seen army service. Among the junior officers appointed, the captains, lieutenants, and second lieutenants, we find such names as Villette, Roux, Navarre, Mabire, Coutras, Dupont; but here again there was no room for Danton. What was the matter? he must have wondered. Had they so little faith in his fighting caliber? They did not even want him as a noncommissioned officer—though they had made his butcher, Legendre, a sergeant. Legendre, a tradesman who knew about nothing except how to cut up meat! Danton, Gély, and Paré were left as private soldiers. To begin with, at any rate. Time enough later to see if any of them rated a noncommissioned officer's stripes.

Camille Desmoulins was not on the muster roll at all. He had no wish to shed his blood; he much preferred the gardens of the

Palais-Royal and the loud plaudits of the crowd. Where popularity was concerned, he meant to secure himself the lion's share. On July 13 and 14 he was at his usual place in milord's park. Perched on a high stool, sweat pearling his forehead, cravat all awry, he exhorted the people, the brigands, the bourgeoisie—everybody, in short—to storm Les Invalides and lay hands on the thirty thousand muskets stored there. It was thanks to these guns that an attempt on the Bastille became a possibility.

Did Camille Desmoulins take part in this famous assault? He did not, in any way. The fiery spellbinder was no military leader; and though he was bold enough with his tongue and his pen, this patriot blenched at the sound of gunfire. Even so, the great rush for loot at Les Invalides, where not a shot was fired, brought him a gun, a bayonet, and a brace of pistols. He wrote about the episode to his father, giving himself a fine leading role in it. But on the subject of the Bastille, that fortified stronghold of the Faubourg Saint-Antoine, he added: "I hurried down there at the sound of the first cannon being fired, but the Bastille had already fallen, after a mere two and a half hours."

Though a much bolder character than his friend, Danton himself did not risk his neck by going anywhere near the Bastille till the following night, when all trace of danger had vanished—not two and a half, but a full ten hours later. The circumstances, moreover, provide a strange mixture of tragedy, burlesque, and pure vaudeville farce.

La Fayette, as Commander-in-Chief of the bourgeois militia, had been responsible for replacing the Marquis de Launay, the Governor of the Bastille, murdered by the insurgents. On La Fayette's recommendation, the elector Soulès had taken over the dead man's office. Very conscious of his heavy burden of responsibility, this respectable middle-class citizen from the Saint-Antoine district set forth to take up his post in the old donjon. When night fell, he did not go to bed. Sometimes attended by an escort, sometimes alone, he kept watch over the walls from the outside throughout the evening of the 14th and well into the small hours.

About three o'clock in the morning he went off on his own, and had just crossed the first drawbridge when he found himself surrounded by four swaggering members of the bourgeois militia, under the command of an officer. None of them wore uniform: the municipal authorities had not thought of such a minor detail. They had muskets in their hands, and baldrics slung over their coats to stop their sabers trailing along the ground.

"Who are you?" Soulès asked.

"I am Captain Danton, of the Bataillon des Cordeliers. I have just been inspecting the Bastille with my company. And who might you be, pray?"

"Soulès, the new Governor."

"Eh? There isn't any Governor now."

"Obviously there is, for I am the Governor."

"You?" Danton said. "Show me your commission."

Soulès brought out the paper signed by La Fayette. As it was dark, Danton could not read it. "A mere scrap of paper!" he exclaimed. "Citizens! Arrest this man!"

The Governor protested. He tried to explain but no one would listen. He called to the sentries for help but his cries went unanswered. No doubt the guards were sleeping off the effects of the wine they had found in the fortress. Danton about-turned his squad and marched back across Paris with his prisoner. On the way he had to protect Soulès from the angry attentions of the mob. The whole population, it seemed, was up and wandering about the streets. Some character being haled off by the militia: obviously a "bandit" or a former defender of the Bastille or one of those who hoarded food to starve the people! *"String him up!"* they shouted. At several crossroads Danton and his men were forced to fix bayonets. Otherwise Soulès might well have gone the same way as the Marquis de Launay.

Danton got back to Les Cordeliers before dawn and ordered the tocsin to be sounded. Roused by the bell, the inhabitants put on their clothes and hurried around to the church. The self-styled captain, ever mindful of publicity, put them in the picture. Aroused not only by the events themselves but by a torrid heat wave and the thousand and one rumors flying around Paris, some even wanted to see the suspect shot out of hand.

Soulès made energetic protests. Instead of panicking, he demanded to be taken to the City Hall, where La Fayette had set up his headquarters. The "American" would recognize and protect him. After all, it was he who had appointed him Governor. Eventually the unfortunate victim gained his point. He was bundled into a carriage—an open carriage: nothing else was available in summer—and driven through the streets in full view of the angry mob, with Danton and his three volunteers jouncing along on the running boards.

When they reached the City Hall, La Fayette was nowhere to be found. Exhausted by the revolutionary events of the previous evening, he was still asleep. The only thing to do was to go down to the Hôtel de Noailles in the rue Saint-Honoré, where he was staying, wake him up, and ask him to come to the City Hall without delay.

Finally he arrived—in a furious temper, as might be expected. But everything was cleared up: La Fayette personally vouched for the status and identity of the new Governor of the Bastille.

Such a piece of buffoonery on Danton's part is really surprising. Normally, he displayed admirable judgment and self-control. How could he have lent himself to this masquerade? And how, having passed himself off as a captain, did he find forty volunteers to follow him to the Faubourg Saint-Antoine, let alone persuade his district to ratify his actions in the monastery chapel?

Marmontel, a member of the French Academy, was later to write in his *Memoirs:* "Many unstable persons took advantage of these troubled times to push themselves forward. I used to see many such noisy, turbulent fellows, interrupting each other's speeches, only interested in attracting attention."

Danton fell squarely into this category. What was more, he no longer had any faith in the régime. Recall what he said to his colleague Lavaux, when arguing for the formation of the Bataillon des Cordeliers: "You don't understand what's going on. . . . The *sovereign* people is rising against despotism. . . . The monarchy is finished, *your position* is lost anyway." The position to which he alludes here was that of Counsel to the King's Bench—an office which Danton likewise held. If he believed that Louis XVI would not be able to maintain his position, an obvious conclusion followed. The King's downfall would, *ipso facto,* bring about the dissolution of the King's Bench, and the post of Counsel to its various courts would vanish at the same time. It was therefore vital to keep a close eye on the development of events and not let the future catch one unawares. Danton *had* to push himself forward, in every possible way.

Marmontel also wrote: "We know that throughout the ages the object of a tribune's eloquence has been to work on the passions of the people; and in our society the only training ground for such eloquence was the bar. . . . The surest method of propagating revolutionary doctrines was, therefore, to win the allegiance of the legal fraternity. . . . One can see what a personal interest this body had in changing reform to revolution, and the monarchy to a republic; what it sought to establish for itself was a *perpetual aristocracy.* Destined, one after another, to be the active leaders of the republican faction, these ambitious men could have found no more congenial goal. Already occupying key positions everywhere by virtue of their learning and talent, they would now also be summoned to hold public office and would become, with few exceptions, France's sole legislators: her leading magistrates to begin with, and very soon her true sovereigns."

Although Danton is not referred to in this passage, one instantly thinks of him while reading it. Not only did he foresee that the fall of the King would topple the Counsels to the King's Bench as well; he also saw in the Revolution a means of compensating for the all-too-probable ruin of his professional career—better still, as the instrument by which that career could be replaced by something better and more rewarding. This is why he made his speech outside the Palais-Royal; it also explains the curious comedy he staged at the Bastille and the City Hall, with poor Soulès as its victim.

La Fayette (despite the fact that he had been routed out of bed at dawn and forced to hurry around to the Place de Grève to save the skin of his own nominee as Governor) was very mild in his reproaches to Danton. The latter might be unknown at present; but La Fayette, too, had to watch his step. He swallowed his fury and smiled with exquisite politeness. For the immediate future, as we shall see, he stuck to this policy of conciliation through thick and thin. In fact, however, he had taken an instant and violent dislike to Danton, from the moment of their first meeting that morning, on July 15.

In the district of Les Cordeliers, Soulès's little misadventure did his tormentor no disservice. Napoleon was to say, later, apropos his return from the Middle East: "If you want to win popularity in France, do something daring and slightly crazy." Put the whole thing in miniature—the arrest of Soulès for the conquest of Egypt, the district of Les Cordeliers for France as a whole—and it becomes apparent why Danton's "daring and slightly crazy" action got him made President of his district. The Assembly of Electors was inclined to criticize him at first; but then, proud of a fellow citizen who showed such initiative, they endowed him with a President's badges of office—the hand bell and the glass of water.

CHAPTER V

The "Beloved President"

POLITICAL LEADERS ALWAYS ENJOY an advantage over the military authorities—especially when they are dealing with mere temporary soldiers, reservists called out for the maintenance of law and order. Having been elected President of the district, Danton brought all his weight—over two hundred pounds of it—to bear on M. Crèvecoeur, Commandant of the Bataillon des Cordeliers. Nothing proved easier, at this stage in the game, than to secure his nomination to a captaincy. Danton's ploy had worked well.

At the beginning of August the municipal authorities supplied the militia with uniforms. Not without a certain glow of pride, Danton donned his blue tunic with its white facings and scarlet collar, the white tan breeches, the black top-boots with yellow reveres. On his head went a black felt cocked hat, with the tricolor cockade. Around his waist he wound the sash belt from which his saber was hung (one hand resting proudly on the pommel). He admired himself in the glass while Gabrielle looked on. She was more in love with him than ever, and thought him vastly handsome despite the ugliness of his features.

On August 13 there was an important ceremonial occasion in the church of Les Cordeliers. Although regularly used for secular meetings, the Franciscan chapel still remained consecrated ground. A priest came in especially to celebrate High Mass there and bless the battalion's new flag. There was much pomp and pageantry. The flag, designed by a committee of local notables, consisted of a blue cross which divided the

material into four squares, like those on a chessboard. Two of
these squares were white, two red: the colors were arranged
diametrically, corner to corner. There was a certain amount of
relish for the cynic in this design. The blue cross satisfied the
clergy, the white squares pleased the Royalists, and the red
ones kept the revolutionaries happy. There was something for
everybody, and the silken tricolor was asperged with holy water
to loud applause from the watching crowd.

The new President, who had luxurious tastes, engaged the
orchestra of the Royal Academy of Music for the occasion. It
was to play a *Te Deum* by Gossec in the presence of the
Commander-in-Chief of the militia, M. le Marquis de La
Fayette. The latter, as we know, detested Danton, who returned
the compliment. But politics and common sense required that
such feelings should be kept carefully out of sight; and so both
of them—brilliant cavalry officer and eloquent talker—went out
of their way to charm each other. La Fayette, as a special
gesture of courtesy, brought his enchanting wife, the former
Adrienne de Noailles; she was still almost a child, certainly in
her infectious gaiety. Indeed, La Fayette himself, this heroic
veteran of the American war, was still only thirty-two. The
couple were madly in love—the one point in which they resembled the Dantons. After the Mass and the blessing of the
tricolor, Mme. de La Fayette went around under the ancient
vaulted beams of the church, taking up a collection on behalf
of the poor of the parish—or rather, the district—while the
crowd, wild with delight, sang a ditty that had been the craze of
Paris for the past fortnight:

> Sound the trumpet yet,
> Let France acclaim
> The heroic fame
> Of La Fayette!

Gabrielle Danton, who had arrived dressed in a light, rustling
summer dress, would have much preferred such tributes to be
reserved for her husband, who was the only great man *she*
recognized. She walked out of the church with her mother and
father, who had come in from Fontenay for the occasion. Danton had left a little earlier, by a side door. Was he bored or
irritated by something? Far from it. The President, at that point,

had had to transform himself into the Captain. The battalion was to march down the rue des Cordeliers, led by a band, while spectators crowded every window. Now they could hear the music and the tramp of the reservists' feet; the noise rose to a deafening climax, and there they were! Captain d'Anton commanded the leading company. His men did not march in step as well as they might; their dressing was irregular and their files tended to be uneven. These middle-class gentlemen and artisans and shopkeepers lacked experience and training. But the fanatical devotion of patriots was at least as worthwhile as the more martial bearing of mercenaries.

La Fayette stood waiting for them on the steps of the church, leaning on his saber as though it were a cane. Despite his receding hairline, the Commander-in-Chief looked tough and proud enough. But Gabrielle had a pleasant surprise in store. Danton at some point had left his company and reassumed the office of President, taking up his position beside Lafayette on the steps. It gave Gabrielle a petty thrill of satisfaction to see how his vast bulk overshadowed the Commander-in-Chief as the two of them watched the march-past that Georges had, earlier, led down the street.

"Long live Danton!" shouted some of the local inhabitants. But the cries of "Long live La Fayette!" remained far more numerous. Of course, the dashing Marquis had freed America from English oppression—though he had had M. Rochambeau to help him, and a whole parcel of volunteers besides. No, M. de La Fayette would not have got very far on his own. Now *there* was a man who knew all about the art of self-advertisement. No matter that during the same period Georges had thought of nothing apart from running after little trollops—or wealthy heiresses. Like that Françoise Duhauttoir, whose wealth was only matched by her elegance. Still, what was the point of dragging up such an unpleasant memory? Georges adored Gabrielle and made her terribly happy. She was not jealous of his past. Besides, had she not—thanks to him—now become Madame la Présidente?

Every evening, between five and nine, Danton sat in open committee at the District Assembly's headquarters. He and his vice-president, Fabre d'Églantine, were on the platform, with

the electors facing them. Behind these worthies crowded the
rabble: the workers, the down-and-outs who made scarcely any
money, and for that reason had no voice in the proceedings.
Nonetheless they were more than ready to applaud or to hiss,
according to circumstances; and Danton always took their
opinion into account. More than that, he actively solicited it.

The Assembly studied the problems both of Paris and of the
nation. A clerk recorded in a ledger the views and proposals put
forward. The transcript of each session would be forwarded,
through the proper channels, to the City Hall. There, in the old
Parloir aux Bourgeois of the Place de Grève, the Mayor and his
fellow Councilors would decide whether or not to implement
the recommendations put before them. This was the system
operated, with varying degrees of success, in all sixty electoral
districts of Paris.

The Mayor, Sylvain Bailly, was a noted scientist and a
Deputy to the States-General. He was also another of Danton's
pet aversions. The President's main criticism of Bailly was that
he had profited by the storming of the Bastille and the murder
of his predecessor in office (who had been known as the
"merchants' provost") in order to feather his own nest and
attain high municipal office. As a result, the district of Les
Cordeliers, in obedience to their leader's instructions, lodged
protests against the decisions taken by City Hall whenever they
possibly could.

A case in point was the arrest of a man called Lepeletier. This
obscure writer (who has nothing to do with Saint-Fargeau's Le
Pelletier) had the audacity to publish a work entitled "The
Triumph of the Parisians." In this supposedly witty brochure,
the author prophesied that Paris would fall a prey to its own
revolution and very soon disappear from the face of the earth.
"In six years," the pamphlet alleged—a dangerous fellow, this
scribbler, "there will be beds of melons on the Tuileries terrace,
and onions growing in the gardens of the Palais-Royal." What
an insult to all the labors of Bailly and La Fayette! The man
must be jailed as a defeatist (the word had not been coined as
yet, but the concept was familiar).

Notified of the facts, Danton forced his district to pass a

solemn vote of protest. As a result, Lepeletier, who was the most
naïve of hacks, found himself suddenly set at liberty.

M. de Saint-Huruge—the renegade marquis and neighbor of
Danton's—found himself similarly incarcerated in the Châtelet.
The old fortress stood on the site of the modern Place du
Châtelet, and behind its thirteenth-century towers and ram-
parts were both a jail and a criminal court. What offense had
the Marquis de Saint-Huruge committed? Here the facts require a longer and more detailed explanation, for which we
must leave Paris for a moment and recapitulate what had been
going on at the States-General in Versailles.

The Deputies had been far from idle. They had elected Bailly
their President, and transformed the States-General into a National Constituent Assembly. They held their sessions in that
magnificent hall, the Salle des Menus-Plaisirs. The aristocratic
Deputies (whether through fear or because the spirit of generosity was catching) made proposals for the surrender of their
ancient privileges. During the famous Night of August 4 they
offered to pay the same taxes as the common people, to share
hunting rights with them, to refuse the pensions paid them by
the Crown, and to abolish the manorial courts and the obligatory
free manual labor performed for them by their peasants. Finally
they voted for the termination of the Sale of Offices, and the
admission of all citizens without distinction to civil and military
posts. The Assembly, almost crazy with delight, passed these
measures by acclamation. All Frenchmen had become equal
under the law; the feudal régime was ended.

The Declaration of the Rights of Man, drafted on August 26
by the Abbé Sieyès, put the final seal on this transformation.
The King promised to give the Declaration his solemn approval,
and the Assembly enthusiastically proclaimed Louis XVI "the
restorer of French liberty." The Revolution, one might have
supposed, was over.

The Assembly's euphoria did not last for long. The King soon
went back on his original undertaking. He made the decisions of
the Constituent Assembly subject to a right of veto which he
required its members to grant him. The examination of this
famous veto provision caused much argument. In the corridors
of the Assembly it was widely supposed that the Queen had

been responsible for it and the sobriquet "Madame Veto" now began to be applied to her.

It was at this point that M. de Saint-Huruge dispatched his dangerous letter to Bailly, as President of the Constituent Assembly, and to his Secretary. If circumstances arose, he informed them, which would lead the "aristocratic coalition" to "tip the scales in the direction of the veto," then the ebullient marquis-turned-radical would require "exemplary reprisals" for such behavior. The essential thing about this letter was the thinly disguised threat of murder it contained. At all times, and under any régime, such an act has been liable to severe penalties, and three officers of the watch were accordingly sent to arrest Saint-Huruge at his home.

That same evening, Danton was presiding over his District Assembly. He announced the fact of Saint-Huruge's imprisonment and spoke up in his defense. The marquis, he said, was a hothead but he was also a patriot. Besides, it was no bad thing that patriotism should be seasoned with a dash of hotheadedness. Without the second, the first was liable to go soft. "We are not eunuchs!" Danton bellowed. Saint-Huruge, he went on, was a fine man, a decent fellow who—even with a gun in his hand—wouldn't so much as hurt a fly. He must be released from the Châtelet at once. The President demanded a resolution from the District Assembly. The Assembly so voted and insisted on Saint-Huruge's release. A letter was drafted and dispatched to the City Hall. Whether out of fear or generosity, Bailly gave in. Saint-Huruge would lie in his dungeon no longer.

Sometimes, however, instead of demanding a man's release, Danton was likely to press for his incarceration. Such was the case with the Baron de Besenval, for instance. This Swiss officer was in command of the mercenaries stationed on the Champ-de-Mars during the events of July. Indeed, for a few days, while Marshal de Broglie was detained at Saint-Denis, he was acting Commander-in-Chief. But being afraid that he might suffer the same fate as the defenders of the Bastille, M. de Besenval deserted on the morning following July 14. On the 19th he reached Villegruis, a village two leagues from Provins. When he was sitting at table in an inn, he was unwise enough to spread out a map in front of him and trace the route to Switzerland with his finger. This gesture aroused the suspicions of his fellow guests. In his *Memoirs* he afterward wrote: "I was on the point of leaving when I heard the tocsin being rung with furious urgency; and within seconds the inn was surrounded by two or three hundred peasants armed with guns, sticks, and spits. Their leader informed me that I was 'very probably an aristocrat on the run,' and asked my permission (!) to imprison me. My cell turned out to be one of the rooms in the inn."

The next day his captors took Besenval to Brie-Comte-Robert, and shut him up in a ruined castle. An attorney named Bourdon, together with a squad of lawyers' clerks, was assigned to guard him. La Fayette, informed of the arrest, sent down an aide-de-camp to Brie-Comte-Robert. "After some polite chitchat," Besenval writes, "this officer told me that M. de La Fayette required my word of honor that I would not attempt to escape if the occasion presented itself. 'Monsieur,' I replied, 'the best possible guarantee I can give M. de La Fayette of my remaining here is the risk to which I would expose *him* were I to escape.' My days were by no means disagreeable: I read, and amused myself observing the pranks that the clerks got up; sometimes I had a game of tric-trac with the local priest. . . ."

It is interesting that Bourdon also notified Danton of the arrest: why him, and not the President of any other district? Doubtless because the attorney knew the Counsel, either personally or by reputation. Danton at once convened his electors and told them of this "plot against the nation, with Besenval playing cards instead of submitting to the lightning stroke of justice." On his request the Assembly passed a motion inviting the other districts to copy that of Les Cordeliers. Fifty-nine similar resolutions were delivered with Danton's to the City Hall, which was thus faced with sixty demands that the Colonel should be transferred to a Paris prison, for "immediate judgment."

In reality, Danton did not care at all about Besenval. This hired officer, this Swiss mercenary, had done no more than carry out the duties he was paid for. He certainly was not guilty of "insulting the nation." What Danton hoped to do by attacking him was to annoy La Fayette and Bailly. If, from a

plain sense of justice, they refused to comply with the demands
of sixty Paris districts—the entire city, in fact—what a splendid
addition it would be to the case he was building against them!

But the General and the Mayor did not fall into the trap.
With some regrets, no doubt, they ordered the transfer of
Besenval to the Châtelet prison. Now all they had to do was to
find various excuses for continually postponing his trial. This
they did with some success. The mercenary was not tried for
another five months, and then he was acquitted. Danton did
not press to have the hearing speeded up, for during those five
months he was already enjoying the fruits of his victory and he
saw his influence over the masses increasing daily.

This incident reveals something fundamental about Danton's
character. He demanded the return of Besenval simply to boost
his own popularity, which he felt was not advancing fast
enough. But once he had got what he wanted, he was quite
content to leave the Colonel to slumber undisturbed in his cell,
because he knew very well that the poor man was innocent. Can
we, perhaps, infer from this that he was by nature a kindly
person?

At Versailles, Marie-Antoinette was becoming panic-stricken.
She, too, had no love for La Fayette and Bailly and Mirabeau;
nor, indeed, for any of those who had labored to bring about the
great social revolution. She regarded them all as enemies. Yet
the Queen was not a bad woman. Overspoiled by the life she
had led, too far isolated from the miseries of the people, she
was wholly circumscribed by her own soft, luxurious universe.
When she saw these lightning flashes playing across the sky, she
suggested to the King that he should flee, with her and their
children, to Metz. From here the army of General Bouillé,
Governor of Lorraine, would be able to escort them back to
Paris and re-establish the absolute power of the monarchy.
Louis allowed himself to be talked into this scheme. In order to
facilitate their departure, he summoned the Flanders Regiment
to Versailles. When this unit arrived, the King's Bodyguard
entertained its officers at dinner. The banquet took place on the
stage of the royal theater. A lady-in-waiting in the palace, feeling
that such a spectacle might reassure the Queen, advised her to go

and look at it, with the King. Marie-Antoinette agreed. Accompanied by her vacillating spouse, she appeared in the theater at the precise moment when—by a strange coincidence—the orchestra was playing Grétry's famous air, "O Richard, O my King, the world abandons you . . ." "It's not true!" shouted the assembled officers. Louis XVI and his wife passed around the tables in a state of great emotion. The acclaiming cheers of the diners lulled their fears. With the help of excellent wine, tempers became somewhat overheated. The following day, October 3, the journalist Gorsas, in reporting the dinner in his *Courrier de Versailles à Paris,* wrote that "the health of the nation had been proposed—and rejected as a toast," and that the "lurching guests had trampled the national cockade underfoot."

This red, white, and blue cockade was a rallying point for all patriots. Since the fall of the Bastille, men and women alike had worn it in their hats—especially after Bailly, nominated Mayor by popular acclaim, had offered it to Louis XVI on July 17, during a royal visit which the "conquerors of the Bastille" had obliged the monarch to make in his own capital. Thus, when other newssheets, taking their cue from that published by Gorsas, also announced that the Queen, the King, and the officers of the household troops had trodden their cockades in the dust of the parquet floor, a general outcry, a hymn of hate, went up throughout Paris.

That evening—October 3—Danton was, as usual, presiding over the daily meeting of his District Assembly. The session opened at five o'clock and soon became an uproar. The President thundered denunciations of "the scandal at Versailles," the banquet held by the Guard officers. How did the speaker—not noted for his ability to improvise—comport himself while delivering this indictment? We have the evidence of an eyewitness, a lawyer from Poitiers named Thibaudeau. The son of a Deputy to the Constituent Assembly, he had come with his father to the District Assembly of Les Cordeliers, drawn by the growing fame of its President.

"The descriptions I had been given," he afterward wrote in his *Memoirs,* "left me with a very inadequate notion of the man. I was very much struck by his height, and his burly athletic

figure; by the irregularity of his features, which the pitted scars
left by smallpox still further accentuated; by his harsh, brusque,
echoing voice and dramatic gestures; by his mobility of expression, and his assured and penetrating glance; by the
energetic boldness which stamped his attitude and his every
movement. . . . He presided with the decision, alertness, and
authority of a man who knows his own power; he drove the
District Assembly toward his own chosen goal. . . ."

On that particular evening the goal he had in mind was an
insurrection in Paris, as a response to the Versailles banquet.
At their President's request, the District Assembly drafted a
manifesto to be posted up all over the city. Brune and Momoro
undertook to print it, and their neighbors in the *quartier* to go
billposting in every street of the capital. Whether Gorsas had
told the truth in his newssheet was a question that Danton never
asked himself. His fiery impetuosity and unbridled ambition
erased all doubts from his mind.

Up to this point he had still retained some respect for Louis
XVI. As a Counsel to the King's Bench he observed a certain deference toward the supreme authority over his jurisdiction—so much so, in fact, that the Master of the Mint had, on
his request, struck a medal which members of the District
Assembly could display for purposes of identification, and which
bore on its obverse the legend "DISTRICT OF LES CORDELIERS:
FOR KING AND JUSTICE, while the reverse was inscribed "Presidency of Georges-Jacques DANTON." But now, in the face of
the King's insult to the tricolor, Danton repudiated all allegiance to a sovereign so far removed from justice. Or at least,
so he declared. According to him, Paris should rise, the whole
city ought to set out in one vast procession for Versailles, and—
do what there? Basically, this agitator was uncertain about the
ultimate end in view. Should they break open the gates of the
Château? Hardly, because they were always open and anyone
who pleased could go inside. Should they lay hands on Louis
XVI and expel him from France? The manifesto stuck up
everywhere by order of the District Assembly did not go that
far. Though its actual text has been lost, it seems a fair presumption that its author stuck to vague generalities. On the
other hand, it did call on La Fayette to demand that Louis

XVI dismiss the troops from Versailles—a move that would have left the monarchy at the mercy of the people. As a forced inducement to this act of disarmament, the text of the manifesto —if we can believe Camille Desmoulins—urged the militia to march on Versailles, with the Bataillon des Cordeliers in the van. What most concerned Danton, in his Machiavellian way, was whether La Fayette, the Commander-in-Chief of this force of forty-two thousand men, would allow himself to be compromised by association with the revolt. The rest, as far as he was concerned, could be decided by the passion of the mob.

Next day, Sunday October 4, he ordered the tocsin to be sounded in the district of Les Cordeliers. At the same time, his manifesto was provoking much discussion in the streets. A man named Maillard, a sheriff's officer to the Court of the Châtelet (another legal type!), took advantage of the emotionally charged situation to get himself some excellent publicity. Accompanied by "Reine Andu," a vagabond girl known to her fellow tramps as "The Queen of Hungary," and one "Coeur de Roi," a pariah who had escaped from some asylum or other, Maillard marched off to Les Halles, beating a drum as he went. Here he preached a vigorous sermon to the herring girls, fishwives, and fruiterers. "You're starving, all of you," he shouted, "and yet the *Austrian woman* is stuffing herself with wine and meat! You no longer have any bread—yet *Madame Veto* tramples the tricolor cockade underfoot!"

This crazy fellow's speech and Danton's manifesto gave the starving rabble just the push they needed. The women of Paris set off for Versailles to find "the baker, the baker's wife, and the little baker's apprentice"—as though the mere presence of the King, the Queen, and the Dauphin could make bread sprout up out of the cobbles. Danton was so alarmed by the storm he had unleashed that he proceeded to back down with some rapidity. He let it be understood by Crèvecoeur, the Commandant, that it might be better if the Bataillon des Cordeliers did not, after all, lead the procession. Crèvecoeur—with five hundred reservists under him—asked nothing better.

The women from Les Halles set out for Versailles, reinforced by others from the working classes and the bourgeoisie, and, finally, by every down-and-out in Paris. The Bataillon des

Cordeliers, together with the other fifty-nine district battalions, followed this screaming mob at a very safe distance. La Fayette, their Commander-in-Chief, marched at their head. Since he could not arrest this flood of humanity, the General decided to follow rather than canalize it—to intervene, that is, only in case of emergency.

As for Danton, he stayed firmly at home. He had not been present at the storming of the Bastille, and he did not go on the march to Versailles. This "poor man's Mirabeau," as he was already being called, preferred to direct the mob's actions rather than become a part of it. Like most revolutionary leaders the world over, he was, in fact, a dyed-in-the-wool bourgeois. Besides, had he not his work to attend to? Ever mindful of his debts and his living expenses, he was at the time engaged on a submission to be presented before the Court of Commerce. His client, a St. Malo shipowner named Benjamin Dubois, had been trying to prosecute one of his captains for the past six years. The latter, an old seadog called Chenard, commanded the *Amalia,* a vessel owned by Dubois. In 1782 he had, without any authorization, sold her and cleared a personal profit on the deal. Doubtless his employer owed him money. Nonsuited by the Parliamentary Court of Rennes, Benjamin Dubois was relying on Danton to get this judgment quashed by the King's Bench.

When the battalion was just setting off for Versailles, Danton told Jules Paré, his chief clerk, and Desforgues, his junior assistant: "If anyone asks for me, say I'll be incommunicado for the next forty-eight hours." Temporarily, it seems, he was repudiating his captain's commission. He shut himself up in his study, wearing dressing gown and slippers, to work on the Dubois case. For two days he never stirred out of his apartment. Indifferent to the storm he had provoked, Maître d'Anton was working. . . .

On the 7th, Paré came to tell him the latest news. The Château of Versailles had been invaded by the mob, and the Queen's chamber broken open. Marie-Antoinette had been awakened by their savage yells and forced to seek refuge with the King, in her nightdress. La Fayette had been driven, by his conscience and his aristocratic interests, to come to the royal family's rescue. Louis XVI, his wife, and his children had been brought back to Paris accompanied by this ghastly crew, who perched screaming on the roof of the royal carriage and waved pikes on which were stuck the heads of the palace guards killed during the assault on the palace.

"The royal family," Paré concluded, "is now lodged in the Tuileries. The Constituent Assembly has no option but to follow them and establish itself in Paris."

"Excellent," Danton said. Then he added: "My petition on behalf of M. dubois is ready. Please make inquiries as to the exact date on which his case will be heard. I am going down to the District Assembly now."

When he entered the hall he was given a tremendous ovation. His audience ascribed the triumph of the previous night entirely to him—not altogether fairly, since Maillard's part in the proceedings had been by no means negligible. In an adroit and, as usual, improvised speech, Danton took no steps to correct this impression. He then turned, abruptly, to the agenda. That day there was a highly vexed issue up for discussion, in which Marat figured as chief actor. In order to clarify it, we must go back a few weeks in time.

The freedom of the press, established on August 26 by the Declaration of the Rights of Man, provoked a sudden eruption of newssheets, published at irregular intervals, the number and contents of which left the populace agape. They produced the illusion that the public was going to be told everything—and nothing but the truth. The output was fantastic. Camille Desmoulins found his true métier: journalism. He founded a broadsheet called the *Courrier de Brabant*, the title of which contained an allusion to the insurrectional movement in the Belgian provinces. There could be no better proof of his scatterbrained impracticality than this. To set up, as the guiding example for a real and vast revolution, a feeble imitation the very existence of which was unknown to most people was something that only Desmoulins could have thought up.

Sometimes a weekly, sometimes a daily (according to the money that Camille obtained from his father in Guise), the *Courrier de Brabant* was a vehicle for the bile-ridden reflections of its one and only director. Thanks to this publication, Mlle. Duplessis's suitor saw his stock rise in the marriage market. The parents of his intended began to take a less intransigent attitude toward him—not that they would entertain, as yet, the idea of his actually marrying their daughter. All the same, this was the man who, from his high stool in the Palais-Royal gardens, had sent Paris out to storm the Bastille; and the immense popularity he enjoyed with the masses in consequence had done something to break down their opposition. Besides, when blows are being exchanged, they must have argued, it's always advisable to keep in with the stronger side. So Camille found himself, from time to time, asked to have supper with Lucile.

Among the other newssheets, there was only one more violent in tone than the *Courrier de Brabant: L'Ami du Peuple* ("The People's Friend"), edited by Jean-Paul Marat. Danton and Desmoulins occasionally met Marat in a gaming house that formed part of the Palais-Royal. It was run by a certain Mme. de Saint-Amaranthe, a tenant of the Duke of Orléans, assisted by her daughter, Mme. de Sartines. Count Alexandre de Tilly, a former page to Marie-Antoinette, was to give a very vivid sketch of these two ladies in his *Memoirs*. The elder of them (still only just forty when Danton made her acquaintance) was a lady of quality who had been reduced to working for her living. The younger—not yet twenty—provided lively competition for her mother's more mature charms: M. de Tilly described her as "an angel of beauty, remarkable for her physical attractiveness."

Danton and Desmoulins used to pay occasional visits to this high-class bawdyhouse—without Gabrielle or Lucile. The nymphs of the establishment did not stir Camille; he had eyes for no one but his fiancée. Danton, on the other hand, took a lively interest in every woman he found there: the two owners, the clients at the gaming tables, even the maids. Though he adored Gabrielle, he felt a strong pull toward polygamy. Yet it does not seem that—at this period, at least—he was unfaithful to his wife. He loved a feminine ambience: throats and breasts redolent of perfume, the suggestive rustle of a dress. His escapades seem to have stopped short of anything more serious. In Mme. de Saint-Amaranthe's establishment all he sought was sensual stimulation—visual, auditory, olfactory—and, above all, connections that would be of use to his devouring ambition.

Jean-Paul Marat was a more regular visitor who brought with him a recently acquired (and carefully cultivated) atmosphere of squalor. He had been physician-in-ordinary to the household troops of the Comte d'Artois, and was the former lover of the Marquise de l'Aubespine, who had launched him in society. Till lately he had occupied a sumptuous apartment in the rue de Bourgogne where he received an aristocratic clientele; he was, moreover, the author of a score of books on physics, medicine, and sociology. But one fine day Marat had discovered he possessed an irresistible urge to be, quite simply, a bum. He threw everything up—his mistress, his past, his luxurious tastes, his bourgeois clothes, and his profession. He dressed in beggar's rags and never went near a bar of soap. From then on, wherever he went he brought a week's growth of beard, the smell of sweat, and a choice display of ulcers brought about by his unhygienic habits. At the same time, he proclaimed his hatred of the wealthy bourgeoisie to which he had belonged, his hostility toward the aristocrats, who had done so much to help and encourage him, and his rancor against the social order from which he had derived so many benefits before his conversion to a life of squalid idleness. One curious fact (which does much to illuminate the futility of the upper classes in the eighteenth century) is that Marat became all the rage, a nine days' wonder, so that when the storm broke he found himself a leader of the new revolutionary fashion.

Though one part of his brain was afflicted with this curious obsession, the rest of it nevertheless displayed intelligence of the highest order. He had conceived—long before Sieyès—a "Projected Declaration of the Rights of Man and Citizen," followed by a "Plan for the Just, Wise and Free Constitution." On September 8, 1789, the author of these manifestoes founded a paper, *Le Publiciste Français* ("The French Publicist"). On September 16 he changed the title, and *L'Ami du Peuple* was born.

Bitter and violent by temperament, Marat was not a man to mince his words. The whole of France found itself pilloried, in the columns of *L'Ami du Peuple,* by his furious invective. The

King, the Queen, Mirabeau, Bailly, all the Deputies, the electorate, the nobility, the clergy, the starving commons who demonstrated their cowardice by keeping quiet—Marat attacked them all. He described the Night of August 4 as a "bad joke," as "tinsel fripperies" engendered "by fear rather than virtue." "The States-General," he declared in print, "have wasted on such minor matters the time that should be devoted to problems of larger importance."

Having dealt with the Constituent Assembly, he went on to attack the municipal authorities, La Fayette, and the bourgeois militia. For him the latter was no more than "a horde of troops that had crushed the multitude." So much for the reserve battalion with whom Danton paraded as a captain.

This was a dangerous man: better to have him as a friend than as an enemy. So Danton, who knew he could be sure of meeting him in the gaming house run by Mme. de Saint-Amaranthe and her daughter, began to frequent this alluring if scandalous resort, and his cheerful, ugly face became a familiar sight there. He spent hours on end chatting with Marat; it is unlikely, however, that he flattered him unduly, for Danton was not the kind of man to toady to anyone, not even the King himself—except when the success or failure of a legal case depended on his doing so. When dealing with this fashionable rabble-rouser he was polite, but no more. Yet even politeness was not always easy. The anarchic and antisocial doctor had a sour outlook on life. One evening Danton, too, called down the vials of his wrath—merely for preferring Corneille to Racine. As Danton told Guellard de Mesnil, Secretary of the local District Assembly: "I am not wildly enamored of this person Marat. He does not lack for spirit, but his cantankerous nature robs one's conversations with him of any pleasure they might otherwise contain."

This rebarbative attitude, combined with the unpleasant lack of cleanliness in his personal toilet, finally alienated Mme. de Saint-Amaranthe's clientele. Seeing that people were tending to give him a wide berth, Marat stopped going to the bawdyhouse and his nasty smell faded from its armchairs. Danton had no further meetings with him there. Providence, however, arranged that they continue to run into each other on occasion. Ever since Marat had rejected his life of luxury, he had been living in a series of varyingly modest (and varyingly flea-ridden) lodginghouses, moving from one district to another as the fancy took him. He finally ended up, with his few ragged possessions, in the Hôtel de la Fautrière, rue des Fossés-Saint-Germain.

Having thus become a resident of the Cordeliers District, he got into the habit of dropping in on the meetings of its deliberative Assembly. He very soon became both the Assembly's butt and the thorn in its flesh, depending on whether he managed to make himself heard or was shouted down by his fellow spectators. Danton himself never called him to order. No doubt he found the presence of this bloody-minded grouch irksome, but he could sense the growing influence which this inspired down-and-out had among the ordinary variety of the breed. Marat published *L'Ami du Peuple* every five or six days—when he could get credit from a printer. Decent people knew nothing of his origins or what he had given up. The have-nots, when they saw this wretched, ragged, ill-shaven creature, used to say: "This is one of our own kind, a victim of arbitrary power." Those of them who could read would devour his fierce, crackling prose, in which demagoguery always got the better of compassion. In the end they made no distinction between the man and the paper he published, so that Marat himself came to be known as the "People's Friend." With such a rival in the field—whether hostile or friendly—Danton had to watch out.

On October 7, 1789, after the District Assembly had applauded its President as the man responsible for bringing the royal family back to Paris, Danton called on his Secretary to read the agenda for the meeting. This consisted of a letter which Marat had sent to "Monsieur d'Anton, President of the Cordeliers District," and which was, in fact, an appeal for help. Eight days previously, Marat's *L'Ami du Peuple* had slung a great deal of mud at M. Boucher d'Argis, examining magistrate to the Criminal Court of the Châtelet. The burden of Marat's complaint was that this official had still, after a quite unconscionable delay, not heard the case of Colonel de Besenval—the officer fetched back from Brie-Comte-Robert by order of La Fayette and at Danton's personal instigation. Since Marat suggested that M. Boucher d'Argis had been bribed by Besenval's friends, and in general treated him as a prevaricator (and, worse, a traitor), the latter had issued orders for Marat's arrest, had commanded the seizure of all copies of his newssheet from the Widow Hérissant (his present printer), and had obtained a warrant to search his room in the Hôtel de la Fautrière. The journalist first hid with Gabrielle's butcher Legendre, and then fled to Versailles. In his letter to "Monsieur d'Anton," he begged the District Assembly to help him.

Though the recipient of the letter personally detested his petitioner, he did not hesitate. He had not the slightest interest in defending Marat; on the contrary, he would much rather have attacked him, denounced his lies, and either secured his imprisonment or else forced him to seek refuge in Switzerland. Either way he would have been rid of an embarrassing nuisance. Nothing could have been more appropriate—had Danton not perceived, in Marat's misadventure, a chance to further his own plans. By springing to the fugitive's defense, he could cause Bailly great annoyance, for the police were under the ultimate authority of the Mayor, and it was the police who were responsible for arresting persons to be tried in the Criminal Court of the Châtelet.

Danton therefore spoke up in praise of Marat and got the district to pass a resolution whereby the Assembly, "being persuaded that the freedom of the press is a necessary corollary to that of the individual," declared that it took "under its protection every writer whatsoever within its boundaries, and will defend them to the utmost of its powers."

"To the utmost of its powers" meant, in plain speech, that it was prepared to call out the five hundred volunteers of the Bataillon des Cordeliers. The President signed this threat of civil war with some reluctance. Then he addressed his two Secretaries. "I am now," he said, "going to give my orders to M. Crèvecoeur, our Commandant. He is to mount defenses outside the Hôtel de la Fautrière and in the rue des Fossés. However much of a fool Bailly is, he would never dare to bring other troops into this area from outside."

But privately he was by no means so sure; and the future was to confirm his doubts.

Among those who heard him speak that evening was Choder-los de Laclos, a reserve officer and the novelist who wrote *Les Liaisons Dangereuses*. At this period what we would call a best seller did not make the fortune of its author. A writer was forced to sell his manuscript outright, for a lump sum, to some bookseller and then look on helplessly while the profits of several large printings went elsewhere. So despite the immense success of *Liaisons*, Choderlos de Laclos was forced to make his living in some other profession and at present was working as the Duke of Orléans's estate agent. Popular rumor held that the Duke had provided the political model for Laclos's fictional Prince, with his *âme damnée*. It was true, in any case, that the novelist's character suffered from his appalling thirst for wealth, and all his actions reflected this trait.

After the session on October 7 it is supposed that he engaged Danton in conversation for an hour or more and—by a process of skillful bribery—brought him over to the Palais-Royal group. There is no way of proving this. Whatever the truth of the matter, though, Danton made the novelist come home to dinner with him and told Gabrielle to lay places for ten. She and her two servants at once set about organizing the meal.

Who, in fact, were the guests? Apart from Choderlos de Laclos, history knows of at least four others: Brune and Momoro, the two printers, Fabre d'Églantine the poet, and Desmoulins, the "Lantern Attorney." He had been given this nickname after the publication of his famous pamphlet, "Discourse to Parisians Concerning the Lantern." This lantern was, in fact, a street lamp which provided light at the corner of the Place de Grève and the rue de la Vannerie. In its shadow a butcher had decapitated the Governor of the Bastille. From its metal standard the mob had hanged a Minister of the Crown, Foullon. In describing these dramatic incidents, Desmoulins had coined the verb *lanterner*, a neologism destined to enjoy considerable success. Instead of howling for blood, he produced the slogan *"À la lanterne!"* It was because of his pamphlet that the "patriots" sang, to the tune of a quadrille that Marie-Antoinette used to play on her clavichord, that famous (and virtually untranslatable ditty:

Ah! ça ira, ça ira, ça ira!
Les aristocrates à la lanterne.

[Ah! it'll come, it'll come, it'll come!
Aristocrats dangling from every lamppost.]

Now the Lantern Attorney was swimming in the troubled waters of Philippe d'Orléans's party. Proud to be included among the Duke's guests at his country residence of Mousseau (of which Monceau Park is all that survives today), he declared to Gabrielle Danton that she was a better cook than the Duke's own chef. During dinner he referred to La Fayette as *le blondinet* ("the blond kid"), a label which stuck to him. To Danton the hero of the American War of Independence was, as he said, "a eunuch."

Sarcastic phrases flew thick and fast during this supper party, which must have been (from the sound of it) rather like the Guards' dinner in miniature. The guests assailed the King and Queen with some most improbable epithets. Bailly, Lally-Tollendal, Sieyès, Malouet, even Mirabeau himself—all the original revolutionaries, in fact—were scornfully pilloried. These "half-wits" could no longer control the avalanche they had set moving. And the guests, in between mouthfuls, reminded one another of Mirabeau's famous remark: "When you become involved in organizing a revolution, the difficulty is not so much to get it moving as to stop it."

This truism is as old as the world, and any comment on it would be superfluous. Every uprising breeds its profiteers, who move in when the work has been done for them. Latecomers, they misuse the windfall provided for them by the generosity of their forerunners in the field. "Jobs for the boys" is their motto. All Gabrielle's guests were touched with this kind of cutthroat opportunism, and barely troubled to conceal the fact.

As she listened to their talk Gabrielle shivered in horror. For several days now she had been suffering from the early symptoms of pregnancy. The death of her son, five months previously, had left her prostrate with grief. Now, thanks be to God and her herculean husband, she knew that the bibs and diapers of the deceased child would, after all, be put to use. How lucky she was, she thought: but . . . would God allow such good fortune to the wife of a man who dreamed of encompassing the downfall, perhaps even the death, of a monarch anointed at his coronation with the Holy Oil?

After three days Gabrielle felt somewhat reassured. Behind all his furious vaporings, her loudmouthed husband was really a staunch traditionalist. On his return home from the District Assembly on October 10, he informed her that he was going, the following day, to pay homage to Louis XVI at the Tuileries. The electors had delegated their President to render thanks to the King for his return—as if the poor man had any option in the matter, with a howling mob besieging Versailles! But such considerations were deemed irrelevant. Danton asked his wife to get his Court dress ready for the occasion: coat and breeches of black satin, waistcoat of Indian silk, with white and blue stripes, white silk stockings, and paste-buckle Court shoes.

The next day he entered the ancient château of Catherine de Medici. Abandoned by Louis XIV, the "Sun King," a century before, the sumptuous Tuileries had remained uninhabited ever since, except by spiders, rats, and mice. The King, Marie-Antoinette, their children, and their personal attendants were sleeping on camp beds or rugs until the furniture removers arrived with some of their household equipment. The château (fated to be burned down in 1871) displayed its magnificent façade between the Pavillon de Flore and the Pavillon de Marsan, both of which still survive.

The delegation from Les Cordeliers was a tiny one, consisting only of Danton and Guellard du Mesnil. Both of them, despite their revolutionary self-esteem, found it hard to control their emotions. As he walked forward under those sculptured ceilings, decorated with frescoes of angels sitting on somewhat discolored clouds, the agitator from the Cour de la Commerce became once more the austere Counsel to the King's Bench. Full of respect and very much the courtier, he bowed before Their Gracious Majesties in the presence of several Ministers and— the one blot on the picture—the Marquis de La Fayette. Did he observe ancient custom and kiss the King's hand? It is scarcely conceivable: such an act would have been reported by La Fayette, who was only too eager to show up his adversary's duplicity. Nevertheless, it appears that Danton was all honey

with his sovereign. Louis XVI looked his huge visitor up and
down and, without listening to him for more than a minute or
two, turned his eyes away.

In fact, Danton's head was far from being turned by his surroundings: his motive was one of calculating self-interest. In
prophetic visions he might see the King toppled from his throne;
but for the time being Louis still reigned, and a week later Danton was due to plead before the Court of Commerce, King's
Bench Division. The case was that of the St. Malo shipowner
we have already mentioned, that Sieur Dubois who sought
justice against one of his captains for allegedly stealing a ship.
The Rennes Parliament had found against the plaintiff, and
Danton was trying to get this decision quashed.

Louis XVI never presided over a Court of the King's Bench
in person, but the magistrates were obliged to send him tran-
scripts of the cases heard, and the King appended his signature
to the judge's verdict. Did he in fact read them before doing so?
On occasion, it seems, though such an event was fairly rare—
except, that is, when he personally knew one of the Counsels
involved. The decisions of the King's Bench were always delayed for a week or a fortnight, so that the papers might be
scrutinized by the sovereign before action was finally taken. By
congratulating Louis XVI on his return to Paris (and in such a
manner that he was bound to remember his visitor) Danton
hoped to dispose the King favorably toward the case he was
pleading.

So when, on October 19, he rose to address the court in the
case of Dubois v. Chenard, he had high hopes of success.
Luckily for his reputation with the populace, the courts of the
King's Bench did not conduct their hearings in public. The
crowds that he aroused against the executive would have been
flabbergasted to hear him "humbly beg His Majesty, who in his
wisdom guards and maintains the ordinances of this realm," to
accept the findings which "with deep respect" Maître d'Anton
presented for his consideration.

The shipowner's advocate was no plaster saint. Besides, as
Danton had learned from an aphorism in that dead tongue
which he knew so thoroughly, life takes priority over philosophy:
Primum vivere, deinde philosophari.

[1] Georges-Jacques Danton, King's Counsel, from a contemporary cameo. (*Photo by Josse-Lalance*)

[2] The first Madame Danton (Gabrielle Charpentier). Portrait attributed to David. (*Photo by Josse-Lalance*)

[3] Citizens from the suburbs of Saint-Antoine and Saint-Marceau on the march, June 20, 1792. (*Photo by Giraudon*)

[4] A recruiting station on the Pont-Neuf during the national emergency of July 1792. Sketch by Prieur. (*Photo by Bulloz*)

The Constituent Assembly followed Louis XVI to the capital. To begin with, it installed itself in the Great Hall of the Bishop's Palace, near Notre Dame. ("Bishop's Palace" is no slip of the pen. The diocese of Paris, ruled over by a plain bishop, was still suffragan to the archbishopric of Sens.) But one Deputy, Dr. Guillotin, a public-health specialist of some repute, warned his colleagues against "the dangerous proximity of the Hôtel-Dieu [the oldest hospital in Paris] and its unhealthy emanations." They then decided to change the scene of their debates to the Riding School of the Tuileries.

This Riding School, which stood near the middle of the Tuileries Gardens, on the north side (where the rue de Castiglione opens today), was now invaded by an army of masons, joiners, and upholsterers. They put up tiers of seats for the Deputies, a dais for the President, a speakers' rostrum, and, at either end of the great hall, a public gallery. These alterations attracted a number of curious spectators every day. One evening Georges and Gabrielle Danton came down there. As he watched the workers going about their task, Danton murmured: "You know, I *should* have been a candidate at the elections, despite everything."

From the moment the Assembly moved into its new home, Parisians stopped referring to it as "the Constituent." In common parlance it was never henceforth called anything but "the Riding School." So it was in the Riding School that the Deputies took up their abode. On November 2 they voted for the confiscation of all Church property. The list of this property was never-ending: it included not only monasteries, abbeys, priories, and hospices but also houses, forests, and estates. By selling them subsequently—after they had had time to organize a competent administration for such a vast project—the Deputies felt confident of being able to refloat the country's finances. Danton gave his approval to this remedy: Gabrielle, on the other hand, was most upset by it. For her, to dispossess the Church was tantamount to laying hands on Our Lord.

Her husband's growing popularity now extended beyond their local area. He was the inspiration behind so many measures in the Cordeliers District. Besides, Camille Desmoulins never missed an opportunity of lauding his friend's activities in his journal. On October 21, for instance, some of the starving poor had seized a baker whom they accused of hoarding flour, dragged him out of his shop, and hurried him along to the Place de Grève—perhaps remembering the words that Desmoulins had pictured the famous Lantern as uttering:

"How many scoundrels have escaped my clutches! Why did they let the Marquis de Lambert go free? Coward! *You* will not escape the Lantern! Why ignore the Abbé de Calonne, the Duc de La Vauguyon, and so many others? . . . Evening is drawing on now: it's a good thing for faithful housedogs to bark at the passers-by—then we need have no fear of thieves in the night. . . ."

Aroused by such inflammatory prose, the crowd hanged the baker from the Lantern.

But Danton was less sanguinary than his friend and could not see this cast-iron gibbet as the remedy for famine conditions. The Abbé Maury, a right-wing Deputy, was threatened one evening in much the same fashion as the baker but disarmed his aggressors with the remark: "When you've strung me up on that thing, d'you think it'll give a brighter light?"—a view which Danton, without any heart searchings, might well have made his own. Courageously, he sprang to the posthumous defense of the supposed hoarder. Informed of the little drama that had been played out in the Place de Grève, he called a meeting of the District Assembly and told them: "The harvest is abundant. Everyone knows this. I'm a countryman myself, and I have precise information on the subject. Let us invite the other districts to join us in making a united approach to the executive, and demand that the requisitioning of grain in the Paris region cease forthwith. Such brutal methods simply encourage peasants and speculators to hold back their supplies. No, what we must do is negotiate directly, by mutual agreement, with the farmers themselves."

This sensible piece of advice was applauded by the entire city. The Riding School passed a motion to the same effect, and Desmoulins wrote it up in his *Courrier*.

On another occasion Danton attacked the organization of the Commune. This consisted of three hundred members, five from each of the sixty electoral districts. Bailly presided over their deliberations, with far too great a show of independence. He made it quite clear that he had no time for the opinions of the sixty Assemblies, and the three hundred Councilors simply let him have his head, so that in effect *he* governed *them*. Danton protested strongly against this kind of thing. What was the point of an elected council, he asked, if the Mayor took no account of their suggestions? "If a law is not the expression of the general will," he wrote, in a vote of protest passed by the District Assembly, "then that law is worth nothing."

This "general will" was to renew, four times in succession, the mandate of so aggressive a President. His repeated successes, however, brought trouble in their wake. In the corridors of the City Hall, defamatory rumors began to circulate. Danton must have bought the votes of his Assembly. But did he make that much money? Well, not at his *profession,* said the most daring scandalmongers: he didn't handle enough cases for that. Perhaps he got it from the Duke of Orléans. It was known that Choderlos de Laclos was a friend of Danton's, and Laclos threw the Duke's money around by the handful.

Rightly or wrongly, Danton attributed these offensive rumors to Bailly and La Fayette. He voiced loud and indignant complaints in the presence of his constituents and admirers. A motion was passed, and circulated around the other districts, paying tribute to "the courage, talent, and sense of civic duty which M. d'Anton has displayed, in the most striking manner, both as soldier and as citizen." By this motion the Assembly intended to manifest its high esteem for the District's "beloved President."

Their beloved President did not, however, allow himself to become intoxicated by success. One day he thought up a way of making his electors believe he was renouncing demagoguery—whereas in fact he was pursuing it in a more intensified form. Here we have one among a hundred such tricks which this eighteenth-century Machiavelli had at his command. All he was doing, in fact, was to change the object of his blandishments. On December 7 he launched a blistering attack on the selfishness of the local inhabitants, accusing them of letting their fellow countrymen in the industrial suburbs die of starvation. Then, with dictatorial highhandedness, he decreed, *motu proprio,* an extraordinary levy of twenty sous from each citizen. This caused a great stir in the district. Danton, they said, was wielding greater absolute power than the King himself. He proceeded to nominate a Charity Fund Treasurer who took up this *ad hoc* tax by a door-to-door collection. The sum realized was sent to the poverty-stricken districts of Saint-Marcel and Saint-Antoine, where it certainly helped to make Danton's name more widely known. And if any citizens refused to contribute to the scheme, one could always employ force to make them change their minds.

The force in question consisted of Crèvecoeur's battalion. Unfortunately, this body was in danger of passing beyond the beloved President's control, as the result of action taken by La Fayette and Bailly, who were beginning to tire of Danton's rodomontades and the influence he had over the other districts. At the beginning of 1790 the two accomplices caused the bourgeois militia some gratification by bestowing a new and unexpected title on them: the National Guard. At the same time, they split the force up into seven divisions, six of infantry and one of cavalry. Commanded by a general on the active list, each of these reservist divisions consisted of the troops from ten districts—that is, of ten battalions. That of M. Crèvecoeur was attached to the Second Infantry Division. It was allotted the number 3, and had to drop the title "Bataillon des Cordeliers" on the grounds that *it was too reminiscent of the old régime—* that régime which the Night of August 4 had done away with. Once again we can detect the crafty influence of La Fayette. Furthermore, now that the Sale of Offices had been abolished, regular regiments no longer bore the name of their former colonel-owner, but a plain number. So why should the volunteer battalions retain the name of their district? The law was the same for all. There was no longer a Régiment de Berchény or a Régiment de Choiseul; so why should there be a Bataillon des Cordeliers or a Bataillon des Feuillants? Each of them would have its number from now on, just like the others.

Crèvecoeur, the commanding officer, resigned in disgust. The

Third Battalion, Second Division received as its new commandant a certain M. de la Villette, who, carefully dropping his "de la," took office as plain "Commandant Villette." Each of his five companies was under the leadership of a captain, a lieutenant, and a second lieutenant. But the list of these officers —brought around to district headquarters by an aide-de-camp of La Fayette's—no longer included Danton. In order to mitigate his fury, the aide-de-camp explained that there was a certain incompatibility between his high office as President and the modest rank of captain. There was a certain amount of truth in this flattering argument. All the same, Danton's antipathy for La Fayette could not but be aggravated by the turn of events.

Judging it more prudent to swallow his wrath, the President nevertheless was determined to get his own back in some way. He thought he had found an opening in the wording of the National Guard officers' commissions, which were taken to all those gazetted by a special messenger from the City Hall. He declared that the form of words was ill adapted to the circumstances, and offered to go and argue the point in the City Hall on behalf of his electors. This, of course, was one more excuse for annoying Bailly, whom he intended to assail with withering sarcasms. Since he could not touch La Fayette, he would argue the toss with his accomplice.

Received in audience by the Commune, he began by reading the text of a specimen commission aloud. Its general drift signified that the citizen appointed had been nominated to the rank he held by "Messieurs le Maire et le Commandant Général" (the Mayor and the Commander-in-Chief). But in his fine oratorical frenzy, Danton misread the first three words. Unintentionally he substituted for them the phrase "Monseigneur le Maire"—as though Bailly were a prince or an archbishop. The audience thought this was a joke, and not one in the best of taste. Voices were raised in protest. Several members demanded a vote of censure against the offender. But Bailly remained calm and imperturbable. With a fine show of scorn, he begged Danton to read the text more carefully. Danton had another look at the parchment scroll in front of him, admitted the mistake, and expressed his regrets. For once, he had turned his audience against him.

About a month before this incident—to be precise, on December 3, 1789—Danton had discharged one of the obligations in his contract with Huet de Paisy. The terms under which he had purchased the office of Advocate required him to pay—among other various maturing bills—a sum of 12,000 *livres* by March 29, 1791. In fact, he paid it sixteen months in advance, together with 1500 *livres* interest.

What was the reason for this extreme haste on Danton's part? The mystery may well be linked with that other enigma, the paternity of Françoise Duhauttoir's son. She was to marry Huet on February 6. In the marriage contract, drawn up by Maître Dosfant, Danton's notary, she made a declaration of property which her insolvent fiancé was quite incapable of matching. It was at this point that Danton (who could legally have waited another sixteen months before discharging his debt) brought the sum in question to Maître Dosfant's chambers. Whereupon Huet de Paisy made over to his "intended" (with whom, we may recall, he was already living on a marital basis) a stipulated jointure of 600 *livres per annum,* this being the income from the capital.

Where did Danton lay hands on such a vast sum as 13,500 *livres?* Scarcely out of his professional income, we may assume. He did not handle enough cases to maintain a home, keep open house, and predischarge a debt that was due to mature so much later. Later, that pretty bluestocking Mme. Roland was to assert, in her *Souvenirs,* that in 1789 Gabrielle could not have managed her housekeeping "if it had not been for a gold sovereign which her father sent her every week." Where did she get this detail? Unless proof positive appears to the contrary, we must dismiss it as mere malicious gossip.

But—unfortunately for Danton's posthumous reputation—there is other, and more striking, evidence of the same sort. According to La Fayette, Louis XVI paid Danton money "to keep his wrath sleeping." Brissot is said to have supplied him with an "Orléans retainer." His relationship with Choderlos de Laclos, the Duke's agent, makes such an assertion at least plausible. The proprietor of the Palais-Royal was not stingy with his gold: it was supposed to have been responsible, *inter alia,* for the attacks on those two factory-owners, Réveillon and

Henriot, in the Faubourg Saint-Antoine, during April of 1789. It was also connected with Maillard's speech in Les Halles on October 4 and the mob violence at Versailles on the 5th and 6th. Philippe d'Orléans, accused of having instigated these incidents, had prudently retreated across the Channel, where he was waiting until the Queen's wrath abated sufficiently for him to return to Paris. Officially he was on some trumped-up diplomatic mission to London, and therefore spent much time in the company of M. de la Luzerne, the French Ambassador. This diplomat was not even aware of Danton's existence. But he heard the name mentioned at the Foreign Office; and (as he reveals in a dispatch to Louis XVI's Minister of Foreign Affairs, dated November 29) La Luzerne told the Duke of Orléans one evening, confidentially, that "there are two particular Englishmen [sic] in Paris, one named Danton and other Paré, whom several people suspect of being agents of the government in London." If this account is accurate, Philippe must have had to repress a smile when he heard it.

It looks very much as though Danton had a foot in every camp—and was paid by everybody for doing so: by the King of France, who imagined that he could control so dangerous an opponent with simple bribery; by the King's cousin, Philippe d'Orléans, who, while not in all likelihood aiming at the crown, nevertheless allowed the ambitious Laclos to draw him into more dangerous liaisons than those portrayed in his novel; and by the King of England, who wanted to pay France out for the aid she had given his rebellious American colonies, and would be only too glad to support such a troublemaker in Paris. All these rumors point in the same direction: one cannot ignore them entirely. Perhaps the worst is that recorded by the printer Louis Prudhomme, an occasional historian and onetime friend of Danton's. According to Prudhomme, Danton once told him, without any shame or embarrassment: "A revolution should bring profit to those who make it. . . . If the kings enriched the nobility, then the Revolution should line the pockets of all true patriots."

Apocryphal or not, such an opinion is worth examining more closely—and in perspective. For centuries a small minority had relied on its special privileges to enjoy a life of leisure. The majority had to toil, not only for its own existence, but also to pay the taxes which supported the minority in idleness. Danton himself belonged to the second category. Among his own family and relatives, among the common people of Troyes and Paris, he had always been familiar with toil and sweat, with the fear of foreclosure, the terrible specter of debtors' prisons, of the justice that condemned men to the galleys. Then, suddenly, history was changed. The Declaration of the Rights of Man gave the common people fresh hope where none had been visible before. They would have been less than human had they not fallen victims to temptation. How could one expect them not to reach out toward delights now, for the first time, placed within their grasp? During the Empire a "Madame Sans-Gêne" ("My Lady Brass" might be an equivalent of this sobriquet) could stand in one of the great halls of the Tuileries and announce cheerfully: *"We* are the princesses now!" Yet what, in fact, had Marshal Lefebvre's wife been originally? A washerwoman who sweated over her tub twelve hours a day, with no free Sundays or holidays. But human beings are not saints, and the hearts of even the most upright always harbor some lurking sense of frustration which—if events explode around it—can be transmuted into the desire for compensation and vengeance.

Between 1789 and 1794 almost all the idols of the people took money from a variety of sources: the Court, the Palais-Royal, the English Foreign Office, Spain, Prussia, or Austria. Everyone either knew or suspected this. (The only politician who, beyond any doubt, steered clear of the general trend was Robespierre: hence the nickname of "The Incorruptible" given him by the masses. Yet this virtuous, militant revolutionary proved himself the most bloodthirsty of all those who helped to create the modern world.) Such jobbery on the part of the builders is a regrettable fact, but one endemic to human nature. This is an explanation rather than an excuse. It is a mistake to magnify events out of their context. Without the profit motive, without ambition—even without that caricature of ambition, mere social climbing—the world would still be in the Stone Age.

When Philippe d'Orléans returned from England, Camille Desmoulins took Danton to see him. The Duke, who had been acquainted with Danton since the latter's admission to the Lodge of the Nine Sisters, asked him to stay to dinner. Another guest on this occasion was Mrs. Dalrymple Elliott. Grace Elliott—the Christian name suited her to perfection—was a young English-woman of twenty-four who led a cheerful, somewhat irregular life. Married when barely sixteen to a man rather older than her own father, Mrs. Elliott had lost no time in escaping from so ill-balanced a partnership. She became the mistress of the Prince of Wales (who sired a child by her) and then threw him over in favor of the Duke of Orléans, who in 1784 was making a short stay in London. She accompanied her new lover back to Paris.

At the outbreak of the Revolution she was still corresponding with the Prince Regent. Her relationship with Philippe d'Orléans was by now one of friendship, and nothing more. Since 1785, Mary Fitzherbert had replaced her as the future George IV's mistress; and since 1788 a certain Mme. Buffon had succeeded her in the affections of Philippe. But both gentlemen retained very friendly feelings for their ex-mistress: indeed, the Duke often invited Grace Elliott to dinner at the same time as Agnes de Buffon. Despite an inevitable feeling of rivalry, the two ladies got on very well together. And it was at just such a dinner party that Danton became acquainted with them both.

Mrs. Elliott was working as an agent for the British govern-ment. She had kept up a correspondence with her former brother-in-law, Lord Gilbert Elliott, and reported to him every-thing she saw going on in France. Early in 1790 this gentleman arrived in Paris on a fact-finding mission. He made the ac-quaintance of several Deputies. One evening, at dinner with the Duke of Orléans, Grace introduced Danton to him, as one of the curiosities of Paris. Since she and Elliott spoke French fluently, the two men chatted on about this and that while Grace fol-lowed the discussion with an amused eye. When Elliott re-turned to London, Danton remained in contact with his cousin, Hugh Elliott, and another Englishman, Augustus Miles, both resident in Paris—and both Foreign Office agents. Miles was also a member of the Jacobin Club, and urged Danton to join, which in due course he did.

There is nothing in all this to prove that Danton was taking bribes. But when, in 1793, the claws of the Terror descended on

Mrs. Elliott—at the precise period of Danton's greatest power—some invisible hand whisked her from prison to prison, in such a way that her name was removed from the record whenever a Revolutionary Tribunal threatened her pretty head. Now it is quite certain that Grace Elliott was never Danton's mistress. Why, then, did he go out of his way to protect this woman who had borne a child by the Prince Regent of England? The answer is not far to seek: he was getting money from the British. A chronological study of his life, though it may not supply formal proof of this, makes it at least a strong probability. The beloved President was an old hand at swimming with the tide.

CHAPTER VI

The Club of Les Cordeliers

THE MANDATE OF THE COMMUNE ran out in January of 1790. To renew it, Bailly ordered all sixty districts to hold new elections. Since the Municipal Assembly consisted of three hundred members, each district had to put forward five Councilors. In that of Les Cordeliers, Danton ran as a candidate himself.

There is something strangely paradoxical about his nature. Even while campaigning hard to get his foot inside the door of the City Hall, he went on breaking lances against the civic authorities. He wanted a seat in the Commune, yet he fought it tooth and nail: in the case of Marat, for instance. The Franco-Swiss doctor was now back from Versailles, where he had gone into hiding after a warrant had been issued for his arrest, and had begun to publish *L'Ami du Peuple* once more. More acidulous than ever, he was determined to outshine Camille Desmoulins in the violence of his invective. The latter had changed the title of *his* broadsheet from *Courrier de Brabant* (which meant little or nothing to most Parisians) to *Révolutions de France et de Brabant*, and its contents were growing steadily more caustic and pungent. Marat, still a determined down-and-out, had gone back to his old lodgings in the Hôtel de la Fautrière. Desmoulins, on the other hand, having received some money from his shadowy relatives, was now established in a pleasant bourgeois apartment overlooking the Place du Théâtre-Français (today the Place de l'Odéon). It was a struggle between the two polemicists to see who could find the greater number of insults to hurl at the "paid revolutionaries," as they described the Mayor of Paris and the Commander-in-Chief of the National Guard. The annual salary voted to the former—110,-000 *livres*—made *L'Ami du Peuple* almost inarticulate with rage. Once again, the insults it leveled at the Mayor were a calculated throwing down of the gauntlet; and once again Bailly picked it up. At his request, the Criminal Court of the Châtelet again took action against the pamphleteer. On January 10, orders were given to arrest Marat, "quietly and without fuss." A sheriff's officer, together with three officers of the watch, went to the Hôtel de la Fautrière. A neighbor, a woman, spotted them from her window and warned Marat, who vanished. He descended on Danton, who at that moment had no thoughts except for his electoral campaign. Yet despite his urgent desire for a place among the members of the Commune, Danton decided to use the Marat affair as a weapon against the City Hall. He called a meeting of the District Assembly and had them vote a motion addressed to the Châtelet, warning the latter that no decree under its jurisdiction could be executed in the district "without having been communicated to the President." "And approved by him" was the clear underlying implication. In any case, the Court took this caveat as read, and did not press the point. By now the authorities were beginning to fear Danton more than Bailly.

Marat took advantage of their retreat to fire a shot or two at this ancient tribunal. In his next broadsheet he wrote: "Any suggestions for reforming the Châtelet would be doomed to failure. The attempt to make a healthy and vigorous body from such weak or rotten limbs is a clear impossibility." He concluded with an appeal to the people, who were told that they should "rise and demolish this Gothic tribunal."

Having read this outrageous piece, the examining magistrate of the Châtelet, M. Boucher d'Argis, requested the City Hall's intervention. Before they went into recess, the retiring Councilors voted, once again, for the journalist's arrest. His response was to describe them as *fripons* (knaves), an insult which carried a far stronger meaning then than it does nowadays. At the same time, Marat denounced "the luxury of the Mayor and his household furnishings, and the sumptuousness of his table, where he consumes in a single meal enough to feed four hundred poor people."

This time he had gone too far. At all costs this slanderous
fellow had to be silenced. On the 21st a top-priority order from
Bailly reached the headquarters of the National Guard: Marat
was to be arrested at once. La Fayette had no option but to pass
on this order to the Commandant of the Third Battalion (formerly the Bataillon des Cordeliers) for immediate execution. But
if Crèvecoeur's successor, Villette, was responsible to La Fayette
as his military superior, from the administrative viewpoint he
came under Danton, as President of the district. He therefore
informed Danton of his instructions. Danton, instead of backing
up La Fayette, ordered Villette to take the battalion and throw
a cordon around the journalist's residence—to protect him.
Caught between two allegiances, the battalion commander chose
the second. His troops took up defensive positions outside the
Hôtel de la Fautrière.

Informed of this move by the public grapevine, La Fayette
ordered General Plainville to intervene. This officer marched off
a force of five hundred infantry and four hundred dragoons
against the rebel stronghold. These nine hundred men, summoned to enforce respect for law and order, only reached their
destination twelve hours later, on January 22, together with a
police superintendent and two sheriff's officers who were to effect
the actual arrest.

By what can only be described as an epic coincidence, Danton
had just reaped the fruits of his electoral campaign. He was now
a member of the Commune: the following day he had to take his
seat in the City Hall and be duly sworn in. At the District
Assembly he received the congratulations of his constituents.
Then there came the sudden tramp of marching feet, as General
Plainville's troops began to occupy the streets around them.
Torn between his duty as an elected Municipal Councilor and his
special prerogatives as District President, what was Danton to
do? He did not show any signs of hesitation: he at once mounted
the speakers' rostrum and denounced this "intolerable invasion."
Though he detested Marat, he was only too glad to block any
action by Bailly and La Fayette. In the course of an impassioned
harangue he exclaimed: "If we listened to nothing but the
dictates of our own righteous indignation, seeing ourselves thus
besieged on our own territory by *two thousand armed men*

[*sic*], who are barricading the main thoroughfares and block-
ing all access to or from the district, we would spring to arms
instantly! If the tocsin were to be rung now, if we sounded the
general alarm, twenty thousand men would rally at our call and
these troops would blanch at the sight of them. But God forbid
that we should do such a thing: our cause is too fine a one to
risk spoiling. The only arms we must employ are those of
reason!"

The orator, then, it would appear, was renouncing any possibility of fraticidal strife—and with good reason. The citizen
militia of Les Cordeliers would never bring themselves to cross
bayonets with the citizen militia from other districts. Fearing
desertions, Danton decided to negotiate with the executive. In
any case, there was no need to sound the tocsin or beat the drum
to bring the crowds into the streets. From her window Gabrielle
could see her neighbors all flocking out to engulf La Fayette's
nine hundred men.

At the headquarters of his District Assembly, Danton proposed
that a deputation should be sent to the Riding School, requesting
the Constituent Assembly to arbitrate in this matter. There was
general applause, and Danton himself was chosen to head the
delegation. He set off at once, together with three of his constituents and his friend and chief clerk, Paré. A vast crowd
cheered them on their way. Outside Marat's house—now cordoned by Villette's battalion—Legendre shouted: "While I am
here the People's Friend is safe! No one shall touch so much as
a hair of his head!"

When they reached the Tuileries, Danton and his group requested a hearing at the bar of the Assembly. The request was
refused. Danton then sent in a note to the Deputy presiding over
that session, a lawyer named Target. The latter—convinced
that Danton, far from seeking a reconciliation, was deliberately
encouraging violence—replied that he was going to lay the
matter before the Constituent Assembly there and then. The
Deputies—after a stern talking-to from Target—passed a motion
calling upon the Cordeliers District to show proper respect for the
law. A secretary was sent out to inform the petitioner, who had
been pacing around the colonnade, that the National Assembly
"disapproved of his conduct" and that it "relied on his sense of

patriotism to permit the execution of the Assembly's decrees rather than obstruct them."

Here was a real setback for Danton. He had to admit defeat, and went back across Paris in a very crestfallen mood. But what was this? Everybody had disappeared: the crowds thronging his route, General Plainville's troops, the battalion protecting the Hôtel de Fautrière, all those serried ranks of uniforms and riders, that vast mob of local inhabitants and screaming women—all gone, vanished as though they had never been. What had happened in Danton's absence?

The truth was that La Fayette, being no more anxious than Danton to provoke a civil war, had capitulated and ordered his subordinate commander to pull out. Marat himself had disappeared. Sacrificing his usual attire—the headscarf, the shirt gaping open at the neck to expose his hairy chest, the old and filthy jacket—he had walked out of his house in a smart frock coat and hat, smiling, clean-shaven, and quite unrecognizable. Thus disguised, he had passed unchallenged through the crowds and the military cordon. Danton, on learning what had happened from the neighbors, went back home to Gabrielle, who had been sick with anxiety during his absence and was only too glad to hear his cheerful laughter once more.

Next day, January 23, the lucky victor went to take his seat in the City Hall. Elected a member of the Commune together with his friend Legendre, he appeared in the old *Parloir aux Bourgeois* and was greeted by much loud whispering. The Chamber was less enamored than ever of this person and of the way he invariably attempted to block municipal decisions. New members took the oath in alphabetical order; when it was Danton's turn, loud protests were voiced. The man was a disturber of the peace who had always hampered the Commune in its lawful duties—had, indeed, fought its decisions tooth and nail within the last twenty-four hours. How could such a pestilential agitator be allowed a place among its members? Faced with such an attack, Danton found himself constrained to plead in his own defense, emphasizing his love of the people, his respect for the law, and his devotion to reason. The eloquence he displayed won him some votes; but without the threat of a new plebiscite in his favor at district level, he would not, it was clear, obtain his validation.

As far as Marat was concerned, the incident seemed to be closed. He had gone into hiding, and that was that. But the sheriff's officers returned to his lodgings the following day. No one made any effort to stop them when they placed seals on the door of his room, nor when they proceeded to immobilize the printing press he employed. For the time being *L'Ami du Peuple* was dead: four months were to elapse before its next appearance.

In Danton's case, the consequences were different. The Châtelet continued to place an unfavorable interpretation on his speech of the 22nd. The judges of this tribunal remembered only his violence, and neglected the spirit of reconciliation which had succeeded it. They therefore instructed the examining magistrate of the Garde des Marets to lay charges against him. This official signed a warrant for Danton's arrest, on the grounds that he had "made speeches prejudicial to public law and order."

Coming so soon after the Marat incident, would an *affaire* Danton finally cut this infernal district down to size? Not yet: the examining magistrate proceeded to go cool on the job. He held the warrant in abeyance, deciding to wait until passions had cooled before executing it. Not surprisingly, every Paris newssheet took cognizance of these events. One pamphlet, sold on the streets and in the public gardens, treated the whole affair in humorous vein. Its title gave the prospective reader a fair idea of its contents:

> GREAT motion on the
> GREAT crime of the
> GREAT M. Danton, perpetrated in the
> GREAT district of the
> GREAT CORDELIERS and upon the
> GREAT retinue thereof.

At last, the ambitious District President was renowned throughout the capital. So at least he declared in the presence of his wife and friends. But this was a mere façade. Underneath he was highly apprehensive at the prospect of his arrest, with officers of the watch arriving and beating on his door. One or two hints that he slipped into speeches before the District Assembly persuaded that body to address a protest to the Constituent Assembly. Danton's electors, declaring that the proceedings now under way "violated both freedom of speech and the freedom of legal assemblies," appealed to the representatives of the people to suppress this "anticonstitutional warrant" and to "forbid the judges of the Châtelet to repeat such actions in future, under penalty of being proceeded against themselves, on a charge of *lèse-nation*."

The Constituent Assembly, presented with this demand, appointed a Deputy from Sarreguemines to investigate and report on it. This person, whose name was Anthoine, exercised the function of examining magistrate (Criminal Division) in the bailiwick of Boulay. Without bothering to make an expert assessment of the facts from a legal viewpoint, he came out boldly on the side of the accused, even going so far as to suggest the prosecution of the Châtelet judges. Luckily for them, the members of the Constituent Assembly hushed the whole thing up.

On the whole, Danton emerged from this murky affair with his reputation enhanced both in the eyes of the Paris proletariat, which saw him as an ardent champion of liberty, and in those of the King, the Court, Bailly, and La Fayette, who now considered him a man to be reckoned with, an opponent of formidable powers, a demagogue capable of winning the obedience and the adoration of an entire district.

On February 6 he dressed up in his finest clothes. He could scarcely avoid being present at the signing of the marriage contract between Françoise Duhauttoir and Huet de Paisy. This, in accordance with the custom of the times, was an occasion to be celebrated in style—though the wedding itself was an intimate affair, the mere regularization of a long-standing illicit union.

Antoine Charpentier, Maître Dosfant's chief clerk and Gabrielle's brother, had been responsible for drawing up the contract. The whole affair was thus kept within the family. Toward the end of the eighteenth century such breaches of professional etiquette were regarded as morally permissible. Among the other goods of the bride-to-be, the contract included a sum which Danton still owed her. Of the 36,000 *livres* Françoise had lent him to help him purchase his situation from Huet, he had already paid off 27,000 *livres* (a further proof that he was in receipt of some kind of clandestine income); this left 9000 outstanding, which Antoine Charpentier included in Mlle. Duhauttoir's assets. There was also a clause regularizing the position of the son by "some person unknown." Huet de Paisy acknowledged this boy as his. At the same time, he admitted the paternity of a daughter whom Françoise had borne early in their relationship.

Since the Constituent Assembly had not, as yet, deprived the parish priest of his duties as local registrar, their marriage was duly recorded in the parish of residence—not that of the rue de la Tixanderie, we may note, but that of the rue des Couronnes, on the heights of Belleville. For the past two years the couple had been living there, in a house belonging to Françoise. When the brief ceremony was concluded, they both went home there, accompanied by Danton's blessings. Were not this pair responsible for his own marriage? One good turn deserved another.

Such minor troubles in Danton's highly complicated life did not take the edge off his devouring ambition. On the contrary, the removal of these millstones from his past left him all the freer to strike out into the future.

Having been disavowed by the Constituent Assembly as a result of the Marat affair, he now set about getting himself back in the good graces of this intransigent body. Though he had no intention of repudiating his original action, he did arrange for his own District Assembly to pass a motion calling for his "respectful submission" to the legislative authorities, and describing as "an infamous traitor to our country any citizen, or group of citizens, that would utter protests against any one of that body's decrees." This motion did not stop Danton pursuing his struggle against the Commune (of which he was a member!) and showing scant respect for the edicts of the Constituent Assembly in the process. But he was not—at least, not officially—responsible for this motion himself; he was merely obeying the decisions of his "infernal district."

Camille Desmoulins had a very different epithet for it in his broadsheet: he referred to it as this "incomparable district." The Lantern Attorney was now loudly singing the praises of the tiny Assembly and its President. In his *Révolutions de France et de Brabant* Lucile's lover showed equal enthusiasm for Robespierre, his former classmate at Louis-le-Grand. Robespierre had just been elected President of the Jacobin Club, and it was prudent to keep in his good books.

The creation of this group went back some little way. At the time when the Constituent Assembly was still sitting at Versailles, the Breton Deputies had formed a Society of the Friends of the Constitution. Wanting to demonstrate their power, they changed the title of their association. Since the word "club" in English also means "bludgeon," they called it the Breton Club. When the Constituent Assembly moved to Paris in Louis XVI's wake, the Breton Club held its meetings in the Couvent des Jacobins on the rue Saint-Honoré: hence the nickname of "Jacobin Club" which the public gave it. By now its membership was no longer restricted to Breton representatives, but to Deputies from any part of France. It was then widened to include the inhabitants of Paris generally, and latterly foreigners also became eligible for admission—always on condition that they could produce a membership card or a personal invitation.

The church could hold about a thousand people. They sat on tiers of wooden benches, erected above the tombs in the nave. Not only Frenchmen, but Germans, Englishmen, and visitors from Holland and Switzerland rubbed shoulders here: an extraordinary mixture of nationalities, religions, and types of intelligence, that was destined, finally, to dictate its own terms to the executive. This explains why Robespierre, who succeeded to the presidency at the precise moment when the Club was beginning to make itself felt as an influence, suddenly became a more powerful figure in Paris than the aggressive ward leader from Les Cordeliers.

Danton was acquainted with the Deputy from Arras, but did not rank among his intimate friends. After Robespierre's election as President of the Jacobin Club, Danton felt he had to get even with his competitor. He pondered this problem between his infrequent cases and the various duties entailed by the need to keep up his popularity in the district.

With so many other calls on his time, one wonders how much leisure he had left to devote to Gabrielle, to enjoy, not only her feminine charms, but also the home which, little by little, she was equipping and decorating. The presence of separate twin beds in their room caused some astonishment among the couple's friends. Did Danton's passion fall short of his affections? These beds stood back in a dim recessed alcove, lined with yellow tapestry. Out in the light of the room proper—decorated with the same straw-yellow motif—Gabrielle had a roll-top escritoire, a large chest of drawers, a seven-day case of razors, done in marquetry work, two armchairs, and six cane-bottomed chairs. In the drawing room, which also served as a waiting room for Danton's infrequent clients, there was a suite consisting of a sofa and six armchairs in purple, an easy chair with a gay printed cretonne cover, and ten lyre-backed chairs arranged around a mahogany table. Between the two windows there stood a clavichord, on which Gabrielle—who had taken lessons while living at the Quai de l'École—could play hits of the day such as the minuets by Boccherini and Exaudet, Bécourt's "Carillon National," and—a little later—the "Carmagnole."

The master's study was decorated in red. It contained a large desk, with a secretaire beside it, a standing desk, and some comfortable armchairs. There were oil lamps to provide light. In the octagonal dining room, scantily lit by a narrow casement looking out over the Cour du Commerce, Danton had fitted up an office where his clerks, Desforgues and Paré, carried out their subordinate duties. These consisted less of legal work than of revolutionary chores.

Where, then, did they eat? In their room, when no guests were invited, and in the drawing room on more formal occasions. Thus they emulated the example of royalty: at this period only the bourgeoisie still earmarked a separate room for meals.

There were one or two pictures hanging on the walls. Among them were the portraits of the tenants which can be seen today in the museum at Troyes. Tradition ascribes that of Gabrielle to Louis David, and that of Georges to some unknown artist. But some writers have challenged such an ascription. According to them, both portraits were the work of the same person— Mme. Victor Charpentier, the wife of Gabrielle and Antoine's elder brother. Françoise Hébert had previously been married to Hugues Taravel, Painter-in-Ordinary to the King. After his death she married Victor Charpentier. Her first husband had passed on his talent to her—a talent which much resembled that of Louis David. Hence the confusion.

On May 18, 1790, Gabrielle bore a second son. Her first had died in April 1789; this posthumous brother was christened with the name, and family name, of his uncle and godfather, Antoine Charpentier. Why, one wonders, was the child baptized at Saint-Sulpice, rather than at Saint-André-des-Arts, in his own parish? Doubtless because Saint-Sulpice, though situated on the edge of the district, was not actually within its boundaries. Danton was beginning to establish his authority over the anticlerical group in his neighborhood, and the blessing of the Church might have offended those "patriots" who came around, as delegates from the local Assembly, to pin a tricolor cockade on his son's cradle.

But Danton's unfortunate district now suddenly found itself under sentence of death, abolished, at a stroke of the pen, by the Constituent Assembly. The same fate had befallen the fifty-nine other districts: all were doomed to extinction. The Deputies had decided to reorganize the administrative divisions of the capital. The sixty districts were replaced by forty-eight "voting areas," where, henceforth, it was illegal to hold meetings or debates except at election time. This measure was obviously aimed at Danton, and it aroused his pride as well as his anger. The authorities must really be frightened of him. Camille Desmoulins, writing in his newssheet, put the following words in Danton's mouth: "O beloved Cordeliers District! Farewell! The bell will be silent now, the President's chair vacant; no longer will the speakers' rostrum resound to the utterance of illustrious orators . . ."

By now the failed lawyer was no longer in straitened circumstances. Since he had begun editing his broadsheet, his life had become positively opulent. The source of this manna was not, certainly, the broadsheet itself, which had a circulation of no more than five to six thousand and carried no advertising (a device as yet nonexistent) to swell its gross revenues. It looks very much as though "the conqueror of the Bastille" was in receipt of secret funds from some source or other. For the first time in his life he was eligible for the "contribution of a silver mark." By virtue of this tax he got his name put on the electoral roll. When he next dined with M. and Mme. Duplessis, he pressed them to agree to his marrying Lucile. But this worthy pair were still hesitant. To have the Lantern Attorney for their son-in-law would doubtless be some sort of protection for a Royal Treasury clerk and his wife—and, *a fortiori,* for their daughter. But if by any chance the monarchy triumphed over the forces of revolution, such a marriage could cause them great harm. So they told Desmoulins to be patient for a few months longer; Lucile was still so young, they said.

Waiting; waiting; always more waiting.

But Danton was not the man to be put off in this way; when *he* set his mind on something he aimed straight for the mark. Since the Constituent Assembly, by substituting these forty-eight voting areas for the original sixty districts, had *ipso facto* suppressed the Assembly of Les Cordeliers, its ex-President launched a blistering attack on the régime at a meeting of the Jacobin Club. With his usual flow of eloquence, and a little luck on his side, he would, he hoped, replace Robespierre as the most influential figure there. He did not so much dislike Robespierre as, at the bottom of his heart, feel envy for his success.

To obtain entrance to the Club on the rue Saint-Honoré required a written invitation. This Danton got from the Englishman, Augustus Miles, a member of the Club and a friend of Mrs. Elliott's. It was, we recall, Lord Gilbert Elliott who had first introduced them. On May 30 Danton entered the Jacobins' meeting hall and took his seat on one of the benches. His appearance was greeted with whispering rather than applause. At that moment a Deputy named Alexandre de Lameth went up to the speakers' rostrum. Although of noble birth, Lameth, who was the member for Péronne, belonged to the left wing of the Constituent Assembly. A veteran of the American War of Independence and a sworn enemy of privilege, he formed, together with his brother Charles and his colleague Barnave, a kind of triumvirate, designed to counterbalance Mirabeau's popularity in the Riding School. This "placed" him politically. In his speech before the Jacobins he attacked the quality of the bread issued to troops in the Givet area. "Adulterated bread," he called it, "made with flour of such poor quality that our unfortunate soldiers are suffering from attacks of colic and vomiting."

Continuing his address, Lameth now turned to the matter of what were known as "yellow tickets." This had nothing to do with the dishonesty of contractors, or the criminal complaisance of senior officers who accepted the goods they supplied. The word "ticket" was used, in military parlance, to denote the certificate of discharge given to a man released for medical reasons or at the end of his term of service. Either by an oversight or through mere slothful indifference, the authorities had printed these certificates on the same yellow paper as was used for "tickets" of *dishonorable* transfer or discharge. When traveling through France, demobilized soldiers were often called upon to show their discharge papers, in the villages, as means of identification. They were thus very often confused, by the local peasantry, with those who had dishonored the uniform they wore. In a calm, unemotional voice Alexandre de Lameth protested against this state of affairs and begged the Club's intervention to bring it to an end.

Hearing these words, Danton felt he had found an excellent opportunity of putting himself forward. He asked Robespierre's leave to speak, and took Lameth's place on the rostrum. What Jaurès was later to describe as "sweating eloquence" was something the ex-President of Les Cordeliers exploited to excess. For half an hour he proceeded to season Lameth's arguments with an admixture of *sauce Danton*. The poisoned bread, the rapacity of the contractors, the corruption rife among military purchasing agents, the negligence of the officers, the yellow tickets, brave veterans, and dishonorable discharges, illiterate peasants who ought to be educated by the nation—this adaptation of Lameth's speech flowed in torrents from the lips of his successor on the rostrum. Danton's gestures were of a sort to match his voice. He banged the lectern with his fist and stamped his foot on the floor of the platform. His oratorical fluency astonished some of his audience but also caused much amusement. This rehash of facts which all those present knew as well as he did, this thundering piece of plagiarism, got most of its applause from the back of the hall. With his usual violence of expression, Danton concluded: "If I had the honor to be a soldier in the French Army, and was given a yellow ticket at my demobilization, I would take this seal of dishonor and soak it in the blood of the Ministers responsible!'"

This hyperbolic sentiment, and the incitement to murder that went with it, earned the speaker some catcalls. Acclaimed by a minority, but hissed and jeered by the bulk of his audience, Danton came down from the rostrum and resumed his seat. His ill-judged intervention did him considerable damage. The members of the Club did not share the attitude toward him which was felt by his neighbors and constituents in the Cordeliers District. The latter were quite ready to excuse his indiscretions because of the stand he had taken over the Marat affair. But in the Jacobin Club he was regarded as a man of devouring ambition, thirsty for popular fame, and always on the lookout for a chance to put himself forward.

There was another group which shared this opinion of Danton: the Club des Feuillants. This society, founded by La Fayette, Bailly, and Mirabeau, held its meetings in a house once occupied by Feuillant monks (a strict Bernardine order) near the Riding School. Originally the Club formed a meeting place for moderate radicals. Later it became a refuge for reactionaries, a fact which led to its dissolution.

After his speech on May 30, Danton became aware that the Jacobins were even more hostile toward him than was the Club des Feuillants. Realizing the tactical error he had made, he kept quiet for several weeks. At the City Hall his reserve was a matter of astonishment to his colleagues. Sprawled out in his chair, he looked like some enormous dog digesting its lunch.

At home, Gabrielle found him much more like the husband she recalled on their honeymoon. Their friends would drop by during the day to smile at little Antoine. Lucile Duplessis came around with Desmoulins. Fabre d'Églantine brought his latest poems and read them out loud in the middle of the drawing room. Brune, Momoro, Legendre, the Roberts, Danton's in-laws the Charpentiers, even his mother, who made the trip up by coach to kiss her grandchild—the apartment was always full of such comings and goings, and loud with cheerful festivities. What lavish dinners took place during that June in 1790! Danton was throwing money about by the handful—and yet it was several weeks since he had touched a case. His two most recent cases had gone against the grain of his political beliefs. In one of them he had figured as the defender of the nobility, appealing to "the sovereign wisdom and justice of His Majesty" in order to obtain confirmation of a certain M. de la Thifordière's titles; in the other, he sought similar recognition for the rights of a "Prince de Montbarey." Such cases might well compromise him in the eyes of his constituents, and the few gold pieces he would pocket by way of fee did not justify the risk.

Did he attend the celebrations on July 14, the Feast of the Federation? There is no record of his presence on the Champ-de-Mars; this orator seems to have had very little liking for the common people *en masse* except when he had a chance to harangue them. When the Bastille was stormed he was nowhere to be seen. He played no part in the attack on the Palace of Versailles. Why should we expect him to put in an appearance during the first annual celebration of these events?

The City Council, however, led by its Mayor, marched in procession to attend this grandiose commemoration, wearing black, and without swords. The crowd was so dense, and the delegations so numerous, that it took the members of the Commune four hours to reach the Champ-de-Mars. While some 400,000 spectators looked on, Monseignor de Talleyrand celebrated Mass on the Altar of the Fatherland. Louis XVI swore to uphold the Constitution laid down by the National Assembly. La Fayette rode in cavalcade through this multitude, while torrential rain poured down on them. Mirabeau, however, complained to the Abbé Sieyès about the near-idolatrous treatment which the Commander of the National Guard had received. "Imagine it," he said. "I have seen Federals fall on their knees before this dictator and kiss his hands, his garments, his boots, the very saddle of his horse!" And Mirabeau concluded, with much bitterness: "What can you do with such people? If I was ever made a Minister, best to slip a knife through my ribs, because in a year's time you'd all be slaves."

That evening, all Paris feasted. Though Danton was absent from the Champ-de-Mars, he nevertheless presided over the celebrations in his own *quartier*. Of the thousands of delegates who had come up from the provinces, some two hundred were

staying in the Cordeliers District. The kitchen ranges of the
monastery were heated up again for their benefit. Danton sat
at the highest table, with all his political friends around him.
After the dessert he made a speech. A good number of his
guests slept off the wine they had drunk outside in the streets,
their backs propped up against the nearest house front.

Now that the Constituent Assembly had nationalized all ecclesiastical property, it was decided that a certain number of
churches should be used as meeting halls and polling stations.
Saint André-des-Arts figured on this list and now housed the
administrative offices of the Thêâtre-Français voting division.
Since the Commune held only a provisional mandate, fresh
elections now had to take place. A certain M. d'Hervilly was
appointed by the retiring members to visit Saint-André-des-Arts
on July 29 to inaugurate the church's civic function and see
new members duly voted in. Both Danton and Bailly had put
their names down on the list of candidates.

Danton, hoping at one stroke to improve his chances against
his opponent and to obtain a fresh platform for his oratory, decided on a bold tactical move. Together with his friends Desmoulins, Paré, Fabre d'Églantine, and Fréron, he founded the
Society of the Friends of the Rights of Man—a deliberate plagia-
rization of the former Society of the Friends of the Constitution,
founded in Versailles a year earlier, and now, after the move to
Paris, reincarnated as that same Jacobin Club of which Robespierre was President. Moreover, since "the Incorruptible" held
his meetings in a monastic house on the rue Saint-Honoré,
Danton wanted to do likewise in his beloved monastery of Les
Cordeliers. But Bailly, who kept well abreast of all the latest
developments in the City Hall, managed to parry his opponent's
attack. Invoking the act covering the seizure of ecclesiastical
property, he had the entrance gates to Les Cordeliers placed
under official seal. Since the Society of the Friends of the Rights
of Man dared not break these seals, it was forced to seek accommodation elsewhere. It found it in a private tennis court in the
rue Mazarine—a fine opportunity for its members to swear their
own Tennis Court Oath. Once more imitating illustrious pred-

ecessors—and in particular Bailly, who had presided over the famous resolution of June 20, 1789—they swore not to disband, under any circumstances, till they had provided France with "strong institutions." But there was no David, or any other well-known painter, who thought fit to record *this* event for posterity.

Danton's electoral campaign was conducted in this covered court. For several days the "hall" in the rue Mazarine echoed to the speechmaking of him and his friends—and to the applause of the common people, who, though still ineligible to vote, nevertheless flocked to election meetings.

Finally the voters made their way to Saint-André-des-Arts to register their choice. As the electoral division did not include more than half the old district and took in parts of several former adjoining districts, Danton could count on less support than in his now defunct constituency. This was a characteristic phenomenon of the age: the lack of adequate press coverage and public transport, together with the nonexistence of photography, isolated each *quartier* from its neighbors, just as they isolated each *département* of adjacent provincial regions.

All these factors go far to explain why Danton—who, though the darling of Les Cordeliers, came in for more than his fair share of abuse elsewhere—only just managed to avoid defeat at the polls. Even so, he scraped in at the bottom of the list. Of the 580 qualified electors of the Théâtre-Français division, only forty-nine voted for him. Bailly, on the other hand, swept home triumphantly, with 478 votes recorded in his favor. Nevertheless his adversary, although only the fourth of five elected Councilors, got back inside the City Hall for a second time—by the back stairs, his enemies were heard to murmur.

Taking a calculated risk, Danton offered himself as candidate for the office of Public Attorney to the Commune—a magistrate who possessed the power to act in the Commune's name. Here he met a further setback, being defeated by a rival named Boullemer de la Martinière. Nevertheless, 129 electors supported him, which represented a net gain on the previous poll. Encouraged by this, he applied for the post of Deputy Public Prosecutor. Once again he failed; yet no less than 197 votes, he learned afterward, had been cast in his favor, a further increase of sixty-eight. There could be no doubt about it; his popularity was on the increase.

Unfortunately, Danton suffered a sharp reverse during a scandalous incident in which he unwillingly found himself cast as the main actor. The order for his arrest, signed by a magistrate of the Châtelet after the part he had played in the Marat affair, had been collecting dust in a drawer ever since February. On the other hand, the Châtelet itself no longer existed. The reorganization of the judiciary, lately voted by the Constituent Assembly, had replaced it with a series of district courts. One of these was anxious to pursue outstanding cases left over from the defunct jurisdiction. A sheriff's officer named Damien, accompanied by two policemen, arrived at Saint-André-des-Arts right in the middle of an election meeting. This time the voting was for seats on the General Council—and once again Danton had put himself up as a candidate. "In the name of the law," Damien cried, "I arrest you."

This caused a sensation among the spectators, and feelings ran high. The crowd at once split into two factions: those who opposed the arrest, and those in favor of it. With a little encouragement, they would have come to blows. Danton's friends, backed in the end by the majority of the electors, were of the opinion that to arrest a candidate—and in the headquarters of the constituency, at that—would constitute an offense against the rights of the electorate. They showed Damien the door, and drafted a protest which was sent to the Riding School. The Constituent Assembly then delegated its Constitutional Committee to rule on the matter. One section of the press rallied to Danton's support, and the court involved quietly dropped its charges.

Despite this, the scandal brought Danton a fresh setback. Of 144 candidates for the General Council, nominated by the forty-eight electoral divisions of Paris, only one found the road barred to him; and that one was Danton. In his paper, Camille Desmoulins deplored this stinging rebuff. "The patriots' most staunch ally," he wrote, "the only tribune of the people who might have made himself heard in the land, and whose voice could have rallied all patriots around the rostrum; the only man whose veto the aristocracy had good cause to fear, and in whom they might have found both the Gracchi and a second Marius —in a word, M. Danton—has been proscribed by every electoral division."

Disappointed, but far from crushed, Danton decided to take a vacation. With his wife and child he set off for Arcis-sur-Aube. When they reached his home town, they stayed with his sister Anne-Madeleine, who had married and was now Mme. Menuel. Her home—a bigger one than the family house on the rue de Mesnil, where Danton had been born thirty-one years previously —could easily accommodate the couple, their child, and a maid.

Around Arcis the prodigal son found, to his surprise, that he possessed a very odd kind of popularity. Since Paris news-sheets did not reach the provinces, his fellow townsmen only knew vaguely, through gossip, that he held high office of some sort in Paris. Not knowing what was meant by King's Counsel, they assumed that he had become Councilor to the King—that is, that their Maître d'Anton was a member of the King's Privy Council. What a source of pride for the inhabitants! When they passed him on the street they greeted him with a degree of respect which at first took him aback and then (after he had found out the reason for it) caused him much amusement. Always cheerful and hail-fellow-well-met, he was just as ready to shake rough hands as soft. Ah, they all said, what a fine gentleman that Monsieur d'Anton is! What an excellent person! (He was "d'Anton" to everybody now.) And he's not in the least standoffish, either; success hasn't turned *his* head. And just look at his wife! Such a lovely Parisienne, so gracious and elegant, always smiling! As for the baby, the whole town soon knew it weighed a good fifteen pounds. Farmers, artisans, and local bourgeoisie, all were equally captivated.

The aristocrats, on the other hand, cherished no such illusions. With their superior education they could see how deadly and implacable an enemy this lawyer was. But they remained a small minority group, which had little contact with the people.

Nor was Mme. Recordain taken in by the general mood of

uncritical adulation. After Antoine's birth she had, we recall, made the trip to Paris to see her grandchild. In Danton's apartment on the rue des Cordeliers she had met and dined with her son's close friends—that disturbing creature Fabre d'Églantine, the ebullient Desmoulins, the huge and bestial Legendre, the ambitious Chaumette who had never a good word for anybody. Then there was Choderlos de Laclos, the author of a scandalous book—another undesirable person! Mme. Recordain was not quite so put off by the Robert family. Even so, this pretty, well-connected girl who had married into the bourgeoisie worried Danton's mother. For the daughter of a de Kéralio to prostitute her noble birth by engaging in revolutionary ideology seemed, to Mme. Recordain, behavior highly unbecoming to a good Catholic. And her son's lavish way of life—so far above his professional income as an advocate—seriously worried her. Though she was shrewd enough not to talk indiscreetly about such things on her return home, she did confide in her husband. So when Danton said to them one day, after coffee: "Let's go out—I have to see Maître Finot, the notary," M. Recordain asked him, on a sudden impulse, whether he was really well off or not. Danton simply smiled, and left it at that.

On his return to Paris, Danton asked Fabre and Desmoulins for news concerning the great project he had left in their charge before taking off for the country. For several weeks now, all three of them had been plotting a simultaneous revenge against the Commune and the Jacobin Club. Danton's plan was to transform the Society of the Friends of the Rights of Man into a revolutionary club. If the Incorruptible could preside over *his* club in the rue Saint-Honoré, why should the Corruptible not launch a Club of the Rights of Man?

Nevertheless Danton, who had read his Machiavelli and learned a lot from the recent setbacks he had experienced, decided that this time he would operate in the background. The poster plastered up around the streets to announce the Club's formation did not include the name of its begetter. The manifesto was signed by one Dufourny de Villiers, as President, and a certain Dulaure, as Secretary. It read as follows:

The main object of the *Club of the Rights of Man* is to denounce, before the tribunal of public opinion, all abuses of authority, in whatever sphere, and any infringement of the rights of man; the Club therefore, after due deliberation, invites any citizen to acquaint it with any instance of oppression or injustice which they may have suffered, or concerning which they possess information, and to furnish therewith the evidence on which such complaints are founded.

The *Club of the Rights of Man,* having satisfied itself as to the legitimacy of such a complaint, will lose no time in giving it the greatest possible publicity, and in exposing the author of the crime to public obloquy. . . .

It hardly seems necessary to add that dozens and, later, hundreds of such denunciations poured in to the Secretary. The new Club would certainly not lack for business.

The original premises were in the rue des Boucheries-Saint-Germain, close to the Abbaye. A person called Cirier, who owned a ballroom, was willing to make it available to "Dufourny de Villiers"—or, in other words, to Danton. The first meeting, announced by means of handbills which Brune ran off, drew only a small audience. There were young girls under the gallery handing out copies of the Declaration of the Rights of Man. The assembled company, led by the President as though by a priest, read this prayer of the new religion aloud, in unison. Then the speeches began. There were attacks on the municipal authorities, the Constituent Assembly, the Throne, and the Church.

As the weeks went by, the audience grew till M. Cirier's ballroom could no longer hold them all. Every evening people had to be turned away. Momoro suggested reoccupying the church of Les Cordeliers, though both it and the monastery were still under seal. To get the seal removed required authorization from the City Hall, where Danton was by no means *persona grata*. Such a request was bound to meet with refusal. The conspirators therefore played a more subtle game. Dufourny de Villiers resigned the presidency in favor of a certain Peyre, or Pieyre, whose name is variously spelled on the Club's official records. When we consider the success of the intervention, it seems likely that the man in question was actually Pieyre rather than Peyre. The latter, a native of the Basses-Alpes, only made his first visit to Paris in 1792, as a Deputy to the Convention. The former had lodgings in the Palais-Royal, where he occupied the post of secretary to the Duke of Orléans. The latter was on reasonably good terms with Bailly—who had just been re-elected Mayor with a big majority. In these circumstances, there is nothing to prevent us assuming that it was the Duke's secretary who briefly held the presidency of the Club—and was nominated to this position with a view to having the Commune remove the seals that barred all entrance to the monastery. This near-certain hypothesis is yet another indication of collusion between Danton and the Duke.

The Commune, then, now permitted the Club of the Rights of Man to establish its premises in the former monastery: hence its new name, the Club des Cordeliers. However, the City Hall would allow it to hold meetings only in the "theological lecture room." But a few days later the Club occupied the chapel by main force, and Bailly dared not object, much less take a stern line over its action.

Chateaubriand, who visited the Club in 1792, left the following sketch of it in his *Mémoires d'outre-tombe:* "The monastery had been stripped of all its veils, curtains, sculptures, and paintings: the basilica was scraped bare, and offered nothing to the eye save its naked bones and vaulting. At the east end of the church, where wind and rain came in through the glassless rose windows, there stood some joiners' benches, which did duty as a desk for the President when the session took place inside the church. The speakers' rostrum consisted of four small propped-up beams, each pair resembling a vertical X, with a plank running between them like a piece of scaffolding."

The Jacobin Club was a quasi-parliamentary association, where one had to show one's credentials to gain admission, and the most marked characteristics in debate were caution and casuistry. At the Cordeliers, on the other hand, entrance was free to all, and anyone who chose could get up and harangue a highly mixed audience, which might well be equally amused or furious. There was only one rule imposed on all speakers: they had to put on the "red cap" before climbing the ladder that served as a staircase. There was a long strip of calico nailed to the wall, which bore the legend *LIBERTÉ, ÉGALITÉ,*

FRATERNITÉ ("Freedom, Equality, Brotherhood"). This slogan was born in the Club, invented by Danton, and destined to become the motto of the various French Republics of the future.

In this assembly the tribune from Arcis possessed a weapon that matched his ambition. He could stand on equal terms with them all now—Robespierre, making his academic speeches to the Jacobins: Bailly, the life and soul of the conservative Club des Feuillants; the Deputies busy with their legislation in the Riding School. The "poor man's Mirabeau" now possessed a megaphone which was to project his brazen voice, his coarse chuckle, and those startling metaphors of his to the four winds of public opinion.

How did he intend to employ this "cannon," as he himself once described the public platform? To begin with, by forcing Bailly to become one of its servants. The anecdote has some unexpected twists to it.

There was, at this period, a certain obscure Deputy in the Constituent Assembly whom Providence and Allah were later to make famous. His name was Menou; he was a baron and the son of a marquis from Touraine. Elected by the nobility of his bailiwick to represent them at the States-General, Menou had gone across to the benches of the Third Estate, where he made loud proclamation of his liberal opinions. (We find him, in later years, a general in Egypt under Bonaparte, Commander-in-Chief after Kléber's death, converted to Islam, given the Moslem name of Abdullah, marrying a Moslem girl, and affecting Turkish costume. Defeated by the English, repatriated to France after the Peace of Amiens, and restored to the bosom of the Church, he was to end his adventurous life as Governor of Venice in 1810, a Grand Officer of the Legion of Honor, and a Knight of the Iron Crown. But at present Deputy Menou's unpredictable and dilettante career still lay ahead of him, and he was devoting himself to attacking Louis XVI's government.) On October 19, 1790, Menou mounted the speakers' rostrum and proceeded to take several members of the Cabinet apart. M. de Montmorin and M. de Fleurieu, who were respectively Minister of Foreign Affairs and Minister of

Marine, were described as "incompetents." He was still more
scathing about their colleagues Champion de Cicé (Minister of
Justice), Guignard de Saint-Priest (Minister of the Interior),
and La Tour du Pin (Minister of War). With evidence that
was at least open to argument, he denounced their "errors, their
tyrannical behavior, their culpable complacency," and wound
up by demanding their dismissal.

This violent speech, on which the Constituent Assembly refused to take action, provoked a great stir in Paris. The parliamentary system was still in its cradle then, and when the debates
of the legislative body became somewhat heated, they generated
a degree of feeling unimaginable today. The men of 1790 were
not yet inured to the effects of political eloquence.

On Danton's request, all forty-eight electoral divisions assembled in the new club. Without bothering to find out if Menou
was mistaken in his facts, deliberately lying, or actually telling
the truth, they passed a motion calling upon the King to dismiss
the Ministers concerned. At the same time, they charged Danton to use what powers he had to make the Constituent Assembly
back their motion when it was presented to Louis XVI.

Danton set off from Les Cordeliers with a delegation. Having
far from pleasant memories of his first approach to the Riding
School, he wanted Bailly—who was both Mayor and Deputy of
Paris—to introduce him among his legislative colleagues. So
instead of making direct for the Tuileries, he went first to the
City Hall. As a Municipal Councilor he had the right to demand a private interview with Bailly.

So at last the two men sat facing each other, a triple gulf between them. First, there was the difference in their ages: fifty-
four as opposed to thirty-one. Then there was their education:
one had been trained as an astronomer, the other as a lawyer.
Finally, there was the matter of their political opinions. At the
time when Georges "d'Anton" was still affecting an apostrophe
in his name, Bailly had long been attacking the nobility and its
entrenched privileges. In 1789 he was responsible for making
the Deputies of the Third Estate take the Tennis Court Oath.
When his objects had been achieved, during the Night of August
4, he felt that the Revolution was over. Equally against an
absolute monarchy and the dictatorship of the masses, he saw

France's salvation in a series of laws that would enshrine the Declaration of the Rights of Man, and which could be passed by peaceful legislation—provided, that is, there were no agitators like Danton around to stir up trouble. For Bailly, his visitor was the most dangerous kind of demagogue. On the other hand, he was beginning to be somewhat afraid of him. So, with considerable misgivings, he agreed to lead the group which his perennial adversary had brought to the City Hall.

Admitted, through Bailly's good offices, to the Riding School, the delegation produced much whispered excitement as they stood in a group at the foot of the speakers' rostrum. When Bailly rose to address the Assembly—not as a Deputy, but in his capacity as Mayor—the great astronomer did not forget (then or indeed at any time) that he was a member of the French Academy. From his distinguished lips there emerged a series of elegant periods, cast in the mold which refined social usage laid down. He urged his colleagues "to consider the anxiety of all patriots after hearing M. Menou's speech, to give a generous hearing to the leader of this delegation from the electoral divisions, the Honorable Monsieur d'Anton."

When the latter rose to address the House, there was a striking contrast in presentation. Speaking now for the first time in the Riding School (where subsequently his voice was to make both men and windows tremble) he astonished his listeners, right from the beginning, by the power of his utterance. Scorning all polite introductory formulas, not beginning with the word "Citizens," let alone "Gentlemen," he plunged straight into the attack. "The National Assembly," he thundered, "has thought fit to decide that there was no cause to debate the motion—already put before it—that the King should be informed that these Ministers no longer command public confidence. . . ."

The speech delivered by Menou three weeks earlier had been published in the *Moniteur,* where Danton had read it—and, with his prodigious memory, he had retained every word of it by heart. Employing the same device that he had overplayed at the Jacobin Club (when he had adopted Lameth's cause about those "yellow tickets"), he recapitulated all Menou's arguments, trimming them up with his own fiery rhetorical devices. But the

booming resonance of his voice, the images which formed his
style, his crimson face, the violence of his language—everything
about him, in fact, which most aroused enthusiasm in a mob
audience—had a quite different effect on the more weighty and
serious members of the Constituent Assembly. Stupefied by his
opening broadside, the silent Deputies began to recover themselves. Loud whispers finally broke into open barracking.

"What a tub-thumper the fellow is!"

"A real marketplace demagogue."

"It's that notorious creature Danton, you know; they say he's
in the pay of the King—"

"—of Orléans—"

"—of anyone with money to spare."

The member for Haute-Garonne, Marie de Cazalès, shouted
at his colleagues: "Let the man speak! We should be prepared to
listen to anything—political absurdities included."

Danton was standing below the tiers of seats, in the middle
of the square that separated them from the speakers' platform,
and behind that Bar of the House which has vanished from the
modern Chambers but was a physical reality then. He raised his
head and stared at his interrupters. Then, bullneck swelling, he
roared: "The Commune of Paris is made up of citizens who
belong, in a sense, to all eighty-three *départements*—"

"That's a lie!" shouted one Deputy. "The provinces are horrified by the excesses of the capital—"

"Anxious," Danton went on, "to carry out its duties as leading guardian of the Constitution, it has lost no time in acquaint-
ing you with the desire of every enemy of despotism. That desire
is for the prompt, indeed the immediate, dismissal of the Ministers involved."

He proceeded to give various "imperious reasons" for these
dismissals. With bludgeon-like arguments he finished off the
Minister of Justice, Champion de Cicé, whom he accused of
counterrevolutionary measures. He next assailed the Minister of
the Interior, Guignard de Saint-Priest. This former Ambassador
to Constantinople, Danton observed ironically, "had brought
back from the East a Damascus scimitar—with which he hoped
to decapitate a few patriots." There was no evidence adduced in
support of such wild assertions. Danton knew the first rule of

political invective: always assert, never prove. His indictment roused furious resentment among right-wing members, drew applause from the Left, and caused laughter and barracking in the crowded public galleries.

"M. de La Tour de Pin," Danton continued imperturbably, "the Minister of War, is incapable of any action appropriate to his office. But he remains an enemy of the Revolution, because he confuses his parchment scrolls and his self-esteem with the true nobility—that of heart and character."

When he came to deal with the Minister of Foreign Affairs, the speaker modified his tone. Addressing himself to the Standing Committees of the Assembly, this formidable prosecutor suddenly turned counsel for the defense. In the silence that fell as a result of this volte-face, Danton said: "You suspended M. de Montmorin pending inquiries. He had been accused of concealing facts concerning British military preparations from you for several days, on the excuse that he did not want to interrupt the celebrations of July 14. But you investigated his motives and honorably acquitted him of any treasonable intent."

Not only did Danton refrain from attacking Montmorin: he was also personally acquainted with him. Nine months previously, on February 5, to be exact, Danton had appeared before him in the Court of the Upper Chamber and asked him to uphold the dubious genealogy of his client, Manceau de la Thifordière. His eloquent pleading, his appeal to "the sovereign wisdom and justice of His Majesty," and his ultimate victory in this very hazardous case had brought him, if not Montmorin's public approval (as a Minister he was bound to frown on demagoguery), at least the interest which a great public servant was bound to take in so skillful an advocate. They met after the verdict, but there is no record of what they said to each other.

Would Danton now, on November 10, be prepared to attack the aristocrat who had honored him with his hand in friendship nine months before? In fact, following the example of the Standing Committee of the Assembly, he gave him an "honorable acquittal." He then wound up his speech by "beseeching" his listeners, in the name of the Paris Commune, to ask Louis XVI for the dismissal of Champion de Cicé, La Tour du Pin, and

Guignard de Saint-Priest, and to institute proceedings against these "unworthy Ministers."

When the thunder of applause and protest finally died away, the President of the Assembly, M. Chasset, turned toward Bailly (who was sitting pale and silent in one corner of the Chamber) and gave him a smile of sympathy and encouragement. Out of regard for the Mayor, he announced that "this Assembly accords the petitioners the honors of the present session." Then he turned to Danton and said curtly: "We will examine your complaints."

This investigation produced a vote of 513 in favor of the Ministers continuing in office, and 340 supporting their dismissal. Yet Danton's move can hardly be called unsuccessful, since La Tour du Pin and Champion de Cicé were so disconcerted by the size of the minority vote that they submitted their resignations as soon as the results were known. Guignard de Saint-Priest was the only one who obstinately held on in office—though not, as events turned out, for very long.

Danton, then, had won a victory on two of his three fronts. This triumph, combined with the fact that the Assembly had actually given him a hearing, was to put the final seal on his power and influence in the eyes of the masses. Clothed in the bare authority of a Municipal Councilor, he had beaten the Constituent Assembly, the government, and the King. When the Abbé Maury—that impetuous priest—saw him walk out of the Riding School with the self-satisfied swagger of a champion, he could not refrain from observing to Cazalès: "Why, the wretched creature will go around boasting that he *scared* us!"

Only one member of the Cabinet had received kindly treatment in Danton's speech, and that was M. de Montmorin. Why this unforeseen generosity? Danton's defenders will say that he appreciated—as did the Standing Committee—Montmorin's virtues or talents. But according to his enemies, the anomaly resulted from Montmorin's acting as the go-between through whom Danton received those sums which Louis XVI paid him "to keep his anger sleeping." La Fayette, as we have seen, employed this phrase in his *Memoirs*. According to him, such disbursements were paid from the secret funds of the Foreign Ministry.

There were others who shared the opinions of La Fayette. On March 10, 1791, four months after this famous session in the Riding School, Mirabeau wrote to the Count de La Marck (who was the regular channel by which his advice reached the Queen) : "My dear Count, it is vital that I see you this morning. Yesterday Montmorin and I learned some quite extraordinary facts from each other, by comparing notes, not only concerning the organization of the press (which is coming out ever more strongly against me and in favor of La Fayette), but also with respect to certain confidential reports and special proposals of a most singular nature. . . ."

Mirabeau indicated the sources of these confidential reports. Besides Montmorin himself, they emanated from three members of the Assembly who moved very much in Court circles. M. d'André represented the nobility of Aix, a town in which Mirabeau (though himself a count) was the representative of the Third Estate. M. de Beaumetz was one of the Deputies for the nobility of Artois. The third, M. Le Chapelier, had been President of the Assembly on the Night of August 4; he had remained on personal terms with the King ever since, *qua* President, he had brought Louis the decrees formally abolishing privileges, in ratification of the Assembly's vote to abandon them. Were these three men sufficiently well informed for Mirabeau to be able to declare without hedging, in his letter to La Marck: "Danton received 30,000 *livres* yesterday, and I have proof that it was Danton who brought out Camille Desmoulins's last number"— a polite way of saying that Danton paid the printer's bill?

Then, going on to discuss the 6000 *livres* which he, Mirabeau, had obtained in order to suborn a spy, the writer added: "This sum was more innocently spent than Danton's thirty thousand. When you come down to it, to avoid being a dishonest rogue in this underworld requires much guile—or gullibility."

To replace La Tour du Pin, Louis XVI called upon Duport-Dutertre. The latter was a lawyer by profession, and since the municipal elections had held the office of Assistant Deputy Public Prosecutor to the Commune. When he was appointed a Minister, he resigned this position and it was the responsibility of the City Hall to find a successor. The moment he heard of the vacancy, Danton submitted his name as a candidate. His popularity and renown, the use of his Club to promote him during the campaign, made him confident of success. But his optimism was soon dashed. Another lawyer, named Desmousseaux, beat him with a majority of more than fifteen hundred.

This time Danton could not slip away to Arcis-sur-Aube to let his rancor cool. Two days later, on December 29, he was to be a guest at Camille Desmoulins's wedding. The Lantern Attorney was at long last marrying Mlle. Duplessis. After three years of resistance, her parents had finally capitulated. They were letting Lucile have her way, and giving her a dowry of 100,000 francs into the bargain. By running with the wolves, as it were, they felt they were safeguarding their own future.

Oddly, Danton himself was not included among the witnesses. There were five of them—and all destined to achieve considerable notoriety: Jérôme Pétion, Deputy in the Constituent Assembly; his colleague Brulard de Sillery, the separated husband of Mme. de Genlis, former mistress of the Duke of Orléans and the governess to his children; Maximilien de Robespierre; Louis-Sébastien Mercier, historian and member of several learned academies; and finally Brissot, known as de Warville, who was to be one of the leaders of the Gironde in the Convention.

A rumor went around that the Duke of Orléans, though not present at the ceremony in person, had offered to provide accommodation for the newlyweds. Subsequently he invited them to the Palais-Royal on several occasions, and also to his estate, Monceau Park, where he still gave parties. Danton and Gabrielle were among the guests on such gala occasions, together with most of their friends. Only Robespierre held out dourly against the Duke's blandishments. He remained, as ever, the Incorruptible. Once, upbraiding Desmoulins for his irresponsibility, he snarled: "I shall stay at home: champagne is the very poison of liberty."

The old intimacy between Lucile and Gabrielle now reestablished itself. The newly married Mme. Desmoulins, who was six years younger than Mme. Danton, made the latter the trusted recipient of all her conjugal problems and emotions. When politics kept their husbands away from them, the two women met almost every day, sometimes in Lucile's house, sometimes in Gabrielle's. Lucile used to play with little Antoine, rehearsing, through him, the role of motherhood which she hoped one day to play in earnest.

Lucile sometimes brought her sister to see the Dantons. It was here that Adèle Duplessis first met Robespierre, who had become a visitor at the house since the marriage of their common friends. The Deputy from Arras felt love stir in him for this young girl Adèle—but quickly thrust down an emotion so incompatible with his general character. Robespierre's heart was no less incorruptible than his honor. He could not afford to divert much of his time and energy into the requirements of a middle-class marriage; his life was dedicated to public service. As a result, Danton, who had quickly observed the early budding of this relationship, now referred to his visitor as "that eunuch"—a label he had already applied to both Bailly and La Fayette, the first of whom was married, and the second the father of a family. With regard to these two, Danton clearly had intended his offensive epithet to carry a moral implication.

The creation of the Club des Cordeliers did not prevent its founder from applying for admission to the Jacobins. His application was successful, despite the unfortunate intervention he had made on May 30. Four days after Desmoulins's marriage Danton walked in with his own membership card; he no longer had to depend on invitations.

Mirabeau was presiding over that particular session. Though he had been one of the founder members of the conservative Club des Feuillants, he nevertheless kept up his connection with the rival establishment, in the hope of bringing it back to its old, more moderate policies. On that January evening in 1791 he suddenly cut Fabre d'Églantine off in mid-speech, having decided that his remarks were becoming far too violent and extremist. At the time the poet was defending the political line taken up by Westermann, the Governor of Haguenau in Alsatia. Westermann was a Republican and in constant conflict with the Royalist municipality of Strasbourg. Mirabeau, himself equally Royalist, did not approve of this improvised plea on behalf of "the patriot Westermann." But when Danton rose to speak in support of Fabre, the Deputy from Aix did not deny him the floor.

Danton had learned a lesson from his unfortunate experience on May 30. With some skill he now put enough honeyed phrases in his discourse to satisfy Mirabeau's academic susceptibilities. His arguments on behalf of Fabre d'Églantine and Westermann were greeted with applause.

From now on he was a frequent speaker at the Jacobin Club. During 1791 alone he took the floor no less than eighteen times. His interventions were always off-the-cuff affairs, and went almost entirely unrecorded, except for vague reports in the newssheets. An examination of these abstracts shows us the two main sides of his eloquence. When he addressed the Jacobins he spoke very formally; this was the advocate in him coming out. But inside his own Club he ranted like any demagogue in the marketplace. These two styles between them served all his requirements. He would employ the first to convince intelligent, educated people (or those who passed muster as such), and the second to whip up the passions of an illiterate mob. He had at last learned to cut his cloth according to his audience. There is only one place to learn a smith's work, and that is in the smithy. Danton had been wielding his hammer, with redoubtable force, for some eighteen months now.

There were others who learned this skill in handling men at the same time as he did—elected bodies no less than individuals. Ever since the fall of the Bastille the Commune had been seeking some sort of *modus vivendi*. Its members thought they had found a solution by dividing the over-all body into several categories. Now they determined on yet another reshuffle. Henceforward the Commune would consist of the Mayor, sixteen administrative officers, a Municipal Council of thirty-two members, a General Council of ninety-six notables, a Public Attorney, and two Deputy Public Attorneys. Once again the electors were required to go to the polls; and Danton, who sensed that his popularity was on the increase, took a risk and submitted his name as a candidate for the next highest office after that of Mayor, that of Administrator. After several recounts, he came in second out of sixteen Administrators elected.

Another of the Administrators voted in on this occasion was

Mirabeau, who also played some part in the success of his rival—
in fact, he recommended Danton to the electorate. This intervention once again raises the problem of Danton's relations with
the Court. Mirabeau was determined to save both the Crown
and the Revolution: the first, because he was of the opinion that
a Republic could not possibly give France lasting stability, and
the second because he considered himself its original champion
and begetter. Through the intermediacy of his friend La Marck,
he gave Louis XVI some excellent advice, which that monarch
saw fit to ignore, but for which he paid Mirabeau very liberally.

As a kind of *quid pro quo* for his kindness during the election,
Danton now campaigned for Mirabeau's admission to the Directory (a consultative body established by the Constituent Assembly in the chief town of each *département*). Even so, that
of the Seine Division must have turned Danton's stomach. It was
presided over by the Duke of La Rochefoucauld-Liancourt, who
was also the Master of the Royal Wardrobe; and its Public
Attorney was the Marquis of Pastoret, who afterward joined the
emigration movement. After their previous quarrels and rivalries,
Mirabeau and Danton were now as thick as thieves. Did the first
pass on to the second a proportion of the retainers he picked up
in the Tuileries? We cannot say with any certainty, but there is
an anecdote which at least makes such a theory plausible.

In 1791, Lord Holland (whose wife was later to soften the
rigors of Napoleon's captivity on St. Helena) was still a very
young man. After finishing his studies, this budding politician
traveled through France *en route* for Rome. During a stay of
several weeks in Paris, the London aristocrat was introduced to
Danton. In response to an indiscreet question Danton is supposed to have said: "People are quite ready to pay a man like
me 80,000 *livres*—but a man like me is not to be bought for
80,000!" If the remark is authentic, such a piece of hairsplitting
might be taken as indicating that Danton did not in fact refuse
bribes—and was even prepared to betray those who had bought
him afterward.

As an elected Administrator of the Commune, Danton was
entitled to "administer" the latter's funds, a task he shared with
his fifteen other colleagues. Among these were Talleyrand, the
Abbé Sieyès, the naturalist Lacépède, a former Jesuit priest

named Cerutti, Alexandre de Lameth (the man who spoke up
against the "yellow tickets"), Mirabeau himself, and M. de
Jussieu, a well-known botanist. It was a talented group, to say
the least. But Danton was not in the least put out by their presence. He drafted a letter of acceptance which showed how well
he had learned the art of rubbing the more awkward corners off
his angry intransigence. Alluding to the "impulsive enthusiasm"
of his own "fiery patriotism, without which one cannot unite
either to achieve or to maintain liberty," he nevertheless was
careful to emphasize his "spirit of moderation, so essential if we
are to enjoy the fruits of our glorious Revolution."

This double profession of faith sets the pattern for all his
future activities. After February 1, 1791, he never deviated from
it. His "fiery patriotism" led him in turn to the destruction of
the monarchy, the creation of the Republic, the victory of Valmy,
the Committee of Public Safety, and the Revolutionary Tribunal.
His "spirit of moderation," on the other hand, by putting a
brake on his "impulsive enthusiasms" was to place him in that
tainted category of people fit only for the guillotine. In three
short years he was to run the whole gamut of violence, passion,
and death.

In the clubs Danton could give free rein to his naturally
choleric temperament. Danton was a carnivore: he could not
do without his prey. One evening in the Jacobin Club, Collot
d'Herbois was singing the praises of a diplomat named Bonne-
Carrère, whom the government had just appointed Ambassador
to Belgium. This was a fine opportunity for Danton to vent his
spleen. He did not know Bonne-Carrère but was nevertheless
unable, he declared, "to regard him as a friend of liberty."
What he had against the poor man was precisely the thing
that elicited praise from Collot. His actual words were: "Bonne-
Carrère has accepted a post in *that enemy body* the executive,
and to speak favorably of him from henceforth is fitting only
for slaves!" This was his oblique way of proclaiming his strong
opposition to the Minister—a remark which, according to *Le
Patriote Français,* was made in his usual "stentorian voice"—
that famous brazen bellow which astonished everyone when he
heard it.

Mirabeau was not present at this meeting. He had been confined to bed, in extreme pain, since the previous evening. His agony continued for five days, while crowds waited uneasily outside his apartment in the Hôtel de la Chaussée-d'Antin.

The day after he died, the Jacobins, standing as a mark of respect, heard his eulogy pronounced by Barnave, one of his fiercest opponents—a fact which gave his speech all the more significance. The audience heard him out in thoughtful silence. They were on the point of dispersing when Danton ascended the steps of the rostrum. Unable to resist his eternal itch to address an audience, he had decided to add his own homage to that of Barnave. In some surprise the audience sat down again. To the words of the Deputy for Grenoble (which he repeated and amplified in his own florid style) Danton added several ideas of his own. Lamenting Mirabeau's passing, he recalled "this great man's promise to hound down factious elements." This phrase was all the more mysterious—Danton knew how effective an ambiguity could be—in that the "factious elements" were obviously located, grammatically speaking, among the enemies of the régime that still remained in force; that is, the monarchy. And it would be a shrewd observer who could decide whether Danton's own inclinations were toward the maintenance in power of Louis XVI (who, it was whispered, had Danton on his payroll) or whether he supported the Duke of Orléans (who, according to various rumors, was also bribing him) or whether he was really working toward the Republic whose virtues he so often extolled (at the invitation of John Bull, according to yet other rumors, who stuffed his purse with British money in furtherance of such a design). Danton closed his address with a demand for the dissolution of the Constituent Assembly and the summoning of a Legislative Assembly.

Next day he attended Mirabeau's funeral. After the service the cortege left Saint-Eustache at sunset. By the light of torches it made its way toward Sainte-Geneviève, now transformed into the Panthéon; the remains of the illustrious orator were to inaugurate its new function as the last resting place of famous men. Sieyès and La Marck walked sobbing behind the coffin, which was borne on a litter by sixteen men of Mirabeau's Grange-Batelière battalion. A fresh relay took over every five hundred yards. La Fayette marched behind them, with drawn sword.

The National Assembly, the clubs, and the municipal authorities all swelled the cortege. Danton walked with the members of the Commune, dressed in black, a head taller than any man present. Crowds packed the roadside, every window was filled; some spectators even sat up on the rooftops. A brass band was playing Gossec's *Dead March*. The revolutionaries wept for the man who had been the first to dare speak of "the people's will." The Royalists repeated his dying words: "Those who mourn my passing will be mourning the monarchy, too; once I am dead, the factious will fight over its tattered remnants." Who the devil, men asked, were these "factious elements" that Danton, too, had spoken of? Danton himself, and his friends, according to confidential information supposed to stem from Mirabeau. But it seems certain that Danton identified them with the partisans of Louis XVI, since his friend Desmoulins was to write in his broadsheet: "Go, then, O witless people, O corrupt nation, and prostrate yourselves before the tomb of this honorable man— the very Mercury of his age, the god of orators, liars, and thieves!"

A curious panegyric for the dead man whom all Paris was mourning! By some miracle, the crowd made no attempt to tear its author limb from limb. But then who will ever understand the sentiments of the people?

CHAPTER VII

The King's Flight and Danton's Retreat

MIRABEAU'S FUNERAL provided no more than a brief pause in the middle of a highly charged and inflammable situation. The new Civil Constitution of the Clergy had aroused particularly violent feeling, since it was mandatory for priests to swear that they would observe it. Some were prepared to do so, others protested against a series of regulations which included the abolition of monastic vows, the realignment of diocesan boundaries with those of the *départements,* the assimilation of the clergy as a branch of the State Civil Service, and, finally, their election by the faithful—with the obligation (for those chosen) to swear an oath of civil allegiance. A war to the death was declared between those who would and those who would not take the oath: between what were termed by the public the *curés jureurs* ("conformist priests") and the *prêtres réfractaires* ("refractory priests").

For all parochial requirements, the electors would meet in the Bishop's Palace and vote on each measure under the eye of the Secretary. This officer was selected from among the administrative staff of the Commune, and the man they chose to look after these small meetings was none other than Danton.

His conduct, in the circumstances, was quite astoundingly fair and unprejudiced. Though under pressure from the anticlericals among his constituents, and at the same time restrained by Gabrielle and his own family tradition (two of his uncles were priests, and one sister was in a convent), Danton presided over these impassioned ballots without ever taking sides. It was an innocent project of the King's that finally drew him out of his neutrality and hurled him into the heart of the religious struggle.

The oath taken by conformist priests caused the King great heart searching. As a monarch of calm and conventional piety, he could not bring himself to see the nation meddling in the affairs of the Church. Furthermore—by a *concordat* which dated back to the reign of Francis I—French sovereigns "by the grace of God" had the right to appoint bishops. Now, it seemed, the Constituent Assembly was stripping Louis of his spiritual privilege. Caught between his Catholic conscience and his duties as a constitutional monarch, he felt that his private moral dilemma would very soon cross the dividing line and become public property. Now, about three months before Mirabeau's death, La Marck had passed on to the King a remark the "plebeian Count" had made, to the effect that "the royal family was lost if it did not leave Paris." With Mirabeau gone, Louis XVI had only one idea left in his head: to follow the dead man's advice.

In order to see which way the wind was blowing, he decided to go away on April 18, 1791, to spend the Easter holiday at Saint-Cloud. He warned La Fayette of his intention, and the Commander-in-Chief of the National Guard took adequate measures to ensure the royal family's safety. He detailed several battalions to cordon off the approaches to the Tuileries, so that the royal carriages could drive through without any trouble. By an unfortunate oversight, the Marquis included the Bataillon des Cordeliers in this detail. It was at this point that Danton, informed of what was in the air by the battalion commander, Villette, emerged from his period of self-effacement and intervened with all his old fiery impulsiveness.

That evening, Palm Sunday, the day before the royal family's projected departure, Danton buttonholed La Fayette in the City Hall. Since the morning a rumor had been going about that a refractory priest, a Jesuit named Lenfant, had celebrated Mass in the Tuileries Palace. At Danton's instigation, the Cordeliers battalion had unanimously agreed to draft a public notice denouncing the "culpability" of Louis XVI, "first public servant, whose duty is to uphold the law, but who prefers to flout it." This poster also called upon other battalions of the National Guard to prevent the departure for Saint-Cloud, instead of

ensuring that it went off without a hitch—in other words, to
disobey La Fayette's orders.

The announcement of this restrictive move provoked a debate
in the Municipal Council. La Fayette, supported by Bailly, asked
members to proclaim a state of martial law and the compulsory
mobilization of reservists. With his sharp, hard-hitting oratory
Danton managed to whip up a majority against the motion—
whereupon La Fayette, in a state of furious annoyance, offered
Bailly his resignation. "Only a coward," Danton growled, "could
desert his post in the hour of peril! And besides, your commission
is not from the municipal authorities. If you want to resign, you
will have to take your resignation round all the forty-eight
electoral divisions that made you a general."

What "peril," in fact, did Danton have in mind when he
spoke? That a refractory priest should celebrate Mass in fact
bothered him not at all. What really made him apprehensive
was the suspicion that Saint-Cloud might be the first stage in a
longer journey—which, if accomplished, would bring Louis XVI
to the heart of La Vendée, where the inhabitants had been in
revolt against Paris ever since the Civil Constitution of the
Clergy.

La Fayette, naturally, did not go around the forty-eight constituencies offering them his resignation. The following morning,
Monday April 18, he arrived at the Tuileries bright and early,
leading the battalions that he had detailed for duty the day before, and counting on his own personal authority and popularity
to get the royal procession safely through.

The carriages were waiting by the front steps of the palace.
The King, his family, and their suite got into them. Alerted by
the posters that had been put up all over the Théâtre-Français
electoral division (which was, of course, Danton's), a vast crowd
had gathered behind the railings. It was making a clear demonstration of its hostility toward the King's departure. The battalions that followed one another in at the palace gates—that of
Les Cordeliers in particular—did not appear much disposed to
let him go, either.

The mob cheered the troops, yelled insults at Marie-Antoinette, and were sarcastic at the King's expense. The royal
children were in tears. Saber in hand, La Fayette galloped from

one battalion to another, no longer capable of making them obey his orders. For two hours he cajoled and argued, but without success. When, at last, Marie-Antoinette retreated up the steps into the Tuileries, she could not help turning to the troops of the National Guard and saying: "You must at least admit that we no longer have our freedom."

The next day Louis XVI went to lodge a complaint before the Constituent Assembly. The session was being presided over by an obscure Deputy named Chabroud. Without addressing Louis as "Your Majesty," much less using the third person, Chabroud replied to his protests: "You must be quite well aware that noisy demonstrations are an inconvenience which always accompanies the progress of liberty!"

When he got back to the Tuileries, the hapless monarch found a somewhat unusual letter awaiting him. It was, officially, from the Directory of the *département,* but in fact had been composed by the inevitable Danton, together with Count Armand de Kersaint. In reprimanding tones it counseled the King to remove from his company all refractory priests, "who shed hypocritical tears over religion." It concluded by enjoining him to send a declaration to the other Courts of Europe that he was living as free as the fish in the ocean. Louis XVI, however, could not write this lie to the monarchs of neighboring countries. He merely drank the bitter cup of his defeat to the dregs, vaguely conscious that once again Monsieur Danton—one of his own Advocates—had triumphed over him.

First at the Jacobins, and then in the Club des Cordeliers, the hero of the day was welcomed with a great ovation. In both places he made a speech, which was largely an attack on La Fayette. "He has resigned!" Danton roared. "Why is he still with the National Guard?" Fréron went further still. Recalling that the Constituent Assembly, when it abolished hereditary titles, had decreed that no citizen might henceforth bear any name "but the true name of his family," printed the following piece of advice in Desmoulins's journal: "Citizens, know who are your friends, and who your declared enemies! Bailly and *Mottié* are unworthy of your trust. It is Danton the patriot you should elect Mayor—and *ça ira!*"

"Mottié" was the patronymic of the Marquis de La Fayette, just as "Vignerot" was that of the Dukes de Richelieu, and "Riquetti" that of the Counts de Mirabeau. Monsieur Danton, it was clear, could no longer cut up *his* name with an apostrophe. In point of fact, it was some time since he had risked doing so. He had laughed too much at the quatrain which Desmoulins, in his *Révolutions de France et de Brabant,* had composed on the origins of the King—the distant descendant of that Hugues Capet whose grandfather had practiced as a lawyer.

> If I may not say it on paper
> Then I'll dig a hole, like the barber,
> And whisper it to the reeds, rather than hold my tongue:
> *Capet, our royal Capet, is a common lawyer's son!*

And if a notary's descendants could hold the scepter for a thousand years, surely an Advocate might aspire to the far more modest rank of Mayor? But Danton did not go so far himself. He left it to Desmoulins and Fréron, his two panegyricists, to demand the highest position in the City Hall on his behalf, and was quite content—no glutton he—to canvass (Villette having resigned) for the command of the Third Battalion, Second Division, of the National Guard, which, despite the new regulations, continued to be known as the Bataillon des Cordeliers.

The volunteers held a meeting at Saint-André-des-Arts and elected Danton by acclamation. But the company of regulars, which formed a quarter of the battalion's strength, argued that "in expiation of the part played by the majority in preventing the departure of the King for Saint-Cloud," the battalion should lose its "henceforth dishonored" name and take instead that of the "Bataillon de l'Observance" ("The Conformist Battalion"). The members of the other three companies, the reservists, flatly refused, and the disagreement nearly ended in blows.

Danton, elected Commandant in the middle of this grotesque quarrel, could not decide how to settle it. Someone suggested referring the matter for arbitration to the Commander-in-Chief. Now it was Danton's turn to refuse. The very idea of appearing before the man whom he had branded as a coward in the City Hall, and asking him to decide whether the battalion should change its name to the Bataillon de l'Observance or remain the

Bataillon des Cordeliers, was out of the question. God forbid that any Danton should so humiliate himself! Preferring to resign rather than to submit to "Mottié," he turned in his commission to M. de Gouvion, the National Guard's Chief of Staff, and went back home, brooding over this new disappointment, cudgeling his brains for a revenge worthy of his character and status.

At this period Paris had no more than 700,000 inhabitants: the capital was still squeezed and corseted within a ring of bastions and military fortifications. Its narrow streets, innocent of any sidewalks, gave it an appearance which is barely imaginable today. Their surface was formed of ill-fitting paving-stones, on which pedestrians frequently stumbled. At night the only illumination was provided by a few glimmering oil lanterns, spaced out at a great distance from one another. They hung at second-story level, suspended from cables that ran across the street.

On June 20, 1791, about eleven o'clock in the evening, Danton came out of the Jacobin Club, accompanied by Fréron and Desmoulins. The three friends strolled back up the rue Saint-Honoré in the summer dusk, talking politics. Outside the Church of Saint-Roch they passed a patrol. The tramp of the soldiers' boots in the stillness made a great impression on Desmoulins. He whispered: "Is it tonight that old Fatty [the King] is supposed to be making his getaway?"

In his pocket Fréron had a letter, delivered that afternoon, and warning him that the royal family intended to escape during the night. "We've heard that one so often I don't believe it any more," Danton said. "Besides, ever since April 18 La Fayette's been very wary of us. His troops are keeping good watch over the Tuileries. How could anyone get through the gates?"

The three parted at this point: Danton and Desmoulins toward the river and the Left Bank, while Fréron continued up the rue Saint-Honoré, in the direction of Les Halles. As he crossed the rue de l'Échelle, he saw a carriage with an escort of cavalry who carried torches to light the way ahead. Fréron craned forward and saw that the person behind the carriage window was La Fayette. The General was on his way home from the Tuileries, accompanied by two of his staff officers. "He was convinced," Desmoulins afterward wrote in *Les Révolutions de Paris,* "that the walls of the Tuileries would safeguard the hostages of the people."

At eight o'clock next morning Danton was still asleep. In a neighboring room Gabrielle was washing little Antoine. The bell rang, and Fabre d'Églantine appeared, his features congested with emotion. He made his way into Danton's bedroom and woke the sleeper. "Get up!" he shouted. "The King has escaped!"

Danton seemed less surprised by the news than his remarks the previous evening would appear to warrant. Had he in fact concealed his real thoughts when discussing the subject with Fréron and Desmoulins? Did Louis XVI's escape, as far as he was concerned, form part of the logical development of events? Or was his antagonism to the King during the past year deliberately used—with Machiavellian foresight—as a weapon to make Louis take the course he in fact did? All he said as he got out of bed was: "La Fayette must bear the responsibility." And then a cry of exultant triumph: "I've got him where I want him now!"

Both he and Fabre pricked up their ears as the church bells began to hammer out the tocsin, warning all Paris of what had taken place. The servants in the Tuileries had awakened to find the royal apartments deserted, the beds empty. They raised the alarm at once, and the news of the King's flight spread quickly through the city. The rumors produced huge crowds outside the railings of the Tuileries. No one knew how the royal family had managed to get through the cordon or, indeed, what had become of them since their escape.

Danton dressed quickly and hastened down to the Club des Cordeliers, to find large numbers of citizens already there. He strode up to the speakers' rostrum and thundered out denunciations of Louis XVI and "the Austrian woman." Had their flight finally tipped the scales of his uncertainty? "By upholding a hereditary monarchy," he cried, "the National Assembly has reduced France to slavery! Let us abolish, once and for all, the name and function of King; let us transform the kingdom into a republic!" The motion was put to the vote and carried, with a rider that a poster should be distributed inviting the people to approve this decision.

Danton next went to the City Hall, where he found his col-

leagues in a somewhat greater state of alarm than himself. They
all set out together for the Riding School, with a small military
escort. When they reached the Tuileries, they saw a vast crowd
milling about in the gardens. La Fayette was the target of much
abuse: the crowd expressed much anger over the failure of his
security arrangements. Danton, scooping up this ball on the re-
bound, shouted: "You're right! M. de La Fayette made himself
answerable for the King's person! Where is he now? Where are
either of them? Your leaders are traitors! You have been betrayed!"

Danton was instantly recognized by his great height, and the
crowd cheered him. "Vive Danton!" they yelled, and some
journalists present also heard the somewhat startling cry of
"Long live *our father* Danton!"

The Constituent Assembly—under the presidency of Alexandre
de Beauharnais, husband of that Josephine who was later to become Napoleon's empress—was in an uproar. Complete disorder reigned: it was not so much a debate as a mere shouting
match. The delegation from the City Hall was admitted to the
Bar of the House but for a long time could not make itself heard.
In reply to a question from the President, its members outlined
the measures they had already taken. The royal apartments had
been placed under seal, the gates had been inspected, and every
member of the staff had been submitted to close interrogation.

When he got back to the Place de Grève, Danton found that
La Fayette's popularity had not suffered so much as he had at
first supposed. The General, in order to test the mood of the
populace, had proceeded from his house to his headquarters on
foot. Though insulted by some members of the public, he found
himself cheered by others; and he arrived at his destination without having been molested *en route*. On his orders, large numbers
of officers set off, on horseback, along all the roads leading out
of Paris. Each of them carried written orders to "rescue the King
from the enemies of the Revolution." Bailly, for his part, remained fully in control of the City Council. Since he could not
attack La Fayette or Bailly either in the Constituent Assembly
or before the Commune, Danton decided to launch his accusation against them at a meeting of the Jacobin Club.

Though such meetings were held daily, the one which took

place that evening assumed particular importance. In his sharp, cutting voice Robespierre delivered a slashing indictment of the government and the National Assembly, both of which he criticized for lack of initiative. He wound up an emphatic speech by declaring that he was ready to offer his life for the cause of liberty.

His audience did not demand such a sacrifice of him; but from his place in the body of the hall Danton roared: "We will die with you, Robespierre!" He rose and took Robespierre's place on the rostrum.

"Gentlemen," he began, without preamble, "if the traitors show their faces here, I swear I will prove that their heads should fall at the feet of the nation they have betrayed. If not, let my own head answer for it on the scaffold!"

Would he actually name the traitors he was denouncing? At this precise moment, by a strange and dramatic coincidence, La Fayette, together with Barnave, Alexandre de Lameth, and Sieyès, appeared in the hall. Danton, on catching sight of his adversary, was at something of a loss. It had not occurred to him that the General would anticipate his attack and come around in person to fight back. But he quickly pulled himself together again. Changing his tactics, he announced, in a solemn voice: "I shall speak now as though I stood before the tribunal of Almighty God—and I am glad to see that M. de La Fayette is here, so that I can say to him, before you all, what I would say before Him who reads the hearts and minds of us all."

Then he paused, trying to work out the line he would take. While so doing, he cast a reproachful glance at Alexandre de Lameth. He had thought he could rely on this man's friendship, but his appearance in La Fayette's company seemed to show that Danton had been mistaken. No matter; such a betrayal merely added fresh fuel to his wrath. He fixed his eyes on La Fayette. He did not, as yet, accuse the General of being responsible for the flight of the King; this charge he held in reserve, as a final clincher. It would be the dessert after the banquet, the set piece that concluded the firework display.

With consummate art Danton began by listing various other complaints. At last he had an opportunity to get them all off his chest. With unholy joy he brought them out, one after another. There was La Fayette's scheme to have two Chambers instead of one: "a most destructive system," Danton commented. There was the plan to torpedo the Society of the Friends of the Constitution, the Club's official title—and this complaint was one to which those present reacted with particular feeling. "You have made the allegation, General," Danton said, "that this Club is composed almost entirely of wastrels and vagabonds, united only in their determination to perpetuate a state of anarchy." At these words, an indignant murmuring arose. La Fayette stood there, very straight and still, taking these body blows without flinching. But his face was unnaturally pale.

Warming to his theme, Danton went through all his victim's activities, including his relations with Danton himself. He described the virtual censorship which La Fayette exercised by systematically persecuting the journals which opposed him, while lending support to those that came out in his favor. Then, turning to "that memorable day April 18," the speaker recalled that La Fayette had come out in favor of letting the royal family leave for Saint-Cloud. That morning, too, it was the reactionary Bataillon de l'Oratoire which found itself posted on guard duties at the gates of the Tuileries. "Will you kindly explain to us," Danton asked, "why *the same battalion* was on guard the previous night?" He regarded this coincidence as evidence of premeditated action.

"Let us make no mistake about it, gentlemen," he went on. "The flight of the King is neither more nor less than the result of a gigantic conspiracy. The only way in which it could have been carried out was through the complicity of leading members of the executive branch. And as for you, Monsieur La Fayette— *you,* who undertook final responsibility for the King's person!— do you think you can discharge the debt you owe by showing your face here? It is not so long since you were describing the Jacobins as mere factious troublemakers. These troublemakers and assassins, you will find, are more generous than you would be in their place. At least they are offering you asylum. What? Nothing to say? Speak up, man!"

La Fayette fixed his eyes steadily on Danton but still remained silent. The atmosphere was tense with emotion. "You swore the King would never get away," Danton exclaimed.

"You went bail for him, you were his surety. One of two things must be true, then: either you are a traitor who has sold his country or—if you made yourself answerable for someone you could not control—you are a plain fool. At the very best, you have shown yourself incompetent to hold your present command."

The insults were chosen with skill. Traitor or fool: Danton left his victim very much on the horns of a dilemma. Would La Fayette finally speak up in his own defense? It seemed not. He still preserved the same scornful silence. In point of fact, this professional warrior lacked the equipment for a verbal conflict. More at home on the battlefield than in the sphere of ideas and words, La Fayette was at a hopeless loss when he tried to hold his own in such bouts of political in-fighting. Danton was perfectly well aware of this: he took advantage of the fact to play with his opponent, much as a cat will play with a mouse it has caught. He recalled the French intervention in America, and La Fayette's resultant reputation, "which has spread from pole to pole." He spoke of the beginnings of the Revolution and of the undoubted part that the General had played in it. Then, with some condescension, he delivered himself of the following words: "You can no longer continue to ignore the suspicions which a large part of the people feel on your account, and the anger which your actions arouse in them. I trust and hope that such involuntary errors of judgment are the worst charge that can be brought against you. France can achieve her freedom without your aid! If you want to show true greatness, become an ordinary citizen once more."

It was over; Danton had had his revenge. Convinced that his victim would never recover after such a trouncing, the butcher strode down from the rostrum, mopping his brow. There was scattered, thin applause. The bulk of his audience appeared flabbergasted. Amid the buzz of whispered comment a few encouraging voices could be heard, calling on La Fayette to make a reply.

Disgusted by Danton's violence, and caught off guard by his astute rhetoric, La Fayette turned in hopeless bewilderment to Alexandre de Lameth. The latter understood his gesture, stood up, and tossed him the following lifeline. "Danton," he said, "has mentioned remarks by me as evidence for his assertions. Though I have had occasion in the past to say harsh things about M. de La Fayette, nevertheless I have always—even when criticizing him most severely—maintained absolute faith in his patriotism and declared that he would die leading his troops in the event of a counterrevolution. I call Danton himself to witness for the truth of this statement!"

Danton, who was sitting beside Camille Desmoulins half rose and said: "It is true that M. de Lameth has expressed himself in this manner concerning M. de La Fayette, on several occasions."

There was an audible sigh of relief in the hall. The audience felt rather sorry for the General, whose behavior resembled that of a child who has been caught doing something naughty. Finally he rose to his feet, and his supporters took fresh hope. In a flat, neutral voice he said: "I am here today because this Society is the place for any good citizen to be on an occasion when freedom is in jeopardy and one must fight to preserve it. You all know that I was the first to say that a people will become free when it truly desires freedom. I have never been so sure of freedom as today, while observing the spectacle the capital presents to the spectator."

"He's climbing down," Danton whispered to Desmoulins. "What an ass the man is!"

La Fayette did not defend himself any further. Pleading the call of duty, he made his excuses and withdrew. All eyes followed him to the door. Either through disdain or fear, he had made no attempt to answer the questions put to him. And while the Jacobins were passing a motion to have Danton's speech printed (shorthand writers had taken it down during delivery), they heard the applause with which the General was greeted by his supporters outside in the street. One discordant voice, however, could be heard in this welcoming chorus. It belonged to a citizen named Nérée-Vacquier, who inquired of the Marquis's supporters: "Since the General swore he would answer for the King's person with his head, will someone tell me why his head isn't stuck on the end of a pike yet?" The questioner was arrested. When Danton was told about the incident, it is said, he laughed till he cried. It was the reaction of a grown-up child, with all the cruelty and injustice that characterize children everywhere.

The following day the motion passed by the Club des Cordeliers was made public. Billposters went around pasting up copies of the proposal which Danton had put forward the night before, demanding the proclamation of a republic.

This motion produced a fresh debate at the Jacobin Club. During the meeting Robespierre asked Danton: "What *is* a republic?"—a question which threw something of a chill over the proceedings. The only genuine republic of which anyone had any knowledge was that recently formed in America, and even this was very sketchily understood, by hearsay for the most part. To top everything, La Fayette himself—the previous night's scapegoat, the man whom Danton had denounced as the King's accomplice—had actually helped to found it. Moreover, the French could not really imagine a country without a king. La Fayette apart, it is doubtful whether there were any real Republicans in the executive; and even La Fayette hesitated at the thought of throwing over, in favor of some system resembling that of the United States, a monarchical tradition already eighteen centuries old. The Duke of Orléans's eldest son, that Duke of Chartres who in 1830 ascended the throne as King Louis-Philippe, later wrote, in his unpublished* memoirs: "The moment the King was gone, M. de La Fayette was all for a republic; but after the King was brought back to Paris, he changed his mind completely. Henceforth his only thought was to strengthen the monarchy and the Throne, by persuading the King to surround himself with constitutionalist ministers. . . . If, as I believe, M. de La Fayette did, very briefly, favor a republic, it was probably through the fear that a regency, or some other such form of administration, might allow my father to seize power." Such a verdict would place La Fayette among the

* Discovered by Mme. Marguerite Castillon du Perron and used by her as material for her book *Louis-Philippe et la Révolution Française* (Paris, 1963).

Duke of Orléans's opponents—and the Duke of Orléans was a friend of Danton's.

Now it so happened—whether by coincidence or design—that the Duke put in an appearance at this second debate of the Jacobins. It had got off to a bad start, as far as Danton was concerned, since he could find no adequate answer to Robespierre's question "What *is* a republic?" The affair which had begun so promisingly the night before was now turning out something of an embarrassment for the great orator. Making an excuse of the emotion which, the previous morning, had provoked his outburst against Louis XVI, he asked that the Club should discuss the republic no further but proceed directly to the order of the day. This surrender caused some murmuring, and Danton began to feel a little embarrassed. It was at this precise moment that Philippe d'Orléans chose to make his appearance. He had just arrived from the Palais-Royal in an English dogcart. Acclaimed by the crowds as he drove through the streets, he had pulled up outside the door of the Club and —since he was a member—found no difficulty in obtaining admission.

This was a real windfall for Danton, a miraculous stroke of luck in his favor. Yesterday it had been La Fayette who materialized just as Danton was about to attack him, and conveniently offered his throat to the knife. Now it was Philippe d'Orléans, a second *deus ex machina,* who appeared at the exact moment when his friend, much embarrassed by this crazy request to define a republic, was looking around for some way out. Danton grabbed this chance with both hands. Adroitly distorting the events of the past twenty-four hours, blackening the absent La Fayette while he sang the praises of the newly arrived Duke, he plunged into a simultaneous indictment of the General and his vanished sovereign—a neat way of hinting that Philippe d'Orléans might be a suitable candidate for the Throne.

"I have made every possible concession to M. de La Fayette," Danton declared. "I did no more than call upon him, in a frank and loyal manner, to explain his actions. His only reply to my words was, in effect, 'I have saved the country.'"

A Jacobin intervened at this point with the observation that the General had lost no time in sending aides-de-camp in every direction "with the object of finding the King and forcibly bringing him back to Paris."

"Bringing him back?" Danton queried. "And with what end in view, pray?"

"Unless the King is deprived of his rights by a vote of the Constituent Assembly," came the reply, "he remains inviolable."

At this, Danton exploded. Forgetting that it was the Jacobins he was addressing, and not the Club des Cordeliers, he let loose a whole volley of insults. "This so-called King of the French," he snarled, "after swearing to uphold the Constitution, has now fled his capital—yet, as I understand it, he has still not forfeited his crown! . . . The day before yesterday his last proclamation was read out to the Assembly. In it he affirmed his intention of deliberately destroying the Constitution. Such an admission brands him as a criminal—unless we deem him mentally defective! What a ghastly impression it would make on the world at large if, with the chance to find a king either criminal or demented, we did not opt for the second choice! The moment this royal person is deemed insane, he can no longer be King!"

At these words, all eyes turned toward the Duke of Orléans. If there was not to be a republic, and Louis XVI had run his course, what remained save a regency, under the First Prince of the Blood? But at the same time, Danton remembered the active rumors in circulation to the effect that he had been bought by the Duke. He searched rapidly for some way of scotching this suspicion, and his fertile brain came up with a somewhat odd form of government. Leaving the Duke to his toadies, Danton exclaimed: "What we need is not a regent but a Council in Lunacy!" Developing the idea with lightning speed, he proposed that Councilors should be chosen by means of a two-stage vote, renewable biennially—a plan which did not preclude the Duke's election to the Council, nor his elevation to the office of President. This accomplished, the game was as good as won.

Ten days later Danton sent up his trial balloon once more. On July 3 he repeated: "It's not a regent we need, it's the sequestration of royalty."

Meanwhile Louis XVI had been found again. On the evening of June 23, 1791, the same day that saw Danton torn between his friendship for the Duke and his desire to escape charges of venality, a breathless messenger informed the Assembly of the King's arrest at Varennes. Three Deputies, Barnave, Pétion, and Latour-Maubourg, were delegated to go and escort the royal family back to Paris.

While the capital awaited their return, the press exploded. In his newssheet Camille Desmoulins referred to "the animal-king" and "the crowned bumpkin" who, by his plan to re-establish the *ancien régime* with the help of Bouillé's army, had "put a pistol to the nation's head." Abandoning all delicacy, Camille described Marie-Antoinette as a "licentious Messalina." The King's sister, that pure and angelic Elisabeth who had accompanied the royal family on its journey, he called a "fat busybody." He also demanded that Louis XVI should "be exposed for three days to public mockery, with a red kerchief tied around his head; that he should then be conducted, by stages, to the border, and on arrival there be kicked bodily across it." As for "his female," the polemicist wanted her "whipped with rods" and shut up in a convent.

The poor creature returned to Paris on June 25, with the King, her children, her sister-in-law, and the three Deputies. A vast crowd surrounded the two carriages. But not a sound was heard; the Commune had ordered strict silence to be kept. Two ranks of soldiers presented arms, with butts reversed as for a burial. The horses' hoofs and the carriage wheels echoed on the ground like a funeral knell. And it was true; the bell was tolling for the monarchy.

The Assembly suspended Louis XVI, and the Tuileries became a prison, a kind of gilded cage, which La Fayette surrounded with guards. Sentinals could be seen even on the rooftops. But the Marquis was still playing a double game. He brought into the palace not only the Swiss Guards, who remained loyal to the King, but also about a hundred gentlemen of the Court and several ladies of the highest rank. With this infusion of aristocracy La Fayette consoled the Queen. With his troopers, whose tents were pitched in rows outside in the palace gardens, he furnished a guarantee to the Jacobins, to the Club des Cordeliers, and—above all—to Danton.

There is some indication that Barnave and Lameth made an attempt to reconcile the two adversaries. If we can trust Marat, Danton and La Fayette took a "friendly" cup of chocolate together in the house of one of these common friends. The only result of this meeting seems to have been a sharp increase in the two men's dislike for each other.

The Deputies, meanwhile, were discussing what measures they should take. Ought they to re-establish the King or remove him altogether? That there had been a conspiracy was no longer in doubt: witnesses who had come from Varennes and Sainte-Menehould all agreed that the Marquis de Bouillé *was* waiting for Louis XVI in Argonne with his troops. Several of his detachments had come within an ace of rescuing the royal family from the citizens summoned by the postmaster. What was more, Bouillé had written a personal letter to the Constituent Assembly, threatening France with terrible reprisals by "all the crowned heads of Europe."

In his broadsheet Marat demanded the appointment of a "military tribune" or, failing that, of a "dictator." As a candidate for this office he suggested Danton. Reading the violent, hyperbolic prose in which this proposal was couched, Gabrielle's husband crumpled up *L'Ami du Peuple* and threw it across the room. "The *dictatorship!*" he growled. "A fine sort of present! Why not the Throne while he's at it? Why not have me anointed at Rheims?"

At the same time, he was beginning to fear the possibility of some official action being taken against him. He himself had never demanded the King's death; but various imbecilic friends of his made no bones about putting such a proposition in his mouth. That brute Legendre, for instance, the President of the Club des Cordeliers, made his fellow members swear before God to "take a dagger to any tyrant who dared attack the Constitution." A rumor went around that Danton, accused of having initiated this oath, was in danger of losing his liberty. Confirmation was supplied when the police arrested the billposters who had disseminated so sanguinary a declaration. Robert had devoted two columns of the *Mercure National* to a

vigorous protest against this infringement of liberty—and was in
prison before nightfall. His wife came, in tears, and begged
Danton to intervene. But what could he do? It would not be
long before he was forced into flight himself, as a result of the
notorious—and, it must be said, decidedly murky—"Affair of
the Champ-de-Mars."

On June 25, the same day as the King returned from Varennes, the National Assembly finally took the step that Choderlos
de Laclos had been working for. As the Duke of Orléans's private
secretary, this ambitious writer had been pressing his chief to
cross the Rubicon and announce himself as a candidate for
the Throne; but this Philippe steadfastly refused to do. So, for
months now, Laclos had been intriguing behind the scenes. He
was determined to present the Duke with a *fait accompli*, to
force his hand, so that he would have to accept either the Crown
itself or at the very least a regency, with himself, Laclos, as
prime minister. On June 25 this unbalanced *arriviste* thought
his hour had come at last. The Constituent Assembly, in public
session, called upon the Duke to take over provisionally from
Louis XVI in the event of the Throne falling vacant.

But Mme. de Genlis was also keeping her weather eye open.
This ex-mistress of Philippe's had kept up a strong and enduring
friendship with him. She had brought up the Duke's two eldest
sons and was still official governess to the third boy and his sister.
What most alarmed her was the thought of these young people
being compromised by their father's intrigues. The moment she
heard of the Constituent Assembly's decision, she went straight
to her former lover. With a forceful array of arguments this
strong-minded woman made the Duke see the dangers that lurked
in such a proposal. She showed him the storm that was already
rumbling against himself and his children, confirmed all his suspicions about Laclos's personal lust for power, and sketched the
very similar motivation of Laclos's friends Desmoulins and Danton. Then, almost word for word, she dictated a letter for the
Duke, in which he disavowed the Constituent Assembly's decision. This letter was sent to the Assembly's official journal. It
contained, *inter alia*, the following words: "If there is to be any
question of a regency, I hereby renounce, now and forever, the

right which the Constitution gives me to exercise that office; I might go so far as to say that, after making so many sacrifices in the interests of the people, and for the sake of freedom, I can no longer leave the class in which I have placed myself, that of the ordinary citizen. . . ."

This was a bombshell for Laclos and his ambitions. But though initially taken aback, the wily intriguer soon recovered himself and lost no time in coming to a private agreement with Danton. Then, sure of the support he needed (there is no formal proof of Danton's part in this affair but subsequent events make it a near-certainty) the novelist asked leave of the President of the Assembly to appear before the Bar of the House. On July 11 his request was granted. In an adroit speech he attacked the notion of a republic, while at the same time acknowledging Philippe's withdrawal; to everyone's surprise, he gave the impression that he was pleading for the present King. But what Laclos in fact was doing, from a practical viewpoint, was giving the Duke's supporters enough time to mount a *coup d'état*.

The conservative majority did not fall into the snare Laclos had laid for them; indeed, they went so far as to use some of this apprentice Machiavelli's arguments to succor the King. Two days after Laclos made his speech, the Standing Committees of the Constituent Assembly presented their report on the flight to Varennes. This document recommended neither the King's removal from power nor the setting up of a regency under anyone whatsoever. Two days after its publication Barnave asked leave to speak in the Assembly. Together with his colleagues Pétion and Latour-Maubourg, he had brought the royal family back to Paris. Moved by the distress of the Queen, he proposed a motion confirming the inviolability of the King's person. The Deputies, who were alarmed equally by the prospect of republic or regency—the first suggested by mob agitators, the second by an ambitious junta—voted in favor of this motion. By declaring the King inviolable, they *ipso facto* restored his powers as a constitutional monarch.

The news of this decree made Choderlos de Laclos almost inarticulate with fury. If an Orleanist *coup d'état* did not take place at once, it would be too late. The Duke's private secretary hurried to Danton. The two men made an interesting contrast:

dashing Colonel of the Reserve and corpulent Counsel, the
one fifty and the other thirty-two—though to look at them one
might well have reversed their ages. Laclos seemed far younger
than he actually was: he devoted a great deal of care to his
appearance. His wig was scrupulously brushed and powdered;
his complexion was miraculously free from wrinkles; he dressed
with dandified and foppish elegance. Danton, on the other
hand, seemed a good deal older; excessive weight put years on
him. Yet Laclos's *Poésies Fugitives* and *Les Liaisons Dangereuses*
had been in all the booksellers' shops at a time when young
Danton was still playing truant from school. Later, when General Marmont was in command of the First Consul's artillery in
Italy, Choderlos de Laclos was his adjutant. In his *Memoirs,*
the aged Marshal devoted one word only to his former subordinate, whom he described as the "celebrated Laclos." Marmont's hand was shaky enough by the time he came to pen
this phrase, but the hint was enough, both for him and his
readers. It is easy to see how much, back in 1791, a person like
Danton could be flattered by the friendship of this elegant
officer. Laclos's eyes were aglint with shrewdness and subtlety;
his high forehead—another sign of intelligence—rose above them
like some gleaming miter. The gigantic Danton, overshadowing
his visitor with his corpulent presence, nevertheless gave the impression of being his foil. Their interview makes one think of the
fight between David and Goliath. But here the object was not
so much to defeat one's opponent by force of arms as to bam-
boozle him with clever arguments.

Whether there should be a republic or a regency did not
matter for the moment. The most urgent and essential thing was
to prevent Louis getting the reins of power back into his hands.
Laclos brought Danton around to the idea of a *coup d'état.* He
had no idea whether, once the King was overthrown, Danton
would opt for one form of government or the other. But he calculated that once victory was assured, he could force the
demagogue's hand in favor of Philippe d'Orléans. As for the
Duke himself, if he found himself with his back to the wall he
would no longer try to shuffle out of his responsibilities.

Though won over to the idea of a popular pronunciamento
(which he had undertaken to bring about by virtue of his

influence over the masses), Danton was still hesitating between the two possible options. Republic or regency? No matter; that could be settled later. He threw in his lot with Laclos—though reserving the right, if all went well, to take whichever side he liked, to proclaim a republic, and, if need be, to throw Laclos himself into prison.

Meanwhile, however, he accepted, from the hands of his fellow conspirator, a petition that had been drawn up by a third rogue. This was Brissot, the founder and editor of *Le Patriote Français,* and another friend of Philippe d'Orléans's— though an unreliable friend who affected a wavering brand of Republicanism and whom Laclos likewise hoped to use for his own ends. The object of this petition was to arouse the people against Louis XVI. On July 16 Danton took it down for approval by the members of the Club des Cordeliers.

A huge crowd filled the Club to hear him. It was a hot summer day and passions were running high, so that the sweat stood out on his listeners' foreheads. From the rough scaffolding which served as a rostrum, Danton read out the text of the petition. Its central demand was for the King's removal from power. The audience did more than applaud: they screamed insults at "the Austrian woman" and "Fat Capet."

Legendre, who was in the chair, delegated forty-eight "patriots" to carry a message to each of the forty-eight electoral divisions. A fortnight previously, the City Council had invited all Parisians to congregate on the Champ-de-Mars on Sunday, July 17. The idea was that they should celebrate—very simply, by the mere gesture of assembly—the anniversary of the events that took place on July 14. (The three days' delay was to avoid the loss of work which this would otherwise entail.) Laclos and Danton intended to use this public gathering for their own purposes. The emissaries of Legendre were instructed to tell each division: "Tomorrow, when the citizens of Paris assemble on the Champ-de-Mars, the petition of the Club des Cordeliers will be offered to them for their signature."

Desmoulins went to the Jacobin Club in person to ask if its members would associate themselves with the venture. But the Jacobins rejected such a plebiscite, on the grounds of illegality.

The removal of the King, they argued, was a matter for the Constituent Assembly, not for the people: *à chacun son métier.*

As for Laclos, he proceeded to thicken the plot in his own idiosyncratic fashion. Since all those thousands of signatures could not be accommodated on the parchment roll containing the referendum, it was necessary to run off a number of copies, and then circulate these to the various electoral divisions in Paris and the provinces. Laclos, given the job of taking the manuscript to Brune and Momoro, the Club's two printers, put it in his pocket and went out. But he stopped somewhere on the way—at a café, no doubt—and inserted a few words in Brissot's text, which Danton had already modified to some extent. The original wording, which equated Louis XVI's flight with an act of abdication, declared that "the undersigned Frenchmen . . . make formal and specific demand that the National Assembly do accept, in the name of the nation, the abdication of Louis XVI, made public on June 21." To these words Laclos added: ". . . and to proceed to his replacement by *all constitutional means.*" This would bind the Assembly, if they accepted the petition, to proclaim the accession of the child Dauphin, with the Duke of Orléans acting as regent.

But once more Mme. de Genlis was to sabotage all Laclos's efforts. This diabolical woman knew all about both texts—the original one and the modified version produced by Laclos. Doubtless she got her information from some member of the Club who heard the speech delivered, and from one of the printers. She lived not far away, in the rue de Bellechasse. She had a whole network of acquaintances in every walk of life and was always on the qui-vive for anything affecting the well-being of the House of Orléans. Perhaps one of her agents brought her the text of this famous petition after taking it down at the meeting. Another agent, some typesetter employed by Brune or Momoro, may have smuggled out a copy to her; and Mme. de Genlis—an intelligent bluestocking if ever there was one—was surprised to find a small but absolutely vital difference between the two versions.

She passed her discovery on to Legendre (who was not regarded as an Orleanist), and he in turn informed Danton. This all took place while the Club was still in session. At the same time Mme. de Genlis contacted the Marquis de Sillery (her ex-husband, and still a good friend of hers) and sent him hurrying off to the City Hall. Sillery revealed the plot to Bailly, and Bailly warned La Fayette. Troops were at once ordered to the Tuileries and the Riding School, to cope with any possible emergency that might arise.

At the Club, Danton fulminated against Laclos's insertion, without, however, giving any indication as to its author. He seemed, indeed, not to know who was responsible. Besides, the manuscript had passed through so many hands. He had the offending phrase officially struck out, and then proposed that the House "proceed to implementation"—that is, that all present should append their signatures to the document. But several members of the Club, with the approval of a section of the spectators, announced that they would not sign the petition unless the Jacobins reversed their decision not to adopt it. Feeling that the scheme was going badly awry, Desmoulins went back to the rue Saint-Honoré to make another bid for Jacobin support. Fréron meanwhile got together about a hundred volunteers as fast as he could, and likewise set off for the rival club, collecting more supporters as he went.

This group arrived just as the Jacobins, having debated the second appeal from the Cordeliers, were preparing to turn it down once more. The crowd led by Fréron burst open the doors and marched threateningly into the building. Their spokesman interrupted the debate to announce: "My friends and I, whose eyes and gestures proclaim the energy, yes, and the courage proper to free men, are here to solicit your approval of the motion calling for the King's removal. I hereby invite the Friends of the Constitution, those true guardians of liberty, to go tomorrow, either singly or in a body, to the Champ-de-Mars and there swear, on the Altar of the Fatherland, never again to recognize Louis XVI as King of the French!" There was applause from the public galleries. The Jacobins, cowering terrified on their benches, bowed to the will of the people.

That night Paris presented the spectacle of a city under arms. The battalions dispatched by La Fayette had moved into position around the Riding School. The ground shook as horses and artillery thundered along. Unable to sleep, the inhabitants leaned out of their windows, watching. Patrols were out in the streets rounding up suspects. As any individual who ventured outside his own house was so regarded, queues soon began to lengthen outside the gates of all the Paris prisons. In order to save space, the police set free all those who had been arrested on obviously inadequate evidence. François Robert, jailed several days earlier for protesting in his newssheet against the arrest of the billposters, now found himself released. He hurried home, embraced his wife, and—warned by her of the turn events had taken—went straight down to the Club des Cordeliers. When he arrived, everyone was just leaving, having arranged to meet on the Champ-de-Mars the following morning.

Dawned that incredible day, July 17, 1791. Drawn by some partisan allegiance, or out of sheer curiosity, a heterogeneous mass of people was strolling about in the vicinity of the Altar of the Fatherland on the Champ-de-Mars. The sun was shining. Hawkers selling gingerbread and coconuts bawled their wares at the passers-by. Men, women, children, entire families, who had either been notified by their local authorities or else had read one of the posters in the streets, were eagerly awaiting the arrival of the Club's top names—Danton, Camille Desmoulins, Fabre d'Églantine, Legendre, Fréron, perhaps even Marat. This was something not to be missed.

Unfortunately, the stars were replaced by stand-ins. Four unknown persons elbowed their way through the crowd and climbed up on to the Altar. It was François Robert, who, accompanied by three obscure citizens named Vachord, Demoy, and Pegré, had brought the petition of the Club des Cordeliers. Nominated for the job by Danton, Robert—a Belgian—had come to invite the French people to press for the removal of their King. Even Marat, the Swiss who had proclaimed himself a "Citizen of the World," remained out of sight all that day. Yet the previous evening the "People's Friend" had been generous enough with his invective from the rostrum; and that same morning, after describing, in his newssheet, the troop movements carried out, on orders, by units of the National Guard, he concluded with the following ironic words: "Rumor has it that M. de La Fayette would not hesitate for one moment to fire on the crowd. In order to put an end to such uncertainty, I propose to have the General assassinated." But *L'Ami du Peuple* had a circulation of no more than five thousand copies; not everyone in Paris could have read it.

In any event, it was François Robert who now stood at the top of the Altar steps to read out the petition. Just as he began, events took a sensational turn. A commission of five Jacobins arrived, five unknown "patriots." In the name of the Club, which had twice refused to associate itself with the referendum and had done so in the end only under duress, one of the messengers thrust Robert aside and, taking his place, proceeded to read the flabbergasted gathering another, still more violent motion. Not content with demanding Louis XVI's removal, it also proposed bringing him to trial. The Jacobins had begun to be alarmed at the competition their rivals now presented. Besides, the Duke of Orléans was a member of their Club; so was Choderlos de Laclos. The condemnation of Louis XVI would make his cousin eligible for the Throne. But Philippe, with sudden pusillanimity, had decided to refuse the burden of the oldest crown in Europe. First Paris, then all France, were being invited to force his hand.

"Bring the King to *trial?*" people muttered; and then, "Well, after all—" and in the end the little notebooks brought along for that purpose were filled with over six thousand signatures. During this lengthy operation a body of volunteers kept the crowd moving in orderly fashion past the Altar. The goose-quill pens were used up at a great rate that morning, as the immense queue shuffled forward. *Your turn, citizen! Next, please! Hurry along there!*

Then came the unlooked-for interruption. What was happening, people asked one another, as the sound of marching feet drew nearer—and what was the reason for those bayonets glinting over there outside the Military College? And on the other side, down along the bank of the Seine? To the right, to the left now as well, on all sides . . . It was only the National Guard, but what were *they* doing cordoning off this crowd?

The battalions advanced steadily. Were they (shades of Marat!) coming to fire on the people? The crowd did not think so. Each battalion consisted of one regular company, made up

of soldiers on the active list; but the other three companies consisted of national volunteers, workers, artisans, members of the
bourgeoisie, the brothers, sons, and fathers of all those men and
women who now crowded the Champ-de-Mars. There was,
people felt, nothing to fear from these reservists. But they continued to advance, marching at the slope, and their very presence
constituted a vague threat. La Fayette could be seen out in front
of them, on horseback, and Bailly was riding with him.

Suddenly a red flag was unfurled beside them, the blood-
colored standard that was, as it were, the warning shot given to
agitators. Ever since a decree passed by the Constituent Assembly
on October 21, 1789, it had been the symbol of martial law. Its
appearance meant, in so many words: "Go on home, break up
your meeting, or we shall fire on you."

What had happened to provoke these stern emergency measures? The answer was that two men had been murdered here:
two drunks, in point of fact, one of whom was a cripple with a
wooden leg. Early that morning, before the crowds had begun
to converge on the Champ-de-Mars, the first arrivals had found
these sodden tramps sprawled at the foot of the Altar of the
Fatherland. Mistaking their keg of wine for a powder barrel,
some simpletons accused them of plotting to blow up the Altar.
After a noisy and argumentative promenade as far as St.
Pierre du Grand-Caillou, they decapitated the two wretches and
paraded their heads, on pikes, through the streets of the capital.
With that special kind of lunacy endemic to popular revolutions and reigns of terror, the nonsensical story of an attempt on
the Altar of the Fatherland reached the City Hall. Partisan
distortion made a full-blown uprising of the incident, which
reports of the crowd signing the petition seemed to confirm. The
Mayor proclaimed a state of martial law and arrived on the
Champ-de-Mars with La Fayette, his troops, and the red flag
while the citizens of Paris—without any hint of excitement or
disorder—were still adding their names to the Jacobins's referendum.

A fatal—and classic—incident took place, almost inevitably.
How did that first volley come to be discharged? According to
La Fayette's adversaries, he ordered his troops to open fire without any prior warning apart from the red flag. His supporters,

on the other hand, alleged that some rabble-rouser fired a pistol at the General, without hitting him, and that this caused an immediate, instinctive answering fire from the front ranks. The muskets went off almost by themselves. The crowd ran in all directions, some of them charging their aggressors, others taking to their heels in headlong flight, leaving about a hundred victims behind them.

And what of Danton, and Laclos, and Desmoulins, and Fréron—indeed all of those who had been responsible for this day's work: Fabre d'Églantine, Santerre, Legendre, Marat, those who had spoken in the previous evening's debate, the printers Brune and Momoro—what had become of them all? No one had seen any of the Club's moving spirits on the Champ-de-Mars. The only persons of any importance from the Cordeliers who turned up were Hébert and Father Duchesne, who signed the petition. What was more, the only leading member of the Jacobins who put in an appearance—and, indeed, exposed himself to La Fayette's musketry—was Robespierre. Why were all the main players in the Great Game so conspicuous by their absence?

The previous night Danton had barely got back home from the Club when a messenger arrived from his brother-in-law. Citizen Jean-Baptiste-Léonard Durand was supposed to be an agent working for Montmorin, the Foreign Minister; it was he, rumor had it, who used to supply Danton with money from the secret funds. But on this occasion he had come to warn him of his impending arrest. "Spend tomorrow in the country," he told Danton. "It's Sunday, after all; no one could question your going."

This news took Danton aback, and he passed it on to his close friends. They all assembled in his study, at crack of dawn on the fateful day, to take stock of the situation. Everyone was there except Legendre, and they all agreed that it would be wiser to wait and see how events developed rather than to chance their heads on the steps of the Altar of the Fatherland. They handed over the text of the referendum to Robert, who had only just been released from prison, and he set off for the Champ-de-Mars, having rounded up three junior members of the Club—Pegré, Demoy, and Vachord—to act as his escort.

Danton's domestic servants were still asleep. Gabrielle served the conspirators with coffee and wine. She was pale, her features drawn after an agonizing night of worry; yet she still managed to smile politely at these men, though in her heart she accused them of being the evil influences that led her husband on. She looked back regretfully to those happy days when Georges dreamed of nothing but getting cases and taking excursions into the country.

At this point Legendre arrived, out of breath, having run all the way from his butcher's shop at the other end of the street. He, too, had received a visit. Two friends, whom he named, had come and told him: "We have been instructed to give you a warning. Leave Paris as soon as you can, today. Get out of town. Take Danton, Desmoulins, and Fréron with you. This is what Charles de Lameth says you should do."

Lameth, a former comrade of La Fayette's in America, had considerable sympathy for Danton. Though he represented the nobility of Artois in the Constituent Assembly, he was nevertheless very far to the Left. He had been elected President on July 5, and had an intimate acquaintance with the machinery of power. Any advice he gave must be taken seriously.

Yet despite everything, Danton hesitated. The fact of his absence both at the storming of the Bastille and from the march on Versailles did not matter too much, since at the time he had been quite unknown. But today an accusation of cowardice could seriously damage his reputation. "Don't let's take off for the country," he told his friends. "Let's wait and see how things develop. Our presence here may become essential. We might as well go on with our work."

The work in question consisted of drafting a new proclamation, in case the original one should prove inoperative. The plotters were not aware that the Jacobins, by demanding that the King be brought to trial, had already outbid them.

About the middle of the morning they heard the distant sound of firing. Half an hour later one of Robert's three companions burst in, panting. It was from his lips they first learned of the events leading up to the slaughter on the Champ-de-Mars. What had become of Robert? they asked. The messenger did not know.

"If La Fayette has fired on the people," Danton bellowed, "he's done for! Those who drink the people's blood die of it."

Always the grand phrase, the striking metaphor: even in moments of intimacy this actor still believed he was on the stage. He turned to his wife and said: "Gabrielle, we're going to have dinner at your father's house in Fontenay tonight. Join us there this evening and bring the child with you."

When they left the house, the defeated conspirators parted. They all went off in different directions, skulking in the shadow of the walls, having arranged to meet again at M. Charpentier's house. To reach Fontenay-sous-Bois took two hours on foot, or thirty minutes by the stage cart. Some of them boarded this vehicle, others preferred to walk. The most important thing was to get away unobserved. Luckily the camera had not yet been invented: the portraits of public figures were not printed in the newspapers. Those National Guardsmen who—through fury or guilt at having killed innocent people—swore they were going to massacre those responsible for the petition, would have been hard put to recognize Legendre, Desmoulins, or even Danton himself. Prudhomme, the bookseller, was mistaken for Desmoulins as he was crossing the Pont-Neuf, and only just escaped his would-be assailants. Fréron was knocked down at the same point and owed his life to some National Guard reservists from his own neighborhood, who placed him under their protection.

Other members of the National Guard vented their wrath on the Jacobins. As they were passing down the rue Saint-Honoré, they stopped outside the Club, shouting insults, and tried to force the door. There was a general stampede inside. Some members jumped out of the windows. At this point Robespierre appeared, having just got back from the Champ-de-Mars. He was stalking along without looking at anyone, grave and meditative, "lean with civic purity and as stiff as virtue." Recognized by his olive-green coat and the thick pebble-glasses magnifying his eyes, the Incorruptible narrowly escaped being beaten. Some women made a protective rampart of their bodies about him. Several shouted, "Long live Robespierre!" and an unknown voice from the crowd called out: "If we've got to have a king, why not him?" There were murmurs of approval. Robespierre, anx-

ious to escape his compromising supporters no less than his
enemies, vanished into the workshop of a joiner, one M. Duplay,
who gave him a rapturous welcome. He offered his visitor a meal
and a bed for the night. His wife and daughters plied the fugitive
with attentions. The whole family insisted, next morning, that he
must come and live with them. Robespierre accepted their offer
and left his lodgings in the rue de Saintonge. This is why his
home, partly through the actions of Danton and Laclos, was
henceforward in the house of Citizen Duplay.

The group responsible for the incident on the Champ-de-Mars
reached Fontenay-sous-Bois during the afternoon, some on foot,
others by stage cart or cab. Their arrival surprised M. Charpentier
and left his wife in a flutter. The little village was bathed in
sunlight. It seemed a hundred leagues from the tumult and confusion of the capital. The forest of Vincennes ran close beside it,
isolating it from Paris and all its agitations.

The fugitives told their host all that had happened. About
seven o'clock that evening a hackney carriage arrived, bringing
Gabrielle and the child, escorted by Antoine Charpentier. Everyone sat down to dinner together. When the meal was over,
Desmoulins decided to go back to Paris. He had to go and
"blackguard La Fayette a bit to the Jacobins," he said, and to
reassure poor Lucile. Fréron, Legendre, and the rest followed
his example. They asked Danton if he was coming. But Gabrielle
intervened at this point, saying that a night in the country, with
the windows wide open, would do her husband a great deal of
good.

"On your way," Danton told his accomplices. "I'll be back
tomorrow."

When the whole household was asleep, a sudden clamor arose
outside. A group of men had gathered outside the wrought-iron
garden gate and were shouting insults at Danton. Suddenly
awakened by the noise, Danton sat listening to the chorus of
abuse. His assailants called him "a creature of the aristocracy,
an enemy of the people, a spy in the pay of Prussia and England."
They shook the bars of the gate but failed to break it open. Then
their footsteps could be heard fading away. Finally they were
gone. It had been a brisk sort of skirmish.

On his return to Paris, Desmoulins sent his wife to stay with her in-laws, at Bourg-la-Reine. The Roberts and Fabre d'Églantine accompanied Lucile. Saying he would join them later, Desmoulins left, together with Fréron and Legendre, for Versailles, where a friend of Marat's called Lecointre was going to put them up.

Next day, July 18, Bailly set the law in motion against those behind the petition. At his request the Assembly passed a decree aimed at "individuals guilty of wilfully advocating disobedience to the law, whether by posters and notices, whether through the spoken or the written word." Such persons were to be "arrested on the spot," brought before tribunals, and condemned to "three years in a chain gang." On hearing of this decree, Danton told his wife and in-laws: "From now on none of us will be able to sleep safely in our own beds."

In furtherance of this decree, the Public Prosecutor of the Sixth *Arrondissement* made investigations with a view to arresting "the authors, abettors, and accomplices of the ill-fated plot which took place on July 17." On August 4 he signed a warrant for the apprehension of Danton, Desmoulins, Legendre, and Fréron.

But by then they were already miles away from Paris. Danton finally made up his mind to beat a retreat on the 18th. He would go to Troyes and seek refuge with a friend of his, the Attorney General for the Aube *département*. If he managed to get there and found he could breathe freely, without fear of pursuit, then he would pass the news on to his wife, and she and little Antoine could then leave Fontenay-sous-Bois in their turn and join Georges at Arcis.

But with his rendezvous now fixed, Danton continued to hesitate. Suppose the police pursued him as far as his home town? He had to anticipate all contingencies—even exile abroad, emigration. It was true that in several speeches he had flayed those aristocrats who, after the fall of the Bastille, had set a frontier between themselves and the people. The man who three years later was to say, "You cannot carry your country away with you on the soles of your shoes," now dictated a power-of-attorney to his brother-in-law which casts something of a shadow over his own patriotism. In 1791 he was very seriously consider-

ing carrying his country away with him on the soles of his shoes.
If he did not intend to by-pass Arcis-sur-Aube and go into exile,
why should he have given Antoine the authority "to manage
and administer all his property and affairs in his name," to
"make over, on the most advantageous terms possible, the
lease of the apartment which the said Sieur Danton occupies,"
to "cancel the said lease," and, above all, to "sell the furniture
of the said apartment."

This authorization to sell is significant. When anyone leaves
his house with the intention of returning shortly, he does not
normally cancel his lease or sell off his furniture.

Deputy though he was, Robespierre, too, could feel himself
threatened by the Constituent Assembly. Was he not the most
representative of the Jacobins? And had he not signed their petition, calling for the trial of the King? Yet despite this he remained in Paris, at the very heart of the danger area. As Bar-
busse remarked over a century later, it takes a major crisis to
show people's true lineaments; and one has to admit that in
1791 Robespierre behaved very differently from Danton.

Having arranged and signed his power-of-attorney, Danton
kissed his wife and son and said good-by to his in-laws. Then he
borrowed one of his father-in-law's horses and had it saddled.
An hour later he was on his way, galloping for dear life.

The same day—this was still July 18, and the warrant was
not issued until August 4—some police officers went around to
the offices of *Les Révolutions de France et de Brabant*. Instead
of Desmoulins, who had left for Versailles, they found his editorial
assistant Roch-Marcandier. This young idiot tried to stop them
searching the premises. He whipped out a pistol and fired one
shot before he was overpowered, beaten up, and hauled off to
prison. Here he found Momoro and Brune, the two printers
who had run off copies of the petition, together with another
obscure Cordelier named Saint-Félix. As usual, it was the small
fry who got caught.

Another such unimportant victim was Victor Charpentier,
Antoine and Gabrielle's elder brother. Together with his wife,
he went down to Fontenay to stay with his family; and when
the police arrived to interrogate Danton, they took Victor for
the fugitive demagogue. As he attempted to defend himself

against them, these louts gave him a thorough going-over. Here we have one more piece of evidence which suggests that despite Danton's size and ugliness, his contemporaries were ill acquainted, on the whole, with his general appearance.

Those who emerged most triumphantly from the events of July 17, on the face of it at least, were La Fayette and Bailly. They received the congratulations of the conservative majority in the Constituent Assembly. Yet their popularity, already shaky after the flight to Varennes (which they had failed either to foresee or to prevent), was a very fragile thing, which collapsed altogether beneath the weight of the red flag. As Count Alexandre de Tilly, an eyewitness of these events, was to write afterward: "The blood that flowed on that day was the unfortunate Bailly's death warrant. His knowledge of heavenly revolutions [an allusion to his work as an astronomer] had taught him nothing about the history of their terrestrial equivalent; though no doubt he had read—and forgotten—while browsing through the dusty tomes in his study, the old truism that *where its former favorites are concerned, the populace has but one reaction, and one gift to bestow: ingratitude, and death.*"

In 1794 the implacable Saint-Just was to criticize Danton for his flight three years previously, which he branded as cowardice. The fugitive's supporters, on the other hand, tried to find excuses for him; indeed, they justified his conduct. According to them, by leaving Paris when he did, Danton was fulfilling a patriotic duty. Conscious of his value in public affairs, he was saving himself for the struggles ahead. If he had been imprisoned and sentenced to three years in a chain gang, the way would have been left clear for the enemies of France and liberty. Unfortunately for this theory—which suggests that Danton did not lack self-conceit—the power-of-attorney which he made in favor of Antoine Charpentier points in a very different direction.

When someone is determined to "save himself" for future action, he will normally save his house and chattels, too. The clause concerning these suggests very strongly that Danton considered Troyes and Arcis—in the event of real danger—as no more than the preparatory stages toward his emigration. He stayed only a few days in Troyes; on July 26 he reached Arcis, where he was reunited with his wife, child, mother, and step-father. They were occupying a small manor house which stood in its own twelve-acre park by the river, opposite the town's single bridge but at a little distance from it. The former owner, Mlle. Piot de Courcelles, had sold this property to Danton on April 13, for 25,300 *livres*. He installed his mother and step-father there—it was a more comfortable place than their own house—and took advantage of his stay in Arcis to go to Maître Jeannet-Boursier's chambers and sign not only the deed of purchase but also a life annuity in favor of his mother, the income from which amounted to 600 *livres* annually.

Safe in his retreat at Arcis, Danton could think of himself as a free man. During the first few days he went out and explored his estates. Then, having observed that he was being trailed, at a distance, by persons he did not know, the refugee gave up his strolls through the streets and fields: he even withdrew from his own residence—the charming manor house opposite the bridge. Warning his wife and mother of what he was going to do, he went into hiding in the house next door, which belonged to his friend M. Courtois, the local tax collector. Built at right angles to his own, it formed a tiny square or courtyard between the two residences. When Gabrielle and her mother-in-law wanted to pay Danton a visit, they needed only to walk across this courtyard (or skirt around two sides of the square).

But there was a stranger in town who observed their movements and guessed the truth. On July 31 this man came and rang at M. Courtois's door. "I know M. Danton is here," he said. "I would like to speak to him, please." Courtois refused to admit him. The visitor protested. In the end Danton agreed to see him and hear his story. He said he was an ex-convict, a victim of arbitrary injustice. He had been present on the Champ-de-Mars and had fought against La Fayette's troops. Recognized in his neighborhood and threatened by the police, he had left Paris so hurriedly that he had not even brought his purse with him. Anxious to get rid of the fellow, Danton gave him nine *livres*. The man thanked him, then said: "I suppose you couldn't put me up, could you? Lend me a bed? I've walked all the way here from Paris and I'm fit to drop. Besides, I'm not very anxious to show my face just now."

Danton could, and did, make the obvious reply—that he was not in his own house. Scenting a spy, some kind of informer who, once established in Courtois's house, could open the door to the police, he said, with absolute finality: "In my position I have to be suspicious of everyone. Be off with you. I may have money to spare for people down on their luck—but I also have a brace of first-class pistols to deal with shifty crooks like you." The man took off without further argument.

There was another, more serious attempt of this sort, but we have no details concerning it: simply the fact of its occurrence, revealed by Danton himself during his trial in 1794. "Assassins," he then declared, "were sent to murder me in Arcis, and one of them was arrested."

But the fugitive was in considerable danger of arrest himself. "That pious old woman Beugnot," as he described the Attorney General for the Aube *département,* warned him that spies were trying to kidnap him. In Paris the Minister of the Interior was trying to persuade the Minister of Justice, Duport-Dutertre, to initiate a prosecution in the Troyes courts. Although he was a friend of La Fayette's, Duport-Dutertre hesitated to do this: he was afraid of Danton.

All these rumors trickled through to Arcis. The majority of the inhabitants, still proud of their distinguished fellow towns-man, took his side. An informer wrote to the Public Prosecutor of Troyes saying that to effect the arrest of such a person would require the help of a military detachment. Orders to this effect were issued.

When he heard this, Danton decided to flee. As it happened, his father-in-law was just then thinking of taking a trip to England. For some while now he had been trying to spin cotton in his workshop, and these unsuccessful experiments had twice led him to the verge of bankruptcy. A man called Mill, an English mechanic, was working on the installation of a spinning jenny in Birmingham. Richard-Lenoir, the Paris manufacturer, sent one of his subordinates named Martin to inspect this machine—which was, in fact, destined to revolutionize the cotton industry. M. Recordain knew all about this: he, too, he felt, should go over to Birmingham. But he could not meet the expenses involved, and spoke no word of English.

Danton, whose English was fluent and who had money and to spare, offered to go with him. A young relative, a cousin named Georges Mergez, accompanied them. All three carried daggers and pistols. Later, Fouquier-Tinville was to call this trip an "emigration." To which Danton replied from the dock: "Despotism still flourished unchecked in Paris. I therefore chose exile. I banished myself and swore not to return to France until liberty had been established there."

Of his intention to return we have one corroborative piece of evidence: he did not take his wife and child with him. But that intention is also implicitly contradicted—again, by Danton himself—in that clause of the power-of-attorney Antoine Charpentier received which required him to terminate Danton's lease and sell his furniture. Besides, the exile could very easily summon his wife by letter to join him.

So on that hot August morning in 1791 Danton was parted from Gabrielle for the first time. The three travelers must have left by post-chaise or hired carriage. We can imagine Danton's sad expression at that leave-taking, and Gabrielle's tears as she held out their son to him. They embraced, and then the driver whipped up his horses and was gone. As he rattled along, Danton may well have felt that Bailly and La Fayette had won the final round.

CHAPTER VIII

Deputy Public Prosecutor to the Commune

AT THIS PERIOD the Austrian Emperor and the King of Prussia were more concerned over Catherine the Great's ambitions in Poland than over Louis XVI's internal difficulties. The Empress of Russia herself, anxious to be left a free hand on the Vistula, was pressing the Courts of Vienna and Berlin to intervene in France. As for England, a revolution which damaged her rival's maritime power could not but be welcome across the Channel. William Pitt, the Prime Minister, was establishing numerous agents in Paris, some English, some French, and some Swiss. Was Danton one of them? Various reports and letters which only came to light long afterward (and which we shall refer to later in the chronological order of their discovery) confirm the probability in a manner tantamount to proof.

Unfortunately for history, little is known about Danton's visit to England. There is no evidence as to where he stayed in London and Birmingham. He wrote few, if any, letters during his time there—not through fear of compromising himself, since he often displayed a quite childish lack of caution (as his property deals make clear); but rather because of his natural bent for off-the-cuff oratory, which left its mark on his way of life in general. Even if he kept up a correspondence with Gabrielle, which might have enlightened us about this period, his family either destroyed or concealed his letters after his death. We know only that he did not dally in England, since he remained there a mere six weeks.

There is very little likelihood that Pitt received him during his visit. The Prime Minister was a man who kept himself aloof. This task was doubtless carried out by his secret agents, who were unlikely to make the fact public. Their department contained numerous filing cabinets, each with its label—"Spanish Affairs," "Polish Affairs," "Prussian Affairs," and so on. Only one had a French title, and that because there was no exact equivalent in English for the thing it described: *Agents Provocateurs.* If a file with Danton's name on it existed in this cabinet, no proof of the fact has survived.

On the other hand, we are less likely to be wrong if we assume that the traveler met Thomas Paine, author of *The Rights of Man,* and Thomas Christie, another admirer of the Jacobins' ideals. But it is not true that it was Talleyrand who introduced Danton to the two Londoners. In August and September of 1791 that revolutionary prelate had not yet crossed the Channel. His official mission to London only began the following year, on January 24, 1792. But despite this, Danton may well have made the acquaintance of both Paine and Christie; and they in turn may have put him in contact with the leaders of the Whig Party: Sheridan, Fox, and Lord Stanhope. The last-named was in fact the Prime Minister's brother-in-law; though he attacked Pitt's policies in public, he privately supported them.

Thanks to this lucky coincidence, Danton could play a double game. He could satisfy his patriotic conscience by attaching himself to the Whigs, who were dreaming of an alliance with the country that had formulated the Rights of Man. But through the good offices of their leader, he could also establish himself on a better footing with the agents of the Prime Minister, who, after all, was the man who held the purse strings. It did no harm, either, that Pitt's secretary and *éminence grise* was none other than his niece, Hester—Lord Stanhope's daughter.

Danton's precise relationship to both these political groups is yet another of the mysteries which crowd his double life, compounded in equal degree of a genuine, and ardent, passion for universal liberty, equality, and fraternity—and a no less powerful love of money.

During his London exile he learned that Leopold of Austria was at long last beginning to take some interest in the fate of his brother-in-law Louis XVI. Together with the King of Prussia he signed, on August 27, the so-called Declaration of Pilnitz. This Declaration, which affirmed their intention of restoring order in France, was a virtual dead letter since the two monarchs made their intervention conditional on the support of the other Great Powers. England, for one—as Danton had some reason to know—wanted nothing more than the prolongation of disorder and anarchy in France. Leopold and Frederick of Prussia, who were well aware of the British attitude, only signed their inoperative agreement at all so as to please the French King's brothers. The younger of these, the Count of Artois, had been living beyond the Rhine ever since the fall of the Bastille; while the elder, the Count of Provence, had left Paris on the same night as the flight to Varennes took place. His luck held better than Louis's did; he reached Belgium without any mishap.

The pressure which these two princes put on the German monarchs, then, came to very little in the end. Except for the *émigrés,* who sat polishing their sabers in Coblentz, there was no army preparing to invade France. Nor had the French themselves any intention, as yet, of exporting their reforms. Before he died, Mirabeau had warned the country against any such plan: "A war, even a just war, would be an immense disaster. . . . We must fall back on ourselves, adopt the defensive stance. . . . What have we to put up against the might of Europe? A deficit of 240 millions in the Treasury, our royal stocks and bonds at rock bottom, a wave of speculation that's ruining Paris, an exhausted and grumbling populace, a slump in trade, lack of unity at home and lack of credit abroad, ill-trained troops and a badly equipped fleet."

Danton and his friends had to bear at least part of the responsibility for this chaos. How could the government and the Constituent Assembly be expected to overhaul the country's finances, reassure the King and persuade him to accept the new régime, pacify the populace to the point where they looked on their elected representatives as friends, reorganize the fleet and the army, and restore general confidence abroad if all the while a handful of men under Danton's leadership kept pouring inflammable spirit on the smoldering embers of public opinion? Indeed, Danton and his supporters were considered such a menace that the Assembly actually considered passing a general amnesty, applicable—without naming them individually—to "all agitators and rabble-rousers."

Danton now decided, either because of information in a letter or as the result of reading the papers, that his return to France would help to bring this amnesty about. What was more, the Constituent Assembly was about to yield its place in the Riding School to a Legislative Assembly, and the country was getting ready for fresh elections. To canvass for votes in the Paris area meant at least showing oneself to the voters; and if the Constituent Assembly did not bring in the promised amnesty before its dissolution, it would, surely, be difficult for the new Assembly to take action against one of its own members. Parliamentary immunity would provide him with all the protection he needed.

But there was still a need, during the election campaign, to avoid provoking the attentions of the Standing Committee of Inquiry. This body was presided over by a lawyer, Maître Garran de Coulon, with a strictness that even the police might envy. Fortunately—and this shows that Danton *was* keeping up a correspondence with friends in Paris—the exile discovered that Maître Garran had been appointed, as from September 1, President of the Court of Appeal. Thus Topino-Lebrun, an eyewitness of the Germinal trials, was enabled to note down the following reply by Danton to a question from Fouquier-Tinville: "I escaped to London. I returned after the news of Garran's appointment." It is true that he did, in fact, take boat for Boulogne after this appointment became effective, and from Boulogne traveled by coach to Paris.

In the rue des Cordeliers he found his apartment and furniture (which Antoine Charpentier had not as yet disposed of) still intact. But there was no Gabrielle to welcome him: at his own request she had remained at Arcis, together with little Antoine. Yet the lusty Danton did not take kindly to a long separation from his beloved. Why, if this was so, should he have ordered her to stay in Arcis when his own destination was Paris? Let us take another look at Topino-Lebrun's notes. After recalling Garran's nomination to the Court of Appeal, Danton is supposed to have added: "They offered Legendre 50,000 *écus* to slit my throat." Who were "they"? The former member of the Revolutionary

Tribunal did not name specific persons. But their identity matters little for our present consideration. It is obvious that, faced with a threat of this kind, Danton decided to keep his wife in the country, far away from the possible scene of any such attempt, which might well cause her extreme alarm. Besides, she was pregnant and must be treated with special consideration.

So when he came back to Paris, he was alone. His first call was at the electoral headquarters of his constituency; from here he went on to the Club des Cordeliers. Despite his rubicund features, he posed as the poor injured victim, and his supporters gave him a rousing ovation. The news of his return spread rapidly through the neighborhood. For two days he hesitated whether to risk going out, crossing over to the Right Bank, and confronting the Jacobins. When he had demanded, on July 16, that they endorse his petition, was not this the original cause of them putting up their own? On September 12 he decided to take the plunge and show his face among them. When he appeared in the Club he was given a rousing welcome. So all was well: the capital had a short memory. Besides, was Danton responsible for the bloodshed? "When La Fayette fired on the people," he said, "I was out of Paris." There was the real culprit: the facts spoke for themselves. And La Fayette's opponent did not omit to remind them of it. For the Jacobins, as for the Cordeliers, Danton was once more the man of the moment.

But not, alas, in the eyes of the law. The next day, September 13, in the middle of an election meeting, M. Damien, the sheriff's officer, arrived at Saint-André-des-Arts. The appearance of this old acquaintance of his, who not so long ago had tried to arrest Marat, gave Danton a nasty shock. Suppose Damien had come for *him?* The newly returned exile's suspicions were confirmed in a moment, when Damien proceeded to serve a warrant on him. But, as things turned out, it was the poor sheriff's officer who spent that night in jail, not Danton. The crowd first shouted abuse at him, then seized him and carried him off to the Abbaye Prison. Somewhat shaken, the gatekeeper dared not refuse this unusual inmate. The whole thing was pure vaudeville farce, with the policeman beaten up and the criminal laughing himself silly. The cell reserved for Danton was occupied by the sheriff's

officer instead; and it was the sheriff's officer who was accused
of "an offense against public liberty."

Danton went to the Jacobins to make a plea on behalf of
this unfortunate man. The result shows what extraordinary
influence the Club enjoyed, though its members enjoyed no kind
of electoral mandate. Thanks to Danton's efforts, Damien was
released after three days' imprisonment; and the National Assembly—as ever, a highly impressionable body—proceeded to
vote, before its final dissolution, for the amnesty that Danton
and his friends had anticipated. No sooner was the decree
passed than they all appeared again, loudmouthed and dictatorial as ever, and went everywhere venting their hatred against
Bailly and La Fayette, those "assassins of the people!"

Louis XVI went to preside over the final session of the
Constituent Assembly. He arrived at the Riding School in
splendid pomp, the procession having followed an immense
detour so as to take in as many streets as possible. Before he got
there, Robespierre protested against one phrase in the closure
report: "The members of the present legislature are eligible for
re-election." On the contrary, declared the Incorruptible, they
should "return to the great body of ordinary citizens and disappear from public view." In his acid voice he concluded: "Let
us be gone, gentlemen! Get out of here, breathe the fresh air of
equality, leave our places to others."

The other members dared not object to this somewhat shatter-
ing request, lest they seem to be displaying greater self-interest
than the Deputy from Arras. They therefore voted in favor of
his proposal. This was a real windfall for Danton—so many
rivals removed from the running at one stroke!

That evening all Paris converged on the Tuileries. La Fayette
lifted the restrictions which turned the Palace into a prison. The
troops withdrew: the crowds surged through the gates, though
they were allowed no farther than the main courtyard. There
were shouts for the King to come out on the balcony. Louis XVI
and Marie-Antoinette appeared, accompanied by their children,
and the cheers with which they were greeted gave them the
impression that the flight to Varennes had been forgiven.

The person whom the masses found it less easy to forgive in

this connection was La Fayette. Besides, they still held the Champ-de-Mars incident against him. His revolutionary past was lost behind the shadow of the red flag. Realizing this, he submitted his resignation and retired, with his wife and daughters, to work off his rancor in his château in the Haute-Loire. He was beginning to appreciate the first law of revolutions: that those who make them invariably end as their victims.

His post was taken over by the Marquis de Mandat, an aristocratic career officer. By accepting command of the National Guard, however, this poor fellow was doomed, *ipso facto,* to become Danton's victim.

Danton himself was busy with his election campaign, making speeches to the Cordeliers, to the Jacobins, at Saint-André-des-Arts, canvassing votes all around. His friends were supporting him in various ways. They sang his praises in their newssheets. There was a popular ditty that went the rounds at this period; its couplets boasted of progress toward liberty, while its refrain went as follows:

> Do you want to be sure
> That all this will endure?
> Then choose good men and true
> For the legislature!
>
> Only vote for such men
> As Danton, and then
> We'll be happy forever,
> Forever, amen!

In one of his addresses, Legendre exclaimed: "The voters of Paris will be dishonored forever if Danton is not elected to the Legislative Assembly!"

But he was not.

On the evening of his defeat, his supporters flocked around to his house to offer their condolences. Blackballed yet again, Danton was sick of politics and had no intention of lingering in Paris. The day after the elections he left town again and returned to Arcis-sur-Aube, glad to be reunited with his family and breathe good fresh country air, redolent of field and woodland.

The first session of the Legislative Assembly was held on October 1. Curious bystanders crowded outside the doors of the Riding School to watch the new representatives pass in. The powdered wigs of the Constituent Assembly had given place to humbler citizens who wore their own straight hair: young, eager, pugnacious men, full of fire and spirit.

The Constitutional Royalists occupied the benches on the right; independent members were grouped in the center, while the revolutionary party installed itself on the left. The latter was drawn from several areas and walks of life and formed a somewhat heterogeneous collection. Among its ranks could be seen Chabot, the Cordelier and former Capuchin friar, and the legless cripple Couthon, who was still wavering between the policies of Danton and Robespierre. There were also a number of Jacobins who had been elected by the provinces—by the Gironde in particular. These Deputies—Vergniaud, Guadet, Gensonné, and Isnard—gradually modified their original extremism, allying themselves first with the Marquis of Condorcet, a physician originally from the Aisne region, and then with Brissot, the journalist and Paris Deputy, to form, jointly, what was known as the Girondist Party.

At first the majority continued to protect Louis XVI. The Assembly received him in great state and encouraged the royal family to appear in public once more. In accordance with this advice, they went to an evening performance at the Théâtre Italien, where the audience—following the lead of its elected representatives—gave the royal visitors a rousing welcome. Women were seen throwing flowers to Marie-Antoinette.

The former Deputy Pétion, one of the three who had escorted the royal family back from Varennes, was said to have fallen very much under their spell during the journey to Paris. More even than the King or Marie-Antoinette, it was Louis's twenty-seven-year-old sister Elisabeth who had captivated him, to the point where people declared he was in love with her. No doubt this was an exaggeration; but Pétion certainly made good use of the royal family's renewed popularity for his own ambitious purposes, and his relationship with Elisabeth must have helped him to do so. He dreamed of succeeding Bailly, who had been out of favor with the people since the shooting incident on the

Champ-de-Mars. But an unexpected candidate put himself up against Pétion: none other than La Fayette. The Marquis, however, did not collect three thousand votes, whereas Pétion received nearly four times that number, and—despite his reputation as a libertine—was duly proclaimed Mayor.

So Danton, through no direct action of his own, had triumphed over his two adversaries, Bailly and La Fayette, who were thus, most providentially, removed from his path. But though the General had retired to his estates, he could at any time return to Paris and become a danger once more. To get rid of him permanently, he had to be given a post well away from the capital. When he became Mayor, Pétion intrigued so thoroughly, and to such effect, that La Fayette found himself given the command of the so-called Central Army, which had its headquarters in Sedan. He went off obediently into exile—receiving the acclamations of the mob as he rode through Paris. This exhibition of public inconstancy only served to confirm the new Mayor's apprehensions.

Now that he was free of both the astronomer and the General, it might have been thought that Danton would promptly leave Arcis-sur-Aube and return to Paris. But as yet he did nothing of the sort. The politician was turning into a property dealer. He let out his Nuisement farm on lease to a man called Boursier, at a rent of 1200 *livres*. On October 28 he bought a stretch of woodland near Chesne, paying 2250 *livres* for it. On November 7 he acquired a garden for 240 *livres,* and on the 8th, a kitchen garden, which cost him 210. Furthermore, no less than five of his neighbors sold him parcels of land which increased the size of his "gentleman's park." All these transactions passed through the hands of Maître Finot—who also had to register a pension of 100 *livres,* which Danton made over to his old nurse, Mme. Hariot. He bought draft oxen, and livestock, and plows, and began to run his estates like any respectable *paterfamilias.* His wealth and courtesy won him universal approval. Out in the country he was known as "that pleasant gentleman Monsieur Danton," and everyone believed that their *nouveau riche* landowner was one of the grandest advocates in Paris.

The seventeen rooms of his manor house now housed Danton's entire family—not only his mother and stepfather, but his un-

married sister Anne-Pierrette, his sister Anne-Madeleine (plus
her husband Pierre Menuel and their five children), and Great-
aunt Anne Camus. The old nurse, Mme. Hariot, acted as
housekeeper; it was she who held the keys to all cupboards and
presses and was in charge of domestic staff.

Gabrielle, now pregnant for the third time, was hoping to
give Antoine a little sister. She had more confidence, however, in
her own Paris doctor than in the local Arcis physician. "We
ought to go back," she told her husband, and Danton agreed:
his friends, in their letters, were similarly urging him to return to
the capital.

Desmoulins and Lucile arrived in Arcis to hasten his decision.
The Club des Cordeliers wanted its leader back. Paris was going
to the polls to elect a new Public Prosecutor to the Commune,
together with a new First Deputy Public Prosecutor. (The
Second Deputy Public Prosecutor had been elected for a two-
year term, of which twelve months were still to run.) Danton
must, they said, run for Public Prosecutor—or, failing that, for
First Deputy. It would make a fine requital for his setback at the
elections for the Legislative Assembly.

Danton and Gabrielle returned to Paris and settled back into
their old apartment. Politics claimed him once more. There was
another election campaign to organize, with speeches to the
Cordeliers and the Jacobins, and at Saint-André-des-Arts. "Danton's waking up again," said his friends.

The election took place on December 2. M. Manuel, a
Jacobin, was chosen as Public Prosecutor, with Cahier de Gerville, a retiring member of the Constituent Assembly, as his
First Deputy. Danton had failed again. But no sooner were
the results known than Louis XVI appointed de Gerville Minister of the Interior. Was this mere coincidence, or was it
evidence of collusion between Danton and the Court? In any
case, the office of First Deputy Public Prosecutor was suddenly
vacant again, thus enabling Danton to canvass for it a second
time. It is hard to decide the truth in this case—though Danton's
relations with the government (denied by his friends, affirmed
by his enemies) leave a certain amount of room for speculation.

Another ballot was held, and this time Danton's candidature

was successful. He found himself elected First Deputy Public Prosecutor, with 1162 votes cast in his favor. His rival, Collot-d'Herbois, received only 654. This victory made Danton a powerful public official. From the material viewpoint, it brought him in a salary of 6000 *livres per annum*—a sum which that out-of-work actor Collot-d'Herbois must have been furious at missing. But to a man who had laid out something like 100,000 *livres* on the purchase of various properties during the past ten months, the 6000 *livres* must have seemed a mere pittance.

All the same, success went to his head. In his delight he told Gabrielle to redecorate their apartment. He himself visited gold-smiths and furniture makers, and soon pier glasses, crates of silverware, and piles of new linen were being delivered, discreetly, to the rue des Cordeliers. Fresh stocks of good bottled wine were added to the supplies already in the cellar. And everything was paid for in cash. Danton had come a long way since the days when he was forced to ask tradesmen for credit. Gabrielle could now enjoy the last stages of her pregnancy in the lap of luxury. Thank God, this child, and its elder brother, would be free from want.

Better than anything else, their father was settling down. In his new role as wealthy middle-class gentleman and respectable government official, he made no attempt to incite the people against the executive while waiting to take up his post. The latter ceremony was fixed for January 20, and Danton had to contain himself in patience for another forty days. It was a good opportunity to relax a little. Wearing a dressing gown, his legs stretched out toward the fire and a book propped up on his knees, the First Deputy Public Prosecutor sat and savored the joys of public success and domestic happiness. No harsh words of recrimination now passed his lips. The inhabitants of Arcis had not been mistaken when they referred to him as "that pleasant gentleman Monsieur Danton."

But the man of means nevertheless kept a close eye on the way events were moving. By now there were between eight and ten thousand *émigrés* gathered under arms at Coblentz, and this force constituted a serious threat to the régime. They were backed by the Emperor of Austria, and their blustering displays of rodomontade left Marie-Antoinette (who was the Emperor's sister) very uneasy. Besides, they were under the leadership of Louis's two brothers, the Counts of Artois and Provence, who were preaching a kind of holy war. Regarding the King as a virtual prisoner, the elder of these "Cains" (as Marie-Antoinette described them) proclaimed himself Regent. He formed a Ministry, presided over by M. de Calonne, and designated the Prince de Condé as Commander-in-Chief of his "armed forces." Faced with very real danger as a result of these personally compromising appointments, Louis XVI wrote to his brothers, requesting that they return to France. This request went unanswered. The King then signed a decree commanding "Monsieur" (the Count of Provence's official title under the terms of State protocol) to be back in Paris within two calendar months.

The Legislative Assembly did more than ratify this decree; they also passed one of their own, summoning the *émigrés* to return before January 1, under pain of being declared "suspect persons" and having their property confiscated by the State. But this time Louis XVI lashed out from between the shafts. His family affairs, he declared, were nobody's business but his own. In a raging fury he availed himself of his right of veto and rejected the decree.

Faithful to the terms of the Constitution, the Legislative Assembly gave way. Indeed, the Directory of the Seine *Département,* which had a large Royalist majority, sent the King a congratulatory address. At this, public unrest began to blaze up again—with Danton's supporters (though not Danton himself) sedulously fanning the flames. At the end of a petition attacking this address tooth and nail there could be seen the signatures of all the leading Cordeliers: Legendre, Camille Desmoulins, Billaud-Varenne, Hébert, Fournier the American, Saint-Huruge, and many others. Danton, still wrapped in his mood of easy-going expectation, did not sign this protest. "He's asleep," grumbled his supporters. "Maybe he's been bought off," his enemies suggested. But only a little patience was needed now. The huge lion was stirring from his slumbers and would soon, when the hour struck, shake the bars of his cage to some purpose.

Despite the clauses which neutralized the Declaration of Pilnitz as far as any practical action went, the Emperor by no
means discouraged the *émigrés* assembled in Coblentz. Faced
with this threat, the French government took steps to defend the
country against attack. Though composed mainly of *feuillants*—
that is, conservatives—the Cabinet nevertheless placed national
security above mere party interests. Three army groups received
orders to place themselves in readiness to combat any attempt at
invasion: those of Flanders, Lorraine, and Alsace. The first was
under the command of Marshal Rochambeau, who had served
as a lieutenant general in the American War of Independence.
The second was led by the unfortunate La Fayette; and the
third had as its commander Marshal Luckner, a Bavarian
mercenary who had been in the service of France since 1763.

On the old and well-tried principle that the best defense is
offense, one section of public opinion was moving little by little in
favor of carrying the war into the enemy's camp. It was at this
point that Danton, blinking into wakefulness like some great
drowsy tomcat, emerged from his torpor to deliver a speech at
the Jacobin Club. He emphasized the dangers of such war;
while admitting its inevitability, he argued that it should be
postponed until the last possible moment.

"Yes," he exclaimed, "the trumpets will sound for battle!
Yes, the avenging angel of liberty will strike down despotism and
all its henchmen! But, gentlemen—*when* should we embark
upon this war?" Not, in his opinion, until the country had dealt
with its internal enemies, who constituted a much greater threat
than the band of *émigrés* assembled on the banks of the Rhine.
Here he found himself in agreement with Robespierre, a resolute
opponent of all open hostilities.

On January 20, 1792, the First Deputy Public Prosecutor to
the Commune took up his duties. He was officially inducted by
Pétion and Manuel, the new Mayor and the new Public
Prosecutor, during a brilliant and glittering ceremony. To their
words of welcome Danton replied with a written, prepared
speech—the first of his political career. He began with a personal
apologia.

"The irresistible force of public opinion has brought me back from my rural seclusion, from my life as a humble farmer working a few fields that I purchased with the public compensation paid me for my now nonexistent position as Counsel. Yet my detractors have blown up this little property of mine into vast estates, paid for by secret agents of England or Russia, whose very existence is unknown to me. . . ."

A cool opening, to say the least of it; yet no bolder than what followed, when the speaker portrayed himself, "at the moment when our country is threatened from all sides, as a front-line sentry" keeping watch over national defense. He feared neither his personal adversaries nor the enemies of France. In a voice powerful enough to make them all quail, he declared: "I have been endowed by nature with the muscular body and harsh features of liberty. Exempt from the misfortune of being born in one of those privileged—and for that reason almost always degenerate—groups thrown up by our ancient institutions, I have preserved, as a wholly self-made person, every jot of my native vigor. Never for one moment, either in my private life or the profession I embraced, did I cease to demonstrate that I knew how to combine coolheaded reason with emotional warmth and firmness of character. If, since the very earliest days of our national regeneration, I have experienced all the most passionate manifestations of patriotic feeling; if I have allowed myself to appear exaggerated in my determination never to show weakness; if I have already been proscribed by the authorities for showing up, in their true colors, those men who wanted to put the whole Revolution on trial and for defending those who were described as the 'rabble-rousers of freedom'—all this was because I could see, very clearly, what one must expect from the traitors who openly protected the serpents of the aristocracy!"

The speaker did not actually name these traitors. Was he thinking of Bailly, La Fayette, Barnave, and Lameth? Yet on this occasion he was surrounded by La Fayette's supporters: the benches were overflowing with them.

Never faltering, Danton continued: "The truth is that my actions are constantly dictated by the eternal laws of justice. I cannot continue any relationship once it has become corrupt, or associate my name with people who do not scruple to apostasize

[5] The storming of the Tuileries, August 10, 1792. Sketch by Prieur. *(Photo by Bulloz)*

[6] The massacres at the Châtelet and at Bicêtre, September 2 and 3, 1792. From a contemporary engraving. *(Photo by Roger Viollet)*

from that religion of the people which they formerly defended. This is what my life has meant."

Having sketched this impression of his past, Danton now blocked in, with large, bold strokes, the general lines of his future. The defunct Assembly had drawn up a Constitution; the King had gone to the Riding School and sworn to uphold it. Time now for Danton to proclaim his allegiance to this charter. He said: "Whatever my individual opinions concerning men and affairs may have been at the time of the Constitution's overhaul, *now that it is sworn* I would demand the death penalty for any man—were he my brother, my friend, or my own son—who raised a sacrilegious hand to attack it. Such are my feelings in this matter. The general will of the French people, made no less solemnly manifest than their adherence to the Constitution, will always be my supreme law. I have consecrated my entire life to the people. No longer will their enemies attack or betray them with impunity. Very soon they will rise and purge the earth of all its tyrants, unless tyranny abandons the league it has formed against them. If need be, I will die in the defense of their cause—"

"We will die with you!" a voice called out, and a chorus of assent rose from the benches: "Yes, yes, we will die, too!"

Danton's peroration was a fine piece of soapbox rhetoric: "The people will have my dying prayers; only the people deserve them. Their courage and enlightenment have raised them from abject nothingness; their courage and enlightenment will render them immortal!"

"Bravo!" cried his audience, and even the moderates could not but help acclaim him. Then the Mayor took the tricolor sash of office and bound it around the First Deputy Public Prosecutor's waist. In one of the front seats, Gabrielle dabbed at her eyes, and her husband blew her a kiss. Proud and happy, he had just outlined, in this ringing yet calculated manifesto, the pattern of his militant destiny. As Aristide Briand was to declare, "a political speech is not a work of literature, it is *an act.*" One hundred and thirty years earlier, Danton had come to the same conclusion. This "act" of his on January 20, 1792, this resounding personal testament, was to make him one of the pillars of the Revolution.

Gabrielle's pregnancy was nearing its term: the doctor gave her another ten days or a fortnight. Lucile Desmoulins was also expecting a child, but she still had over five months to wait. The two women visited each other regularly and went out for walks together, the one displaying her condition, the other her beginner's fears concerning that unknown quantity, motherhood.

Since he did not want to tire his wife unduly, Danton no longer invited friends home to dinner. He was proposing numerous reforms in the Commune and in order to win support would entertain the waverers at meals in the Palais-Royal chop-houses. This cost him a good deal of money, and his detractors made such burdensome "love feasts" a ground of complaint against him, claiming that he spent anything up to 300 *livres* a head on them.

What came a good deal cheaper, on the other hand, were the long sessions Danton spent in Zoppi's, a café on the rue des Fossés-Saint-Germain (today the rue de l'Ancienne-Comédie). Zoppi himself was an Italian, who, like his illustrious forerunner Procopio, made the best mocha coffee in Paris. On the chairs where Danton rested his vast hams, men such as Boileau, Racine, or La Fontaine, and, later, Voltaire, d'Alembert, and Diderot, had sat before him. Everyone knew the history of this famous establishment. Procopio had come to Paris from Palermo in 1684, with the idea of spreading the coffee-drinking habit among Frenchmen. He opened a little shop in the rue des Fossés-Saint-Germain, opposite the Comédie, the most fashionable theater of the day. He served his customers with nothing but this blackish brew of his, to the exclusion of any other beverage. Mme. de Sévigné, whose literary and gastronomical predictions were equally shaky, declared that "Racine is a passing fad, like coffee." She did not like this new drink herself, and was irked by the spectacle of carriages stopping outside the "café" (a neologism coined for the occasion) while the occupants had a cup of the stuff brought to them without leaving their seat. Inside, in a large room with walls painted to resemble marble, a subdued gathering did homage to the new fashion and sat sipping the strange nectar from tiny ritual cups.

When Zoppi took over, this exclusiveness ended: in 1792 not

only mocha coffee but every other kind of drink was available. Zoppi was a native of Florence, and a fellow countryman of Danton's mother-in-law, Mme. Charpentier. With the one, as with the other, Danton enjoyed chatting in Italian. *"Mi da un cappuccino bollente,"* he would say, heavily stressing the tonic accent, and Zoppi would reply: *"Subito, Signor sostituto!"*

Another customer *chez Procope* was Legendre, who did not envy Danton his linguistic skill: all a butcher needs to know is how to cut up meat, and his friend remembered the 50,000 *écus* that were offered Legendre as an inducement to perform that service on Danton himself. Without Legendre's declaration, Danton would never have known a thing about this murderous project. The two of them spent many hours together at Zoppi's, talking politics with d'Églantine, Marat, Hébert, Saint-Huruge, or Momoro, whose support for Danton was mingled with a certain jealousy; of all his companions there was only one who felt nothing but admiration for him, and that was Camille Desmoulins.

While their wives were embroidering bibs or discussing their coming *accouchements,* the two friends were doing the rounds of the theaters. They were often to be seen at the Théâtre du Palais-Royal, then known as the Théâtre Montansier, from the pseudonym of its director, Marguerite Brunet. The First Deputy Public Prosecutor, according to gossip which he did his best to suppress, was one of the Montansier's sleeping partners. From the auditorium of this celebrated theater he would applaud famous actors and plays with revolutionary themes. Backstage, in Mme. Brunet's apartment, he met the admiring circle who paid court to this great performer. Conversation would go on far into the night, to the accompaniment of champagne and *petits fours.* It was here that Danton met the beautiful and coquettish Agnes de Buffon, still determined to lure him, by the promise of her favors, into joining her beloved Philippe's party. When the Duke of Orléans approached the pair, did he observe the dangerous game his mistress was playing? With a man like Danton, any woman was best advised to be on her guard. Or did the Duke intend to draw the demagogue over to his side at last by deliberately shutting his eyes until the crucial moment was reached? Incapable of arresting the movement he

had set in motion three years before, Philippe no longer knew
which way to turn. Laclos, after his defeat by La Fayette on
July 17, had returned to the active list and was now commanding an artillery regiment somewhere in the provinces.
With his secretary gone, the Duke was wavering between the
various factions laying siege to him. Sometimes he was taken in
tow by the prudent Mme. de Genlis, sometimes by Agnes de
Buffon, who urged him toward further intrigue; and sometimes
he went to lay his unhappy head on the breast of Grace Elliott,
that beautiful Englishwoman who came between Mme. de Genlis
and Mme. de Buffon, chronologically speaking, in the catalogue
of his mistresses.

Of these three women, only one was not on visiting terms
with Danton: Félicité de Genlis. The other two behaved very
amiably toward him; and if Mrs. Elliott had no desire to submit
her satin-smooth skin to the embraces of this hairy and energetic
monster, it looks as though Mme. de Buffon would not have
scrupled to do so had she thought it might help to win Philippe
the Regency. But there is no evidence that Danton had made
her his mistress by the beginning of 1792; at this period his
emotions were very much taken up with Gabrielle's imminent
accouchement.

The happy event took place on February 2: a second son was
born in the rue des Cordeliers. His parents named him François-
Georges, and they put him out to nurse with a farmer's wife in
l'Îsle-Adam, nine leagues outside Paris.

The situation on the borders remained disturbing. The
émigrés were still arming, and Austria continued to support
them. The Legislative Assembly wanted the government to present the Emperor with an ultimatum. But the various Ministers,
in their anxiety not to offend the Queen, postponed making a
decision for so long that the Assembly, losing all patience with
them, passed a vote of no confidence. The conservative Cabinet
was forced to offer Louis XVI its resignation, and the latter
had no option but to call on the Girondists to form a government. Among them were two men destined to play a vital part
in Danton's future: Roland and Dumouriez.

Roland was a native of Lyons, a former factory inspector

whose office had been abolished by the Constituent Assembly. He was spending the winter in Paris with the object of establishing his claim to a pension. Though he had no political talent, this senior civil servant nevertheless joined the Jacobin Club; their general attitude pleased his liberal instincts, while their relative moderation appealed to his sedately rational mind. His experience in administration had brought him a wide circle of acquaintances, which his wife's beauty duly transformed into more or less firm friends.

Twenty-two years younger than her husband, Manon Roland was the daughter of a Parisian engraver. More or less self-educated, this attractive girl had acquired during the course of her reading—mainly from Plutarch—a love of courage and the Republican virtues. Her *mariage de raison* gave her the pleasure, as a capable woman, of leading her husband by the nose just as she felt inclined. Cultured rather than educated, an odd mixture of seriousness and impulsive spontaneity, Mme. Roland nursed a dream of becoming—thanks to her mediocre husband —a kind of political Egeria. She shone both in her own salon and in other people's, so that every intelligent man in Paris was captivated by her. Her beauty did the rest. Manon, in fact, was the main reason for Roland's elevation to a ministerial post. On the advice of those Deputies who cultivated her friendship, Louis XVI offered the ambitious Mme. Roland's husband the portfolio of Minister of the Interior.

As for General Dumouriez, the new Minister of Foreign Affairs, he was an old acquaintance of Danton's. Both were Freemasons and had belonged to the Lodge of the Nine Sisters since 1786. They saw little of each other, however, since Dumouriez commanded the Cherbourg garrison; though whenever he came up to Paris on leave, the little general seldom missed a session at the Jacobin Club. Here he would meet Danton and converse with him. He was a poor public speaker and very rarely addressed the Club; but in private discussion his remarks proved him no less skillful or liberal-minded a thinker than any person present, and just as rich in original ideas. So it came about that when Louis XVI was compelled by the Legislative Assembly to dismiss his conservative government and call in the Girondists, the latter advised him to give Dumouriez the post of Foreign Minister.

Ever since the occasion of Robespierre's famous question— "What *is* a republic?"—the notion of such a régime had been gaining ground. Apart from Dumouriez, who remained a staunch traditional Royalist, all the new Ministers hoped for its establishment. Mme. Roland encouraged them in their aims. Having made herself the *éminence grise* of the Cabinet, this clever middle-class woman (who was very conscious of her own status) could not tolerate a situation in which Marie-Antoinette imposed her decisions on the King, while she herself, the engraver's daughter, was similarly manipulating the government. One or other of them had to go. And how could one bring about the overthrow of the monarchy without a war against Louis XVI's brother-in-law? If the campaign proved successful, and the Emperor was defeated, Louis himself could scarcely avoid abdicating. If it ended in disaster, the people were certain to turn against the person ultimately responsible—which meant, again, the King. This was why Mme. Roland was arguing in favor of war, and why every Minister except one, General Dumouriez, was making inflammatory speeches: to the Jacobins, in the Riding School, at Cabinet Committee level, or inside the Tuileries Palace.

The French army, however, was hardly in any state to fight. The emigration of many of its regular officers—who were drawn from the nobility—meant that replacements had to be recruited from more plebeian sources, and then trained. Furthermore, insubordination was rife in barracks; the mutiny of Château-vieux had by no means been forgotten, and was to cause Danton, in 1792, one of his biggest discomfitures as a public speaker.

The incident went back to August of 1790. Some Swiss Guards of the Châteauvieux regiment, on garrison duty at Nancy, had staged a mutiny. From his headquarters at Metz the Marquis de Bouillé dispatched nine battalions, posthaste, to deal with the rebels. This task force re-established order with such energy that the Commission of Inquiry sent out by the Constituent Assembly reported to the President: "It is not a town we have come to, but a graveyard." Thirty-two mutineers

were condemned to death by court-martial, and another forty
sentenced to thirty years in the galleys.

Eighteen months later the Legislative Assembly reprieved these
forty galley slaves. They were brought back from Brest, and
Paris gave them a heroes' welcome. The wagon on which they
traveled was smothered with garlands and bouquets. Its occupants, who were more dazed than delighted, still had on the
clothes and the special red cap issued to galley slaves. This cap
was in fact copied from the Phrygian bonnet worn in ancient
Rome by enfranchised slaves. The Jacobin Club organized a
banquet in honor of these forty unfortunates. The conservative
Club des Feuillants, anxious to curry favor with the populace,
took up a collection on their behalf in the Tuileries electoral
division.

Now this division's wealthiest constituent was none other than
Louis XVI himself, who contributed 110 *livres*. A messenger
was sent to the Jacobins by the Feuillants and presented them
with a sum totaling 1445 *livres*. But when he made allusion to
the King's generosity, Danton sprang up and took the floor. "I
am delighted," he thundered, "to see that the royal family has
become aware at last of the harm wrought by agents of the
executive. But can authority expiate its faults with such cheese-
paring acts of charity? The contribution is an insult!" While
congratulating humbler citizens on having subscribed to this
"fund of brotherhood," Danton asked, angrily, "by what right,
and what effrontery" Louis XVI could now offer money to the
men whom he should have defended eighteen months before
against "the traitor Bouillé." "How could a Châteauvieux soldier
who possessed the least spark of self-respect accept such a
gratuity?" he concluded. "I call for the *rejection* of this sum!"

"Reject! Reject!" cried the audience.

Such a hubbub arose in the end that it drowned everything
else—Danton himself no less than his critics. Judging that he
had gone too far, he decided to climb down a little. Hammering
the rostrum until relative silence was restored, he then consented
"to leave the matter of Louis XVI on one side," and suggested
that the King's courtiers had taken advantage of his good will.
Though he did not return to his earlier proposal of returning
the King's contribution, his final words were: "We shall ensure

that in future the King's advisers furnish him with proposals
worthier of a great nation."

His philippic was over: so much sound and fury expended on
so small a matter, a mere 110 *livres*. Yet the sum could, nevertheless, have brought relief to those poor devils in their misery;
had Danton forgotten that? As always, the most important thing
for Danton was to make his voice heard. Since Louis *had* made a
contribution, it was an insult to the Swiss Guards. But imagine
how eloquently Danton would have lashed the King if—alone
of all the well-to-do citizens in his constituency—he had failed
to donate a penny piece to the collection! Knowing Danton as
we do, it would be easy enough to compose this alternative
speech, in which the sovereign would be castigated for his
avarice.

Not, it would seem, that Danton himself had any cause to
complain of Louis's closefistedness. In the last resort his conduct
remains an enigma; unless, perhaps, we apply to him the judgment which Sainte-Beuve made on Mirabeau, the "plebeian
Count": "Mirabeau," said Sainte-Beuve, "did not sell himself;
he merely allowed people to pay him. There is a subtle distinction
between the two." If Danton accepted money, he certainly did
not feel that this bound him in any way. Moreover, since he
received it from such mutually hostile sources as Louis XVI, the
Duke of Orléans, and Pitt, he obviously steered his favors,
according to circumstances, in the direction of the highest
current bidder. Such a hypothesis, of course, also takes into
account his puerile need to sound off before an audience, to
spread himself, to impose his commanding presence on people.
There was a strong element of childishness in this herculean
character's makeup.

Robespierre was a very different proposition, as became apparent when the Incorruptible rose to speak against Danton's
proposal, on March 4, 1792. With his habitual lack of passion,
the former Deputy conceded that to return the King's offering
was a gesture that "had something right and generous-minded
about it, something worthy of Danton's patriotic feelings." But
could the Club dispose as it thought fit of sums that were not its
property, and had been raised for the alleviation of distress?
"The royal family's behavior as private individuals does not

concern us here. If, in their capacity as public servants, they do good, we shall willingly recognize the fact. If they do not, then we shall take steps to remind them of the people's rights." This more or less implied that—in sharp contradistinction to Danton —"The King would deserve our censure only if he had made *no* contribution."

The Jacobins followed the lead of their prophet. Robespierre ensured that those 110 *livres* reached the forty ex-prisoners for whom they were intended. But though he had been defeated, Danton bore no malice against the man responsible. To do him justice, such resentment was simply not in his nature. He was an odd character. In France—a nation so in love with eloquence that its Assemblies possess a speakers' rostrum—people are less prone to condemn Danton than in England, where the Chamber possesses no orators' podium, and each speaker addresses the House from his own place—an arrangement which tends to curb verbal flights of fancy. It may be desirable, in the present context, to quote Ralph Korngold, whose study of Saint-Just contained the following portrait of Danton:

> Danton was an exact equivalent of the contemporary American "boss" or ward heeler. Such men are generally corrupt, but they possess, incontestably, the gift of magnetizing mass audiences. They tend, for the most part, to be tall, jovial-looking characters, indulgent to vice and loyal to their friends. It is their primitive virtues which make them a menace to society and historical truth. Without those virtues, their political influence would be negligible, and if even so they chanced to become historical figures, biographers would not be tempted to set them on a pedestal which they ill deserve. Danton was a hedonist. Saint-Just remarked of his party: "They want to be happy and enjoy life." A legitimate desire, and one common to all mankind—but one to which only a hedonist would be capable of sacrificing all else.

If by "hedonist" we mean an adherent of that doctrine which sees pleasure as the prime object of life, then Danton was a hedonist to his fingertips. But pleasure, for him, took several different forms. There was the pleasure of being a good family man, never so happy as when surrounded by his wife, his children, and his possessions. There was the pleasure of the lover who used to boast that he rendered homage to his wife's charms every night of the week. There was the characteristically bourgeois pleasure to be derived from amassing a fortune and watching it bear fruit. There was the pleasure of being a dutiful son who settled annuities on his mother and his old nurse and was supporting almost all his immediate relatives in his manor house at Arcis. There were the pleasures of literature: did he not spend whole evenings reading French, Latin, Italian, or English writers? There was the pleasure of being an orator, a man who would, at the drop of a hat, take the floor on any topic and—carried away by his own natural eloquence—improvise arguments at random, sometimes with quite staggering good sense, sometimes with a crassness that called down reproofs on the speaker's head. Finally, there was the pleasure of destroying in order to rebuild, of wiping out the past in order to put a more justly ordered future in its place. A curious, Janus-like figure, one feels. France, the world, the cause of liberty—all owe him so much that we should hold his memory in the very deepest respect; yet on closer acquaintance it is almost impossible not to feel contempt for him.

It would be hard to conceive a more striking contrast than that other founder of the modern world, Robespierre. Here, certainly, was a man for whom pleasure held no temptations. His quarters in the house of M. Duplay, the joiner, consisted of a maid's garret, reached by a staircase so chilly it might as well have been a ladder. He had neither wife nor mistress— "a eunuch," Danton had called him—and his life was dedicated to public service. One peasant woman later exclaimed, when she heard of his tragic end: "Then there'll be no more happiness for us poor folk; they've killed the man who really loved us." This cry of anguish expressed the beliefs of millions in France. Yet did Robespierre *really* love the "poor folk" all that much? He let too many of them go to the scaffold for us to be certain. Yet he regarded these victims as enemies of social justice—or at least as indifferent to it, which in his view came to much the same thing. Besides, was he not accused of being responsible for atrocities which he had never ordered, which he opposed with all his strength, and often knew nothing about? Robespierre was not—this must be emphasized—a more bloodthirsty character than Danton; yet it took a hundred and thirty years of patient research before historians realized the fact. Fifty years ago Danton already had his own street and statue in Paris, whereas only one suburb, Montreuil, had thought of naming one of its thoroughfares after Robespierre. A tardy way of honoring the man whom Napoleon called "the scapegoat of the Revolution."

But in 1792 neither the Incorruptible nor his corruptible rival was concerned with this posthumous fame; both, in their very different ways, were fighting to achieve liberty. Robespierre saw in it the fulfillment of his ascetic ideal, while for Danton it promised to satisfy yet another aspect of his omnivorous hedonism.

The two men may have opposed each other over a minor matter such as whether or not to refuse the King's contribution to charity; but when it came to a vital issue like the war, both were in complete agreement. While the Girondists, together with Brissot and Roland and their respective supporters, were all in favor of declaring war on Austria, Robespierre and Danton roundly condemned such a policy and made no bones about the hazards it would involve.

Robespierre was now regretting his successful motion to debar retiring Deputies from re-election, since it meant that he could not argue the case for peace before the Legislative Assembly. He therefore fell back on the Jacobin Club and used it as a forum in which to debate this national issue. Danton, meanwhile, taking advantage of his official position as Deputy Public Prosecutor, was urging the cause of peace in the City Hall. But the majority of the Council were conservatives who supported La Fayette, and therefore aligned themselves with Brissot and his followers over the war issue. Their motives, however, were somewhat different. They did not believe that war was the way to bring about a republic (which the majority opposed in any case); on the contrary, they believed that a victory over Austria, won by La Fayette, would bring him back into favor and make him dictator of the country. On April 19 they protested vigorously when Danton, recalling the numerous and "useless wars of France's tyrants," demanded that their statues be removed

from the City Hall. Protestation swelled into uproar as the
speaker leveled a vengeful finger at the busts of Bailly and La
Fayette (which were presiding, as it were, over the proceedings)
and requested their sacrifice as well. Argument degenerated into
abuse, and from abuse it was a short step to physical violence.
Manuel, the Public Prosecutor, and Pétion, the Mayor, rushed
to Danton's aid. The three of them became the center of an
angry fracas, and a moment later knives flashed out to reinforce
the fists of their attackers. The National Guard had to be
called in to restore order. Danton went home to Gabrielle with
a split lip, torn clothes, and fury seething in his heart.

Brissot's policy of war with Austria gained ground steadily.
This influential member of the Legislative Assembly was supposed to be an innkeeper's son from the village of Ouarville,
near Chartres. Before the abolition of titles he had changed
the spelling of his birthplace, so as to give himself the flattering
name "Brissot de Warville." In actual fact, his baptismal certificate describes his father, Guillaume Brissot, as a master tailor.
But in any case, whether he was the son of an innkeeper or a
tailor, Brissot (a journalist by profession) was determined to
show the Emperor that France's armed forces—even after losing
many regular officers to the *émigrés*—still remained superior to
those of Austria. That would teach the Emperor's sister a lesson.
Some years previously, in 1784, Marie-Antoinette had had "M.
de Warville" thrown into the Bastille: it appeared that he had
composed a pamphlet impugning her virtue. Released from
jail through the good offices of Mme. de Genlis, at this time
the Duke of Orléans's mistress, Brissot called at her house to
thank her, was shown in by a maid, one Mlle. Dupont, and fell
in love at first sight with the maid. A little later he and Mlle.
Dupont were married. In 1792 he made a great play for Mme.
Roland; but the Minister of the Interior's wife did not bestow
her favors on all and sundry, even if they bore a name like
de Warville. Her pro-war activities made Brissot cultivate her
all the more—no doubt with the hope of leading her into close
combat of a more pacific nature. He declared, to everyone who
would listen, that "we should not allow ourselves rest until peace
reigns among men, and the world is made one country." And
how was this peace to be achieved without marching on those

who would have none of it and cannonading them into submission?

Such were the depressing antecedents of a war that was destined to last twenty-two years, and to bathe France—indeed, all Europe—in blood throughout Revolution, Consulate, and Empire. Girondists and supporters of Brissot saw such a conflict as a lever to topple the monarchy; conservatives, on the contrary, calculated that it would strengthen the King's position; while La Fayette's partisans thought it essential for their own leader's rise to power.

Torn among three doubtful and ambiguous allegiances—to the monarchy, the dream of Republicanism, and the Orleanist party—what was Danton to do? That, said his enemies, would depend entirely on financial considerations: he would throw in his lot with whichever leader—Louis XVI, Pitt, or the Duke—offered him the largest subsidies. No, his adherents declared, it was a matter of patriotism: he would be swayed by nothing except his conscience as a Frenchman.

Meanwhile he remained a mere spectator of events. He attended meetings of the Jacobin Club but no longer spoke there; and he would spend hours sprawled in the public gallery of the Legislative Assembly, listening to hotheaded speeches from the floor. To the Jacobins, Robespierre argued energetically against "a war contrived by enemies of the Revolution"; while in the National Assembly, Brissot, amid great general excitement, declared: "A people that has won its freedom after twelve centuries of slavery needs a war to consolidate it. . . ." Fears that other countries would join Austria Brissot swept aside with a wave of the hand. "The English nation is well disposed toward us," he said, "and their government would shrink from going against the nation's wishes. Spain is intimidated. Prussia will not dare to move. This war cannot last for long, and is unlikely to have any great effect on trade."

Robespierre replied to this harangue in the Assembly with a speech delivered from the rostrum of the Jacobin Club. "Before you rush off to Coblentz," he said, "at least make adequate preparations for fighting the war first! It would be madness to open hostilities now. We need to manufacture guns. The people must be armed. . . ."

The battle of words went on and on. For Robespierre the war "would be utter disaster unless it was a holy war." For Brissot, it would firmly establish the conquests of the French people. "You do not *decree* a holy war," the Incorruptible retorted, "you *preach* it. Then the masses will rise against the crowned heads that oppress them. But in such a case it is the various foreign powers involved who must give the signal for battle. Are we to offer the sovereigns of Europe the role of peace lovers, and to put the appearance of right and justice on their side? No, no—set your own house in order before you attempt to bring the blessings of peace elsewhere!"

For some time now Camille Desmoulins had been one of Brissot's supporters. In his patriotic fervor the Lantern Attorney was baying with the wolves. In his newssheet he described all those who opposed the venture as "petty shopkeepers, more afraid of revolutionaries than of uhlans."

And what was Danton waiting for? Why did he not join this universal concert, bang the big drum with the rest of them? He was keeping quiet, reserving his strength, watching for the right moment. That impenetrable wall of silence behind which he had retreated was a source of amazement to his friends. "Danton's asleep," people said, not for the first time. When the remark was reported to him he replied: "Have patience: Danton will wake again." His duties as First Deputy Public Prosecutor were not arduous; Manuel, his superior, though very well disposed toward him, left him little work to do.

Between Brissot's propaganda and the fear of the *émigrés*, all France was rapidly succumbing to war fever. With both the Legislative Assembly and the *vox populi* urging him on, Louis XVI could equivocate no longer. His Ministers, too, were pressing him to act—above all, Roland, spurred on by the promptings of his wife. Even Dumouriez was won over to his colleagues' viewpoint. The little general, who had served the Kings of France for thirty years, remembered their traditional policy —the overthrow of the House of Austria. Now this dynasty had changed its master. Leopold had died on March 1, to be succeeded by his son, Francis II. The latter—Marie-Antoinette's nephew—was a fiery militarist; Metternich described him as "a prince with statesmanship in his blood." For the new Emperor, the Revolution was a chancrous growth, to be burned out with a red-hot iron. One more reason to defend France by stealing a march on this future adversary!

On April 20 the Legislative Assembly, by a huge majority, voted for war. Only seven Deputies were against the motion. Having no option but to implement this decision, Louis XVI declared war "against the King of Bohemia and Hungary," a subtlety designed to avoid hurting the feelings of Marie-Antoinette, "the Austrian woman." In order to pay the various army contractors, who were only too delighted by the turn events had taken, the Treasury was forced to issue more promissory notes than the actual state of the country's resources warranted. Here was the first flaw in Brissot's ill-forged blade. And though he had asserted, in a recent speech, that Prussia would not dare to move, nevertheless the Prussians—invoking their treaty of alliance with Austria—now came to her defense.

The Austrian and Prussian armies advanced upon the French border, by the northern route. Their approach caused panic in General Théobald Dillon's two army corps. After retreating as far as Lille, they mutinied and murdered their Commander-in-Chief. At Quiévrain, the Duke de Biron's division similarly disintegrated at first sight of the enemy.

Faced with catastrophes of this magnitude, would Danton break silence at last? At the Jacobin Club people crowded around him, plied him with questions. In moments of panic France always found a hero to save her. Would Danton emerge as the new Messiah? To force his hand, a majority vote was passed offering him the presidency in succession to Alba-Lasource. Danton accepted the offer. To loud acclamation he was installed in the presidential chair, and presented with the official hand bell. So the founder of the Cordeliers became the President of the Jacobins. All public opinion was now his to mold in those powerful hands of his. But he chose to inaugurate his new office by paying tribute to Robespierre, with whose views, for once, he found himself in agreement. He did not, like the Incorruptible, stigmatize the declaration of war as a tragic blunder (no point in wasting time on a *fait accompli*); instead, he took advantage of a ridiculous debate to extol the former Deputy from Arras.

That asinine character Tallien proposed a motion debarring tax defaulters from admission to the Club. "Since soldiers pay the State with their blood," he declared, "civilians should pay in taxes." An arguable proposition in different circumstances, Robespierre declared, rising to speak against Tallien. The Revolution had destroyed credit and ruined the small tradesman. The people were hungry. Like customers anywhere, they felt resentment against their suppliers. Tax defaulting was a natural consequence of such a state of affairs. For months now Robespierre's audience had been worked on by the warmongers, and his reasoned argument produced an uproar. For half an hour he struggled to make himself heard amid jeers and insults. What his interrupters were really attacking him for was his foresight. They had wanted this war, and it had begun disastrously—just as the Incorruptible had predicted it would. What fools can never forgive is a prophet who is proved right by events. Amid the loud hubbub individual words of abuse were audible. "Despot!" someone shouted.

At this, Danton exploded. Rising in his presidential seat he brought the meeting to order. "M. Robespierre," he shouted, "has never exercised any despotism here save that of pure reason."

"Well," someone observed, "the demagogue's awake."

"I am not a demagogue," Danton replied, "and for a long while now I have kept silent with very great difficulty. I shall unmask those who boast of having served the commonweal; I shall contribute all I can to the triumph of liberty. A time may well come—and that time is not so far off—when there will be grave need to speak out against those who, for the last three months, have been impugning the courage of a man to whose bravery the whole Revolution bears witness. It is not so long since his enemies were describing that courage of his as obstinacy and ruthlessness: but they never slandered him as his present opponents have done!"

So Danton, without hesitation, spoke out in defense of Robespierre's courage and honesty; though whether he approved of the Incorruptible's politics is another matter. Of that, the future would judge. In any case, he disappointed those who were relying on the leader of the Cordeliers—now the leader of the Jacobins—to bring some spark of hope into the general mood of panic.

The situation on the border was getting steadily worse. Marshal de Rochambeau was forced back from Furnes by the combined Austro-Prussian advance, and retreated as far as Tournai. In the Ardennes, La Fayette saw his advance posts compelled to fall back on Maubeuge, and set off thither himself, abandoning Sedan. Then, suddenly, came the news that three regiments —the Royal German Regiment, the Saxony Hussars, and the Bercheny Hussars—had gone over, bag and baggage, to the enemy. The Minister of War, panic-stricken, submitted his resignation to the King. To replace the Marquis de Grave, Louis sent for General Servan. This friend of Roland's got the Legislative Assembly to pass one public-security measure: a force of twenty thousand National Guards was to be concentrated outside the walls of Paris. Why did Louis XVI apply his veto to this decree? Doubtless Marie-Antoinette—"Madame Veto"— was in some way connected with the mutiny. Better still (or much worse, depending on how you looked at it), he proceeded to dismiss three of his Ministers. Servan went first—a natural casualty of the veto. He was followed by Roland and Clavière, respectively Minister of the Interior and Minister of Finance. As for Dumouriez, the King switched him from Foreign Affairs to the War Ministry.

At this point Danton suddenly woke up completely. "I hereby undertake," he declared before the Jacobins, "to put the fear of God into this perverse Court! The only reason why the executive has showed such audacity is because we have been too easygoing."

How did he plan "to put the fear of God" into the occupants of the Tuileries? First, by forcing the Legislative Assembly to make a more equitable distribution of the war levy, so that the wealthy were forced to pay proportionately more than the poor. Next, by once more compelling the Legislative Assembly—on the threat of calling out the mob—to pass a law which would oblige Louis XVI "to repudiate his wife and send her back to Vienna, with all the consideration, amenities, and safeguards to which she is entitled." Thus "the House of Austria, which has always brought troubles upon France," would no longer have any private or dynastic motives for interfering in her domestic politics.

This was to neglect the fact that it was France, not Austria, who had declared war; but Danton cared nothing for such logical quibbles. It also left out of consideration the personal will of a sovereign who, appearances to the contrary, did not lack for stubbornness.

If this scheme of a royal divorce caused amusement among the plebs, it thoroughly alarmed Dumouriez, and left La Fayette speechless with rage. Dumouriez resigned on June 16. While the King was forming a new Cabinet of obscure conservatives, the Legislative Assembly received a letter from La Fayette, in "the entrenched fortress of Maubeuge." This communication begged them to safeguard the fate of France by taking some thought for the French army, which was desperately short of all essentials—men, munitions, food, and clothing.

"Do not reject this plea," La Fayette wrote. "It comes from those who are the true friends of your authority." To this request he appended certain others, concerning the immunity of the executive and the independence of the sovereign, as laid down by the Constitution. Finally—and here was the bomb that was to explode in Danton's hands—the General demanded that "the régime of the clubs be extirpated at your hands, and replaced by the rule of law; that their usurpations of power give way to the firm and independent exercise of properly constituted authority, and their anarchic slogans to the two principles of freedom; that their frenzied fury yield before the calm and unwavering courage of a nation that knows its rights, and is determined to defend them; that their sectarian conflicts be subordinated to the true interests of the country as a whole, which, in a moment of crisis, should unite all those *who do not regard its enslavement and ruin as a subject for vile rejoicing and infamous speculation.*"

This red-hot verbal broadside of La Fayette's was obviously aimed at Danton and his supporters. Since he felt no fear of them, he was able to write, in justification of his outspokenness: "Here, among my brave troops, timid sentiments would be unthinkable." Was he relying on these "brave troops" of his to restore order in Paris—and, if need be, to carry him, La Fayette, to power?

In the Legislative Assembly, for all that the Girondist Guadet described him as "a second Cromwell," most of the Deputies approved of the General's attitude. For some time now the unwarranted interference practiced by the clubs in political matters had been irritating them considerably. After all, Deputies were elected by the people; they regarded themselves as quite experienced enough to conduct the business of legislation without any advice from the Jacobins and the Cordeliers, whose membership did not depend on public suffrage. They were getting thoroughly fed up with these irksome nuisances. However, they did not dare make an open attack on men such as Danton, Robespierre, or Marat. After a heated discussion, therefore, they decided to take no immediate or dramatic action on the letter from Maubeuge, and passed to the order of the day.

But at the Jacobin Club it was a very different matter. Danton had found a sublime, magnificent, and quite unexpected chance to attack his old adversary, with all the invective at his command. After Collot d'Herbois, Robespierre, and Desmoulins had worked off their indignation, Danton took the floor. He began, ironically: "Doubtless we should regard the day on which La Fayette reveals himself in his true colors to all France as something of an auspicious occasion. Now all the masks are stripped away, he can never again be quite so dangerous." Then, in more serious tones, he demanded the dispatch of two petitions: the first to the National Assembly, asking that it should request the General to appear before the Bar of the House; and the second to all the constituencies, begging them to send similar petitions to the Legislative Assembly themselves.

Danton also flattered himself that he could foresee La Fayette's reaction: even if the Deputies did not refuse such an appeal, the General was sure to. "He will not obey, I am convinced of it," Danton declared. "He'll go over to the enemy, without a doubt."

At the same moment, a similar debate was going on in the Club des Cordeliers. Danton had attended the Club's meetings less often since he had found Legendre and Marat acquiring

an influence over them that rivaled his own, and—above all—
since a newcomer called Santerre had arrived, bringing with
him his reputation as "the Father of the Back Streets." This
was what the humble folk in the *quartier* called him: Santerre
was always ready to lend a sympathetic ear to their troubles. A
brewer by trade, he had been present at every major affray of
the Revolution. He had fought beneath the walls of the Bastille
and had, besides, saved the lives of several wounded defenders
whom he took into his own house and had nursed by his family.
As a battalion commander in the National Guard, he had
followed La Fayette to Versailles on October 5, 1789, and
attempted, though unsuccessfully, to protect the palace. A partisan of the Revolution (though opposed to pointless atrocities)
Santerre was experienced enough to sense, the evening before
June 20, 1792, the first warning symptoms of the storm that
was to culminate in the famous invasion of the Tuileries.
Whipped into a frenzy by mob orators, the whole of Saint-
Antoine swore to take revenge for the dismissal of the Ministers
by slaughtering the royal family. La Fayette's letter was the
last straw, the ultimate excuse for an outburst of mob violence.
Agitators from the Jacobins and the Cordeliers, eager to fish in
these troubled waters, hurried down to the Faubourg Saint-
Marcel and urged its inhabitants to join their comrades from
the Quartier Saint-Antoine.

Since he could not arrest this torrent, Santerre resolved to
place himself at its head and canalize its flow, so as to avoid
the worst. Accordingly he preached revolt throughout his constituency. He was joined by Pétion; and so it came about that
the Father of the Back Streets and the Mayor of Paris found
themselves leading a memorable demonstration, in which Danton
played no part. The brewer maintained discipline of a sort
among those who profaned the sanctity of the Throne; and
though he could not stop the crowd manhandling Marie-Antoinette and forcibly adorning Louis XVI with the red cap
of liberty, at least he saved their lives.

For about four hours the people filed past that little group—
the King, wearing a galley slave's bonnet; Marie-Antoinette,
worn to breaking point yet still maintaining an outward air of
impassivity; Louis's sister, Madame Elisabeth; and the royal

children. Finally a junta consisting of three Deputies—Isnard, Vergniaud, Merlin de Thionville—together with Pétion, the Mayor, Manuel, the Public Prosecutor, and Santerre himself, managed to get the crowd out of the palace. By eight o'clock in the evening the Tuileries were empty again. Louis XVI tore off his Phrygian bonnet and trampled it in his fury.

When Danton learned from Prudhomme how far the courage displayed by the King and Queen had restored their prestige in the eyes of the masses, he exclaimed: "This bitch of a Revolution's done for: the patriots have got nothing out of it, nothing!" And when Legendre boasted of having told Louis XVI, to his face, "Sir, you are a traitor!" Danton spat at him: "And where do you think *that* will get you, you half-wit?"

CHAPTER IX

The Mystery of August 10

WHEN HE ASSERTED that La Fayette, on being summoned before the Bar of the Assembly, would take fright and go over to the enemy, Danton was very much mistaken. Though in fact the General received no orders to appear before the Deputies, he nevertheless did so, of his own volition. When the news of the march on the Tuileries reached Maubeuge, he was horrified —so much so that he temporarily turned over his command to Marshal Luckner and set off at full speed for Paris.

On June 28 he appeared in the Riding School and insisted on being given a hearing. When he rose to speak at the Bar of the Assembly, the Right applauded, while the Left maintained a reproving silence. The Girondist Deputy Isnard declared: "Since none but the most pressing reasons can have made a Commander-in-Chief abandon the post in which his country has placed him, I demand that M. La Fayette be given an undisturbed hearing."

The General spoke for no more than five minutes. Since he mistrusted his own powers of eloquence, he had prepared a written speech. As he read it, he placed before the Assembly various addresses composed by "the officers, noncommissioned officers and men" whom he commanded, his "brave companions in arms," who, he said, shared his own indignation at the offense committed against the Constitution by this violation of the King's personal immunity, which it guaranteed. Red in the face with emotion, he concluded: "I beg the National Assembly, first, to order that the instigators and ringleaders of the acts of violence committed on June 20 be brought to trial and punished as criminals, guilty of *lèse-nation;* and second, to stamp out a certain *sect* which is usurping the sovereignty of the nation and tyrannizing its citizens, and whose public debates leave no room for doubt concerning the abominable nature of the projects envisaged by its leaders." Quite plainly, La Fayette was referring to the Jacobins and Cordeliers. Since, like many Parisians, he believed that Danton was behind the outrage inflicted on the King, the General made no bones about attacking him. In doing so alone and far away from his army, he displayed considerable courage.

The Girondist Guadet, who had described La Fayette as a "Cromwell" after the reading of his letter, now rose to question the legality of his presence in Paris. "Maybe," he observed ironically, "we have no further enemies beyond the frontiers. Doubtless the Austrians have been defeated." Then, becoming serious again, he demanded that the Minister of War, who was present during this debate, should be "questioned by the President of the Assembly, to find out whether he had granted M. La Fayette a leave of absence in order to come to Paris."

An acrimonious discussion followed, which ended with the Legislative Assembly voting, by 339 votes to 234, against authorizing its President to interrogate the Minister along these lines. It further decreed that the Committee of Twelve should examine the Commander-in-Chief's petition.

One eyewitness, a bookseller named Eymery, left this sketch of what took place next: "On leaving the Assembly, the General went to seek audience of the King. Some were alarmed by this move, others took it as a hopeful sign: but it left everyone curious, with the result that a large crowd followed La Fayette to the Tuileries and was still waiting when he came out. He was escorted home to numerous shouts of 'Long live the nation!' mingled with frequent cries of 'Long live La Fayette!' A Maypole was set up outside his door, adorned with red, white, and blue ribbons, symbolic of liberty. A section of the National Guard offered him a guard of honor, with their compliments."

This resurgence of La Fayette's popularity—courage always pays off—did not please Danton at all. Instances of La Fayette's gallantry (without including the American campaign) now included the events of July 14, 1789, those of October 5 and 6 in the same year, that of April 18, 1791, and, finally, the incident of the Champ-de-Mars—four affrays in which Danton had been conspicuous by his absence, and the last of which had precipitated his flight to England.

Faithful to this habit of his, he lay very low during La Fayette's stay in Paris. It was not that he feared the General himself so much as the mass of his supporters. But when the Marquis—after a sojourn of only forty-eight hours—took off again for Maubeuge, Danton at once let fly. The Cordeliers marched in procession, with great ceremony, to the gardens of the Palais-Royal, where they proceeded to burn La Fayette in effigy; and the electoral district of the Théâtre-Français called for "the sword of justice to descend on the head of Bouillé's accomplice."

Such actions did not prevent the Directory of the Seine *département,* who had been much impressed by the General's appeal, from suspending Pétion and Manuel from office for the part they had played in the events of June 20. Though they evicted the Mayor and the Public Prosecutor, they did not include Danton (the Public Prosecutor's First Deputy) in the list of those suspended. By leaving him where he was, they were making a *de facto* admission that he had played no part in the affair. So Danton's supporters could argue that he, faithful as ever to the Constitution, had never associated himself with any act that violated it; while his adversaries and rivals could murmur, behind the scenes: "Naturally—the King's paying him not to."

Though the pressure on the border was becoming more intense, as yet there had been no direct and formal encounter between the French army and the forces of Austria and Prussia. But on July 6—three days after La Fayette's return to Maubeuge—Louis XVI sent the following message to the National Assembly: "The advance of Prussian troops, to the estimated number of fifty-two thousand, and their massing on our frontier, is proof of concerted action between the governments of Vienna and Berlin. Hostilities in this region are imminent, and I am counting upon all Frenchmen to present a bold, united front, so that we may combat and repulse these enemies of our country and of liberty."

Whether Louis XVI drafted this proclamation himself or simply put his signature to a text supplied by his Ministers, he was in either case demonstrating his fidelity to the Constitution. At the same time, he was betraying the cause of the *émigrés* assembled at Coblentz, who had sworn to restore his absolute power. If they proved victorious, these ultra-Royalists might even bring the King to trial; his proclamation certainly entitled them to do so. They considered their cause as sacred, and now Louis XVI himself had betrayed it. His position was a terrible one to be in. Sending secret subsidies to the exiles and lending clandestine encouragement to their activities, the unfortunate monarch had attempted a difficult double game, one far too complex for his mediocre intelligence.

Alarmed by his message, the Assembly formally declared a state of national emergency. On July 11 it ordered steps to be taken for the enlistment of volunteers. Throughout the country platforms were erected, decked with red, white, and blue ribbons, where (from the 22nd onward) recruits were signed on. There was one at the Carrefour Buci, a few yards down from Danton's house. He went and made a jingoistic speech there, but did not enlist himself. Nor did any of his friends.

Camille Desmoulins was in a state of vague but cheerful euphoria. Since July 6 he had been a proud father. Lucile had given birth to a baby boy, named Horace after the Roman patriot. The child was put out to nurse at l'Îsle-Adam, with the same farmer's wife who already had the Dantons' younger son in her charge. Lucile, seeing the way events were shaping, wanted all her time free to support her husband: the wife in her triumphed over the mother.

The capital was also being invaded by large numbers of Federates from the provinces. This was the name given to delegates from the various *départements* to the new Feast of the Federation on July 14. As in 1790, it was celebrated on the Champ-de-Mars. Six hundred men of Marseilles marched through the streets singing the "Hymn to the Army of the

Rhine." Composed in Strasbourg by an officer whose name nobody knew, and subsequently carried to Marseilles by various
travelers, this tune was now taken up in Paris and given the
title of the "Marseillaise."

Danton harangued the leaders of the delegations at the Club
des Cordeliers, while Robespierre preached to them in the Club
des Jacobins. Danton was present on this latter occasion and
took the opportunity to reopen hostilities against La Fayette.
"What can the Federates do for the safety of their country?"
he cried. "Either their presence must establish the reign of
liberty forever or else that liberty is doomed. The nation is
counting upon them. They must swear not to disperse until the
traitors in our midst have been punished by law or, better,
have fled the country. There exists, under the Constitution, a
means of expressing and satisfying the national will. The right
of petition does not lie buried beneath the Champ-de-Mars
with the bodies of those whom *they* have slaughtered there!"

Despite this incitement to riot, the new Feast of the Federation passed off calmly enough. Once more the King swore
fidelity to the Constitution on the Altar of the Fatherland.
Everyone present repeated the words of the oath after him. But
the lighthearted atmosphere of 1790 had been replaced, two
years later, by an oppressive sense of foreboding. Both the people and the Court felt that dire events were in store. Marie-
Antoinette, ensconced in her pavilion, could no longer restrain
her tears. Pétion and Manuel, now restored by the Assembly
to their positions as Mayor and Public Prosecutor, attended the
ceremony *ex officio,* together with Danton as First Deputy. All
three were dressed in black, with the tricolor sash across their
front; and all three were as tense as the rest of that vast assembly—the royal family, the Deputies, the Federates, the
crowds jostling one another across the Champ-de-Mars.

Everyone was nervous, though nobody could have said precisely why. The most apprehensive of all were those men who
had believed themselves in charge of events and now saw the
situation getting beyond their control. Uneasily, the revolutionaries began to feel the Crown regaining its influence over public
opinion—aided by a war-induced mood of pessimism. Some of
them thought the best policy was to foster fear deliberately,

whip it up to the limit, as a way of giving their partisans fresh heart. Danton did not share this view; but circumstances soon arose which made him change his mind very rapidly.

A certain public letter-writer named Dupart, who lived near the Church of Saint-Eustache, received—from some supporter of Philippe d'Orléans—a very singular commission. His client showed him one letter written by Bertrand de Molleville, the former Minister of Marine, and another by the Queen. Dupart, who happened to be an expert forger, set about the mysterious task demanded of him: to compose a certain list of names, which was to pass as being drawn up by Bertrand de Molleville and annotated by Marie-Antoinette.

One curious aspect of this affair is that the forger was not paid in cash, or even promised cash and then bilked of it. The bait in his case was a woman, and one calculated to tempt any man: that famous, unbalanced, impulsive amazon Théroigne de Méricourt. Dupart had been paying court to her, unsuccessfully, for months. Later, on August 10, this young virago was to kill a journalist with her own hands. Now she expressed herself as quite willing to sleep with Dupart. Had he not accepted the frightful risk involved in forging the handwriting of the Queen and a former Minister simply for the pleasure of holding Théroigne in his arms? Besides, it was all in a good cause. When one was a Republican, what would one not do to bring about the abolition of the monarchy? She lived in the rue de Tournon, a few yards down from the rue des Cordeliers. Danton knew her well and regarded her, on the basis of her unconventional qualities, as an emotionally disturbed person.

At the time he had no inkling of the extraordinary bargain that had been struck between her and Dupart. He had just packed his wife and little Antoine off to stay with his in-laws at Fontenay; some premonition had told him to get them out of the way. Since his evenings were now free, he accepted an invitation from the Duke of Orléans. Philippe gave occasional dinner parties for his friends at the Château de Mousseaux; a chosen few would stay the night. For a long while now the populace had given up calling him the Duke of Orléans, and instead referred to him by the semimocking sobriquet of "Philippe Égalité," in reference to his revolutionary tendencies. He had been one of the first to accept the abolition of titles, and in the end he took "Égalité" as his official surname.

So Danton found himself asked down to Mousseaux by Égalité where his fellow guests included both Orleanists and Republicans. There was good food and drink, much desultory conversation. It is not possible to fix the precise date of this occasion: it must have been between July 15 and 20. The details of the scene after dinner are provided by the Count de Lamothe-Langon, Permanent Secretary to the Council of State under the Empire, Prefect of Toulouse, a protégé of Cambacérès, the Lord Chancellor, and author of a volume of *Memoirs* published in 1837. This is the source for the story of M. Dupart, the public letter-writer of Saint-Eustache: there can be no question, this time, but that Lamothe-Langon actually composed the reminiscences in question.

Among the guests was Roederer, Public Prosecutor for the Seine *département* (an authority separate from the Municipality of Paris); and it was Roederer who in 1815, as a Count of the Empire, was to communicate this extraordinary story to Cambacérès, in the presence of Lamothe-Langon, who reproduced it in his *Memoirs*.

"As I recall," he makes Roederer say, "it was at a dinner party at Mousseaux, between July 15 and 20, 1792, that we were shown a list written in a hand said to be that of Bertrand-Molleville, the former Minister of Marine, and annotated by Marie-Antoinette. Unless some extremely clever forger had been at work, what we had here was a list of three hundred names, divided into five categories: (1) those to be executed; (2) those to be sent to the galleys; (3) those condemned to life imprisonment; (4) those to be banished in perpetuity; and (5) those to be imprisoned or exiled for limited periods. All categories were equally liable to confiscation of property *in toto*. In the first column [that of those condemned to death] were the names of three Dukes—Orléans, Biron, Aiguillon—and sixty members of the Constituent Assembly, together with Robespierre, Pétion, Lameth, and Marat, though our group was not represented. The second column contained almost as distinguished a collection (I had the honor to appear there myself, in very good company); the Duke of Liancourt headed the third, and 'Monsieur,' the King's brother, the fourth."

This mixed bag was not only eclectic, but chosen with some skill. Along with the revolutionary group (which included both nobles and commons) there had been included "Monsieur," the self-styled "Regent," who was posing in Germany as deputized guardian of the Crown, and who—through his incitement of the *émigrés* against France—had been originally responsible for Louis XVI's adventures in double-dealing. Inclusion of a prince whom the Queen had referred to as "that Cain" was calculated to give any list which bore her annotations a certain air of authenticity. This was rendered even more plausible by the fact that Danton's name did not figure on the list of victims— which agreed very well with the belief that he had been bought off by the Court.

"This infamous piece of work," Roederer is reported as declaring, looked absolutely genuine. According to Pétion, he had got it from Madame Campan, which was quite untrue; but at the time one was ready to believe anything—especially anything alarming. The Duke of Orléans looked quite flabbergasted, while Sillery and Voidel practically collapsed. Barbaroux—who already saw himself, together with Vergniaud, toiling away at a life sentence in the galleys—asked what we intended to do, and then said: "I've taken *my* decision. All I'm waiting for is the men of Marseilles. When they come, I'm going to put myself at their head, march on the Palace, and kill the King and Queen—or die fighting my way in."

As his account goes on, we see Philippe Égalité's guests becoming increasingly panic-stricken. Among them was the Incorruptible, constrained by the gravity of the times to prostitute himself at the Duke's table. Philippe wanted "to go back to England" and have Robespierre accompany him.

Suddenly Danton burst out: "I'll cut the throat of any bastard who pulls out now! F—— it, the thing's done, we've got to go through with it. Talking won't get us anywhere. Barbaroux is right—let's follow him and storm the Tuileries. Strong action will take the Royalists off their guard—they'll panic and retreat, and then we'll have won the whole game hands down."

Pétion then mentioned one obstacle that stood in the way of this murderous project: the National Guard, apart from two or three battalions, were all staunch monarchists. He spoke of "removing" General de Mandat, La Fayette's successor as Commander-in-Chief.

"What do you mean, *remove* him?" Danton said. "Kill him, man! The dead can't come back."

"This suggestion for getting rid of poor Mandat," Roederer went on in his 1815 account of the episode, "astounded several of us who were present. Danton's reply to our comments was: 'Better to eat the lion than be eaten by it.' We could have argued that such an attitude lacked common sense, not to mention honor; but no one spoke up. So it was decided to launch an attack on the Palace as soon as sufficient Marseillais could be found to give the Parisian mob a lead."

Referring to Philippe's financial embarrassments, Roederer concluded with these words: "A certain *person,* who was constantly being promised the Crown, supplied what money he had left to pay the men of August 10. Here was one person who found himself conned all along the line—and richly deserved it. The party broke up at this point. We all went off to tell our friends about the aforementioned proscription list. . . ."

So, if we are to believe Lamothe-Langon and Roederer, it was the fear provoked by a forged list of men, supposedly condemned by the Court, which spurred those listed to overthrow the agents of their condemnation. A people's destiny depends on odd things. And if Danton was really in receipt of payments from the Crown, was his terror of being added to the list the reason for his break with the monarchy? In his *Memoirs* La Fayette asserts that one of Louis XVI's agents paid Danton 50,000 *écus* "to turn the coming insurrection in the King's favor." The "person" referred to by Roederer (i.e. the Duke of Orléans) may well have also greased Danton's palm. Whom are we to believe? It is practically inpossible to disentangle the thread of all these mysterious undercover deals, only known to us through *Memoirs* which must be treated with infinite caution as a source of evidence.

Whatever the truth of the matter, it is certain that Danton now began to make every preparation for the overthrow of the royal family. Having taken command of the movement, he began by enlisting the support of the very lowest strata of society. Hitherto such persons had contributed little to the Revolution—which was made by a bourgeois group for the benefit of the bourgeoisie—except contingents of rioters and assassins. The real "people," the great mass of workers and honest wage earners, remained aloof from these events. They were the less concerned in that the revolutionaries (all of them of the middle-class, if not of noble stock) continued to discriminate against "passive" as opposed to "active" citizens. Only the latter, who paid a tax equivalent to three days' wages, possessed the right to vote or run for office. For the first time, Danton raised his voice in protest against such an injustice. Elected President of the Théâtre-Français electoral division, he had the audacity (quite unheard of in his day and age) to uphold the rights of "passive citizens" and to urge "active citizens" to vote in favor of universal suffrage. So Danton, the tainted, corrupt tub-thumper, was nevertheless the man who invented—the word is no exaggeration—the electoral charter for this modern age, political equality between rich and poor. Here is one more item to set in the credit balance when we are judging this enigmatic Janus of a man.

Thanks to him, a vast sense of hope was born among the masses. Yet his Political Declaration of July 30 went further still. Hitherto, only "active citizens" had been permitted to enlist in the National Guard and rally, like the nobles of the Ancien Régime, to the defense of their country. Now here is the motion which Danton had passed at Saint-André-des-Arts: "The Théâtre-Français electoral division hereby declares that when the nation is in danger, *all* Frenchmen whatsoever should be called upon to defend it; that what the aristocrats formerly termed 'passive citizens' no longer exist; and that those who bore this unjust appellation are entitled not only to serve in the National Guard, but also to participate in the debates of their constituencies and their primary assemblies."

After "this first bomb thrown into the Court," as Chaumette described it, fate proceeded to detonate another, the Brunswick Manifesto, which was to have even more dangerous repercussions for Louis XVI. This time Danton had nothing whatsoever

to do with it. The manifesto was drafted by the Duke of
Brunswick, Commander-in-Chief of the combined Austrian and
Prussian armies, in his headquarters at Coblentz and addressed
to "all the inhabitants of France." Brunswick declared his intention of "delivering the King, the Queen, and the royal family
from their present captivity"; of protecting those towns and
citizens "that submit to the King," but of utterly destroying
those which offered any resistance to the German armies and
of punishing "there and then, with all the rigor that the rules
of warfare permit," such inhabitants as might rise against the
invader.

For Paris, in particular, the Commander-in-Chief announced
the most fearful reprisals. Holding all Deputies, members of the
Commune, National Guards, magistrates, and officials responsible, "on their heads, to be judged by court-martial without
hope of pardon, for the least violence, the slightest outrage,
committed against Their Majesties the King, the Queen, and
the royal family," Brunswick warned them that in the event
of the palace being invaded again, the Emperor of Germany
and the King of Prussia would exact "an exemplary and never-
to-be-forgotten vengeance, by condemning the city of Paris to
utter destruction, and its inhabitants to the firing squad."

It would have been hard to conceive more barbarous penalties. Destroy Paris and shoot its citizens? "By God!" people said
when they read the proclamation. "Does this little Prussian
Generalissimo take the French for a flock of sheep?" This lack
of psychological insight, this indirect challenge to Gallic pride,
was destined to produce an effect exactly opposite to that which
Brunswick had hoped for. Instead of spreading terror, it triggered off an outburst of patriotism. Far from reassuring Louis
XVI, it filled him with such apprehension that the unhappy
sovereign, sweating with fear, lost no time in condemning the
manifesto in a letter to the Legislative Assembly.

But his protestations could not dam the flood that had been
unloosed by Brunswick and, before him, by the atmosphere of
panic which the Duke of Orléans's guests had exemplified in
their behavior. For them, the Prussian threat confirmed the
authenticity of the list attributed to Bertrand de Molleville and
annotated by the Queen. It simply increased their conviction

that a secret plot was the only way out. Danton, on the other hand, acted in broad daylight, for all to see. On his recommendation, the forty-eight electoral divisions demanded the King's removal from office; and Pétion read out their petition at the Bar of the Legislative Assembly—a spectacular way of scotching the rumors which claimed he was in love with Madame Elisabeth.

Santerre himself now put an end to his charitable impulses. Convinced that Louis XVI was in league with Brunswick, the brewer made a fighting speech to the Marseillais in the Faubourg Saint-Antoine. The Deputy Barbaroux (whose revolutionary violence had, if anything, increased since that evening at Mousseaux) persuaded Danton—not that much persuasion was necessary—to use his authority as First Deputy Public Prosecutor to obtain five thousand cartridges from the municipal police. The latter duly handed them over, and the conspirators distributed them to their "troops"—not only to the Federates of Marseilles and Brest, but also (if we are to believe Roederer) to "about a thousand jailbirds, thieves, pilferers, bandits of every description; for all that furthered the sacred cause was justifiable." And he added: "Those who seek to achieve an end must use the means at their disposal. We could hesitate no longer; August would either bring back the Ancien Régime or see it destroyed forever."

By the 4th, all was ready for the battle. In the Quinze-Vingt division, Santerre was stirring up the people to revolt. The overthrow of the monarchy, he told them, would bring about that "universal suffrage" which Danton had invented. Danton himself was holding the men of Marseilles spellbound with his speeches in the Théâtre-Français division. Throughout the industrial slum areas people were beginning to sing the "Marseillaise."

On the 6th, Santerre warned Danton that, in his opinion, the mob could not possibly be restrained past the 9th. That was absolutely the last moment for the National Assembly to pass a decree of deposition against the King—otherwise the people would launch an attack on their own, like a shot fired from a gun. "Go for the 9th, then," Danton said; and his friends in the Legislative Assembly got the motion set down in the order of the day for August 9.

At this point, however, Danton's audacity was suddenly mitigated by doubts. More exactly, he lost his nerve. What would become of his wife and children if this revolt proved abortive? Suppose he fell into the hands of the Royalists and found himself before a firing squad? How was he to ensure that his family would not lose its stay and support? Should he lie low, as he had done during the attack on the Bastille and the march to Versailles? Or should he get out of town, as he had preferred to do after the slaughter on the Champ-de-Mars? Gabrielle and little Antoine were still at Fontenay, and François-Georges with his wet nurse in l'Îsle-Adam. What was there to keep Danton in Paris?

On August 7 these friends of Danton's who called at his house in the rue des Cordeliers were told by the maid: "Monsieur Danton left yesterday for Arcis-sur-Aube." The news caused astonishment and anger. Obviously, Danton was happier organizing riots than participating in them.

Twenty months later he was to tell the Revolutionary Tribunal, during interrogation: "I had gone to Arcis, as a dutiful son, to spend three days with my mother—to say good-by to her and put my affairs in order." He added: "I can produce witnesses."

That was incontestably true. He had something better than witnesses: signed documentary evidence. There was a statement, attested in the presence of Maître Finot, the Arcis notary, by Danton himself, his mother, and his stepfather. This curious deed of gift guaranteed to M. and Mme. Recordain, for the rest of their lives, the right to occupy their generous son's manor house. It looks very much as though he was afraid that Gabrielle (in the event of his predeceasing her) might show her mother-in-law the door. So to the sentiments of a "dutiful son" we must add another motive: that of a distrustful husband. The new arrangement scarcely flattered his wife's integrity.

For two days Danton paced his estates trying to reach a decision. Should he stay or go? What ought he to do? On the

8th, a letter arrived from Fabre d'Églantine. Speaking on behalf of the Cordeliers, the poet begged him to return. Robespierre and Desmoulins felt his presence to be indispensable. How could a plot be carried through without the master plotter? This finally decided Danton. He hired a post-chaise and returned to Paris as fast as he could.

He arrived in the rue des Cordeliers, unannounced, on the morning of the 9th. Here he found Gabrielle and his elder son, who had returned from Fontenay the night before, and a few close friends from whom he learned what had been going on in his absence. It was impossible to control the slum districts or the Marseilles contingent much longer. A recent decision of the Legislative Assembly had added fresh fuel to their wrath. By 406 votes to 224, the Assembly had rejected the motion to bring La Fayette to trial for his unauthorized trip to Paris. When the Deputies emerged after the session was over, the crowd booed them. Some members were seized by the scruff of the neck and forced to defend themselves against physical assault.

That same day, August 9, the Assembly at last discussed the matter of the King's deposition—though the debate was so brief that it is hard not to regard this, too, as an element in the plot. "The real signal for the insurrection," wrote Eymery, the bookseller, "was the adjournment of the 'Deposition Debate.' And here one might vindicate the Legislative Assembly of the charge that it was unduly influenced by the 'patriotic' societies—in other words, by the Jacobin faction." In fact, nothing could have been more apt to arouse the mob against the King than a delay in his deposition. This truth appeared so self-evident that Roederer took the floor to denounce a motion approved by Santerre's Quinze-Vingt constituency, which declared that "if by Thursday, August 9, the National Assembly had not approved the King's deposition, tocsin and drum will sound at midnight and summon the people to revolt."

"This motion," Roederer told the Deputies (who knew very well what was afoot), "was circulated to the other forty-seven constituencies. Only one division, that of Le Roi-de-Sicile, has repudiated it." It is all plain enough; by adjourning the debate

on the King's deposition, the Assembly was cooperating with
the anti-Royalists—which meant, in effect, with Danton. It was
a strange kind of plot, since, contrary to what one might
logically expect, everything went on in the open—in the streets,
the clubs, even in the palace itself. Here Louis, who received
hourly reports on the development of events, seemed sunk in
a mood of apathetic resignation and indifference to his fate.
In this he made a striking contrast with the Queen, who displayed great courage and a stubborn determination to resist at
all costs. To her still-faithful Swiss Guards and the few aristocrats around her who had not fled with the rest, Marie-
Antoinette transmitted a mood of astonishing coolness and self-
confidence.

Danton, too, was making the rounds of his *quartier,* though
more with the intention of attempting to calm the people than
with the aim of arousing them further. This did not stop him
from announcing: "Tomorrow the people will be victorious, or
I shall be dead!" Meanwhile Madame Elisabeth was telling a
group of intimate friends in the Tuileries: "There's no danger:
Danton will take care of us." In her innocence she believed
that the demagogue had been *bought* by her brother; whereas
in fact he had merely been *paid*. There is a subtle distinction
between the two.

Lucile Desmoulins was to leave a vivid sketch of the night
of August 9 in her *Journal*. Since her baby (together with
François-Georges Danton) was away in l'Îsle-Adam, the young
mother was able to help her husband entertain several Marseillais at dinner. It was a cheerful meal, spiced with the broad
accents of the Midi and all the more lighthearted because the
guests were convinced that the monarchy's last hours had come.
They took their leave after the dessert, and Desmoulins and
Lucile walked down the rue de l'Odéon to spend the rest of
the evening with Danton.

But when they arrived they found Gabrielle in tears and
Mme. Charpentier vainly trying to reassure her daughter. The
moment he saw Desmoulins, Danton announced his determination to finish off the Throne that very night. "I'm worried,

though," he said. "I'm afraid I may not be able to carry the people with me."

"Oh yes," Lucile insisted, "the plan will go through all right, never fear."

What made her so certain? Perhaps something she had heard from her Marseillais dinner guests. She was a little tipsy, chattering away brightly and laughing without restraint.

"How can you *laugh* at a time like this?" Gabrielle demanded.

Her spirits suddenly evaporating, Lucile lowered her voice: "It'll bring me tears enough later. Perhaps tonight."

Mme. Charpentier rose; it was time for her to be going—not back to Fontenay-sous-Bois, but to her son's establishment in the rue de la Vieille-Monnaie, where she sometimes stayed when she was in Paris. Anxious to have a moment alone with Desmoulins, Danton suggested that Gabrielle and Lucile walk a little of the way with Mme. Charpentier.

The three women went out together. It was a fine, clear evening, and, though France was on the edge of a volcano, the neighborhood seemed very peaceful. After strolling a little way, they sat down outside a café. Suddenly a detachment of cavalry trotted past, followed by a group of "patriots" singing obscene songs. Lucile and Gabrielle took fright again, but Mme. Charpentier remained unperturbed. She said good-by and proceeded on her way alone. The two scared girls ran all the way back to the Cour du Commerce.

Danton and Desmoulins were no longer alone in the apartment. There were about a dozen men there, stacking guns in one corner by the light of oil lamps. Beside them stood pretty Louise Robert, watching these preparations for battle with some emotion. The sight of Desmoulins holding a musket made Lucile burst into tears. She asked Louise if they would sound the tocsin. "They're sure to," Louise replied. Lucile hated the noise of the tocsin; she found it peculiarly depressing.

Among those present was Stanislas Fréron, who took advantage of the occasion to make Lucile one of his usual disguised declarations of undying love. As he picked up a gun (while she looked on) the would-be lover proclaimed, in a melodramatic voice, that he was tired of life and would welcome

nothing more than death. Lucile shrugged her shoulders. Then
she went out and hid herself in the unlit drawing room, where
she lay down on a sofa to try and get some sleep. Overwhelmed and exhausted, poor Lucile was now losing heart altogether. She trembled for Desmoulins, for herself, for everybody.
And all the time the iron footsteps of the patrols continued to
tramp past over the cobbles.

When the men had gone, Gabrielle and Louise Robert tried
to console Lucile. "What are our husbands *doing?*" she asked,
between sobs.

At the City Hall, Danton found the General Council still in
session. Manuel was present to hear the debate, but not Pétion.
The Mayor had been summoned to the Tuileries and had disappeared; he was not seen again at the Commune all that night.

Guard contingents from the various electoral divisions were
assembling in a separate chamber. The numbers of these "patriots" rose steadily: when there were eighty-two of them, they
chose their own President, a customs clerk named Huguenin.
Led by him, they passed a motion expressing their "desire
to save the country." Robert and Simon the shoemaker joined
them, as representatives of the Théâtre-Français division.

Danton at once saw how this illegal assembly could be turned
to good account. What he had to do was to get rid of the
Commune and replace it with this Insurrectionary Commune.
The attack on the Tuileries would thus be made a great deal
easier. Danton accordingly gave the necessary orders, though it
is hard to enumerate them with any precision. If we are to
believe "Two Friends of Liberty," the anonymous eyewitnesses
who published a *History of the Revolution,* Danton was responsible for the strategy of the riot throughout. "It was on
him that the various ringleaders of the insurrection depended;
it was his orders that they carried out."

Such was also the opinion of Dr. John Moore, the physician
attached to the British Embassy. Something of a *littérateur*—
and something of a secret agent, too—Dr. Moore left a most
interesting *Journal Written During My Sojourn in France.*
According to him, Danton was personally responsible for ar-
ranging the assembly of divisional delegates in the City Hall.
This gathering, he asserts, "was not brought about by means

of a resolution carried in the various divisions"—far from it, in fact. The whole operation was "planned by a faction of which Danton may be considered the leader, and of which the divisional electors were the instruments." This opinion agrees with those of Garat, Billaud-Varenne, and Beugnot.

Having issued his instructions, Danton left the City Hall. As though it were a perfectly normal occasion, he went home to bed. He reached his house about midnight and found Lucile Desmoulins and Louise Robert there with Gabrielle, all three of them still dressed and in no hurry to retire. He went through to his room and flung himself down on the bed without removing his clothes.

Then the tocsin sounded, and all the bells in Paris took up that quick, throbbing *ding! ding! ding!* Lucile and Gabrielle were nearly driven out of their minds by it. They lay on the sofa by the drawing-room window, weeping, in a state of near collapse. Louise tried to calm them, but without success. Danton, too, found it impossible to sleep. He came out of his room and stood looking at the three women.

"Where is my husband?" Louise asked. "Where have you sent him?"

Danton pulled a wry face. "How the devil should *I* know where he is at this time of night?" he said, and went back to bed.

The hours dragged by interminably. At one point Lucile, now quite beside herself with anxiety, cried out: "O God, if there is a God, save the men who are worthy of You!"—by which, of course, she meant Desmoulins. The blindness of love . . .

Someone rang the doorbell, and Gabrielle answered it. The caller was an emissary from the Commune. Danton was asleep, she told him, and must not be disturbed. She would take a message.

The bell rang again, several times: more messengers, further reports on the progress of the rising. These tiresome intruders insisted on seeing Danton. While Gabrielle was taking them through to his room, Louise Robert said to Lucile: "If my husband doesn't come back, I can't face the thought of life without him. And as for Danton—the rallying point of the whole attempt!—if Robert's killed, honestly, I'll take a knife to that swine myself!"

The emissaries from the City Hall took their leave. The last to go was a former Prosecutor at the Châtelet, a cousin of Camille Desmoulins's. Despite this person's hangdog appearance, Danton called out to him: "Fouquier-Tinville, I'm going to make you my aide-de-corps—report to me for duty tomorrow."

About two o'clock in the morning Danton strode rapidly through the drawing room. "It's no good," he muttered. "I have to go down there." The front door slammed behind him, and the sound of his footsteps faded on the stairs.

When he reached the City Hall, he found the divisional Guard detachments in control of the building, having ejected the Commune by force. Danton arrived just in time to proclaim the establishment of an Insurrectionist Commune. Everything was going according to plan. There was loud applause, and cries of "Long live the nation! Death to all traitors!"

The aristocratic Marquis de Mandat, Commander-in-Chief of the National Guard, decided to come around to the City Hall himself—a stupid and, as it turned out, fatal decision. He had his office there, though since the previous evening he had been stationed at the Tuileries; as La Fayette's successor, he was responsible for the protection of the King and the National Assembly. Orders to that effect had been given him by Pétion, the Mayor—to keep him out of the way, obviously, since Pétion was privy to the plot.

A second order, carried by a delegate from the new Commune, enjoined Mandat to leave the Tuileries and come to the City Hall to make a report on his arrangements for enforcing security and public order. He was naïve enough to walk straight into the trap set for him. Leaping into the saddle, he galloped along the *quais* toward the Commune. Observing the presence of threatening armed crowds, he summoned the Commandant of the Place de Grève duty battalion and ordered him "to disperse the procession marching on the Palace by attacking it in the rear." A somewhat bloodthirsty decision, perhaps, but quite compatible with Pétion's general instructions.

The battalion commander took this written order and showed it to Rossignol, the police commissioner of Santerre's constituency, Les Quinze-Vingt. Rossignol rushed into Danton's office and thrust the document under his nose. The two of them went to Mandat's room together, and Danton demanded that the General accompany him to the Throne Room (where the new Councilors were sitting) to explain his action. Mandat refused. "This so-called Commune of yours," he said, "is nothing but a bunch of seditious rebels, and I have no intention of appearing before them." At this, Danton sprang on him, seized him by the scruff of the neck, and shouted for help. Hauled out of his office by a yelling mob, the unfortunate Commandant was dragged into the Throne Room, questioned, and finally locked up in the City Hall prison. At Danton's request, the insurrectional municipality at once appointed his successor. The new Commandant of the Guard was Santerre, the brewer from the Faubourg Saint-Antoine.

Mandat was left in his cell for two or three hours. When he was brought out (on the pretext of being transferred to the Abbaye Prison) it was only to be shot by Rossignol on the steps of the City Hall. Though the latter actually fired the pistol, Danton later acknowledged his part in this act of murder before his judges: "Mandat," he said, "had given orders to fire on the people. I therefore transferred the death sentence to him." He seemed proud of his decision. Furthermore, Danton had given a very clear warning of his intentions to Philippe Égalité's guests at Mousseaux. To Pétion's suggestion of "removing" Mandat, we remember, he had replied: "Kill him, man; the dead can't come back." (At any rate, we have Roederer's word for it that this is what Danton said.)

Mandat's ill-timed move was thus of great help in the uprising. But even if the commander of the duty battalion had not shown the order to Rossignol, and Rossignol had not shown it to Danton, it is fairly certain Danton would have found some other excuse for putting him out of the way. The death of the Commander-in-Chief disorganized the palace defenses; the fact of his obliteration made it an easy task to overcome the defenders themselves.

The same source provides us with another anecdote, slightly more susceptible to proof. In the early hours of the following morning (August 10) "when it was already light," Danton was

still organizing events from the City Hall, having drunk a very
great deal to keep himself awake. Half drunk, he went to
Roederer's apartment and found him getting up.

"We're going to burn our boats," he told him.

"You had better be sure you won't need them," the magistrate warned.

"Oh no, the whole thing's planned, we're sure to win. But
the thing is, *people are set on killing the King today, and I
don't regard this as necessary in the circumstances.* In fact, it
could prove a real liability. All those who honestly want the
Duke of Orléans in power would be only too glad to see Louis
out of the way. But his death would complicate things enor-
mously, and *I am therefore against the whole idea of the King's
execution.* What I want *you* to do is put the fear of God
into him—*persuade him to leave the Palace and seek asylum
with the Assembly.* There we shall have him surrounded, and
can proceed to arrange his deposition at our leisure."

Roederer hesitated over undertaking so perilous a mission. At
this, Danton scrutinized him "with wild eyes." Then, the narrator continues, "this giant of a man took me by the throat
and nearly throttled the life out of me. 'Take care,' he said.
'In this tragedy everyone has his allotted part to play. Anyone
who thinks he can be a mere onlooker will find it costs him
his head. Don't falter now, or you'll regret it later. I will be
watching you; you'll be treated according to your deserts.'"

Roederer succumbed to these threats and promised to do
what was asked of him. "It was agreed that, as President of
the *département,* I should go to the Palace and try to get the
King out of the place. We were still talking when the can-
nonade opened up. 'Do you hear that?' Danton cried. 'The
ball has begun! This time we are calling the music, and people
must dance to our tune!' With that he rushed off like a mad-
man. I dressed myself in formal attire and went down to the
département."

To the day of his death Danton never mentioned this encounter with Roederer, and Roederer himself did not do so
until 1815, in the presence of Lamothe-Langon, who enshrined
it in his *Memoirs.* If the anecdote is true, it would lend support
to La Fayette's assertion that Danton received 50,000 *écus* from

the Court just before the events of August 10, and it would explain Madame Elisabeth's remark: "There's no danger: Danton will take care of us."

If this was indeed the case, why did Roederer make no mention of this remarkable visit in his own *Memoirs?* Doubtless because at the time of their publication in 1795, he still feared that the Royalists might take revenge on him. Can one doubt the word of a man concerning whom Sainte-Beuve, in the nineteenth century, had this to say: "To any impartial reader, it is clear today that during the events of June 20 and August 10, Roederer conducted himself, as a magistrate, with propriety and integrity: that, despite his lack of sympathy for the Royalist cause, he showed himself honorable, scrupulous, and conscientious."

The alternative hypothesis is that Lamothe-Langon invented the whole Danton-Roederer interview. Such a thing is possible, but it is hard to find a motive for it. In 1837, when his *Memoirs* were first published, the Revolution already belonged to the remote past. Besides, M. de Lamothe-Langon was a Councilor of State and a former Prefect—positions which, despite everything, do posit some loyalty in their holder. Since his testimony is unique and unsupported, history cannot record it without some reservations.

And yet the whole plan, from the capture of the Tuileries to the rescue of Louis XVI, went off exactly as Danton had foreseen, including the part he had delegated to Roederer. On the morning of the 10th the forces of insurrection marched from the City Hall to the palace, which was defended by a force composed of Swiss Guards, National Guards, and aristocrats. Since Mandat's disappearance, however, they no longer had a leader. Their assailants, on the other hand, were commanded by an Alsatian named Westermann, a former non-commissioned officer who had joined the revolutionaries and had been promoted to the rank of general for the present operation. Santerre, the brewer, who had been made the new Commandant of the National Guard, lent him valuable support by virtue of his ascendancy over the masses.

Before the first shots were fired, Louis XVI sent several messages to the Legislative Assembly, which had been in continuous session since the previous day. Although the attack on the palace was being mounted before their very eyes, the Assembly made no reply to these communications. The King then summoned several of his advisers in order to sound their opinion. "A few moments later," wrote Louis's *valet de chambre* Cléry, an eyewitness of these events, "there entered the members of the Paris *département,* and several Municipal Councilors, with Roederer—at that time Public Attorney—leading them. Roederer, *doubtless by arrangement with the conspirators,* earnestly besought His Majesty and the whole royal family to come across to the Assembly. He emphasized that the King could no longer rely on the National Guard, and that if he stayed in the Palace neither the *département* nor the Municipality of Paris could take any further responsibility for his safety."

"Doubtless by arrangement with the conspirators": if this deliberately italicized phrase does not prove collusion between Danton and Roederer, at least it shows that someone like Cléry believed that defense was still possible, that by his retreat to the Riding School the King was destroying the monarchy, and that he would have been better employed putting fresh heart into his troops. As Roederer himself wrote afterward: "Despite all the Queen's efforts, the King could not bring himself to organize a resolute defense. He should have shown himself in military uniform, wearing the white plume of Henri IV, on horseback, booted and spurred. Instead, he appeared in a violet coat, the color of mourning and ill-fortune, with short breeches, silk stockings, and diamond-buckle shoes . . . and made a very cursory inspection of the National Guard. Some of them insulted him to his face. Yet they would all have obeyed his orders blindly had he dared give them a lead. Barbaroux personally told me that if the King had shown himself, the bourgeoisie would have come out on his side and a counterrevolution would have taken place."

But what Louis XVI and his family actually did was to follow the narrator to the Legislative Assembly, a distance of some five hundred yards. Demoralized by the King's flight, the National Guard contingent went over to the ranks of their comrades, who were just coming up under Santerre's command to attack them. The Swiss Guards, seeing their late comrades-in-arms turning against them, had only one thought: to save their own skins. Why should they fight for a monarch who not only renounced the struggle himself, but also had drafted—in his own hand—an order which is preserved in the museum of Carnavalet, and which reads: "The King commands the Swiss to lay down their arms instantly and return to their barracks."

To the strains of the "Marseillaise," Guardsmen and Federates fought their way through the palace, staircase by staircase, corridor by corridor, room by room. When they were in complete control of the building, they set about hunting down the fugitives, who were defending themselves as best they could outside in the gardens. The carnage went on until evening; there were over eight hundred victims. The losses on the attacking side were about half that figure. Swiss Guardsmen were massacred in the nearby streets; some were even killed in the City Hall, where ninety-six of them had been taken. Robert was an eyewitness of this slaughter and must surely have described it to his wife, Lucile, and to Gabrielle when he returned to the Dantons' house that evening.

Danton himself did not leave the Commune all that day. Messages kept coming in for him, and an endless stream of orders went out. A day was to come when Saint-Just, recalling his absence from the Tuileries, was to call him "a deserter in the hour of danger." While his wife, in her innocence, thought him battling for the palace, and trembled anxiously for his safety, he was in fact sitting behind the scenes, pulling the bloodstained strings of his puppet theater.

Poor Gabrielle was in such distress that, toward the end of the night, Lucile took her home with her. From the windows there was a view of the Odéon, and behind it the trees of the Luxembourg Gardens, an oasis of seeming calm. Gabrielle slept on a camp bed that Lucile had hastily put up for her. Leaving his chief to look after matters of strategy, Camille Desmoulins came back and joined his wife in bed. Louise Robert, whom Lucile had also taken in, was stretched out on a sofa. As her hostess wrote afterward, "she was no longer giving audible expression to her agony of mind, but she was so tense with anxiety that she looked quite yellow." As for little

Antoine Danton, Lucile makes no reference to him in her *Journal;* perhaps his mother had left him with Mme. Charpentier.

Next morning Desmoulins went back to the City Hall. Between nine and ten the three women heard the sound of gunfire: battle was being joined at the Tuileries. Gabrielle turned pale, put her hand to her heart, and slid to the floor in a faint. Jeannette, the Desmoulins's maid, began to "moan like an old nanny goat." Her mistress, with the help of Louise Robert, got Mme. Danton undressed. Now breathing more freely, she came to again. The morning dragged on, punctuated by a series of distant explosions. In order to calm their nerves, the three friends read aloud to one another. At one point Lucile went out to buy some bread. First the baker, then the other customers recognized her—and began to cover her with abuse. They regarded Desmoulins as the person responsible for the massacre. Lucile fled and returned to her own apartment quite out of breath.

When they had just finished their meal, Desmoulins came in, accompanied by Fréron, to reassure his wife and leave again almost immediately. Both of them looked drawn and pale; they had just been at the Tuileries, and their eyes were still dilated by the recollection of the butchery they had witnessed. They had not taken part in it themselves but merely followed in the wake of the combatants. There was no news of Danton or Robert.

After they had gone, the three recluses began to tremble for their husbands again. "Let's go back to my house," Gabrielle said. "Perhaps we'll be kept better informed there." They went out into the street. In the Place du Théâtre-Français, groups of people were engaged in animated discussion. When they reached the rue des Cordeliers they found it impossible to get into the Cour du Commerce; in a fit of alarm the porter had locked the main door and refused to answer the bell. A shopkeeper recognized Lucile and, like the baker earlier that morning, assailed her with abuse. Luckily Gabrielle managed to make herself heard by those inside the building. The door swung open on its hinges, and the three frightened women hurried up the stairs. It was with some relief that they found themselves in the Dantons' apartment again.

More interminable waiting. The guns had fallen silent again now. Crowds surged past in the street, bellowing the "Marseillaise"; there could be no doubt that the people had been triumphant. But what had become of Danton and Robert and Camille?

The bell rang. A Cordelier stood in the doorway. "They're smashing the mirrors in the Palace!" he blurted out. Then he tossed the three women "some sponges and hairbrushes from the Queen's dressing table."

Toward evening there was a great commotion on the staircase. A group of men burst in all shouting at once: Fabre d'Églantine, Legendre, Collot d'Herbois, Robert, "General" Westermann, and, at last, Danton himself, cheered on by his supporters who told Gabrielle he was the hero of the day. Swaying with exhaustion and intoxication and pouring with sweat, he took Gabrielle in his arms and hugged her.

The poor woman fainted again.

"Come on, out of here, all of you," he told the others. "I'm exhausted." He lurched through to his bedroom, flung himself down, and fell asleep almost immediately. He had not even bothered to take his shoes off.

In the Riding School the Assembly had now been in uninterrupted session for twenty-four hours. An acrimonious discussion was raging among the Deputies on the subject of the King's suspension. Louis himself, together with his wife and children, Mme. de Lamballe, and Mme. de Tourzel, was present during the debate—not in the Chamber itself, since that was forbidden by law, but in the reporters' box, the window of which opened directly on to the Chamber just behind the presidential dais.

The debate was constantly being interrupted by various delegations. All of them had come to demand the deposition of the fat thirty-eight-year-old man who was clearly visible up there behind his little window, indeed, and could now be seen busily satisfying the proverbially vast Bourbon appetite. Clutching a chicken in one hand, he was systematically working through its carcass. Marie-Antoinette, her sister-in-law, and

the two ladies-in-waiting had other things besides food on their
minds. The two children lay asleep in one corner.

Suddenly a deputation appeared from the Insurrectionary
Commune. Their spokesman declared: "Those who now stand
before the Bar of your House are the new magistrates of the
people. Present events, and the danger facing our country,
made our election necessary. . . . Legislators, you no longer
have any duty save to support the people. We have come here,
in the people's name, to ask that you decree certain measures
for the public safety. Pétion, Manuel, and Danton are still our
colleagues."

Why were none of these three men among the members of
the delegation? The speaker did not say. In fact, Pétion had
been barricaded inside his house since midday, through fear of a
group calling itself The Knights of the Dagger which had sworn
to assassinate him. He had a bodyguard of armed citizens to
ensure his safety. Manuel, through pressure of official duties,
had not been able to leave the City Hall. But what was the
reason for Danton's absence? Why, knowing his ambitious nature, had he not come down to trumpet his victory abroad in
the Riding School? Was he afraid that the King, or Marie-
Antoinette, or Madame Elisabeth might accuse him of treachery? Or was he genuinely abjuring the mixture of publicity,
profit, and self-interest which had always, till now, dictated his
every action?

In fact, Danton was simply asleep, in a state of utter exhaustion. But the victor had by no means lost his head. While
he slumbered, Desmoulins was working on his behalf. At
Danton's request he had contacted Brissot and told him that
the "patriots" wanted Danton given a ministerial appointment.
Would Brissot oppose his nomination?

"On the contrary," the Deputy replied. "I shall vote for him
myself. It will be a pledge of reconciliation." Furnished with
this guarantee from Brissot to Danton, from the war party to
the peace party, Desmoulins carefully spread the news behind
the scenes in the Riding School. Every member he met got a
full account of his friend's activities and was subjected to much
energetic propaganda.

Guadet, who was presiding over the Assembly when the

delegates from the Commune spoke up in praise of Danton, replied by congratulating them on the sentiments they had expressed. Vergniaud proposed the dissolution of the Legislative Assembly in the near future, to be followed by the election of a National Convention and the suspension of the King—"until such time," he said, "as this Convention shall have passed such measures as may be needed to guarantee the sovereignty of the people." Meanwhile the royal family would be lodged in the Luxembourg Palace "under the protection of the citizens and the law."

The Assembly approved this measure unanimously. Imitating the motion which Danton had had carried in his local constituency, they also voted for the emancipation of "passive citizens." It was by "universal suffrage" that France chose its next Assembly of Deputies. There were only two conditions: voters must be over twenty-one, and the candidates themselves over twenty-five. There was one odd anomaly: the Legislative Assembly did not extend voting rights to domestic servants—nor, obviously, to women.

The Assembly further recalled to office the three Ministers—Roland, Servan, and Clavière—whom the King had dismissed in June, and announced new appointments to the Ministries of Marine, Foreign Affairs, and Justice.

Two hours later Camille Desmoulins and Fabre d'Églantine burst in on Danton, who was sleeping peacefully in the knowledge of work well done, with Gabrielle occupying the other twin bed beside him. Thrusting aside the maid who had answered the door, the two men—undeterred by Gabrielle's presence, nightdress, and all—shook their friend awake.

"You'll have to take me on as Secretary!" cried Desmoulins.

"And give me a place in the Chancellery!" d'Églantine added.

Danton rubbed his eyes. "What sort of Secretary?" he asked Desmoulins.

"Private Secretary to the Minister," the latter told him. And Danton learned that the Legislative Assembly, by 222 votes out of a total of 284 cast, had elected him Keeper of the Seals and Minister of Justice.

In point of fact, he was to be much more than an ordinary

Minister. Since the King had been suspended, France no longer possessed a head of the executive branch of government. This was an essential office; and so the Deputies had decided, before the ballot, that final authority in the Council would rest with whichever of the three Ministers now elected received the greatest total vote. Since Danton's share outstripped that of Monge and Lebrun, he became, in a sense, both Prime Minister and Head of State: he replaced Louis XVI. Here was a miracle indeed.

The following day, with characteristic frankness, he told the Assembly: "If I had failed, I should have been treated as a criminal." This is the first law of revolutions: success is always heroic, and failure criminal. As *de facto* President of the Council, Danton would be called upon to bring his defeated—and therefore criminal—opponent to trial. Then Louis XVI, instead of having the Luxembourg Palace for a dwelling-place, would be sent with his family to brood over this final reverse in the Tower of the Temple.

CHAPTER X

The Minister of Audacity

ON THE MORNING OF the 11th the Provisional Executive Council appeared before the Assembly. It consisted of seven members: Danton, Minister of Justice; Roland, Minister of the Interior; Clavière, Treasurer; Servan, Minister of War; Monge, Minister of Marine; Lebrun, Foreign Secretary; and Grouvelle, Minister without Portfolio. Each of them swore to "maintain liberty and equality or die at his post." To this simple formula Danton felt called upon to add: "I hereby undertake, before the National Assembly, to protect the men within its precincts; I will march at their head, and be responsible for them."

Among these persons was the aristocratic Marquis de Condorcet, not only a Paris Deputy but also a scholar of world-wide reputation. An opponent of Danton when the latter stood as First Deputy Public Prosecutor, he had now voted in favor of his appointment to a Ministry. This caused considerable surprise. To those who reproached him for his decision, the mathematician replied: "The Minister had to be someone who possessed the confidence of the agitators lately responsible for overthrowing the monarchy. He had to be a man with sufficient personal authority to control this advantageous, glorious, and necessary Revolution's most contemptible instruments. He had to be a man of such eloquence, spirit, and character that he would demean neither the office he held nor those members of the National Assembly called upon to have dealings with him. Danton alone combined all these qualities. I chose him, and I do not regret my decision."

A song was composed which translated this tribute into somewhat more popular language:

> Condorcet said of an evening
> To more than one confrere:
> I have a scheme in my noodle
> Which you may like to share:
> What we must establish, you see,
> Dear friends, in this countree
> Is a *ré ré ré*
> A *pu pu pu*
> A *ré,* a *pu,*
> A *république*
> Of form unique.
>
> Danton he wanted Louis
> To sit upon the throne—
> But Danton quickly changed his views
> To mine, and mine alone;
> For he thinks, just like me,
> Nothing better can be
> Than a *ré ré ré*
> Than a *pu pu pu,* etc.

There were two more stanzas in the song; one wonders whether Danton ever got a premonitory shiver when he heard the following lines:

> A hero is honored no longer
> Than it pays to have him about:
> We reap the fruit of his labors
> And then we boot him out.
> This may not be fair play
> But it's still the usual way
> With a *ré ré ré*
> With a *pu pu pu,* etc.

Whoever wrote this verse was a true prophet. More than one French Republic was to adopt the technique it describes.

There was another practice, even less seemly and still very much in vogue, which can be summed up by the perennial slogan "Jobs for the boys." Danton could hardly be expected to break with so very human a custom.

Hitherto one official had combined the functions of Private Secretary to the Keeper of the Seals and Permanent Private Secretary to the Ministry of Justice. The new Minister soon abolished this economy. Camille Desmoulins was appointed to the first post, and Fabre d'Églantine to the second, at a salary in each case of 12,000 *livres*. Robert, whose ambitions were more modest, was well content to be made *chef des secrétaires particuliers,* an office roughly equivalent to head of the Civil Service. We do not know what salary it carried—only that, his duties obliging him to sleep at the Ministry, Robert drew 2400 francs from the Secret Fund in order to purchase the necessary furniture but never did so, since it was provided from existing supplies.

Danton's departmental staff appointments included Jules Paré, his former chief clerk, Collot d'Herbois, Barère de Vieuzac, and a former King's Bench Counsel named Dupont. Robespierre was offered a position, but refused; he did not wish, he said, to become a financial burden on the State. Danton also found places for several old friends outside the Ministry of Justice. Brune, the Cordeliers' regular printer, was put in charge of the Horse Requisitioning Center, which supplied mounts for the cavalry. Armed with an Adjutant General's commission, he set off for the provinces in full-dress uniform, and this appointment of his was the springboard, as it were, which afterward made him a Marshal of France. Marc-Antoine Gély, Danton's fellow tenant, had suffered by the abolition of the Paris Parliament, in which he held a post as court usher. When his neighbor on the floor below became a Minister, he found Gély an identical appointment in the Ministry of Marine. Danton, in fact, took the whole Gély family under his wing—especially little Louise, who was now fourteen and a constant companion of Gabrielle's. A very mature girl for her age, Louise also used to have political discussions with Danton himself. Finally, the Minister freed Lucile from the embarrassing attentions of that overromantic soul Fréron, whom he sent off to the Moselle region as Commissioner of the Executive Council in Metz. The salary was a mere pittance of 1500 francs.

Installed in the Place Vendôme, which had been renamed the Place des Piques, Desmoulins drafted the inevitable "Report to

the Sovereign People." France had to be informed of the changes
that had taken place in the capital, and Desmoulins, the group's
literary figure, was skilled in the art of misrepresenting facts. To
the various *départements* he explained that "a vast plot in the
Tuileries Palace recently came to a head when the Swiss, by an
infamous strategem, lured the Federates of the eighty-three
départements into their lair and proceeded to massacre
them. . . ." This was why the Parisians, hurrying to rescue these
imperiled provincials within their walls, had toppled the King
from his throne, and, in the process, had killed a certain number of his hired assassins. But it was not to be thought that
France as a whole should follow the example Paris had set. The
government was responsible for maintaining order, and intended
to do so. "The sword that we must turn against all traitors and
enemies of our country is the sword of the law. Let the courts
begin to render justice, and the people will cease to take the law
into their own hands."

Danton's signature is appended to this circular, but had he
in fact read it? Did he, we may well wonder, so much as pick
up a pen and scribble his name at the foot of the text? Probably
not. Even during his spell with the Commune, in the Public
Prosecutor's department, Danton already possessed a signature
stamp. This stamp he entrusted, when he became a Minister, to
Camille Desmoulins, who lent it on occasion to Fabre d'Églantine, Robert, and Paré. Many notes signed "Danton" Danton
himself never saw at all. Fabre d'Églantine took advantage of
this state of affairs to feather his nest very extensively. To begin
with he submitted his financial requisitions for approval; but it
was not long before he dispensed with this preliminary. If a
government department was to run efficiently, it had to have
money. One day it would be a draft for 3000 *livres* on some
Minister's funds, the next for 20,000. The various treasurers
always paid up for the warrants bore Danton's signature. But
there seemed to be no end to such demands.

The new Minister was not unaware of this racket, but he had
to rely very heavily on his subordinates. Already overwhelmed by
the pressure of top-priority work, he had no time left to deal
with lesser matters. National defense, purging the country's unreliable elements, relations with foreign powers, speeches before

the Legislative Assembly, all the ceremonies in which a Minister becomes unavoidably involved—there were so many responsibilities on his shoulders.

The first of these ceremonies was the public funeral laid on for the "Victims of August 10." Not the Swiss or the aristocrats, since these could not possibly be described as "victims." No, the latter were those patriots who had been "lured" into the Tuileries Palace and massacred by such "traitors." Four solemn mass funerals moved in cortege through the city. Danton followed that of the Marseillais, which numbered about a hundred coffins. It set out from the Théâtre-Français division (now renamed the Marseilles) and paused *en route* for a sort of exhibition in the Tuileries Gardens. The focal point of this exhibition was a hastily erected pyramid, surrounded by banners, sepulchral monuments, flaming cressets, benches for distinguished mourners, and a speakers' rostrum. "Goodness," Lucile Desmoulins wrote afterward, "what a spectacle it was; we all felt terribly sad."

That night she and her husband slept at the Dantons' house. Recalling the insults her baker had hurled at her on the 10th, Lucile, illogically enough, admitted that "we felt a vague sort of fear about staying at home; it seemed to me that we would not be really safe there." In any case, they were soon to change their domicile. Danton, together with his colleagues Paré, Robert, Fabre, and Desmoulins, took up residence in the Ministry itself, on the Place des Piques. Desmoulins wrote, in a letter to his father: "So here I am, living in the palace that once housed men such as Maupeou or Lamoignon. Despite all your predictions that I would never amount to anything, I have now been promoted to the highest post which a man in our walk of life could hitherto expect. . . . I have no doubt that your fellow townsmen in Guise (an envious lot at the best of times) will become positively splenetic about what they are likely to term my good luck."

This palace in the Place Vendôme (where French Ministers of Justice still hold sway) had formerly belonged, in the time of the Regency, to an *affairiste** called Bourvalais, a jumped-up ex-

---

* *Translator's Note.* There is no exact equivalent for this word in English. One dictionary renders it as a "politician who uses inside knowledge to feather his nest," which conveys its main implications admirably.

servant who lived there in great luxury. Ruined as a result of his speculations, he was driven out of this splendid residence by his creditors, whereupon the royal government bought it up. De Fourqueux, the Minister of Justice of the day, kept, as a curiosity, two massive silver champagne buckets—real museum pieces —from the sale of Bourvalais's household goods.

Enormous rooms, paneled walls, ceilings covered with murals portraying clouds and lascivious deities, furniture produced by the very finest cabinetmakers—such was the setting in which the victors of August 10 were henceforth to have their dwelling. Danton, Desmoulins, and Robert settled in there, with their families, by the end of the month. Fabre, too, moved in— though Danton refused to let him install his mistress, the actress Caroline Rémy.

While waiting for the real move to take place, the three families compromised, between August 11 and 28—by having their meals in the Place Vendôme. While the husbands worked in their various offices, the wives "passed the time cheerfully enough in one another's drawing rooms," as Lucile, the group's secret historian, noted at the time. Their cheerfulness, however, was overshadowed by one fatal accident. In the middle of the square there stood an equestrian statue of Louis XIV. The populace, bent on vengeance, decided to pull it down. Cables were fastened to the bronze charger, and draft horses hitched up to them. Gabrielle and her friends watched this operation from their balcony. But one woman, Reine Violet, who had tied a cord around the great King's neck, was crushed under him when he fell: yet another victim of the Bourbons!

On the 13th the Legislative Assembly, debating the motion that Vergniaud had made three days earlier, voted for its own dissolution. As chairman of this session, Condorcet expounded "the motives which had led the Assembly to proclaim the convocation of a National Convention."

On the 17th the Deputies set up a special Criminal Tribunal, charged with "trying the plotters guilty of crimes committed against the people during the day of August 10." Later ages were to know this court as the Tribunal of August 17, from the date of its institution. (It should not be confused with the Revolutionary Tribunal, which only came into existence later.) It consisted of judges, who were elected from the City Hall, and government Commissioners, nominated by the Minister of Justice. One of those whom Danton appointed was Jules Paré.

The Tribunal was housed in the Law Courts, in the old Chambre de la Tournelle. Its first hearings took place on the 21st, when three "conspirators" were found guilty and condemned to death: Collenot d'Angremont, administrative officer in the National Guard; Arnaud Laporte, Secretary of the Civil List; and finally a journalist called Durozoy, on the staff of the *Gazette de Paris*. Except for Durozoy, whose execution Danton postponed, they perished under the knife of a new machine invented by a piano maker named Schmidt and attributed to Dr. Guillotin.* First employed on April 25, to decapitate a robber, the guillotine now came into regular use, being set up either in the Place de Grève or else in the Place du Carrousel, opposite the main gates of the Tuileries.

But after these first three condemnations, the Tribunal of August 17 found itself out of work. There was a shortage of sufficiently important "conspirators." True, the Swiss Guards who had survived the massacre of August 10 were still held in the Abbaye Prison; but Danton was not overanxious to turn such small fry over to the stern mercies of his special Tribunal—especially since most of the judges, including Robespierre, were refusing to sit, and several National Commissioners (for reasons of conscience) were reluctant to make them do so. The Ministry had to appoint some new ones. Using Danton's signature stamp, Fabre d'Églantine nominated several. Among them was a cousin of Desmoulins's, the man who had been Danton's aide-de-camp on August 10: that onetime Prosecutor to the Châtelet, Fouquier-Tinville. With his arrival the Tribunal of August 17 was to take on a new character. First, however, there had to be some "conspirators" for him to try.

Danton was holding one major victim in reserve—La Fayette. Thanks to an affidavit drawn up by four Girondists—Guadet, Gensonné, Delmas, and Brissot—he felt there would be no difficulty about putting the General in the dock. They claimed that

* For a full account of this instrument, see Robert Christophe's *Les Sanson, bourreaux de père en fils pendant deux siècles* (Paris, 1960), also available in an English translation (London, 1962).

Marshal Luckner, while on leave in the capital, had told them, at Msgr. Gobel's: "La Fayette suggested to me that we should march on Paris." But other eyewitnesses refuted this statement. Luckner himself wrote saying that the bishop's guests had misunderstood his remarks. Though in the service of France, he was a Bavarian, with a very imperfect command of the French language.

Danton, however, refused to admit defeat. Determined to force La Fayette into committing some kind of desperate act, he suggested that the Council should send out a Commission of Inquiry to question him. With Cabinet approval he chose three Deputies—Kersaint, Peraldi, and Antonelle—and dispatched them to Sedan, where La Fayette had once more set up his headquarters after that somewhat precipitate withdrawal to Maubeuge.

Their appearance annoyed the Marquis, and he refused to undergo any kind of interrogation. When they resorted to threats, he had them locked up in the city's castle and ordered his deputy commanders, Generals Dillon and Dumouriez, to make their troops reaffirm the Oath of Loyalty to the 1791 Constitution—which guaranteed the King's inviolability. This gave Danton just the opening he was after. With a fine show of indignation he denounced La Fayette's contumacy before the National Assembly. The latter passed a vote removing the General from his command and ordering "every citizen and soldier to take all possible steps to secure the person of the said Mottié-Lafayette."

Warned of this move, La Fayette played his last, desperate card. This time he made it unmistakably clear that he *did* intend to march on Paris. But several of his regiments mutinied, and there were some officers who wanted to place him under arrest and hand him over to the government. For La Fayette, this meant the Tribunal of August 17 and the guillotine. In disgust he made a very grave decision: he slipped across the border and surrendered himself to the Austrians. However, the deserter was out of luck. Instead of being treated as a prisoner of war, he found himself a political internee. For six long years the Austrians kept him immured in a dungeon of Olmütz Castle—

though this incarceration at least saved his life. For the new France, La Fayette no longer existed. The old-guard revolutionary had been eliminated by Danton.

Danton installed himself and his family in the Place des Piques. To sleep in the bed where Chancellors of France had slept before them must have been an intoxicating experience for the café proprietor's daughter and the provincial from Arcis who had reached Paris without a sou in his pocket.

Although the Assembly had given the Minister of Justice preponderant authority, he decided that all seven Ministers should preside over the Council in turn—a neat way of smoothing away jealousies. But in fact Danton's turbulent personality imposed itself on his colleagues from the very beginning. A velvet-gloved dictator, he masked his threats with polite blandishments; he was especially careful to keep on good terms with Roland—not because he saw this mediocre person as a possible successor, but on account of his wife, that domineering political amateur of the rue des Petits-Champs. It was in this street that the Ministry of the Interior was located (it vanished in 1828 during the construction of the rue Méhul). Evicted from these splendid lodgings by Louis XVI, the Rolands returned there in triumph on August 11. Manon lost not a moment in starting her *salon* again. Important Girondists were to be found here, as well as the pretty hostess's lovelorn courtiers. On all alike she lavished smiles—but nothing more. She exercised such power that Danton told Fabre d'Églantine one day: "I haven't cultivated her enough. Devil take all women who meddle in politics! But since Mme. Roland shares the Ministry of the Interior with her husband, I suppose I must pay the little bitch the compliments she's so susceptible to, and confer with her on matters of State."

Manon, for her part, would whisper to her intimate friends: "Such a pity that the Council is ruined by Danton." Between these two characters a curious duel began. Each was equally determined to steal a march on the other by demonstrations of feigned friendliness. Neither of them was the other's type as far as physical involvement went. Danton had no liking for intelligent women: all he wanted from the weaker sex was submission.

And Mme. Roland could not so much as set eyes on that colossal figure, made still uglier by his youthful exploits, without a feeling of terror and repulsion. She could not conceive this bladder of lard stretched out on a woman's body. How, she asked, could Gabrielle possibly "allow this great stuffed turbot to make love to her?" The insult was borrowed from Vadier, a former Deputy in the Constituent Assembly, and repeated to the Minister of the Interior.

Nevertheless, Danton and Manon were always lavishing on each other compliments of a gallant, semiflirtatious nature. Every evening, after his session with the Council in the Place des Piques, Danton would go pay court to the lady politician of the rue des Petits-Champs. It was a clumsy display, however, for Danton was better at stripping and tumbling a woman than engaging her in drawing-room chatter. With his unceremonious, hail-fellow-well-met manner, he normally settled back in the best armchair and let other people do the talking.

But in the Council it was quite another matter. Mme. Roland was not present and could intimidate no one; Danton had full scope to exercise his powers of domination—all the more so since he despised his ministerial colleagues. General Servan, the War Minister, displayed too visible and public an admiration for "Coco" Roland (as her husband called her); Danton was unlikely to have any great opinion of *him*. Lebrun, the Foreign Secretary, had been too long in administrative jobs and had the civil servant's nervous distaste for taking responsible decisions, which he preferred to leave to Danton. He was, in fact, the eternal yes-man. Monge, the mathematician who had been appointed Minister of Marine, tended to lose himself in detail. He worked far too hard for Danton's taste, and was too cringing when they met: a beast of burden, on whom the Chief Minister could always impose.

Clavière, the Minister of Finance, was a walking reminder of how much the new régime continued to be infiltrated by the old. A Geneva banker, like Necker, he had been placed in charge of Finance because the Deputies believed that the Swiss were more adept than the French at managing public funds. Since he was used to hazardous speculation, he fell into line too readily with Danton's commercial schemes. The result was that the latter considered him a mere lackey. Grouvelle, Minister without Portfolio, was a man of letters. To Danton, who never wrote anything, this colleague seemed the very quintessence of uselessness. Lastly there was Roland—or, more exactly, Roland de la Platière—the elderly husband of a too-clever woman who influenced his every action. Danton did not care for this; in his view, a woman was for nothing but to comfort a warrior's leisure hours. "Can't that old fool Roland tan his little trollop's backside for her?" he asked Fabre d'Églantine on one occasion.

Yet the engraver's daughter wielded such influence that, despite everything, she persuaded Danton to transfer the seat of the Council from the Place des Piques to the Tuileries. The Ministers would now confer in the *salon* where Louis XVI had presided over *his* Council, and Danton would occupy the King's own chair—a prospect which he greeted with hypocritical protestations. Mme. Roland reckoned that in such surroundings Danton's dictatorial control over his Ministers would become less effective. But her hopes were soon dashed; he showed himself no whit less authoritarian in the Tuileries Palace than he had in Bourvalais's town house.

He continued to visit the Rolands after Council meetings and made some effort to adapt himself to the company. But drawing-room gallantry sat ill on the rabble-rouser. When, in an effort to soften Manon, he told her, with coarse familiarity, "I've come to take potluck with you," he saw her flush angrily.

One evening Roland was voicing his anxiety over the troubles now boiling up in the provinces. As Minister of the Interior he had the responsibility for suppressing them. At one point he let slip the contemptuous word "populace." Danton exclaimed: "Are we not of the rabble ourselves? We come from the gutter, Roland. It is this *populace* of yours that has raised us to power. If we ever forget *that,* we shall be making the most disastrous mistake of our lives."

With prophetic insight he told Manon: "You play at revolutions just as the Austrian woman used to play at being a shepherdess. If you're scared of blood, you shouldn't have let these cutthroats carry you so far!"

The blood that Mme. Roland feared was, indeed, to flow in rivers. Marat used his broadsheet to fan the flames of resentment; the People's Friend was now demanding the arrest of all aristocrats and nonconforming priests. Let these traitors, he wrote, join the Swiss Guards, who have been lying on prison straw since August 10. In the City Hall the new Commune was even more fiercely denunciatory than Marat. These priests and nobles must be put where they could do no possible harm to anyone!

As Principal Private Secretary to the Minister of Justice, Fabre d'Églantine discussed the matter with Danton. The poet was, in a manner of speaking, the municipality's representative at ministerial level. If the Minister of Justice had not yet ordered any arrests, that did not prevent the Commune from doing so. A former page to the Queen, that Count Alexandre de Tilly whom we have already met in these pages, heard that while he was away the police had broken into his apartment. Ought he to seek refuge abroad? "I was still trying to make up my mind," he wrote, "—after all, to flee one's country is a very great sacrifice—when the Abbé d'Espagnac, whom I met at the house of a friend, advised me to go and see Danton, and offered to accompany me himself. I was received very civilly, and with some interest, although Danton made it clear from the outset that he knew my principles and general way of thinking. He preferred my attitude, he said, to the pseudo-Jacobinism affected by most members of my class, and would prove how much more congenial he found my frankness than the hypocrisies of false patriotism, that wild passion which certain men professed for a revolution which in fact they detested. In short, he promised to save my life, and was as good as his word.

"But triumvirs in all ages have fallen out among themselves over their victims, and are forever bargaining, bullying, or making concessions to one another over their disposal. Next day I learned from Manuel—*and I am certain Danton used him as an intermediary to warn me*—that for the sake of peace and quiet he had sacrificed me to Fabre d'Églantine's importunities; that my head, in fact, had been a subject of altercation between them!" (The italicized words were underlined in the original text.)

This anecdote is taken from the *Memoirs* of a fervently Royalist aristocrat, who nevertheless bore witness to Danton's generosity of spirit. Twenty-four years afterward he returned to the subject once more. Before he committed suicide, in 1816, M. de Tilly corrected the manuscript of his *Memoirs,* which finally appeared in 1828. At the bottom of the page referred to above he added this note: "I saw Danton two hours before quitting Paris; his bloody hand clasped mine, yet I felt not the slightest twinge of alarm. I listened to his voice—that booming diapason, with its faintly somber and sinister overtones—and found nothing terrifying about the protection he now guaranteed me."

Such aid was all the more surprising in that Tilly, who occasionally dabbled in journalism, had compromised himself on July 27, 1792, by publishing an open "Letter to the King" in which he urged that any assault on the Tuileries be met with strong resistance. Such an article rendered its author liable to public retribution, yet despite this Danton did not hesitate to save him.

As the Duke of Brunswick's armies advanced, so did the threat he represented. Since August 19 this force, some eighty thousand strong, had been on French soil, and the soldiers of the Revolution were in full retreat before it. It had captured Longwy, penetrated the Argonne region, threatened Verdun, passed across part of Champagne, and opened up the road to Paris.

Though Danton was in no way responsible for a war that had been wished on France by Brissot's party and Manon Roland, he threw himself heart and soul into the problem of national defense. He left the affairs of the Ministry of Justice in the hands of Desmoulins, Robert, and Fabre d'Églantine, and henceforth concentrated exclusively on saving the country from military defeat and keeping up the morale of its citizens. Their general state of panic and alarm was manifest at all levels—in the streets, in the houses, at the Riding School, in the Cabinet itself. Danton had to rebuke Roland severely for suggesting the evacuation of Paris.

In his *Memoirs,* composed long enough after the event to be free from the constraints of flattery, Dumouriez wrote of Danton: "When there was the gravest danger of a Prussian victory, he alone stood above the general public consternation and had no part in it. He strongly opposed the removal of the Assembly,

and of the King, to some point beyond the Loire." This indicates
the degree of panic prevalent in Paris at the time. Once Roland
had made his suggestion, the whole government wanted to bolt:
to Orléans, or the Cévennes, or Provence—even to Corsica. A
conference was called in the garden of the Ministry of the Interior to study these proposals. There were several other persons
present at the meeting besides the seven Ministers. They included Dr. Duhem, a northern Deputy whose news from Lille
was anything but reassuring; Fabre d'Églantine; Pétion, the
Mayor; and the aristocratic Count of Kersaint, who had just got
back from a mission to General Staff Headquarters. In a flat,
dull voice he said: "Brunswick will reach Paris in a fortnight—
and take it, too, as surely as a wedge splits wood under the
hammer."

This prediction raised gooseflesh on all who heard it: all,
that is, except Danton, who roared: "Come back to my apartment in the Place des Piques! You'll find my wife there, and
both my children, and—most important of all—my seventy-year-
old mother. I have brought my whole family here. Sooner than
see the Prussians enter Paris, I would let my family die with me,
and have twenty thousand torches put to the city simultaneously
so that nothing remained of it but a heap of smoking ashes.
Roland, you are not to mention even the possibility of retreat.
Remember that the people might overhear you!" *And follow
your example* was the clear if unstated implication.

Obviously, the most urgent need was to make everyone stay
put and offer their sons for the defense of the realm. In fact,
though, did Danton promote such a cause by bringing his
mother to Paris? The truth was that if Mme. Recordain had
stayed in Champagne, she might well have fallen into Brunswick's hands. A more valuable hostage would be hard to imagine.
Once again the Minister was showing the two complementary
sides of his character. He refused to set the country a bad example by running away, and brought his own mother to Paris.
However, his idea of a provincial evacuation went no further.
That same evening he was to declare before the Assembly: "Our
enemies have taken Longwy, but Longwy is not France! We still
have two armies intact, those of Dumouriez and Kellermann.
Let us not exaggerate our fears. We can still save the day. It is

time to tell the people that they must fling themselves against the enemy *en masse.*"

Alluding to the Commune's plans for disposing of the Swiss Guards and aristocrats who had been in prison since August 10, Danton added these terrible words: "When a ship is wrecked, the crew throw overboard anything which might place their lives in peril. Similarly, all potential dangers to the nation must be rejected from its bosom."

To implement this rejection, he advised "the arrest of some thirty thousand traitors." In Paris itself "the Commune" was "to have the right to seize all suspected persons"—in other words, it was free to raid private houses and apartments. This measure had a double purpose: it was designed to find and imprison conspirators, but its secondary aim was to "confiscate the arms of hostile or indolent citizens" and redistribute them among the nation's defenders. "When our country is in danger," Danton concluded, "it has first claim on everything!" The Deputies rose to applaud him; a wave of enthusiasm surged through the Riding School, and Danton obtained the authorization he sought.

He left the Assembly at midnight, got in his carriage, and drove to the City Hall at full gallop. The onetime Deputy Public Prosecutor to the Commune had returned as a dictator. He passed on the Legislative Assembly's decree to the Commissioners for each electoral division. It embodied a general standing search warrant applicable to all suspects' houses. Any arms discovered were to be turned over to the arsenals, and all conspirators arrested were to be held in prison. The Commissioners would have the assistance of troops from the National Guard; and the whole operation would be directed by the Committee of Public Safety. The members of this Committee were Billaud-Varennes, Rossignol, Bourdon de l'Oise, Marie-Joseph Chénier, Xavier Audouin, Robespierre, Fabre d'Églantine, Hébert, and Marat. Panis, "General" Santerre's brother-in-law, together with an obscure Cordelier named Sergent, took on the administration of the Committee, while Méhée de la Touche was appointed its Clerk.

Raids began the following day. Grudges of all sorts, both large and small, played a considerable part in the decision as to which houses were suspect. A lover's jealousy, commercial competition, the urge to bring oneself into notice, or plain stupidity—all these things guided the Commissioners' footsteps. Far fewer arms than conspirators came to light, and if the arsenals did not benefit greatly, the prisons were soon full to overflowing. At the Abbaye and Les Carmes and the Châtelet, at the Salpêtrière and the Conciergerie and La Force, prisoners flowed in by the hundred, sometimes on foot, sometimes in cabs, but always under the escort of men inflamed by *L'Ami du Peuple* and *Le Père Duchesne,* by the prose of Marat and Hébert. In the course of ten days nearly three thousand arrests were made.

Neither the events in Paris nor the news of the war could stop the election campaign from going forward. The Legislative Assembly was to be replaced by a Convention, and innumerable would-be members were canvassing on their own behalf. When the Chamber voted in favor of universal suffrage, it had envisaged a two-stage electoral procedure. The citizens of the capital (with the exception of domestic servants) designated nine hundred electors, who in turn had to elect the twenty-four Paris Deputies.

Danton was a candidate. So were Robespierre, Collot d'Herbois, Manuel, Billaud-Varennes, Camille Desmoulins, Marat, Legendre, Panis, Sergent, Robert, Fréron, Fabre d'Églantine, David the painter, and the Duke of Orléans. Registered under his pseudonym of "Égalité," the last-named felt it advisable to send the following letter to the City Hall:

> Citizens: it is with deep gratitude that I accept the name bestowed upon me by the Paris Commune. It could not have chosen one more in agreement with my sentiments and my opinions. I hereby swear, citizens, to remain constantly mindful of the duties which this name imposes on me, and from which I will never deviate. I remain, Your fellow citizen,
>
> L.-P. Joseph ÉGALITÉ.

His elder sons, the former Dukes of Chartres and Montpensier, were both serving in the revolutionary army. The first, Louis-Philippe, was on Kellermann's staff. Thirty-eight years later the chances and hazards of politics were to make him King of France. Unaware of the future Providence held in store for him, this eighteen-year-old officer was at present known (as a result of his father having renounced the title) as plain "Colonel Égalité." He was also destined, after his promotion to General, to be entrusted by Danton with some very remarkable and confidential information. . . .

The Chief Minister felt that his power over the provinces was very shaky. The whole country by no means approved of Louis XVI's removal from power. If Paris failed to swing France into line behind her, it was the end of popular emancipation: Brunswick would win the war and turn France into a vassal state. As Danton saw it, to save freedom meant concentrating the reins of power in the capital. To uphold this dictatorial régime he could no longer count on the Legislative Assembly which, in any case, had only a few days of life left. His best hope, it seemed, was the new Commune, which he had himself established in the City Hall. But this municipal body appeared to believe it was still in mid-insurrection. There was no need for *L'Ami du Peuple* or *Le Père Duchesne* to encourage its murderous instincts. The Councilors' faces wavered between expressions of defiance and suspicion: they felt Brunswick's threats looming inexorably over them. The *émigrés,* with foreign support, were coming back to reclaim their old privileges, and the exiles' fathers, brothers, and sons—now incarcerated all over Paris—found themselves threatened by the vengeance of the people. Frightened officials had begun to cast bloodthirsty glances in the direction of the prisons. Danton knew this and was apprehensive about the possible consequences. But he had no other instrument available with which to defeat Brunswick.

It was true that the national emergency had produced abundant volunteers. Every day thousands of young men joined the army—though with more enthusiasm, it is true, than seasoned courage. But there was so little time in which to train them; how many even knew how to handle a gun? Conscious of their own inferiority, large numbers of them complained, deserted, or mutinied against their leaders who could no longer enforce their orders. The effects of their insubordination soon made themselves felt. During the night of September 1, a disastrous piece of news broke: Brunswick had occupied Verdun. His troops were now only two days' march from Paris.

The Council met at once and sat in deliberation till a late hour. When Danton finally got home, he told his wife: "Get my scarlet coat ready. If anyone really wants to make himself heard, he's got to catch his audience's eye first. Tomorrow morning I'm going to address the Assembly. And you're coming with me, Gabrielle."

"I couldn't go to the Riding School! You know how crowds always terrify me—"

"Never mind, you come along. You can sit and listen to the debate beside dear Queen Coco, the Messalina of the rue des Petits-Champs. And wait till you see how scared they all are! My God, I'll have them sweating with fright—*and* put fresh heart into them at the same time."

Gabrielle finally agreed. Next morning, September 2, she arrived at the Assembly wearing a taffeta dress and a lace cap. On the ministerial bench Danton's scarlet coat caught everyone's eye. After Vergniaud had called upon Paris to "take the most energetic steps possible," the Minister of Justice ascended the rostrum. With imperturbable self-assurance, he began: "It is a satisfying duty, gentlemen, for the Ministers of a free people to have to inform them that their country is going to be saved. The nation is roused and ready for action, impatient to join battle. . . ."

He went on to outline the decisions the government had taken. Trenches would be dug around Paris, and arms issued to those citizens who volunteered for the city's defense. The Assembly itself would elect a War Committee to "direct the lofty movement of the people." All this meant that the Minister must be granted plenary powers.

The Assembly approved this blank check by acclamation. Then, in an atmosphere of generally heightened emotion, Danton cried: "Whoever refuses to serve in person, or to return his arms, will suffer the death penalty. When the tocsin sounds, it is not an alarm signal; it sounds the charge against our country's enemies. And to defeat them, gentlemen, we need *boldness, and yet more boldness, boldness at all times,* and France will be saved!"

A gigantic ovation rose from the benches and poured down from the galleries. Danton had galvanized everyone's energies: even his fiercest enemies applauded him. As one of them afterward wrote: "When he uttered those final words, this hideous man was beautiful." Yet how—since shorthand as we understand it did not yet exist—could history preserve a record of this famous tirade? Beneath the speakers' rostrum there stood a circular table, around which there worked fifteen secretaries, sitting side by side. Each of them would memorize a sentence, or part of a sentence, as the speaker delivered it, or perhaps an interruption from the body of the Chamber. Then, jogging his neighbor with his elbow, he would hastily jot down this sentence, or intervention, on a numbered sheet of paper. The next secretary, following the same procedure, would also listen to a short bit of the speech, or some fresh interruption; then, as he was about to note it down, he would jog the third copyist, who would go through the same procedure with the fourth, and so on till the flow of speech had been picked up all around the table and came back to number one again. Then all that was necessary in order to obtain a transcript of the proceedings was to arrange the notes in numerical order. This work of synthesis took place in the shorthand writers' box—that same little room through the window of which Louis XVI had, on August 10, observed the debate which led to his dethronement.

Inevitably, errors crept into the shorthand writer's transcript. For this reason it is not certain that Danton, when he improvised his famous aphorism, actually delivered it in the traditional order ("boldness, and yet more boldness, boldness at all times, and France will be saved"). But did he say every word of this? Merlin de Thionville afterward wrote that "Danton saved the country with these words: *Boldness, and yet more boldness, and yet more boldness still!*" There is a third version: according to several papers, he said: "Boldness, boldness at all times, and yet more boldness, and France will be saved!" Here the natural crescendo from "yet more" to "at all times" is reversed; yet however illogical it may seem at first sight, this arrangement of the phrase strikes me as more in keeping with Danton's personal style. Having proclaimed that what was needed was "boldness, boldness at all times," he reinforced the permanence of "at all times" by tacking on that "yet more," which crowns and amplifies it, as though, in his patriotic fervor, he wished to prolong what was already eternal. This hints at the major artistry of Danton's eloquence; it explains why Choudieu, the Deputy for Maine-et-Loire, rushed up to Gabrielle, exclaiming: "My God, how splendid he was! There's never been anything so moving. . . ."

But Mme. Danton would have felt happier had he been a splendid family man or lawyer, rather than aspiring to the perilous splendors of a politician's career. She said as much to her husband when she congratulated him. "Be on your guard against all these men," she warned him. "They may be acclaiming you now, but tomorrow—who knows?—they could turn and tear you to pieces." Then he promised her, in his cups, that when the enemy had been driven back across the border, he would go back to live at Arcis, in the peace of the countryside. For him, as for all true patriots, to believe in victory was to be victorious already.

Meanwhile the Prussian advance continued. Now their armies were no more than sixty leagues from Paris. The dictator's call for boldness removed any lingering scruples that still existed in the City Hall. Since the Chief had commanded it, they would indeed use boldness—in the prisons. Sergent and Panis, the Administrators of the Committee of Public Safety, dictated the following translation of the concept to Méhée de la Touche, the Clerk to the Committee: "Before hastening to the border, we must be sure we have left no traitor or conspirator behind us."

The Committee appointed a number of "judges," who were to go around the prisons and personally to recruit the men to carry out their sentences. How many such amateur executioners did they find? The answer is about five hundred—not, as legend later asserted, the entire population of Paris. But if these good folk were not actively responsible for the September massacres, neither—being thoroughly terrorized themselves—did they make any effort to stop them.

On learning of the measures being taken by the Committee, Roland's Private Secretary hurried around to the Chancellery and informed Danton. According to tradition, Danton's response was: "I don't give a f—— for the prisoners, they'll have to take their chances." When the tocsin—as foreseen in his speech the previous day—began to ring out all over Paris, Prudhomme, the librarian, similarly hastened to the Place des Piques. "Don't be alarmed, it's the tocsin of victory!" Danton told him.

"But there's talk of a massacre—"

"Yes," Danton said, "we might *all* be massacred tonight—the most loyal patriot as soon as the next man. But the people are aroused. They're determined to take the law into their own hands."

Desmoulins, who was present during this exchange, modified the statement a little: "The innocent will not be confused with the guilty. All those vouched for by their local authorities will be handed over to them."

Partially reassured, Prudhomme took his leave.

Dr. Saiffert came to request the release of his patient, the Princess de Lamballe, who was interned at La Force. Danton told him: "I cannot do it. Anyone who tried to oppose the justice of the people would be regarded as their enemy."

In the general atmosphere of panic, Ministers even began to fear for their own safety. There was a remark of Mme. Roland's which went the rounds at this time: "Robespierre and Danton hold the big knife over us all. Danton is the man responsible for this mob, behind the scenes." (At one point she really thought her last hour had come. An unruly crowd, stinking of alcohol, forced its way into the Ministry in the rue des Petits-Champs and called on Manon—by now half dead with fright—for arms to deal with the traitors and to march on Verdun.) In the City Hall the Administrators signed warrants condemning Roland, Brissot, and a score of other Deputies. Danton spotted these documents on the Public Prosecutor's desk, slipped them into his pocket, and showed them to Pétion, the Mayor, who nearly fell through the floor. Without Danton's intervention Roland and Brissot would have joined Mme. de Lamballe in La Force.

In order to canalize this "justice of the people" somewhat better, the Minister of Justice had decided that the Council should conduct its deliberations in the City Hall. When he left Pétion's office, he found his colleagues awaiting him in a nearby room, where he had summoned them for a meeting. Together they settled down to such problems as recruiting, the food supply, armaments, and the requisitioning of horses—all the laborious business subsumed under the heading of National Defense—undisturbed by a single allusion to the massacres. Yet blood was flowing in rivers at Les Carmes and the Conciergerie, at the Châtelet and the Abbaye and the Salpêtrière, and at La Force itself, where a mob of down-and-outs had assuaged their hatred by murdering the Princess de Lamballe. The Committee of Public Safety was actually holding its own deliberations in a room next door to that occupied by the Ministers, and had sent Billaud-Varennes to encourage the butchers and promise them money.

Danton was well aware of what was going on, since—in the midst of all his other tasks—he took steps to rescue several friends from this fearful holocaust. The previous day he had provided his colleague Lavaux (a former Counsel to the King's Bench) with a passport to leave Paris: all roads out of the city had been closed by order of the Commune. He also received a letter from Mme. Adrien Duport, the wife of a Criminal Court judge, imploring his help. She and her husband were on vacation at Bazoches, where they owned some property. Because of this they had escaped the house-to-house raids in Paris; but Duport had just been arrested in his own garden, taken off to Nemours, and thrown into prison. On being notified of his arrest, the Committee of Public Safety ordered the local authorities to transfer the prisoner to Paris. On receipt of Mme. Duport's letter, Danton sent a dispatch rider posthaste to the governor of Nemours Prison, with a formal order forbidding him "for reasons of public security" to let Duport be taken out of his custody. In this way he escaped the Paris butchers.

Another suspect whom Danton saved was Omer Talon, formerly Chief Civil Magistrate to the Châtelet. Some time before, he had been accused by Camille Desmoulins of "selling justice," but had brought action against Desmoulins for libel and obtained damages to the tune of 1200 *livres*. As a member of the Constituent Assembly, he had been noted for his Royalist beliefs. He was also a client of Maître Dosfant's, the notary whose business Antoine Charpentier had taken over, and was on friendly terms with Danton's brother-in-law. Though well aware that in 1791

[7] An evening session of the National Convention, by Paul Chenavard. (Danton at center, foreground.) (*Photo by Josse-Lalance*)

[8] Louis XVI before the National Convention, December 1792. (*Photo by Bulloz*)

Talon had advised Louis XVI to join General Bouillé, could the Minister of Justice refuse a passport to this friend of his in-laws? So Talon left for Le Havre, whence he took ship to England.

The story of Dr. Chévetel, whom Danton similarly rescued, is one that might well have inspired Machiavelli. Chévetel, though an honest Cordelier, nevertheless also had dealings with the Royalist faction—the real plotters, now planning an uprising in Brittany. As a double agent he had gone there on several occasions, to meet the Marquis de la Rouairie, who was charged, by the Count of Provence, with the task of launching this insurrection just as Brunswick approached Paris. In order to make his cover story look more convincing, the doctor also undertook missions to various aristocrats in the capital. His reports were extremely useful to Danton, who knew just how much, and what, to believe in them. He now used this spy to organize a line of retreat for himself in the event of Brunswick and La Rouairie winning a joint victory. As the myrmidons of the Commune suspected Chévetel and intended to throw him in jail, Danton came to his rescue, furnishing him with a passport to Brittany and a confidential letter for the Marquis de la Rouairie. In this letter he proposed an alliance between them. The object of this move was to unite all men who feared the prospect of complete political chaos and were anxious to restore order in France —even, if need be, to bring back a constitutional monarchy. Thus, Danton killed two birds with one stone: he rescued Chévetel from the Committee of Public Safety, and he provided himself at the same time with an out. At thirty-three he had the devious, Machiavellian brain of a seasoned politician.

Though Danton obtained the release of such people as Guillaume, the banker, the Abbé Llomond, and one of Fabre d'Églantine's servants who had been imprisoned for theft, he made no effort to get Montmorin out of the Abbaye. As the person responsible for supplying the royal family with false passports prior to their escape attempt, the ex-Minister had been jailed several days previously. If La Fayette and Brissot were not lying when they claimed that Danton had been drawing a regular retainer from Montmorin for the last three years, it shows singular ingratitude on Danton's part that he made no attempt to help his former benefactor. Unless, that is, he was afraid of compromising himself over what he believed to be a hopeless case—or felt that Montmorin's death would be a very useful way of eliminating so dangerous a witness. That, in all likelihood, is why we find Montmorin being executed, in the rue Sainte-Marguerite, immediately after his condemnation by the Maillard Tribunal.

For three days the butchery went on in every Paris prison. Using sabers and pikes, one hundred and fifty ruffians executed the Swiss Guards who had survived on August 10, various priests and aristocrats arrested during the house-to-house raids, and suspects of every kind including common-law prisoners and some women incarcerated in the Salpêtrière. There were some twenty-eight hundred persons being held in custody at the same time, and the exact number of victims was never known. But it seems that the death roll was 1465, and that 1335 were acquitted by the Commune's "judges"—a fact too often forgotten.

As regards Danton's part in these massacres, it was several weeks before a pamphleteer plucked up courage to say that he had "washed his hands of them." In January of 1793 the *Chronique de Paris* published over Girey's signature, a "carol" in which various politicians were shown arriving in Paradise:

> Jesus thought it was Pilate
> When Danton reached the place;
> Joseph, a hearty democrat,
> Reviled him to his face.

The real "people" were so terrorized that they dared not intervene. Most of the time they were cowering in their houses and went out only to reach their place of work. If they passed a cart loaded with corpses, they hurriedly retreated; they dared not show their lack of enthusiasm for such executions, let alone the active horror they felt.

Gabrielle herself may have conveyed this sense of outrage to her husband. According to a story spread by their two maids, Catherine Motin and Marie Fougerot, she asked Danton, point-blank: "Is it true that *you* were the person who ordered these massacres?" And Danton replied: "Oh God *no!* Don't tell me *you're* going to throw this business in my face, too? Leave questions like that to Roland's wife, can't you? No, I'm not responsible for this butchery—but I was powerless to prevent it. Don't follow the example of all those half-wits who are blaming it on me—that would be a hateful thing to do."

From that day on, or so their friends felt, the Dantons' marriage seemed noticeably less happy. Despite her husband's protestations of innocence, Gabrielle felt that a rift had opened up in their love. It looked henceforth as though she had at last seen Danton in his true colors and was simply tolerating him as best she could. Her old admiration had vanished. Danton, for his part, could not bring himself to forgive Gabrielle her suspicions. He made no attempt to bridge the gulf that had opened up between them; instead, he sought consolation in the arms of other women.

From August 26 onward all France was involved in the nomination of the grand electors for the Convention. On September 3, when the butchers were beginning to tire of their revolting task through sheer exhaustion, the nine hundred Paris electors met in the Bishop's Palace to choose twenty-four members of the Convention. Finding the room at their disposal somewhat cramped, they decided to move in a body to the Jacobin Club and conduct their ballot there. On its way from the Île Saint-Louis to the rue Saint-Honoré, the procession had to pass the Conciergerie and the Châtelet. Outside the doors of both prisons lay piles of corpses. Terrified, the electors looked the other way.

Once at the Jacobin Club, they took several days to complete the voting and declare the results. Of the nine hundred electors, almost two hundred deserted; Danton therefore was elected by 638 votes, Desmoulins by 465, Robespierre by 338. After them the following also obtained places in the Convention: Collot d'Herbois, Manuel, Billaud-Varennes, Marat, Fabre d'Églantine, Robert, Fréron, Sergent, Panis, Legendre, and Philippe Égalité—to name only those who were the Minister's personal friends.

Danton and Desmoulins, then, had come out at the head of the poll. To celebrate their victory they made the rounds of the most fashionable restaurants accompanied by girls of very dubious reputation. Danton was on the point of abandoning his fidelity to Gabrielle, while Desmoulins had been unfaithful to Lucile for some time already. Moreover, gossip had it that Lucile herself was cuckolding her husband, and that he had become a *mari complaisant* in return for her agreeing to overlook his own peccadilloes. In the mock carol quoted above, with its irreverent picture of Paradise, Girey also included Desmoulins:

> Then Joseph saw, beside Robespierre,
> Desmoulins pass that way:
> "How are you, brother worker?"
> The wily Saint did say.
> Camille, not at a loss,
> Answered: "Good morning—boss."

By giving grounds for such rumors, Camille and Lucile laid themselves wide open to every kind of libelous attack. Camille talked, in a cynical manner, about his wife's supposed boy friends. He was proud of Lucile's beauty and seemed, in his profligate way, to get positive pleasure, as Louise Robert said, "from the advances which Danton used to make to her." Yet Lucile herself wrote, apropos Fréron's return from his mission to Metz: "He always looks as though he's sighing. . . . Oh you poor simpleton, what possible hope are you nursing? No, no, my dearest Camille, this friendship, this pure love we have will never exist for any other person but you!"

But the "other persons," Danton especially, went on paying court to her; her husband seemed to derive a kind of erotic pleasure from appearing as the cuckold. His pride in possessing so attractive a wife was such that he would gladly have made her strip in front of his friends to arouse their envy of his good fortune. There was something decidedly pathological about Desmoulins. But though Lucile received all her admirers' declarations without blushing, she never allowed them full consummation of their passion. Her private diary, which she never intended for publication, was to confirm this. Danton, who would have enjoyed nothing more than a tumble with her, had all his trouble for nothing.

He therefore turned his attentions to Mme. de Buffon, Philippe Égalité's mistress and daughter-in-law of the famous naturalist. The delectable Agnes occupied a house in the rue Bleue, which the Duke had rented on her behalf. Danton's friends used to refer to her in conversation as "the lady from the rue Bleue." She had succeeded Mrs. Elliott as the Duke's favorite in 1787. The young Englishwoman, who remained a staunch adherent of the monarchy, had this to say concerning her successful rival: "Mme. de Buffon's policy was different from my own." Where Grace Elliott had been trying to keep Philippe for herself, Agnes de Buffon was doing her best to push him into power. Was it in pursuit of this goal that she succumbed to Danton's advances? The great man of the day never boasted of this intrigue, and Mme. de Buffon herself did not shout it from the rooftops. But there were persistent reports—though perhaps no more than rumors—that when Philippe was staying at Monceau, the Minister was to be seen passing through that door in the rue Bleue. Later, when four Deputies —Buzot, Lanjuinais, Chabot, and Robespierre—asked the Convention to unseat their colleague Égalité and, this done, banish him from France, Danton requested his former colleague Lamarque to speak on the Duke's behalf (to do so himself would have been too risky). Such details, if they do not prove the liaison with Agnes, at least suggest that the lady from the rue Bleue had acquired some influence with the Minister.

Indeed—and this was one undoubted weakness in his character—Danton could be influenced by any woman, provided she was pretty enough. In his *Memoirs* Alexandre de Tilly refers to a person whom he calls, discreetly, Cécile. One September evening, Cécile went to see Danton in the Place des Piques. She told him that the Duke de Broglie, General de Biron's Chief of Staff, had been thrown into prison at Langres, where a group of *sans-culottes* was attempting to organize a minor repetition of the Paris massacres. M. de Broglie, who had fought in America and been a Deputy to the States-General, afterward embraced the popular cause and became a member of the Third Estate. But since August 10 he had refused to swear any oath of allegiance except to the old Constitution; which was why he now lay in Langres Prison in danger of suffering the same fate as his fellow captives in Paris.

With truly feminine audacity, Cécile asked Danton to release her protégé. The Minister, incapable as always of resisting a pretty face, granted her request. "Very well, Madame," he said, "I will let you have him back. But make sure you tell him that we have no confidence either in him or in those of his kind. Tell him to go to sleep, and let people forget his existence. Tell him to leave the hard business of demagogy and the dirty requirements of *sans-culottisme* to us."

And Tilly, the aristocrat who reports this little scene, shows no less admiration for the "champion of democracy" in his comments on it: he praises Danton's loyalty and plain speaking, and "the energetic drive so characteristic of a strong man." Strong enough, perhaps—except when faced with Cécile's charms.

Though almost swamped by the task of national defense, Danton still did not forget his duties as Minister of Justice. With some diligence he set himself to reorganize the administration of justice. New tribunals replaced the old ones; but the magistrates delayed taking up their appointments, for fear that the Duke of Brunswick might prove victorious, and thereupon bring all the judges to trial, as he had promised in his manifesto. At this point Danton drafted a barbed memorandum to the procrastinators: "The more stormy events become, the less time should any official lose in betaking himself to his post." This piece of advice was a thinly veiled imperative; behind it lay the threat that those who failed to comply would find themselves transferred from the Bench to the dock. The Tribunal of August 17 was not convened in order to be a dead letter. Although the Committee of Public Safety had, for three days, stolen the Tribunal's stock of aristocrats, priests, and other suspects, there still remained work enough for the properly appointed magistrates to perform.

For example, there were certain crooks who had used the massacres to help them fleece their unsuspecting fellow citizens. Decked out in false uniforms, these rogues marched into house after house, ordering the inhabitants to hand over their gold coins, watch chains, shoe buckles, and the like "for the defense of the country, and by order of the Commune." Some of them actually brought scales along with them to weigh the jewelry, and issued receipts for each contribution "in the name of the nation." Genuine municipal officials tried to hunt these imposters down, and Parisians got the two categories badly confused. "General" Santerre sent out patrols, which arrested con men and *bona fide* officials alike. The prisons, which had miraculously emptied after the massacres, began to fill up again. There was work enough for the tribunals now, and Danton ordered the reluctant group of new judges to proceed to their duties.

Then, suddenly, the press announced a theft which put all others in the shade. This time it was the State that had been robbed. The Crown diamonds, which were kept locked up in the National Archives, had disappeared—the "Regent," the "Sancy," the "Dragon," the "Tavernier," the "Blue Diamond," all the brooches, necklaces, and diadems confiscated from the ex-Queen, the Dauphin's priceless toys, his father's damascened pistols. Nearly everything was gone. Of a collection worth some 24,000,000 *livres,* according to the previous year's inventory, all that remained was the equivalent of 600,000 *livres* in jewelry.

Although this mystery may at first glance seem out of context here, nevertheless Roland, the Minister of the Interior, and Danton, as Minister of Justice, were linked up with it in so bizarre a manner that we must, unavoidably, devote some space to its elucidation. The really crucial question is whether the theft of the Crown diamonds in any way helped to bring about the victory at Valmy. In the following chapter an attempt is made to shed some light on this problem.

CHAPTER XI

The Mystery of Valmy

BEFORE THE EVENTS of August 10, 1792, the present Place de
la Concorde was known as the Place Louis XV. When the
monarchy was overthrown, the new Commune changed the
square's name to the Place de la Révolution. In it there stood
two large buildings with pillared façades, built by Gabriel thirty
years earlier. On one side of the rue Royale (or the rue Nationale, as it was rechristened) stood the Hôtel de Crillon;
on the other, a monumental edifice which today houses the
Ministry of Marine but was then occupied by the National
Archives. In this vast and magnificent building the State stored
its spare public movables, its tapestries, its works of art. Before
the Court's removal from Versailles, there was an apartment in
the National Archives kept as a pied-à-terre for the Queen,
when she came—strictly incognito—to spend a night in Paris.

Toward the end of the eighteenth century the Place de la
Révolution did not present the same animated appearance as its
modern successor the Place de la Concorde. Since immediately
to the west of it were then either suburban slums or forests, it
could be regarded as marking the boundary of the city. Little
frequented by day and altogether deserted at night, it was not a
spot that many people chose for a stroll. And as the guillotine
at this time was operating in either the Place de Grève or
the Place du Carrousel, there were as yet no curious spectators
outside the National Archives waiting to enjoy this new and
gruesome entertainment.

At night Parisians regarded the square as a death trap, especially since there were no street lamps except for two isolated lanterns, at the end of the rue Nationale and the corner of the rue Saint-Florentin, both of them attached to the side walls of the National Archives building. This explains how the thieves were able, without being disturbed, to reach the main floor by means of the lamp cable (or perhaps with a ladder) and get in through the window. They kept well away from the main entrance in the rue Nationale, where the *concierge* and the guards were stationed—all now sound asleep. But neither in the rue Saint-Florentin, nor in the square itself, nor in the building's colonnade was there any danger of interruption. The best proof of this is that the *coup* came off successfully.

Citizen Restoul, the chief curator, had been worried by the possibility of such an attempt. Having been made responsible for the Crown Jewels only a bare three weeks before, he still felt very nervous about them. They had been transferred from Versailles in 1791 and placed in the custody of Restoul's predecessor, Lemoine-Crécy. Their inventory took up fifty full pages.

Restoul had sent several letters on the subject to Santerre, now Commander-in-Chief of the National Guard. These formal complaints, which may still be consulted in the Archives today, reveal the extent of the curator's anxiety. He was not being given enough soldiers to maintain adequate guard over the building. He had wanted twenty for each main door, or sixty in all; yet he never obtained more than a dozen. One day he wrote: "Is it through negligence, forgetfulness, or deliberate malice that the guard is often left without relief for forty-eight or even sixty hours at a stretch?" Though he reinforced his written complaints with more personal approaches, the poor man did not succeed in persuading Paris's new masters to grant him a single extra guard. The answer to his requests was, in essence, that no danger existed; the doors of the chamber containing the diamonds were locked and bolted and had wax seals on them, while any would-be robber had to pass the *concierge*'s lodge in order to reach the stairway. It seems clear that no one gave a thought to the windows behind the colonnade, which looked out over the Place de la Révolution.

Yet a certain friend of Danton's observed something very strange indeed going on there. Maître Camus, that obscure

namesake of Mme. Recordain, was an officer in the National
Guard. In this capacity he was required to take a detachment
on patrol duty through the streets of the city. Despite his various
distinctions—he was a member of the Académie des Inscriptions
et Belles-Lettres, a former Deputy to the Constituent Assembly,
and a newly elected member of the National Convention—the
old lawyer nevertheless donned his uniform, buckled on his
saber and pistol and cartridge belt, and set off with his twelve
men. During the night of September 16 he was proceeding in
this manner across the Place de la Révolution, decked out in the
blue uniform frock coat of a National Guard officer, and thinking about the imminent opening of the Convention which was
scheduled for the 21st—the day after the dissolution of the
Legislative Assembly. He was also, according to his own subsequent testimony, staring "vaguely" at the black, majestic sil-
houette of the two great mansions built by Gabriel.

As he and his squad approached the National Archives from
the direction of the Seine, they perceived a man standing in the
colonnade, throwing down various objects. A second person,
stationed on the paving below, was picking them up in the
coolest manner imaginable and stuffing them into his pockets.
Thanks to the light cast by the lantern at the corner of the rue
Saint-Florentin, Camus could observe the activities not only of
these two unknown individuals, but also of a third person who,
clutching a basket, was on his way up to the main floor—
either by means of the lamp cable or else on a ladder placed
against the wall. It was too dark for him to be certain which it
was, as he testified afterward before a court of inquiry.

On perceiving these three men behaving in so curious a
manner, Camus at once ordered his squad, not to swoop on the
thieves and arrest them—and this is where the affair begins to
get mysterious—but to march down the square, the whole length
of the building, turn right into the rue Nationale, ring the
front-door bell at the National Archives, and wake up the
concierge to inform him what was going on. This was Camus's
way of sounding the alarm; it must have taken him at least
five minutes. The porter, on being roused from sleep, took a
little time to put on his clothes but finally hurried off to rouse
the curator, M. Restoul, and call out the guard. Another ten

minutes, if not more. Then all these officials, together with Camus and his men, went up the internal stairs, dashed down endless corridors, and finally reached the entrance to the Jewel Chamber. Was it permissible to break the seals without a Commissioner being present? After some hesitation and argument the door was finally broken open. During this little comedy the thieves, of course, had made a clear getaway.

The police were then notified and began their investigations at two o'clock in the morning. Roland, roused from his bed by a messenger of Camus's, left his home in the rue des Petits-Champs and reached the National Archives at some time after four. His first act—the mystery deepens—was to order the police to abandon their inquiries. "This," he informed the stupefied investigators, "is a matter for a government commission." As he stared at the gaping cases and empty caskets and smashed windowpanes, the Citizen Minister, it was observed, had a very thoughtful expression on his face.

The news of the theft sped around the various government departments and finally reached the Riding School. The Legislative Assembly, which had only three more days to run, was completely flabbergasted. Various Deputies interrupted Roland, blaming him for the inadequate size of the guard. To which Roland replied: "Do these gentlemen suppose that the Minister of the Interior's duties consist in nothing but safeguarding the National Archives? I have a vast correspondence to deal with. I am responsible for keeping watch over the whole of France—a far more important task than keeping watch over the National Archives!"

Mme. Roland wrote in her *Memoirs:* "The day after this serious theft took place, Fabre d'Églantine came to see me at eleven o'clock in the morning—d'Églantine, who had never once shown his face in my house ever since the September massacres! . . . He did not find me in; I had just left with Mme. Pétion. Nevertheless, he waited a good two hours for me. When I got back I found him in the courtyard, and he came up with me uninvited. Though I did not so much as offer him a chair, he stayed for an hour and a half, bemoaning the previous night's robbery—which, he said, deprived the nation of such solid wealth—in highly hypocritical tones. He asked

if no one had the slightest knowledge as to who might have done
the deed, and expressed amazement that nothing had leaked out
about it in advance. . . . I let him rattle on, said very little
myself, and revealed nothing of my inner thoughts. Eventually
he took his leave, and I never saw him again.

"When my husband and I next met, I told him: 'One of the
men who robbed the National Archives was here this morning,
to find out if he was under suspicion.' My husband asked who it
was. 'Fabre d'Églantine,' I said. 'How do you know?' 'How do
I know? So bold a move can only have originated with our
master of boldness—I mean Danton himself. Whether this will
ever be proved, in the formal sense, I don't know; but I'm
absolutely sure it's true.' "

Though Manon Roland was an intelligent woman, with excellent sources of information, her evidence must be treated
with caution. She composed her *Memoirs* in the Abbaye Prison:
her alliance with the Girondists—as we shall see later—had cost
her liberty and, ultimately, her life. By now she had come to
regard Danton, who was at least partly responsible for her incarceration, as the devil incarnate. Nevertheless, the behavior of
the Minister of Justice, as revealed in the course of this analysis,
does leave room for suspicion.

Government Commissioners, appointed by Roland, now took
over from the police officials whom Restoul had called in; and
a group of jewelers, under the direction of Lemoine-Crécy, the
previous curator, made an expert appraisal of those diamonds
which the thieves—owing to Camus's sudden appearance—had
not had time to remove.

In the box of documents pertaining to this affair (now
housed among the archives of the Public Record Office) there
is one very curious letter. Written by Roland and dated September 18, it advised one M. Gerbu, a goldsmith in the rue du
Harlay, that two individuals would be calling on him that same
day (i.e. the day following Camus's discovery) to offer him
some pieces of jewelry "stolen from the National Archives."
Roland urged this goldsmith "to take all available steps to
recognize these men, and to secure their arrest."

Now September 18 was less than twenty-four hours after the

discovery of the theft. How did Roland happen to be so well informed? If Danton was in fact involved in the affair, it does not look as though Roland could be entirely innocent. According to the version he produced later, a version contradicted by the note referred to above, it was only *three or four days after the robbery* that he received a visit from two police informers. "Citizen Minister," they told him, "we have some extraordinary revelations to make to you." The two men were called Lamy-Evette (sometimes known as Brière) and Cottet. According to Roland, the following represents their stage-by-stage account of the conspiracy.

On August 10, various looters mingled with the Federates who were fighting their way into the Tuileries Palace. These profiteers laid hands on so much valuable plunder that they were arrested and locked up in La Force Prison. There they made the acquaintance of a character called Miette, who was serving a sentence of several years for fraud. Miette dumbfounded them by suggesting that they should do a job on the National Archives. He knew the interior of the building well. The treasure was kept inside five locked cases, in a chamber the doors of which were under seal. But no seals had been placed on the windows that looked out on the open-air colonnade. To get up there the only equipment needed was a good long ladder. The danger of being spotted was negligible. Nobody ever came near the square at night. Once up in the gallery, all one had to do was to break a window and put one hand through to slip the catch.

"That's all very well," said one of the prisoners. "But we've got to get out of here first!"

Miette roared with laughter. Get out of La Force? An easy task. A warder would open the gate for him whenever he liked.

History does not relate how Roland, at this point in the two informers' story, chose to accept a version which cast grave suspicion on the integrity of a service directly responsible to his colleague M. Danton, as the Minister of Justice. One cannot help thinking of Fabre d'Églantine, now Danton's Principal Private Secretary, and of his visit to Mme. Roland.

However, let us stick to the official thesis for the moment. Miette admitted about forty prisoners to the plot. They left La

Force in several successive groups. The first lot, comprising ten men, was let out by a jailer. (The authorities, we may note, never made any serious attempt to discover this accomplice.) The ten escapees made their way across Paris from the rue du Roi-de-Sicile, where the prison stood, to the former Place Louis XV. No one raised the alarm in La Force, and no one attempted to apprehend the group elsewhere. Yet they took their time, and did not conceal themselves. They made various visits and collected enough accomplices to keep watch for them while they were breaking into the Archives. A quick climb up a ladder and the thing was done. They crammed their pockets with fabulous loot but were unable to take everything at one go— to begin with because there was too much of it, and also because they had promised to leave some for their fellow crooks.

The following evening a new group went into action, led by a man called Meyrand. Again, it comprised about a dozen thieves; and again, all of them had got out of La Force— "escaped" is hardly the word, since they had no more trouble in leaving that most curious prison than Miette had had the day before. After these, the third team had its turn. Under the direction of one Deslanges, it followed the now well-beaten trail blazed by its predecessors, but had even better luck, picking up both the "Regent" and the "Sancy." The first, a diamond by which Marie-Antoinette set great store, weighed 137 carats and was a stone of the very highest quality. It was an heirloom from Louis XIV's nephew, the Regent: hence it's name. This ancestor of Égalité's had bought the famous brilliant from a Hindu, in 1717. The Sancy was an equally fine stone, though it weighed only fifty-three carats.

When Deslanges and his fellow robbers met Miette, Meyrand, and *their* gangs (on the premises of a café-proprietor named Retour) to divide the loot—some hundreds of stones—they quarreled so violently that they failed to reach any kind of agreement. Just as the argument was on the point of degenerating into a brawl, a man called Douligny pulled them all up short by remarking: "There's enough jewelry still left in that strong room to give everyone a fair share."

So it came about that a fourth raid was carried out. It took place two nights later, thus allowing the thieves a day's rest be-

fore the attempt. This time no lookouts were posted; such precautions, they thought, were superfluous. The previous three
operations had gone undisturbed by anyone—police, military
patrols, or casual passers-by. The burglars no longer even preserved complete silence while they worked. To avoid tiring themselves unduly they did not carry their loot down by means of the
ladder or the lamp cable; they tossed the heavier pieces over the
edge of the balcony. Two solid gold statuettes of Fame thudded
down on the flagstones, to be followed by the Dauphin's toy
cannon, a splendid piece of wrought silver studded with diamonds. There was also his rattle; its golden bells, similarly en-
crusted with precious stones, tinkled as it fell. There was another statuette—this time of Bacchus astride a wine cask. There
was a saber that had once belonged to François I; and,
lastly, a collection of brooches, bracelets, and ring caskets. Some
of these precious objects lay where they fell; but others (depending on their shape) rolled away in all directions, and members of the gang went after them on their hands and knees. It
was a fantastic haul.

Since this raid (on the night of September 16) was to be
the last of the series, the gang decided to celebrate their exploit
by having a candlelit supper—in the chamber now used as a
drawing room by the Minister of Marine. They brought along
hampers packed with food, and bottles of vintage wine. But
two passers-by—the first in a long time—saw the candlelight
flickering through the windows and were surprised enough to
go and investigate. On the corner of the rue Saint-Florentin
they were seized by members of the gang. What was to be done
with these intruders? Kill them? Hardly. Burglars they might
be, but not murderers. The best solution, they decided, was to
stop their mouths by forcing them, under pain of death, to
become accessories in the affair—to join the supper party and
get a cut of the loot. The two terrified citizens agreed to this.
They were hauled up to the main floor, along with the last
food hamper. It was just as one of the gang was hauling this
basket up the wall that Maître Gaston Camus (as we saw before) appeared at the head of his patrol.

Suspected of negligence, if not of active complicity in the
crime, Camus had a poster printed and stuck up all over Paris,

with the heading: "REPLY to a broadsheet entitled *The Truth About the Robbers of the National Archives*." In justification of his behavior he claimed that his patrol had arrested *one* of these responsible. But his refutation was dated September 25 and by then seventeeen members of the gang were under lock and key. Which of them had been put away by Camus? An academic question, since their arrest had been ordered by Roland and was accomplished as a result of the statements made by the two police informers, Lamy-Evette and Cottet.

These seventeen—some accused of stealing the jewels, others of receiving them—not only found themselves back behind bars; this time the doors were well guarded. Yet thirty-four others, who had likewise been denounced, were able to get away with their loot, in the shape of comparatively modest stones. Meanwhile some of the biggest diamonds had been recovered, but from such unlikely and highly contested places—according to the official record—that no alternative explanation of their reappearance can be dismissed out of hand. The Regent turned up either under a heap of builders' rubble in the Champs-Élysées, or else in a storehouse down the allée des Veuves. The Sancy was found under the roof tiles of a garret; and Anne of Brittany's Ruby was returned to Paris by a citizen of Hamburg. Others, of lesser renown, trickled back in a similar fashion; yet as late as 1806 the Blue Diamond of the Golden Fleece was to figure as *one of the Duke of Brunswick's heirlooms,* and this piece of evidence brings us back to that same Brunswick who was author of the manifesto and the tradition—whether historically sound or not—that he was the principal beneficiary of this incredible theft.

When we ask who was responsible for his good fortune, the answer appears to be: Roland and Danton. Though the rift between them argues against such a supposition, nevertheless the way in which Roland conducted the inquiry into the affair was so dubious that we cannot dismiss such an explanation out of hand. Danton himself wielded absolute power both at the City Hall and in his Ministry; one cannot help thinking, in this context, of Fabre d'Églantine's strange visit to Mme. Roland and the way he kept questioning her for an hour and a half. We should not forget that Fabre was both a member of the

Committee of Public Safety and Principal Private Secretary to the Minister of Justice.

Nor can we ignore the attacks made upon Pétion, the Mayor of Paris, and Manuel, Public Prosecutor to the Commune, both of whom were supposed to have had a hand in the plot. On the other hand, the public had no way of guessing that Fabre d'Églantine was possibly involved, too; nor was it generally known that Maître Camus was either a relative or an intimate friend of the Minister of Justice.

Boldness, boldness at all times. If it is true that Danton, with Roland's connivance, organized the robbery in order to bribe Brunswick (the pay-off being victory at Valmy) we must admit that he displayed boldness of a very high order indeed. However, to clarify the argument, let us now take a closer look at the actions of the various *dramatis personae.*

Haloed with thirty-five years of military glory, the Duke of Brunswick had marched into France as Supreme Allied Commander of the Prussian, Austrian, and French *émigré* forces. Now he was flattering himself that he would reach Paris without a single blow being struck. In fact, the Duke—ruler over an important principality in his own right—had raised violent objections to signing the manifesto which was to make him an object of hatred throughout France. But both the King of Prussia and the Emperor of Austria had been adamant; and finally, with a very bad grace, the great *condottiere* yielded to their demands. He was much in sympathy with the latest ideas; and he had a secret agent in Paris who, incredible though it may seem, claimed that Brunswick could become King of France. Though too astute to bank on such grand promises, Brunswick could not help brooding, albeit without any great conviction, over so agreeable a prospect.

The agent who held out these flattering hopes to him was called Carra. A native of the Ain region, he had, some years before, been falsely accused of theft, and had fled to Germany. His connection with the Duke dated from this period. The fact that they were both Freemasons helped to consolidate their friendship. Carra was also a member of the Jacobin Club, and —before the manifesto appeared—used to sing Brunswick's praises there. On the very morning when the Duke, sick at heart, obeyed the King of Prussia and put his signature to that terrible ultimatum, Carra published the following in *Les Annales Patriotiques:*

> There is nothing more stupid than those who believe, and would like to make others believe, that the Prussians intend the destruction of the Jacobins. . . . The Duke of Brunswick is the greatest soldier and statesman in Europe. Perhaps all he lacks now is a crown to make him, I do not say the greatest king in Europe, but certainly the true redeemer of European freedom. If he does reach Paris, I would wager that his first act will be to visit the Jacobin Club and don the red cap of liberty.

Carra delivered himself of this ill-timed puff on July 25. That same day he met Santerre and Danton at the Auberge du Soleil d'Or and suggested organizing a mob riot against the Tuileries, with the object of bringing down the King. How Santerre and Danton responded to this proposal we do not know, but we do know that Frederick of Prussia and the Austrian Emperor were aware that such a scheme existed. Danton and Santerre talked about it in their circle, and one of their friends —there were plenty of spies about—passed the information on to both monarchs. The interests of these sovereign rulers were not compatible with Brunswick's more or less genuine ambitions. The Emperor, in particular, was being hoodwinked by certain *émigrés* into the vain expectation that he would get Alsace as a *quid pro quo* for his military aid. Therefore, as far as Austria was concerned, Louis XVI had to be kept on the throne, and that meant defeating both the Revolution and Brunswick's fond ambitions. By forcing their Commander-in-Chief to sign this manifesto, King and Emperor compromised him in the eyes of all Frenchmen; but they also supposed that such a move would push France into capitulation, and here they were very much mistaken.

Nonetheless, Brunswick was confident, in private, that a demonstration of generosity would go far to cancel out the effects of the ultimatum. He had made up his mind to use powder and shot only in the last extremity, and he was convinced that a simple route march would carry him to the gates of Paris. Faced with the iron discipline of his Prussian troops, the Revolution's "ragged battalions" were bound to disintegrate. And the easy victories at Longwy, in the Argonne, and at Verdun provided support for Brunswick's thesis. In the last-named town the Duke was astute enough to find a way of getting himself cheered by the inhabitants. But it was the news of this victory that triggered off the September massacres in Paris.

Dumouriez, the new commander of La Fayette's army, was now ordered to make immediate personal contact with Brunswick—who was, like himself, a Freemason. The French general had already been sent on a similar mission beyond the Rhine by Louis XV and knew his opponent well. Ever since that earlier encounter the two men had kept up a friendly correspondence. This did not, however, prevent Dumouriez writing to Danton: "Verdun is taken: now I await the Prussians. The passes of the Argonne are France's Thermopylae—but I shall have better fortune than Leonidas did."

This dispatch was dated September 1. As soon as he received it, Danton sent out General Westermann to Dumouriez. (Westermann was the former noncommissioned officer who captured the Tuileries on August 10; by now the Minister of War had confirmed him in his new rank.) He reached Dumouriez's headquarters sporting a fine new uniform and armed with very extensive powers; his real function there was to act as Danton's "eye." On September 10 he sent the Minister of Justice a highly enthusiastic letter. Dumouriez, he said, "has restored confidence and morale. Every day he goes from one camp to the other, talking to the soldiers, dealing with their needs, organizing his staff, and preparing the army for action."

On this same date the first robbery of the National Archives took place, with further raids following on the 11th, 14th, 16th, and 17th. According to the investigations carried out by the government commission, it was on either the 11th or the 14th that the Blue Diamond of the Golden Fleece disappeared. We should not forget these dates or the identity of the diamond: both are crucial to the unraveling of the web of mystery surrounding the theft of the Crown Jewels.

On the 17th the Paris Commune appointed Tallien and Carra their delegates to Dumouriez's headquarters. It was the

Mayor—a friend of Roland's—who nominated Tallien, and Manuel, the Public Prosecutor—an intimate friend of Danton's —who secured Carra's appointment.

The latter's propaganda—just before the appearance of the manifesto—in support of Brunswick as a candidate for the French throne seems not to have done him any harm. Far from it, in fact—which suggests that the country as a whole, though fed up with the Bourbons, was still scared by the idea of a Republic. Six *départements* had just elected Carra to the Convention. As a veteran of August 10, he was on good terms with Dantonists and Girondists alike. When he set out on his mission to the army did he, being *persona grata* with so many factions, perhaps have some of the Crown Jewels concealed in his saddlebags? Above all, did he take the Blue Diamond of the Golden Fleece? And was he to use his personal connection with Brunswick as a means of getting this manna safely into the Duke's hands? In any case, it was still necessary for Dumouriez —the indispensable go-between—to maintain diplomatic relationships between himself and his opponent as long as possible before finally resorting to powder and shot.

This in fact—as Danton learned from one of Westermann's dispatches—was exactly what he did.

On the 14th, three days before Carra left Paris, Brunswick sent an emissary to Dumouriez under a flag of truce. Major Massenbach had two tasks: first, to arrange a meeting between Brunswick and Dumouriez and then to convince the latter of the Duke's peaceable intentions. But the French general, apprehensive of Westermann's observant eye, arranged for Massenbach to be received by an old regular called Duval, who completely missed the equivocal nuances in his visitor's conversation. However, he reported what had been said to Dumouriez, who at once grasped the real purpose of the interview.

That same day a strategical error on Dumouriez's part put his army in great potential danger. An *émigré,* Count Roger de Damas, reported this to the Count of Artois—that brother of Louis XVI's who was accompanying the Prussians with his regiments of French exiles. Artois at once hurried to Brunswick and informed him of the situation. But the Commander-in-Chief refused to believe what he heard, and so, as Roger de

Damas later wrote, missed "an easy opportunity" to defeat the foe. "I accuse him of treason," Damas added. But he saw nothing more in this "duplicity" than Brunswick's desire "to be the controlling spirit in the affair." In Damas's view, the Duke had not been "bought" by France; he was sparing her for some obscure purpose of his own.

Nonetheless, the Duke's negligence on the 14th allowed Dumouriez to join up with Kellermann; and the two French armies, now reunited, once more found themselves facing Brunswick's forces. The date was September 20, and the place a level plain dominated by a building destined to achieve immortality: the windmill of Valmy.

On that same day, the Legislative Assembly ended its existence. But not all the Deputies said good-by. A number of them would meet the following day, on the same benches as they had occupied hitherto. Their new Assembly, however, was known as the Convention.

At Valmy an artillery duel began. All through the day the opposing sides bombarded each other. About a hundred and twenty cannons joined in this exchange. When it was over, Kellermann stuck his cocked hat on the point of his saber, shouting: "Charge! Long live the nation!" As one man, the tricolor battalions shouted back: "Long live the nation!" Their intention, clearly, was to advance on the Austro-Prussian forces and cross bayonets with them in the best military tradition. But this aim was frustrated by Brunswick. From the elevation on which he had been observing the battlefield he shouted to the King of Prussia: "We will not give battle here, under any circumstances." Frederick protested: he had not come all the way from Berlin in order to go home empty-handed. "Look at the troops we have to deal with," Brunswick said. "These Frenchmen are just waiting till we're almost on them before charging us!" Then, without offering any further explanation, the Commander-in-Chief had the retreat sounded.

That was the end of the battle. Revolutionary France had defeated Europe. Yet her troops had not been engaged, and the artillery duel had produced a total casualty list, on both sides, of no more than nine hundred killed or wounded. A moral victory was claimed; faced with the stern determination of Kel-

lermann's "cobblers, tailors, and blacksmiths," Brunswick had
decided to pull out his hitherto invincible regulars. Not so,
argued the angry and disappointed *émigrés*. According to them,
Brunswick had been bribed by Danton. Through the agency
of Carra and Dumouriez, both Freemasons, Danton was said to
have conveyed no less than 5,000,000 *livres* to that other Freemason the Duke. And since the Treasury could not supply so vast
a sum, Danton must have sold the Crown Jewels to raise the
cash.

But those who argued thus forgot that the date of the final
raid on the jewels, September 17, militated against their theory.
Between then and the 20th, the day of the battle, how could
the Minister have possibly found time to collect all the jewelry,
negotiate its sale, pack up the proceeds, and dispatch this sum
to Brunswick? Besides, did not the Duke already possess one
of the greatest fortunes in all Germany? He was the reigning
prince of Brunswick, Lüneburg, Wolfenbüttel, and Blakenburg;
brother-in-law to the King of England, and richly paid for his
services as a mercenary by the King of Prussia; the owner,
moreover, of a castle famous for its "Babylonian staircases,
and its doors of bronze, malachite, and ivory." No, the Duke of
Brunswick was not the man to be tempted by a miserable
5,000,000 *livres*.

On the other hand, he suffered from that strange monomania
which affects certain art collectors. He did not go in for pictures, *bonbonnières,* or clockwork dolls; his speciality was
precious stones. The fact was known among the Teutonic aristocracy. Was it also known in Paris? Did Carra and Dumouriez,
who had both enjoyed the Duke's luxurious hospitality, remember this expensive hobby of his? Very often the collector's attitude borders on the pathological. Brunswick was not such an
extreme case. Nevertheless, when he died in 1806 his legal executor found no less than twenty-four hundred diamonds in his
strongboxes—of all sizes, variously cut, rosettes, brilliants, and
briolettes, the latter being a heart-shaped pattern. Several dozen
of these stones had belonged to Marie-Antoinette or Louis XVI;
and among the latter was a really splendid stone, none other
than the Blue Diamond of the Golden Fleece. But a part of it
was missing.

There are two possible explanations. Either some professional "fences," knowing the Duke's passion, had approached him and sold him these stones at some point between 1792 and 1806; or else Danton, with Roland's connivance, had organized the robbery in order to buy Brunswick off. The first supposition requires no further analysis. It is perfectly plausible and does not come within the scope of a historical investigation.

But the second, that of a plot on the part of the government, justifies close critical study of the recorded facts. Let us, to begin with, assume the theory proven and examine the sequence of events in terms of a political scheme operated by Danton with Roland's assistance. At once everything falls into place— and not least the ease with which the doors of La Force swung open, secretly, for Miette and his crew. The prison came under the authority of the Ministry of Justice; Danton himself was the Minister, and Fabre d'Églantine his Principal Private Secretary. There were no less than four separate breakouts, on four different nights, between September 10 and 16. The escape of these fifty ruffians would lend some credence to the idea that the crime was an ordinary robbery. But one or two of the ringleaders were secret agents of the Minister and brought him the jewels earmarked for Brunswick, which must have been collected during the raids of the 10th, 11th, or 14th. It was, in fact, on the 14th that the Blue Diamond was stolen, and on the 17th that Carra left for Dumouriez's headquarters.

The reason why Roland hurried around to the National Archives at four o'clock in the morning and informed everyone there that the investigation was a matter for government-appointed Commissioners was to prevent them stumbling on the truth. Similarly, the reason why Danton sent Fabre d'Églantine to question Manon Roland was to discover whether her husband, for once, had managed to keep a secret from her when told to do so. For an hour and a half the poet spun a web of lies in order to discover the truth. He coaxed the truth out of "Queen Coco" and left reassured. Roland had not spilled the beans.

When Colonel Égalité came on his mission to Paris, Danton said to him: "Tell your chief that he can sleep soundly; he will defeat Brunswick when they come to an engagement." A neat way of notifying Dumouriez, without giving anything away to young Orléans, that the affair was in the bag. This is why, when Dumouriez made the strategical error that Damas pointed out to Artois, and Artois to Brunswick, he himself did not worry about its possible consequences; he *knew* that Brunswick would not attack him.

The cool and careless self-confidence displayed by the thieves, the fact that no patrol came anywhere near the place during the early raids—all this argues in favor of governmental complicity. A little disorganization was necessary to avoid the suspicion of a too-well-planned operation. Out of about fifty burglars and fences, one or two may have known the real object of the *coup,* but the rest served as a convenient "felonious alibi" for Danton's patriotic machinations.

Gaston Camus, who was responsible for the security of this particular neighborhood, did not patrol the Place de la Révolution till the 17th; he had left the field free for the robbers ever since the 11th and assumed, therefore, that the operation was now over. His clumsy error was to cost him a great deal of trouble. During the next eight weeks or so he was under so much suspicion and so ceaselessly grilled by his colleagues in the Convention that Danton began to fear he would not be able to hold his tongue any longer. So, on December 1, he sent Camus on a mission to Belgium.

But Danton's most skillful (or most blackguardly) maneuver was that by which he turned the storm of public opinion against Roland, whom he personally detested. This emerges very clearly during the trial of the Girondists in 1793. On the excuse of ill-health Danton stayed away from these debates and went off to Arcis-sur-Aube for a holiday. But Fabre d'Églantine, giving evidence at the bar of the House, accused Roland—who was not present and therefore could not answer the charge—of having taken part in the plot for motives of gain: "Lemoine-Crécy, the curator of the National Archives, had been replaced, almost on the very eve of the theft, by Roland's creature Restoul. I accuse Roland, and his entire faction, of the responsibility for this theft!"

Vergniaud, one of the leading Girondists, replied indignantly: "I really do not feel I have sunk so low that I need to defend myself against accusations of larceny!" It is obvious that he, at least, knew nothing about the plot.

Here we have strong indications of governmental complicity. Yet if the theft *was* conducted with the intention of buying Brunswick off, we may still legitimately ask why it was necessary to cut up the Blue Diamond, removing a forty-carat section from its total weight of 115 carats. This type of mutilation is commonly practiced by receivers and would suggest that the Duke purchased the stone. If he was given it by Carra, it would probably have been left intact. But there is quite a possibility that Brunswick himself was responsible. He could have divided the Blue Diamond at any time between 1792 and 1806—the year in which his executor, while making an inventory of the estate, discovered a blue brilliant of seventy-five carats, which experts identified as the Blue Diamond minus a forty-carat section. This missing fragment turned up in the crown of George IV, King of England, on the day of his coronation in 1820. In 1795, three years after the theft of the French Crown Jewels, George had married his cousin, Caroline of Brunswick, who was the Duke's daughter. It is quite possible that Brunswick had the forty-carat stone cut for this occasion and that he gave it to his daughter as part of her dowry.

There is further evidence to show that the smaller of the two Blue Diamonds did, in fact, come from the bride's father. It no longer occupies a place on the Crown of England today. Since Caroline found herself unable to get on with George IV, she left him, and thereafter she made no secret of the fact that she was living with another man. Shortly after her husband's coronation, a scandal-ridden hearing (the Bill of Pains and Penalties in the House of Lords) gave her her freedom. She was allowed to take back her *personal jewelry* and to bequeath it to friends in her will. Among these pieces was the forty-carat Blue Diamond. The person who inherited this magnificent stone sold it to an Italian, who in turn disposed of it to an American millionaire named Hope—hence the name of the "Hope Diamond" by which history now knows it. The gem is now on display at the Smithsonian Institute in Washington, D.C.

The theory of a government plot is also supported by the mystery surrounding the trial of the thieves. As stated before, Roland had seventeen persons arrested, fences as well as burglars; and a further thirty-four slipped through the net. These seventeen prisoners were no longer Roland's responsibility after their arrest, but Danton's, as Minister of Justice. In due course they were brought to trial. The court showed no mercy to some but was very lenient with others. Twelve were condemned to death, and the remaining five acquitted. Of the twelve thus condemned, however, *only five* were actually executed. The sentence stated, by way of warning and reprisal, that the executions would be carried out "on the Place de la Révolution, in front of the National Archives." Thus the theft of the diamonds was responsible for the scaffold being set up in this particular square, where three months later the King himself was destined to die by the guillotine.

The five unlucky ones were beheaded in October, on different days. Among them was a receiver named Louis Lyre. His turn was fixed for the 23rd, and one of his accomplices was to be guillotined at the same time. Just as they were about to climb onto the cart, the two men "offered to make certain revelations if their lives were spared." At least this is what the executioner, Charles-Henri Sanson, who was present at the time, afterward asserted. He added: "The theft was of such importance, and the objects purloined of such great value, that the Criminal Court of the *département* applied for a stay of execution." Confusing Pétion with Guadet, the master executioner continued: "Pétion was presiding over the Convention, which alone, from now on, had the power to authorize such a request. He refused to give the undertaking the men asked for, and promised no more than that he would intercede on their behalf with the Assembly if they revealed the truth first. Their evidence led to the recovery of various pieces of stolen property, hidden in the Champs-Élysées; but *since they obstinately refused to identify the ringleaders of this audacious enterprise,* the sentence was duly carried out."

This was no usual sacrifice. At the very least it shows that Lyre and his companion did not regard Miette as the prime mover in the affair, but that they suspected a State secret although they lacked knowledge of its genesis. Luckier than they were the seven men condemned to death who had their sentences reviewed. On Danton's orders they were sent to Beauvais; there they were given a fresh trial, some nine months later, as a result of which they were sentenced to short terms in prison. Why did they receive such favorable treatment? And why were they allowed to keep the jewels they had stolen? Was this a way of buying their silence? Some of them, indeed, founded very considerable fortunes on this act of clemency, fortunes which their descendants continued to enjoy throughout the nineteenth century.

On the other hand, the diamonds acquired by the Duke of Brunswick brought good fortune neither to him nor to his heirs. He himself lost both his eyes at the Battle of Auerstädt in 1806 and died of his injuries within the week. His son perished at Quatre-Bras, two days before Waterloo. This victim of Napoleon's penultimate battle left two sons. The younger died without issue; the elder, who was only eleven at the time of his father's death, became sole heir to the Brunswick name and fortune—including the famous diamonds. Fate did not look kindly on him, either. The only reason for recalling the details of his tragic life here, however, is that it adds something to the thesis which sees his grandfather as the beneficiary of the great robbery in 1792.

This Duke of Brunswick was overthrown by a revolution, driven out of his principality, and forced to wander from one country to another clutching a valise stuffed with diamonds. He survived numerous attempts on his life, finally reaching Geneva, where in 1871 he died. Conscious that the end was near, he made a will bequeathing his entire fortune, estimated at 65,-000,000 *livres,* to the city of Geneva, on condition that "our body shall be laid to rest in a mausoleum, above the ground, to be erected by our executors on some suitable and prominent height within the city limits."

This is why, ever since then, travelers to Geneva have seen— on the left of the lakeside port and overlooking it—the spectacular tomb of a German duke, whose collection of precious stones, inherited from his grandfather, finally passed into the possession of Calvin's city.

It seems clear that the municipal authorities of Geneva converted these treasures into hard cash. The issue of *Le Monde* for June 18, 1963, announcing the death of Victor Lyon, the financier, "at his Geneva residence, the Maison Royale, 46 Quai Gustave-Ador, aged eighty-five," gave one interesting detail concerning this famous and most generous patron of the arts: "He was the owner," declared *Le Monde,* "of the famous 'Blue Diamond.'"

All this does not amount to absolute proof of a government plot in 1792. But it almost does. Danton was certainly capable of such a devious scheme. There may be further confirmation in a speech he delivered on October 4, at a time when the enemy was still besieging Lille. Danton chose this occasion to ask that the Convention declare Paris out of danger. The Convention did not comply with his request, despite the glowing declaration of confidence in Dumouriez and Kellermann which he made them, and a mysterious allusion to "successful plans on the part of the Ministers." Would he have proposed the easing of wartime emergency measures if he had not been certain that Brunswick had renounced his ambitions?

Moreover, Danton felt no embarrassment about suggesting, a year later, that France should try to get Toulon back from the English by offering them 4,000,000 *livres* for it. During his speech on September 6, 1793, he included the following example of boldness: "Where cannons fail to force an entry," he said, "we should try infiltrating with gold." By the end of 1793 France commanded sufficient resources to bribe her enemies; the government had a "secret contingency fund" of 50,000,000 *livres*. But immediately after the capture of the Tuileries, the income from taxation was so much in arrears that the government could not afford to provide arms for the Saint-Georges cavalry division. For all these reasons, an official and secret plot to raid the Crown Jewels strikes one as highly probable.

It has been argued that, instead of stealing the diamonds, Danton could have called upon the Legislative Assembly to offer them to the Duke. But this would have been quite impossible. Through Dr. Chévetal, Danton was in correspondence with La Rouairie, the aristocratic conspirator who was to raise the flag of revolt in Brittany when Brunswick reached the gates of Paris. By proclaiming *publicly* that he was trying to bribe the Duke,

Danton would automatically compel the latter to refuse his offer—unless he wanted to have La Rouairie, the King of Prussia, the Emperor, and the *émigrés* all accusing him of treachery. The whole elaborate plot, the prime object of which was to compensate for French military weakness, would then have collapsed like a house of cards.

This is why, though we cannot be certain that the precious stones found among Brunswick's heirlooms were brought him by Carra two days before Valmy, it is equally impossible to assert as a fact that the Commander-in-Chief *must* have bought them from some receiver, for cash.

In one of his novels Hugo devotes seven lines, no more, to this murky affair. He pictures Robespierre, Marat, and Danton arguing fiercely with one another in a bar down the rue de Paon. The date is 1793. Hugo makes the People's Friend ask Danton, angrily: "What about the robbery from the National Archives? What about the Crown Jewels?" Eventually, after trying a dozen times to dodge the issue with some irrelevant answer, Danton replies:

> "I halted the enemy's advance. I barred the way to the Austro-Prussian alliance."
> "Prostitute!" said Marat.
> Danton rose to his full, terrifying height.
> "Yes," he cried, "I am a whore. I admit it. I sold my body—but I saved the world!"

In fact, what he had saved was the Declaration of the Rights of Man—which amounted to much the same thing.

CHAPTER XII

Deputy or Minister: The Hour of Decision

SINCE MARCH 30 the Marquis de Chauvelin had been the King of France's ambassador in London. But it was M. de Talleyrand, the former Bishop of Autun, who really represented the government. As unofficial ambassador, Talleyrand proved a useful mentor to the twenty-five-year-old official diplomat. Both were well known for their liberal views, and the government of August 10 therefore confirmed them in their posts.

On the other hand, the British government no longer recognized the Marquis. Alarmed by the overthrow of Louis XVI, Pitt and his Ministers preferred not to maintain official diplomatic relations with France. However, they allowed both Chauvelin and Talleyrand to remain in England—a neat enough way of keeping up contact while severing public communications. The link was all the more useful to the two countries in that Danton, with his habitual cunning, was dangling the offer of a French colony in front of Pitt's nose, in return for England's guarantee of neutrality during the war.

Lebrun, the Foreign Minister, was in correspondence with both Chauvelin and Talleyrand. The latter pleaded France's case at the Court of St. James along the lines Lebrun laid down; he was at great pains to emphasize Louis XVI's bad faith and double-dealing during the events which led to his downfall. With discreet allusions to the death of Charles I, the Bishop argued that by deposing the King and confining him to the Temple the victors of August 10 had saved his life and were now holding him in reserve.

Chauvelin, for his part, took advantage of the suspicion with which he was regarded to make approaches to the opposition and urge them too toward a position of neutrality. But he went about the job without finesse, and Lebrun was obliged to repair his diplomatic gaffes by sending him a second mentor, the ex-Abbé Noël, who was accompanied by two of Danton's nominees: his mother's stepson, Georges Recordain, and his cousin Mergez. Recordain was a daring young man who, with the impulsive enthusiasm of his twenty years, had volunteered to act as a courier between London and Paris, carrying mail too dangerous to entrust to the post. It was absolutely vital that England should remain neutral—an object which Talleyrand, Chauvelin, Noël, and Georges Recordain, obscure advocates of a great cause, successfully achieved.

It was in the full flush of this diplomatic victory that Danton appeared before the Convention on September 21, the day of its opening. His eyes shone with self-assurance, his step was brisk and confident. Knowing the strength of his position, he received with a cheerful smile the ovation which greeted him as he entered the Riding School. Wearing a blue coat and a white cravat, he strode into the Chamber, shaking hands as he went. There was a fresh burst of applause as the galleries caught sight of him. Yet news of the victory at Valmy, eighteen hours earlier, had not yet reached Paris.

Less through any false modesty than to make his own position quite clear, Danton ignored the ministerial bench and took his place on the Left of the Assembly, with the "Mountain," where his various friends—Jacobins, Cordeliers, Orleanists—were gathered. From here he could observe the Right, which comprised the Gironde, Brissot's group, and the various hangers-on of Roland and his wife. These two major parties were separated by the "Plain," or "Marsh." Deputies who occupied the Plain, and showed, by their cautious attitude, that they would rather pursue a policy of opportunism than express frank and possibly dangerous opinions, were known as *crapauds,* or "Toads."

Now Danton mounted the rostrum and, for the first time, spoke there not as a Minister but as a Deputy. Better still, and a great surprise to his audience, was the following declaration: "The incompatibility of the executive and legislative powers force

me to make a choice. I am no longer anything but a mandatory
of the people, and it is in that capacity that I offer, before you
all, to resign the ministerial functions that I accepted at a time
of national emergency."

Since it was certain, he said, that Kellermann and Dumouriez
had by now joined forces, he believed that their combined armies "can, must, and will defeat the enemy." Consequently
there was no further need for him, Danton, to retain a ministerial appointment for the purpose of directing National Defense.

The Assembly applauded, but would not hear of his resigning
in this way. Declaring that he would return to the subject later,
Danton next proposed a motion which the Deputies ratified on
the spot: "That the protection of all persons and property shall
be the State's responsibility." "Let us," he cried, "declare that all
property, whether public, private, or industrial, shall be maintained in perpetuity!" He himself was enough of a landed
proprietor to fear the danger of what would be known to the
future as collectivism. One of Robespierre's acquaintances was
an Italian named Buonarrotti, who had been trying—hitherto
without success—to interest him in the theories of Babeuf. For
any man of property Babeuf was a disturbing phenomenon. In
his *Tribune du Peuple* he demanded "absolute equality, and
community of goods." Danton, nervous lest the Incorruptible
be infected with this new plague by Buonarrotti, decided to take
the initiative. On the very day of the new Assembly's inaugura-
tion, he got the Deputies to confirm Article 17 of the Declaration of the Rights of Man: "Ownership is a sacred and inviolable right."

This was one good thing accomplished. The Minister of Justice now passed on to more general affairs. He approved—
though he did not propose—the following motion: "That the
National Convention pronounce a decree abolishing the monarchy in France." Thus at their very first meeting, and in less
than two hours, the Deputies contrived to destroy an edifice
fourteen centuries old and replace it by a régime which protected
property, whether acquired by hard work, brains, or through inheritance. Danton had good reason to be pleased with himself.
He might very well have assented to the principle formulated by
Thiers in 1871: "The Republic will be conservative, or nothing."

In suppressing the monarchy the Deputies displayed some courage. They had not yet learned of the victory at Valmy. Part of France was occupied by the Austro-Prussian forces, and Brunswick's threats were still unpleasantly fresh in everyone's memory.

The great news from Champagne reached Paris toward the end of the afternoon. At that moment the Cabinet was in session at the War Ministry. Danton himself had suggested this location since Servan was confined to his bed with an attack of influenza. The Ministry stood in the rue Grange-Batelière, opposite the Hôtel de Choiseul. Servan's colleagues were conferring with him in his bedroom. His face was flushed and feverish; Roland, Lebrun, Clavière, Monge, and Danton came and went around his bedside. Papers, memoranda, and top-secret State documents were spread all over his sheet and counterpane and shifted with every movement of his legs. On his head he wore a cotton nightcap, and when he nodded in an emphatic manner, the pompom brushed his nostrils.

He suddenly looked across toward the door, an expression of surprise on his face, and the others, seeing this, followed suit. A very young man stood framed in the doorway. The newcomer had entered without being announced by an usher. He had on a colonel's uniform, recognizable by the narrow stripes of gold braid on his tunic. (A general's gold braid was four times as wide.) Yet around his waist the intruder also wore the blue sash of a brigadier general. The combination showed that this officer had been recently promoted, so recently that he had not yet found time to change his narrow braid for the broad stripes of a general.

At the sight of him, the Ministers of the Republic exclaimed, "Your Grace!" almost involuntarily; for this was none other than Philippe d'Orléans's eldest son, the Duke of Chartres, nowadays known as General Égalité. He had been dispatched by Dumouriez to announce the victory of Valmy, and his account of the French triumph filled those who heard it with joyful excitement. When he finished, he had to spend some moments answering a barrage of questions. Afterward he put forward a personal request. Before the battle he had received, from Servan, his promotion to the rank of general and an appointment as

military governor of Strasbourg. He was, he declared, too young
to assume such a post. Moreover, he did not want to be taken
out of the front line, and requested to be kept on either in
Kellermann's army or that of Dumouriez. Servan could not com-
prehend the motives behind such a request. "But you won't be
risking your life any longer in Strasbourg," he pointed out. This,
of course, was precisely what Louis-Philippe objected to. As the
son of a prince who had now become the people's representative,
he possessed a doubly compelling motive for exposing himself to
shot and shell.

During this cross-purpose discussion Danton's heavy paw descended on the young Duke's shoulder. "Come over here a
minute," he said under his breath. "I want to have a word with
you." He drew Louis-Philippe away from the bedside, and
Servan sank back into his pillows once more.

"Don't listen to that half-wit," Danton whispered when he
had the boy beside him in the window embrasure. "Come and
see me at the Chancellery tomorrow morning. I'll settle your
little problem for you."

The dashing young general returned to the former Palais-
Royal, now known as the Palais-Égalité. Here he saw his father
and met several other friends and relations. As was to be expected, he discussed the Battle of Valmy at length.

When he appeared in the Place des Piques next morning,
Danton received him immediately and informed him that he
would remain with the combatant forces—not in Kellermann's
army, but under Dumouriez. Louis-Philippe expressed his grateful thanks. He was delighted to have this interview with a
Minister of such strong and forceful personality. At last, he
thought, an intelligent man! In this bloated giant, with his pink
and flaccid jowls, the Duke felt he had found a sense of realism
that the others lacked.

He was just about to withdraw when he heard these words:
"You may have finished with me, General, but I have not
finished with you."

"What do you mean?"

"You are very young, despite your rank."

"I am nearly nineteen."

This was precisely what was bothering Danton. Young people

were incapable of keeping their mouths shut. Less than twenty-four hours after Louis-Philippe's arrival in Paris, the Minister had already heard something of his views, as expressed in conversation.

"What views?" Égalité inquired.

"Those you expressed yesterday evening about what took place in the prisons. I know all about it. I keep myself well informed."

What Danton was referring to was the matter of the September massacres. Louis-Philippe had indeed come out openly against them the night before, during a discussion at the Palais-Royal. How had the account of his hostile attitude reached the Minister's ears? Perhaps through Agnes de Buffon, or by the agency of some other eyewitness unknown to history.

On being thus upbraided by Danton, Louis-Philippe exclaimed: "The massacres! How could anyone help finding them horrible?"

Danton did not reply at once. His face clouded over. After a moment he said, with brisk self-assurance: "Now listen to me. You're a clever young man, and you ought to have a successful career. But there's one weakness you must be on your guard against. You talk too much. That candid manner of yours is dangerous. It could very easily bring down lightning on your handsome young head."

"How could I restrain my indignation?" Égalité exclaimed. "I embraced the defense of a cause; and now I see that cause stained with the blood of murdered men, slain without trial—"

"Nonsense. Just who *were* these victims whose fate you now deplore in so generous a fashion? The sworn enemies of you, your father, your entire family. They were hand in glove with the *émigrés,* and their own sanguinary plans were common knowledge. They circulated a black list which contained the name of every Deputy—indeed, every notable person—who subscribed to the new radical ideas. Everyone on that list was condemned, in advance, to be hanged or drawn and quartered alive when the *émigrés* were finally victorious. Your father and I figure prominently on that list. Have you read it? You have? Then what the devil is all this childish indignation of yours about?"

"Perhaps the *émigrés* did intend to do such things. But even so, that still could not justify the massacres."

At these words Danton lost control of himself. Clenching his huge fists, he hissed: *"I* was responsible for those massacres! Parisians are the scum of the earth—I wasn't going to have all those young recruits going off to Champagne until they had blood on their hands, the sort of blood that was a guarantee that they'd stay loyal to us. I wanted to put a river of blood between them and the *émigrés*. You're too young to understand such things. Go back to the army—that's the only place today for a man like you and of your rank. You've got a future ahead of you: but don't forget—keep your mouth shut."

Louis-Philippe was rooted to the spot with horror when he heard these words, and turned deathly white. Forty years later, when he was King of France, he passed them on, in confidence, to one of his intimate friends. This person (who some think was the Duke of Aumale, the King's own son) repeated the anecdote to the Marquis of Flers, who inserted it in a study of Louis-Philippe published in 1891. Several subsequent writers reproduced Danton's words, though with reservations as to their historical value. The terrifying frankness and monstrous brand of patriotism they revealed seemed too much to swallow in their entirety. These remarks were consistent with Danton's general character; but since they were transmitted through one source only (the King's confidant) and noted down by only one historian, they had to be treated with some caution.

In March of 1963 there appeared a work entitled *Louis-Philippe et la Révolution française*. Its author, Mme. Marguerite Castillon du Perron, had been at work on it since 1954. She had obtained permission from the Count of Paris, descendant of the last King of France, to consult his ancestor's archives. Going through the "thirty or so trunks" which housed them, and which were stored in a strong room of Coutts' Bank in London, Mme. Castillon du Perron discovered a manuscript bearing the inscription: "My Memoirs, begun at Twickenham in 1802."

"I could scarcely believe my eyes," she wrote in the preface to her book. "No historian, to the best of my knowledge, had ever mentioned the existence of the King's Memoirs. . . ." Naturally she added them to the rest of the evidence she had amassed for the documentation of her narrative.

For over a century and a half these recollections had remained buried and unread. Did Danton's distinguished visitor not intend to publish them? Any firm then in existence would have tried to outbid its rivals for so tempting a manuscript. In 1802 Louis-Philippe was a not-very-well-off exile. If he had sold his *Memoirs,* he would have enjoyed a literary success and gained an appreciable income as well. But he got no profit from his literary efforts; he would seem to have written solely for his own benefit or that of his family. He returned to France after Waterloo and ascended the throne in 1830. Now that he had come back from exile and recovered both his position and his fame, he could all the more easily have published his *Memoirs* had he so desired. The obvious conclusion is that he did not want to. If he was not writing for gain, General Égalité had no reason to conceal, distort, or embellish the truth in order to make his work more accessible to the general public—and thus more remunerative. Here his reminiscences stand in sharp contrast to most: what they reflect is a genuine attempt to tell the truth. So it is significant that he includes (as Mme. Castillon du Perron shows) those horrific words which Danton addressed to him on September 22, 1792.*

An open-and-shut case, one might suppose. Danton admitted his responsibility for the massacres to the young Duke, who, very much taken aback, believed what he was told. But does that necessarily mean that we should do the same? The whole tenor of the Minister's conduct during those days of slaughter described above tends to contradict his admission to Louis-Philippe. Danton's role more resembled that of Pontius Pilate. He did not want such a holocaust; though he was unable to stop it, the last thing he wanted was to direct its progress. His sinister boast before the Prince, the cutthroat's role he assumed in order to emphasize his power is utterly unconvincing. It merely confirms the childish element in his character. His memory is stained

---

* In fact, there are minor differences of expression between the conversation as Mme. Castillon du Perron reports it and the version transmitted by the Marquis of Flers. But the general sense is identical.

with enough bloodshed already; we do not need to blacken it further by accusing him—merely on his own assertion—of having engineered the September massacres for patriotic ends.

After Louis-Philippe's departure Danton went down to the Convention. Disdaining the official Chancellery carriages, he set out for the Riding School on foot—perhaps with the aim of collecting a little public acclamation *en route*. Since the previous evening all Paris had known about the victory at Valmy. To get from the Place des Piques to the Convention meant threading one's way through a network of narrow alleys between the various buildings belonging to the Monastère des Feuillants. A brisk walker could do it in three minutes. The Riding School stood at the present junction of two streets which were only opened in the nineteenth century: the rue de Rivoli and the rue de Castiglione.

The Assembly was Danton's favorite audience, and his torrential eloquence—greeted by the plaudits of a near-delirious crowd —burst upon them not only that day, but for many weeks to come. To catalogue all his speeches during this period—the useless and stupid ones as well as those sparkling with intelligence and originality—would lead us too far afield and be a wearisome task. Almost every session saw him take the platform. His words, Condorcet noted on September 23, were now "words of righteousness; the wicked will no longer dare claim him as their friend."

He made a determined attempt to heal the breach with the Right; unfortunately, the Rolands were becoming more and more aggressive. In the Council, as a preliminary to trying the same move on the Assembly, Roland called for an accounting of all disbursements from the secret funds. Danton would have been hard put to it to comply with this demand, since he had left such disbursements to Desmoulins, Robert, and Fabre d'Églantine.

Nowadays he no longer invited himself to take potluck with Manon. "You ought to take her up again," Fabre told him. "What the little bitch really resents is your never going there." "But the food's so frightful," Danton protested. "Besides, I dislike unfaithful wives. Oh, I know all Queen Coco's affairs are strictly platonic—but that doesn't make her husband any the less of a cuckold!"

Danton was wrong to talk of affairs in the plural. Whatever her conduct might have been in the past, at present Mme. Roland's love was reserved for one man alone and lavished upon him with wild and unstinted abandon. The object of her passion, a Girondist named Buzot, was himself equally infatuated with the chaste Manon but could have wished her a great deal less virtuous. However, any move in this direction had to be kept from Roland, since Buzot had a great regard for his inamorata's husband. While dreaming of melting this icicle he became her political spokesman, denouncing "the anarchic and ruffianly behavior of the Paris Deputies," and the threat to the Convention which their election represented. This caused a fine scandal in the Riding School. Undeterred by heckling from the galleries and, in particular, by "the abominable Marat," Buzot went so far as to propose "that each *département* should provide, for the safeguarding of the Convention, four times as many men as it had elected Deputies."

Buzot's speech encouraged another provincial, an official named Alba-Lasource, to regale the Assembly with a further attack on the capital. He accused Danton, Robespierre, and Marat of conspiring to secure dictatorial powers. The result was a real hue and cry—and all because of Buzot's adoration for Mme. Roland! Robespierre tried to speak, but was shouted down with cries of "Sedition!" and forced to abandon the platform. With resolute mien Danton took his place and made a speech that altered the whole tone and nature of the conflict. Furious at having Marat's exploits bracketed with his own, he now publicly disowned the People's Friend. "I am sick and tired," he shouted, "of people saddling me with the authorship of this man's writings!" But he was ready to excuse Marat's cantankerousness; the poor man had been forced to go into hiding so often, he said, that his spirit was permanently embittered by a "subterranean existence."

Then the Minister spoke out in defense of the Paris Deputies, dealing with each of them by name. "As for myself," he said with a smile, endeavoring to soften his stentorian voice, "I do not belong to Paris; I was born in a region to which my heart always returns with pleasure. But none of us is restricted to this or that *département;* we belong to France as a whole. . . ."

In conciliatory mood he now made a most statesmanlike declaration. "It has been claimed that there are men among us who wish to parcel out France among themselves. Let us banish such absurd notions by decreeing the death penalty against authors of them. France must be an indivisible unity. Very soon we shall all belong to the same great family. . . . I propose that the Convention pledge itself to establish unity of representation and of executive power. The Austrians will shake in their shoes when they learn of this sacred harmony!" And speaking in the present tense, as though the thing were already accomplished, he exclaimed: "Then, I promise you, our enemies are dead men!"

The Assembly rose and cheered him as one man. Then, without a dissenting voice, they voted for the now-famous definition of their new régime: "The French Republic, one and indivisible."

His successes in the Convention did not stop Danton from keeping a firm hand on Cabinet affairs. This applied especially to National Defense, where Servan figured, at best, as a brilliant second-in-command. Having decided that General de Montesquiou, who commanded the Army of the Midi, was not giving sufficient proof of his loyal intentions, Danton dismissed him from his command without so much as notifying him of the fact. He did, however, forewarn the National Assembly of his decision. "Let us show we are men to be feared," he told them. "The preservation of freedom calls for strong-mindedness."

Montesquiou was a careful general. He refused to rush his plans for the invasion of Savoy, but this did not mean that he had made no preparations at all. Not knowing that he had been dismissed, he had every intention of conquering the country. Presently a dispatch reached Paris announcing that he had done so. Danton was mortified at having made such a tactical error—especially since the Convention applauded the victory, loudly, in his presence. Determined to justify his opinion, he persuaded the Assembly to send a three-member Commission to Montesquiou's headquarters. He now feared this general, just as he had feared La Fayette when the latter was the darling of the mob. After his triumph in Savoy, Montesquiou might very well show up in Paris to complain at the way he had been maligned. Fast action was called for.

The only solution was to send out this Commission, at once, and put such pressure on the man that he either rebelled or fled the country. This maneuver had worked very well in La Fayette's case: he had been driven into exile. So Danton, that skillful toreador, now proceeded to plant some sharp banderillos in Montesquiou's prudence and restraint. In a private letter to Montesquiou's chief of staff he wrote: "Keep a very careful eye on the general's conduct; if he orders a retreat, blow his brains out." Sapping the morale of subordinate officers was hardly, one might suppose, the best way to make field commanders victory-minded. But Danton was a civilian and had no understanding of military problems. On the other hand, he knew every trick in the book when it came to making people lose their tempers. The unfortunate Montesquiou, finding himself an object of suspicion to the Convention's emissaries, finally rebelled against their presence. Arraigned by them as a result, he preferred to slip across the border rather than face the guillotine. So France lost a good general, and for this Danton must take the blame. No matter. "The enemy," he declared, "must be made aware of the Convention's existence."

Danton found this new Assembly progressively more attractive than his ministerial tasks. All demagogues need a stage. His offer to resign from the government was put forward again toward the end of September. On the 26th, the people's representatives had decreed that no Deputy was henceforth eligible for any public office. On the 29th, one member inquired whether his colleagues intended the term "public office" to cover ministerial appointments. The report of this debate in *Le Moniteur* continues: "It was unanimously agreed that no member of the National Convention could serve as a Minister"— a resolution which upheld the principle of keeping the executive branch separate from the Legislature. Danton at once tendered his resignation, and his colleagues were obliged to accept it. But they decided, by an overwhelming majority, to keep him at the Place des Piques for another ten days, so that he could brief Garat, now elected to succeed him, on all outstanding problems.

After October 9, then, he was able to concentrate exclusively on his role as representative of the people. The decision was his own, and when one remembers how sharp a nose for profit he had, the choice may strike one as surprising. When he resigned as Minister, he lost a salary of 1250 francs a month. All he would get from the Convention was an eighteen-franc allowance for each session. Even if we assume that the Assembly deliberated daily, and that Danton never missed a debate, his monthly income would still be no more than 547.50 francs.

It is possible that his resignation was partly brought about by the ministerial decree which had been under discussion since September 28. The whole episode is a trifle obscure. When Danton resigned on the 29th, Roland, the elected Deputy for the Somme division, was forced to do likewise. But while the Convention invited the Minister of Justice to remain in office until October 9, Buzot proposed to his colleagues that Roland's tenure be extended until the end of January. In other words, Manon's lover wanted her husband to be given privileged status. The noisy debate which followed did nothing to clarify the problem, and a decision on it was postponed till later.

Meanwhile Servan had resigned his seat on the Council for reasons of ill-health. His portfolio as War Minister was transferred to Pache, a willing and disinterested supporter of Roland's. The new Minister—who had once been Marshal de Castries's clerk—at once demonstrated how patriotic he was by proposing a decree "that our military forces shall not lay down their arms or go into winter quarters until the enemies of the Republic have been driven back across the Rhine." All Ministers supported this motion except Danton, who on October 4 (as we have already seen) attempted to make the Convention proclaim that France was no longer in danger, that the emergency was over. Right up to the 9th, the date of his final resignation from the government, he refused to associate himself with Pache's motion. Even when he was gone, his influence continued to be felt for another fortnight. It was not until October 24 that the decree was finally published, over the signatures of all Ministers then in office.

It is arguable that Danton resigned in order to avoid endorsing this polemic document. On such a hypothesis his decision would provide supplementary evidence as to the part he played in the robbery of the National Archives. When Buzot proposed keeping Roland in office until January, Danton could very easily have used his influence to get himself bracketed with Roland and obtain an equal length of reprieve for them both. His reason for wanting to resign on his own was, no doubt, because of his private agreement with Brunswick. Since the latter's troops were not retreating to Germany fast enough for Pache's liking, Danton ordered Dumouriez to harry their rear—but with a lack of aggression that must have struck anyone not in the secret as very odd indeed. Granted these premises, Danton would have resigned from the government to avoid making a public repudiation of his secret agreement by signing the decree his colleagues proposed. But if his resignation—which he could have postponed as long as Roland's—reinforces the theory that the theft of the Crown Jewels was a government plot, it also reveals something about Roland. Though he was Danton's accomplice in squashing the police investigation, he either held aloof or was excluded from all diplomatic negotiations with the Duke.

These negotiations actually took place, and every historian acknowledges their authenticity. Whether the supposed gift of diamonds in fact formed a basis for discussion or belongs more properly to the realm of unproven hypothesis, it cannot be denied that Danton and Brunswick were in contact with each other through intermediaries. Publicly—on the rostrum, in the clubs, and at meetings of the Cabinet—the "poor man's Mirabeau" proclaimed the need to pursue the retreating army, cut it to ribbons, annihilate it. From his tone one might have assumed that Dumouriez's failure to cut off the enemy rear guard verged on deliberate treachery. Yet he took advantage of his extra ten days in the Place des Piques to send Dumouriez a confidential letter—with instructions not to destroy the Prussian army "since Prussia is not the natural enemy of France."

On the other side, Brunswick also was acting out a very similar comedy. *Officially* he was prepared to evacuate France immediately in return for the release of Louis XVI and the latter's safe arrival on German soil. But at the same time the great *condot-*

tiere was trying to dupe his employer, Frederick of Prussia. If he succeeded in extracting the captive monarch from prison and delivering him in Berlin, he would also be furthering his own personal ambitions by the elimination of a rival for the French throne. *Officially,* again, Danton charged Sillery and Carra with the mission of "making Brunswick see reason." It was a classic poker game, in which each side endeavored to outbluff the other. Brunswick dangled the tempting offer of evacuating French territory; Danton played with a more or less dubious promise, if not of the French crown, at least of the diamonds which had adorned it. (In this case the jewels' purpose would not have been to obtain victory at Valmy so much as a Prussian withdrawal after the battle.) The life and liberty of Louis XVI were being used as a bargaining point. With all these stakes in their keeping, a constant stream of negotiators—Massenbach, Von Manstein, Lombard, and Lucchesini for the Duke; Tallien, Carra, Sillery, and Thouvenot for the French commander— shuttled to and fro between the two generals' field headquarters.

Danton, whose powers as an orator were matched by his astute diplomacy, hoped to put pressure on Brunswick by exploiting his ambitions, real or disguised—not to mention his collector's mania. Without ever pushing him too hard, he was making the Prussian commander withdraw his troops, little by little, from French territory so that the armies of the Republic could then attack the Austrian and Piedmontese forces occupying Nice, Savoy, and Belgium.

The plan succeeded beyond all expectation. General de Montesquiou, as we have already seen, conquered Savoy, and Savoy voted for union with France. General d'Anselme entered Nice without firing a single shot. The Duke de Biron and the Count de Custine (now metamorphosed from noblemen into Republican generals) followed at a circumspect distance behind Brunswick's army, *carefully avoided destroying it,* and entered Germany at its heels. Then, on orders from above, they suddenly took the offensive. They occupied Spire and Mayence, crossed the Rhine at the latter town, and sent Houchard marching into Frankfurt behind a brass band. Several factors had contributed to produce this success: talented commanders; an upsurge of enthusiasm among the rank and file, whose discipline had improved notably since Valmy; and, above all, Danton's tactical skill in the warfare of secret diplomacy. Tainted this man may have been, but beyond a doubt it was he who saved France.

Since Roland's retention on the Council had only been conceded by the Convention *en principe,* Buzot now asked for a definitive ruling on the case. This proposal drew general applause from the Girondists. Meanwhile Philippeaux, speaking from the Mountain, took advantage of the debate to demand a comparable extension of Danton's tenure. But the latter once more refused, declaring that "such an invitation is not worthy of the Convention's dignity." This inept remark triggered off an acrimonious discussion. Suddenly Danton, out of patience with the argument, interjected: "No one appreciates M. Roland's qualities more than I do; but I would suggest that if you decide to invite him to remain in office, you should extend the same courtesy to his wife. Everyone knows that Roland did not run his department single-handed; whereas I most certainly did."

A sally of this kind merely added to the uproar. The orator had overstepped the mark, and his scandalous suggestion was at once picked up by the press—approvingly in the case of Marat's paper, which described the husband of "the woman Roland, Minister of the Interior" as "this kitchen scullion whom she leads by the ear"; whereas *Les Révolutions de Paris* repudiated his remarks, the editor observing that it was not Citizen Danton's business to lift, in public, the veil concealing the natural private intimacy of a respectable married couple who take no action without consulting each other first. One could have wished that Citizen Danton had been as well served in *his* department."

This shaft was obviously aimed at Fabre d'Églantine, Robert, and Desmoulins. Could it also have been intended for Lucile and Gabrielle? Lucile, perhaps; she was believed—quite wrongly— to be overgenerous with her favors, especially where Danton was concerned. As for Gabrielle, everyone knew that she, like Molière's heroine, qualified for the label "charming but prosaic."

On the evening of October 9, Gabrielle moved back into their old apartment overlooking the Cour du Commerce. Since her husband was no longer a Minister, she had reverted to her ordinary status as a petty-bourgeois housewife from the rue des

Cordeliers. It was with some relief that she found herself in the
same home, and occupied by the same daily round, that she
had abandoned fifty-nine days before. That she no longer slept
in the canopied four-poster once occupied by Chancellors of
France did not distress her at all. She had got back her old
room, complete with its twin beds. She had even begun to regain
her husband's affections—somewhat in abeyance after the reproaches she had leveled at him on September 4. Though she
had not forgotten her grievances, at least she was now prepared
to forgive her husband his Pilate's role in the September massacres. Poor Gabrielle, it was lucky she remained ignorant of
Danton's terrible confession to Louis-Philippe. Besides, she was
once more suffering from the early symptoms of pregnancy—
her fourth. The child, she calculated, was due about the beginning of February: four more months of patience and precautions.
The doctor insisted on her going to bed early.

Danton took advantage of this regimen to go out in the evenings without his wife. He, Fabre, and Desmoulins were often
seen together in the Palais-Royal restaurants, accompanied by
women of dubious reputation. Was he ever seen crossing the
threshold of "the lady from the rue Bleue?" There is no clinch-
ing evidence on this point one way or the other. Agnes, who
was still passionately devoted to Philippe d'Orléans, had no
further motive for keeping in with Danton after his resignation
—or at least, so she thought. Deputy Danton and Citizen
Égalité were now equals in the eyes of the law; they sat side by
side on the benches of the Assembly, among lawyers, merchants,
carriers, and horny-handed sons of toil. For a descendant of St.
Louis this seat on the Mountain represented a terrible comedown.
Drawn on by his inevitable destiny, the unhappy Duke did not
realize how fatal the course upon which he had embarked would
prove. He no longer desired the throne, which in any case had
slipped beyond his grasp. Doubtless, too, his son did not return
to the army, after that interview with Danton on September 22,
without telling his father the gist of the following remarks that
the Minister made: "This Republic we have just proclaimed
won't last long. There'll be a great more blood spilled yet; but
France's vices, and maybe her virtues too, will bring her back

to the monarchy. Not the Ancien Régime, that's gone forever . . . A democratic monarchy will be established. And while France will never again tolerate the senior branch of your family, in your own case it's another matter. You have fought under the tricolor flag, and you stand a very good chance of ascending the throne. Your duty, therefore, is to hold yourself in reserve." Louis-Philippe did hold himself in reserve—until 1830.

On October 14 Dumouriez reached Paris and was given a tumultuous ovation by the crowds. When invited to speak at the Jacobin Club on the Battle of Valmy and the Prussian retreat, the little general's first action was to embrace Robespierre. Danton, welcomed with equally enthusiastic applause, accepted the presidency of the Club. "We are not exhausted by any means," Dumouriez told them at the end of his lecture. "Very soon I hope to have a force of sixty thousand men with which to pull down kings and save the common people from tyranny."

Ah-ha, his listeners thought, so freedom was to become an article of export, was it? Camille Desmoulins took the same line in the Convention on September 28, when he came out in favor of a "war of conquest"; Danton dared not point out how fallacious this argument was, since the majority of those present shared the same attitude. He therefore fell back on the well-tried gambit of siding with the strongest party, and expanded on the theme that Desmoulins had sketched. "Let the Convention," he thundered, "become a General Committee of Insurrection against all monarchs throughout the world!" (And why not? Hadn't the Regent, the Sancy, and Anne of Brittany's Ruby all been recovered? Plenty of good fresh troops there . . .) But when his rhetorical temperature fell to normal again, Danton felt he had once more overstepped the mark. Though he avoided repudiating his actual statement, he nevertheless turned his coat. ("The really absurd man," as Barthélemy was to say later, "is the one who never changes.") As far as this war of conquest was concerned, Danton's speech on April 13, 1793, went back on the opinion he had expressed during October of 1792. He even got the Convention to pass a motion declaring that "the Republic would not interfere in any way with the governments of other powers."

Meanwhile—still on October 14, 1792—Danton applauded

Dumouriez's misleading lecture as loudly as anyone. That evening Mme. Roland invited the General to dinner. She thought it a clever move to confront her pet demagogic aversion with the victorious warrior, across the same table. But she also had a surprise in store. The party was not held at the Ministry of the Interior, but in the Tuileries Palace. For five days now Danton had ceased to be a member of the Council. Manon had taken advantage of his absence to install *her* Ministry in the King's Palace. She and her husband were now occupying the apartment that had belonged to Mme. de Tourzel, the former royal governess. (Danton remarked that, despite everything, "Queen Coco" hadn't had the nerve to occupy Marie-Antoinette's chamber.) He accepted her invitation; but the food, which was no better than that in the rue des Petits-Champs, soon triumphed over his false bonhomie. Two hours later he turned up at the Opéra, accompanied by Dumouriez. The audience recognized them both—Danton such a huge figure, the General so diminutive—and a tremendous ovation greeted them when they appeared in their box.

Danton was no longer living like a Parisian, but rather in the style of some provincial in town without his wife—so much so that friends and relatives had given up inviting her, in the certain knowledge that the invitation will always be turned down.

Gabrielle had her consolations—though these did not include the company of Lucile or Louise Robert, from both of whom she was drifting steadily further apart. Lucile's reputation was being blackened by so much gossip nowadays that Gabrielle could hardly help regarding her as a rival. In Louise's case, it was she who had fallen out with the Danton *ménage* rather than *vice versa.* Besides, Gabrielle's fourth pregnancy, unlike the others, was proving a difficult one. She scarcely went out at all, except to take her children for a walk in the Luxembourg Gardens. Often her little neighbor from the floor above would accompany her on these expeditions. As she grew older—if one can apply such a phrase to passing the age of fourteen—Louise Gély was acquiring an air of self-assurance unusual in a girl of her age. Intelligent, understanding, and reasonably pretty, she very soon became Gabrielle's dearest and most intimate friend. The two little boys, Antoine and François-Georges, looked on her as a big sister. She would play games with them, and generally take over from their mother when Gabrielle's pregnancy kept her in bed.

When Danton got home exhausted by his political battles (or a gay night on the town), he would often see little Louise edging discreetly toward the door on his arrival. He would stop her and chat awhile; the young girl's conversation, her beauty, and her adolescent enthusiasm were like pure refreshing water to his spirit—though from time to time he would give her a quick concupiscent glance as well.

In the Convention he had to defend himself against his enemies —and there were enough of those after his resignation from the government. Similarly, he had fewer friends and supporters to back his endless motions. He himself, on the other hand, never hesitated to break a lance on behalf of his Mountain colleagues when they were assailed by the Girondists.

Robespierre, for instance, found himself once more convicted of aspiring to dictatorial powers. The Right demanded his arraignment. The Incorruptible parried their attacks with his habitual weapons: calmness, perspicacity, and two pairs of glasses. Would these suffice without Danton's assistance? His nickname of the "Incorruptible," incidentally, Robespierre owed to Marat: the People's Friend had printed it some while back in his bloodthirsty broadsheet. To make it quite clear that while he himself had a high regard for Robespierre he did not at all approve of his dangerous champion, Danton began by warning his fellow Deputies: "I hereby declare to the Convention, and the country at large, that I do not like *this person Marat.* I am too well acquainted with his temperament; to put it bluntly, he is at once explosive, cantankerous, and unsociable."

This person Marat. There was another man who would never forgive Danton. Once again that fatal oratorical fluency of his had carried him too far. Then, turning back to Robespierre himself, the speaker proposed adjourning the debate for eight days, so that accusers and defenders alike might have time to prepare their cases. The Convention agreed. A week later the Incorruptible was triumphantly vindicated. That day, November

5, was to mark the beginning of the great struggle between Montagnards and Girondists.

The following morning, November 6, a Girondist named Valazé read out from the rostrum a report on the conduct of the King. His denunciation contained so many trifling or nonsensical statements concerning the prisoner in the Temple that the Montagnards began to wonder whether the aim of his party was not to secure the adjournment of a trial which they themselves were insisting should be held. Valazé attacked Louis XVI as a "hoarder of wheat, sugar, and coffee." The "monster" he portrayed was little more than an ordinary speculator. Moreover, he declared, according to the 1791 Constitution the King's person was inviolable. Could one bring him to trial when there were no legal provisions for doing so? For several days the Convention quibbled over this infringement of a principle solemnly enshrined in the Declaration of the Rights of Man—that no law should be retroactively binding.

Soon after the beginning of this lengthy debate, on November 8, news of a splendid victory reached Paris. Dumouriez, leaving Custine and Biron to dog the heels of the Prussian forces in Germany, had defeated the Austrians at Jemmapes two days previously. This success came as the apotheosis to all Danton's maneuvers. Dumouriez, moreover, exploited his victory to the full. He pursued the routed enemy, occupied Mons, Brussels, Liège, Namur, and Anvers, and freed Belgium from the yoke of Austria, which had been treating her as a colony since 1714. Although barely two months old, the Republic was triumphing on all fronts. Danton could feel legitimately proud of these victories. If it had not been for his shady deal with Brunswick, Frederick of Prussia and the Austrian Emperor would be occupying the capital and the Revolution would have foundered.

When Danton first heard the news of Jemmapes, he was not in Paris but at Sèvres, near Versailles, taking a holiday. Gabrielle's health required fresh country air, and her parents had recently acquired some property consisting of a large park and two houses. One of the latter they now occupied themselves (they had decided to leave Fontenay-sous-Bois); the other would make a pleasant vacation residence for their daughter and her husband. The purchase had gone through on October 6.

So Georges and Gabrielle were relaxing at Sèvres, together with both their children and Gabrielle's family. The place had a charming name, "The Fountain of Love"; it seemed to engender a corresponding affection in the Danton *ménage*. Hitherto they had made all their journeys in Paris and its immediate environs by gig. Both horse and vehicle were kept in a stable-*cum*-coach-house, scarcely more than a shed, down the rue du Paon, which ran quite near the Cour du Commerce. This stable was far too small to accommodate a second vehicle and several horses. But the outhouses of The Fountain of Love had no such drawback, and Danton was anxious to ease Gabrielle's pregnancy as much as he could by sparing her the rough jolting motion of a gig. So he purchased a carriage, and it was in this princely vehicle that the Deputy to the Convention, with his wife and children, reached the gates of the Charpentiers' new park. In a period of such social topsy-turvydom and social vindictiveness (Danton's own career reflects this trend to some extent) it took real "boldness" to fly so openly in the face of criticism and, ignoring anything the gossips might say, exhibit signs of wealth such as could never be explained by any number of eighteen-franc attendance tallies at the Convention.

When he learned of the victory at Jemmapes, Danton left his wife and family at Sèvres and returned to Paris posthaste. He appeared at the Riding School to find the King's opponents busy airing the question of a trial once more. Mailhe, the Deputy for Haute-Garonne, read out another report on the King; this one, unlike Valazé's, was incendiary stuff, and the debate on it lasted for a fortnight. Battle was joined between staunch defenders of the law on the one hand, and the opponents of royal inviolability on the other. Long speeches were delivered by such Deputies as Morisson, Saint-Just, Fauchet, Robert, Rouzet, Grégoire, Payne, Faure, Serre, Buzot, Legendre, Jean-Bon-Saint-André, Barbaroux, and Robespierre. The Assembly finally voted in favor of putting the King on trial—not in court, but before themselves.

Though Danton attended every session throughout this dramatic fifteen-day debate, he never once took the floor. His silence astonished those who knew all about the part he had played in mounting the *coup* of August 10; but it came as no surprise to

many others. There had been so much talk about Danton being
bribed by the King that they felt it was only natural for him to
refrain from biting the hand that fed him.

They did not know about the mysterious visitor whom Danton had received before his departure for Sèvres. The visitor
himself recorded this encounter for posterity in his *Notes and
Souvenirs*. Provided that he did not make the whole thing up
(as we know, unsupported testimony must always be handled
with caution) what happened was this. He went to Danton's
house one morning, rang the bell, and was shown into the ex-
Minister's study. Danton gave a visible start of surprise when he
recognized his caller as Théodore de Lameth.

"My poor friend," he said, in lowered tones. "What on earth
are you doing here in Paris? You're a proscribed person; your
life's in danger!"

The two men shook hands. Lameth said: "I am a soldier. I
have come here on a mission." Then he begged Danton to save
the King.

Danton, far from showing him the door, invited him to sit
down and discuss the problem. Louis's innocence, culpability,
and double-dealing were gone through again and again. The
important point was, could a formal trial be avoided? A king
brought to judgment was a king condemned. Danton must talk
to all the really bloodthirsty Deputies, people such as Saint-Just
and Robespierre and Marat. If he failed to convince them, then
he must arrange Louis's escape somehow. To a man of his
achievements, such a thing would be the merest child's play.

"Now listen to me," Danton told him. "I'll be as honest with
you as I can. Though I don't believe the King is entirely blameless, both justice and expediency demand that he should be
extracted from his present situation. I'll do everything I can to
save him within the bounds of ordinary prudence. If I think
there's a chance of my succeeding, I'm prepared to risk my own
neck. But if I lose all hope, don't rely on me. In such a case,
I freely admit that I shall vote with those who condemn the
King. When his head rolls, I have no wish for mine to follow
it."

"Why did you add those last words?" Lameth asked, half
pleased and half vexed.

"To be honest."

So, though Danton attended the debates that decided whether the King was to be put on trial, he took no part in the controversy himself; he was there merely to hear each side's case and keep a sharp eye on the way things developed.

While these stormy events were going on, Danton, too, was forced to defend himself—against charges of squandering public funds during his period in office. The Convention was dealing with several issues simultaneously. Between two consecutive debates on the matter of the King, they found time to discuss no less than thirty-six other subjects—among them the handling of public monies by the Cabinet of August 10. For some while now Manon had been planning her revenge against Danton's attacks, and pushing her husband to demand a statement of accounts from him. With a somewhat hypocritical mien the Minister of the Interior one day announced from the rostrum: "Since I have no secrets to hide, I would like to give an open account of my stewardship. Here is a statement of all expenses I personally authorized on the fund of two millions—400,000 *livres* to each Minister—which the government then in office had at its disposal."

At these words, all eyes turned toward Danton. He went pale. Accounts were something he would find it very hard to furnish. He remembered a sum of 30,000 *livres* given to Santerre for the manufacture of pikes, to be distributed among the citizen body when Brunswick was at the gates. There was also a sum of 17,000 *livres* paid to the clerks in the Place Vendôme for special assignments; and the 2400 *livres* which Robert took to buy the furnishings he needed in the Chancellery. As for the rest, Fabre and Desmoulins had the use of the Minister's signature stamp, and they were not too punctilious about informing him every time they employed it. But Danton could not plead this as an excuse; the men were both his friends and his fellow Deputies. When he himself had to pay anyone for services rendered, he simply dipped into the till without bothering to record the disbursement. As he said later: "Do you suppose I always had time to think about such details?"

In these circumstances what answer could he make when so

insidiously invited to follow Roland's example? And how could
he satisfy the wishes of that financial expert Cambon when he
called for an explanatory statement?

On several occasions, between the two debates concerning
Louis XVI, various Deputies returned to this dangerous question. Since Danton could no longer turn a deaf ear to their prob-
ings, he decided to bring up his heavy oratorical artillery. He
mounted the rostrum. Theatrical gestures, grave and resonant
voice, booming delivery—every weapon in his arsenal was de-
ployed to raise the tone of the debate.

"When the enemy occupied Verdun," he explained, "when
panic spread among even our best and most courageous citizens,
then the Legislative Assembly told us: 'Spare no expense, pour out
money like water if that is the only way of restoring public confidence and giving all France fresh stimulus.' This was what we
did. We were forced to incur expenses far above the normal,
for most of which—I freely admit it—we did not obtain legally
valid receipts. There was great urgency, and everything had to
be done in a hurry. You wanted the Ministers to act in concert:
we did so. That is our account of our stewardship."

A lame argument, the listening Deputies thought; after all,
Roland had supplied them with full details with respect to *his*
administration. Danton could see censorious faces all around
him, and he heard angry mutterings from the benches. Then
he added: "Had the Council spent ten millions more than it
actually did, not one single enemy soldier would have set foot
on French soil, let alone have carried out an invasion."

"It's true! He's right!" shouted several Montagnards. Their
companions applauded, but there were protestations from the
Girondists. The Deputy presiding over this particular session
was Danton's friend Delacroix. His proposal that they should
now pass to the order of the day raised a fresh outcry. The
only way out of this impasse seemed to be by calling upon *all*
Ministers to justify their disbursements, within the next twenty-
four hours. The Convention voted in favor of such a decree. It
was then realized that Danton would have to go back to the
Place des Piques in order to look through his papers. This would
never do. His former colleagues, Roland in particular, had no
desire to see him back anywhere near the Council. Indeed, they

were so delighted at having got rid of him that they now began to back down. Finally, after five more sessions largely taken up with the question of the King's trial, the Assembly, little by little, began to drop *l'affaire* Danton. Deputies who already had their hands full deciding what was to be done with Louis XVI completely forgot the business of ministerial expenses when they heard, from Roland, about the discovery of the so-called *Armoire de Fer,* or "Iron Cupboard."

Roland had been informed of its existence by Citizen Gamain, the Tuileries locksmith. This Iron Cupboard was really a safe, concealed in a wall of the palace and used for storing the King's correspondence. Receipts, letters, reports signed by various well-known political figures—all testified eloquently to the monarch's policy of double bluff. There was material enough here to raise goose-pimples on all those who had not fled the country; enough to make Mirabeau turn in his grave. Yet in all these files the name of Danton did not appear once—a great relief for him, and a powerful argument of his defenders, then or later. *Danton bribed by the Court? Come now, really . . .* But we know that before Roland revealed his discovery to the Convention—which nominated a committee of twelve Deputies to study the King's papers—he had gone through the material himself: a clandestine operation which the Deputies on the Mountain were quick to condemn. They instantly assumed that the Minister's motive was to suppress letters which compromised his friends. Though he detested Danton personally, Roland had allowed his colleague to involve him in so many shady schemes that he well might have destroyed such documents as implicated both of them. A simple enough hypothesis, too simple perhaps; but one cannot help thinking of it when one recalls that La Fayette, Brissot, and Molleville all declared that they had seen, with their own eyes, receipts signed by Danton. That three men of such widely disparate views should concur on so specific a point of detail is striking, to say the least.

Another possibility is that Danton's receipts were never deposited in the King's files at all. During the period of house arrests, as we have seen, the Minister of Justice had issued a passport to Omer Talon, the magistrate who was able, thanks to this gesture on the Minister's part, to get safely away to England.

Now the name of Omer Talon turns up in the Iron Cupboard. Louis XVI had sent him 200,000 *livres* "to police the *faubourgs* (slum districts) and maintain order in them." When Omer Talon returned to Paris in 1802, under the Consulate, criticisms of his way of life began to be heard. Old memories stirred, old incidents were raked up, and Bonaparte had Danton's former protégé arrested. When put on trial Talon declared, under oath, that he had been no more than an intermediary between Louis XVI and Danton himself, and that the sums which he received had gone straight into the demagogue's pocket.

Obviously none of this was known by the Deputies in 1792. The absence of Danton's name from the King's private files afforded him a striking renewal of political virginity. With a reputation for integrity (at least in his relations with the Court) he regained the formidable ascendance which had been somewhat impaired by investigations into his ministerial expenses.

Dumouriez's difficulties in Belgium gave Danton the opportunity to reinstate himself still further in his colleagues' favor. The victor of Jemmapes urgently needed to purchase food, clothing, and transport, but lacked ready cash with which to pay for them. Belgian contractors were refusing to accept the Republic's promissory notes. No such things as a quartermaster corps or a finance corps yet existed; pay and provisioning were in the hands of civilian camp followers known as "army purveyors." Their contract authorized them to make a reasonable profit, but not to profiteer; and their operations were checked by the Quartermaster General and Paymaster General of the army group to which they were assigned.

The official purveyor to the Army of the North was the Abbé d'Espagnac; the Quartermaster General, one Citizen Malus; and the Paymaster General, a person called Petitjean. The priest boasted that he had exchanged his breviary for a sword. A former friend of Calonne's, he had made a fortune under Louis XVI by speculating in the activities of the East India Company. D'Espagnac also had ties with Danton, and it was from Servan that he had obtained his contract as purveyor. Though he lined his own purse in the most scandalous fashion, he had made himself indispensable to Dumouriez. With tireless ingenuity he always managed somehow to find the rations, fodder, equipment, and horses that the troops needed. He even loaned money to the Paymaster General when the Treasury was late in sending it. Thanks to the Abbé d'Espagnac, the army got its pay and seldom went short of rations.

But one Deputy, sent on a mission to Dumouriez's headquarters, came back in a state of high disgust at the personal harvest this curious priest was gathering in. He asked the Convention to dismiss not only d'Espagnac himself, but also Malus and Petitjean. To replace them, he suggested the nomination of a Bulk Buying Commission, consisting of three merchants and two civil servants, and presided over by Hassenfratz—a chemist who was now Minister of War Supply and had formerly worked with Lavoisier.

When Dumouriez heard about these proposals, he exploded with fury. Although he knew quite well that d'Espagnac was making a good thing out of his commission, the General had no intention of losing him. The priest's methods might be morally debatable, but at least the troops had boots on their feet and some kind of food in their mess kits. Pache, the new Minister of War, came out in support of the Bulk Buying Commission, however, and Dumouriez, more angry than ever, sent a delegation consisting of General Westermann and d'Espagnac himself to Paris. There, Westermann pleaded the latter's case before the Convention. As this was a matter of some urgency, Cambon proposed that four Commissioners be appointed to make on-the-spot investigations. The Assembly voted in favor and nominated four of its members for this task.

First there was Danton, who had intrigued for a place on the Commission: when the trial of Louis XVI was held, he would be well out of the way, and in a position to sidestep the promise he had given Lameth. The second Commissioner was Camus; Danton had arranged for his appointment because, being naturally anxious to refute any suspicion of complicity in the theft of the Crown Jewels, he was talking too much. The third was Delacroix, or Lacroix as he now preferred to call himself: another of Danton's old friends. Lastly, the Assembly chose a Deputy called Gossuin, on the grounds that as a native of Avesnes and the member for a northern constituency he was better acquainted than his colleagues with the idiosyncrasies of the Belgian temperament.

Camus and Gossuin left on the same day as the motion was passed, November 30; Danton and Lacroix, twenty-four hours later, on December 1. (The delay was to give Danton time for a flying visit to Gabrielle and his children in Sèvres, just long enough to kiss them good-by.) Lebrun, the Minister of Foreign Affairs, provided Danton with the sum of 100,000 *livres,* not in promissory notes but in cash, and earmarked for "secret expenses." The four Representatives of the People with the Armed Forces traveled in formal city dress. No one, as yet, had thought of making this black, quasi-clerical garb an object of mockery: later it was another matter.

In one of the notebooks which Mme. Roland later used for the composition of her *Memoirs*—not a day went by without some sort of entry—she wrote at the time: "Danton is off to increase his riches in Belgium. He admits, without shame, to a fortune of 1,400,000 *livres.* He preaches *sans-culottisme* but pursues luxury, and sleeps on the piled-up bodies of his victims." The size of his fortune given here is an undoubted exaggeration on Manon's part. Even if he did "admit without shame" to such opulence in her hearing, no doubt his object was simply to make her envious.

CHAPTER XIII

"I Vote for Death"

SOME DEPUTIES PERCEIVED that Danton's departure from Paris was a way of avoiding involvement in the trial of Louis XVI. To allay their suspicions, Danton declared, before he left: "All true Republicans feel indignant at our procrastination in this matter. Tell the people, plainly and without circumlocution, that *the ex-King will be brought to trial with the least possible delay.*" By urging the Convention to get the whole thing over as soon as possible, he was killing two birds with one stone. Granted reasonable luck, his military mission would outlast Louis XVI's trial.

The "sleeping carriage" in which he and Lacroix traveled went by way of Nanteuil-le-Hardouin, Soissons, Laon, La Capelle, and Avesnes. It was raining; showers of blackish water spurted up from the horses' hoofs and the wheels of the carriage. As they approached the border, the travelers observed numbers of soldiers, alone or in groups, slouching along in the mud on the road to Paris and carrying their arms and equipment with them. They looked very much like deserters. At Danton's request, the coachman pulled up. On being questioned, the soldiers replied that they were volunteers. Some of them, considering their contract terminated, were going back to their families. Others were simply "fed up," as they said, with tramping through dirt and slush, freezing half to death, and fighting. This low state of morale came as an unwelcome surprise to Danton and Lacroix. They set off again, and the carriage went rattling at full speed through Thuin, Charleroi, and Namur before finally reaching Liège, where Dumouriez had his winter quarters.

The general had taken up residence in the magnificent Palace of the Prince-Bishops, and it was here that he welcomed his visitors. Camus and Gossuin had been his guests since the night before and told Danton the results of their preliminary inquiries. The military pay chest contained no cash and a mere handful of promissory notes. Dumouriez, when questioned about this, said: "Well, you deprived me of d'Espagnac." Danton's answer was: "Till a firm decision is reached, you still have Ronsin. A Quartermaster General ought to be able to stand in for a purveyor who's been, let us say, unavoidably detained. What we intend to do now is make a complete inspection—camp sites, outposts, hospitals, stores, everything. Afterward we shall draft our report to the Convention."

On almost every occasion Danton and his three companions divided the work between them. They inspected troops and supplies at Liège, Mons, Brussels, Malines, and indeed in every town where the army had to live off the countryside. Their mission had begun as a strictly economic one, but very soon it began to extend into military and political fields as well. Besides observing the wretched quality of rations and clothing, and the primitive conditions in the hospitals where sick and wounded were often forced to sleep on the floor, Danton and his friends were also subjected to a barrage of complaints from Dumouriez. The Minister of War did not want the general to wait until spring before attacking the enemy in the vicinity of Aix-la-Chapelle and Cologne, and driving their forces back beyond the Rhine. Dumouriez was of a different opinion. In his view, he could not hold the present front along the Meuse unless Maestricht and Venlo were occupied. Before making a forward thrust, he had to secure his left. Nor could he mount any offensive at all until he had money to pay the workmen and contractors and peasants, who stubbornly refused to accept promissory notes. England had been forging imitations, and her spies were flooding the country with them; this was the main reason why the Belgians were so uncooperative. But since there were no further reserves of good, well-minted currency, the purveyors had somehow to be talked into accepting promissory notes instead. This situation had already produced a great deal of argument and dissension; it could not be allowed to go on.

But there were still more serious matters afoot. In accordance with instructions issued by the Council of Ministers, Dumouriez had respected Belgian sovereignty. The furthest he went was to make proclamations to that nation; and he had upheld both the privileges of the nobility and the taxes which they imposed. The common people, under the heel of a sacerdotal as well as a secular aristocracy, were incapable of bursting their bonds un-aided; and Dumouriez intended to do nothing (unless on specific orders) to help them attain this goal. Since he thought of Belgium as "liberated" rather than as "occupied" by his forces, he imposed no special levies on the country. Indeed, his convoys paid exactly the same dues at the customs posts between the various provinces as did the Belgians themselves. Nor did he use military force to make the inhabitants open their warehouses to him. He was, in fact, applying in Belgium the philosophical principles of the new régime in France—to the detriment both of his own troops and of the Belgian people.

The solution was clear enough. Dumouriez must either be authorized to treat Belgium as "occupied territory" or furnished with enough cash to obviate such a necessity. The ultimate and most radical alternative was simply to go ahead and annex Belgium to France. Danton leaned toward the last of these alternatives; Dumouriez felt it was too hazardous. Having al-ready been hailed by the *vox populi* as Belgium's liberator, he had no desire to be branded now as a modern Attila. This was a red-hot political question; the Commissioners' investigation had gone far beyond the original terms of their inquiry. The Convention had to be informed of the situation without delay.

Which of the four would undertake this task? Gossuin and Lacroix were ruled out immediately, since at the time when the decision had to be made they were miles away from Liège on a tour of inspection. But someone had to report back to Paris. Though he kept his reasons to himself, Danton was very loath to send Camus. At the time of their departure from the capital, not all the twelve men condemned to death for partici-pation in the theft of the Crown Jewels had actually been ex-ecuted. During October only five had mounted the scaffold

set up opposite the scene of their exploit. There were still seven
left for the executioner; and the delay, it was rumored, was due
to a whole series of "revelations" which the poor wretches had
made, or were about to make, in piecemeal installments. Neither
the Deputies nor public opinion at large could understand the
reason for all this shilly-shallying, and they pressed for the
sentence to be carried out forthwith. (In fact, as we recall, the
sentence was quashed and the seven prisoners transferred to
Beauvais, where at a second hearing they received nothing worse
than light prison sentences.) Members of the Convention kept
up a ceaseless attack on their colleague Camus. He had caught
the thieves red-handed: why had he been so dilatory in proceeding to their arrest? The Deputies demanded an explanation.
It looks very much as though this was Danton's reason for getting Camus put on the Belgian Commission of Inquiry. To send
him back to Paris at this juncture would mean a renewed risk
of his talking indiscreetly. Camus was a very pious man, and a
former Counsel to the Clergy of France; lies were beneath him.
Everyone knew that his room was furnished with a large crucifix
and that he spent long hours kneeling before it in prayer. Was
it wise to risk his facing a moral and religious dilemma which
might drive him to confess?

The only alternative was for Danton to go to Paris himself—
a hard decision, since it meant once more becoming involved
in Louis XVI's trial. Yet the thing had to be done. Dumouriez
could not be left to struggle with his financial, strategic, and
political problems single-handed.

Over this choice between Camus and Danton biographers
disagree among themselves. Some hold that it was Camus who
returned to Paris; others plump for Danton. Those who hesitate
between the two rival theories do not appear to believe that
the identity of the messenger matters very much—too facile a
way of skating over a difficulty. None of these historians has
really sifted the enigma presented by the theft of the Crown
Jewels, or sought for a possible tie-up with French military
strategy. Almost all of them, whether rightly or wrongly, regard
the incident as an ordinary crime. I maintain, on the other
hand, that the name of the Commissioner dispatched from Liège
to Paris has considerable significance. Now the claim for

Camus having made the trip depends on the merest hearsay; but there is one really striking piece of evidence which points to Danton as the messenger. It was on December 8 that he and Camus discussed the political situation with Dumouriez. On the 9th they decided that one of them must return to Paris. On the 13th Danton was in Maître Finot's office at Arcis-sur-Aube, where he signed the deed of purchase for "the coppice known as Les Quittainies," at a price of 600 *livres*. And on the 15th the Convention ratified the decree requested by whichever of the two Deputies had returned to Paris for this purpose. But the one who left Liège must have been Danton: his signature on the notary's deed at Arcis proves it. The distance between Arcis and Paris is less than a hundred miles, and a glance at the map shows that such a detour on Danton's part would have been quite feasible.

The decree which the Convention approved on December 15 had been worked out by Danton in Liège and was put before the Deputies by Cambon. Its text made no specific reference to the annexation of Belgium, but laid down a series of principles governing the occupation of Belgian territory—and, in general, of any foreign territory which the French army might subsequently invade. The decree contained a dozen clauses. It commanded the victorious generals to proclaim, there and then, the "sovereignty of the people," together with the abolition of feudalism, the nobility, and entrenched privilege of any sort. The people were to be convened in primary assemblies for the purpose of electing a provisional government. All property confiscated "from the Treasury, the monarch, his abettors, and from all bodies and communities, whether lay or clerical" was to be placed in the keeping and under the protection of the French Republic. Proclamations were to be made to the effect that the Convention would nominate National Commissioners, chosen from its own members, to go and "fraternize with this provisional Assembly, and take counsel jointly with it and with the French generals as to what defense measures were desirable and what methods should be employed in order to procure such clothing and rations as were necessary for the armed forces." The provisional administration would end as soon as the inhabitants "organized a free and popular form of government."

Lastly, France "would regard as her enemies" all those who, "rejecting freedom and equality," attempted to "restore or treat with the monarch and members of the privileged classes."

When Dumouriez received notification of this charter his anger knew no bounds. In his proclamations to the Belgian people he had promised them liberty; and now he found himself compelled to act like a conqueror. His chagrin and fury were such that he had the decree printed and posted up without appending his signature to it in token of approval; and so hard did he chafe on the bit that from now on he scarcely ever left the Palace of the Prince-Bishops. (In his *Memoirs* he declared that this ukase was partly occasioned by Danton's determination to have his revenge on the little town of Ath, which had refused him a lodging for the night during his journey. No doubt this statement is exaggerated; but it has a certain air of plausibility.)

When Danton left Paris on the evening of December 15, it does not look as though he found time for a quick detour to Sèvres to see his wife. He wrote her from Liège on the 17th—an indication of the speed with which he habitually moved around the country. "Don't forget to take care of sending my saplings to Arcis," he told Gabrielle. "And remind your father to go ahead with the arrangements for his house in Sèvres. Give Antoine lots of kisses from me, and tell him that Daddy will try not to be away too long." In another letter he wrote: "I hope to be with you on January 1, after spending a day or two in Arcis." But Brune, who was still Commandant of the Horse Requisitioning Center, told Gabrielle that her husband's mission would keep him in Belgium for a good two months. Disappointed, she wrote to Danton, who replied: "Our friend Brune really does exaggerate."

Brune was, in fact, pretty near the mark. Danton saw a lengthy task ahead of him, and one that would monopolize all his energies. The Belgians refused to accept the decree of December 15; they disliked bullying tactics. Arguments flared up between them and the thirty National Commissioners of the Convention, who had been sent out to help Danton, Lacroix, Camus, and Gossuin enforce the law. The four of them parceled out the political organization of the country between them. Danton and Lacroix took the provinces of Namur and Liège, as far as Aix-la-Chapelle. They attempted to impose "fraternization" in the towns and villages, with varying degrees of success. Sometimes they had to call in the troops to help them. Nevertheless, Danton himself was never responsible for any atrocities—which is more than can be said for the National Commissioners. Still, he upheld the latter with his authority. "What did the Belgians think we'd send them?" he remarked one day. "Young ladies?"

Personally, he was anxious to please all those under his administration, especially representatives of the fair sex. Though he loved his wife, he was not averse to a little variety. While he was at Liège, Merlin, the Deputy for Douai, saw him "occupied with his pleasures." A man named Foliot described him, in a letter to Carra, as "always sitting down at table, surrounded by girls." He was so constituted that he could not help being unfaithful to Gabrielle. A great drinker and trencherman, this massive, oak-like figure generated an overabundance of sap. Besides, many women were offering themselves to the victors, if only to save a father, a brother, even a husband who had been arrested by the occupation authorities for some offense against their troops. Could the bull from Arcis resist such temptations?

Meanwhile in Paris the King's trial had got under way. Since December 11 the Convention, transformed for the occasion into a court of justice, had been subjecting his actions to a close and relentless scrutiny. Louis XVI made a very bad defendant. It was not a role with which he was familiar, and he floundered badly under interrogation. Sometimes he told such open, unblushing lies that he seemed doomed in advance.

Dumouriez at the time was very anxious to return to Paris. He had two ends in view: to prevent the King being condemned, and to get the decree of December 15 annulled. By pleading overwork and exhaustion he obtained thirty days' leave. Before he set out from Liège he had a discussion with Danton and the latter's London agent, the former Abbé Noël. Among themselves they worked out a scheme for saving the King. Noël had just arrived from France, where he had met Miles, the Englishman Mrs. Elliott had introduced to Danton some time previ-

ously. Noël said he was certain Pitt would willingly pay out two
millions through Miles to buy support in the Convention—
first and foremost Danton's support. If the sum was not sufficient, the balance would be made up by the Spanish diplomat
Ocariz. Mrs. Elliott, Dumouriez, and Mme. de Buffon knew a
good many Deputies who might be susceptible to such blandishments. Agnes still dreamed of one day seeing Égalité on the
throne, but not at the price of his cousin's life.

Dumouriez therefore traveled to Paris in order to set the
project afoot. He reached the capital on January 1, while Danton was still in Belgium. Brune had been right in his estimate;
Gabrielle was not reunited with her husband by New Year's
Day. Unhappily she moved back to the Cour du Commerce. It
was too cold for her in Sèvres. Both children came with her;
Antoine was now three, and little François-Georges eleven
months. Gabrielle's fourth pregnancy had nearly run its term.
It was proving far more uncomfortable than the previous three,
with painful symptoms that made it difficult for her to sleep,
and numerous complications. She was afraid the child might
be born prematurely; the idea of this happening while her
husband was away on his travels scared her. Still, she had her
two devoted maids, Catherine Motin and Marie Fougerot; and
she knew that Louise Gély and her mother would hurry down
from the next floor at the first warning signs and send the
coachman off for the midwife and, if need be, the doctor. But
good friends and loyal servants were not the same as a husband.
Dear God, she prayed, don't let him be too late.

Heaven heard Gabrielle's prayer. Danton left Liège on
January 12, 1793, and arrived in Paris on the 14th, with
Lacroix. They had returned under orders from the Convention,
which wanted to hear a version of the story other than
Dumouriez's. Danton and his wife embraced lovingly; absence
had made the heart grow fonder. The proud father dandled
his two boys on his knee. But more serious matters soon claimed
him. His desk was stacked high with the mail that had accumulated during his absence. Wrapped in his dressing gown,
Danton skimmed quickly through the pile—nothing very interesting. Then, suddenly, a letter from Bertrand de Molleville

caught his attention. It was dated December 11, 1792—over a month before.

This was what de Molleville, the ex-Minister who was now an exile in London, had to say:

> I do not feel, Monsieur, that I should any longer keep you in ignorance of the fact that, among a pile of papers which the late M. Montmorin left in my safekeeping toward the end of June last year, and which I brought abroad with me, I found a memorandum containing details of various sums paid over to you from the Foreign Office secret fund—complete with dates of payment, the circumstances in which you received them, and the name of the person through whose intermediate agency these sums were negotiated and made good. Your relationship with this person is made clear by a note in your own handwriting, which, insignificant though it may be in itself, leaves no doubt that the person in question is acting on your behalf. This note is attached to the memorandum. The authenticity of the latter is further confirmed by its having been written, throughout, in M. de Montmorin's own hand. Up till now I have made no use of these two documents. But I hereby give you warning that they are both attached to a letter I have written to the President of the National Convention, and which I am dispatching—by the hand of the same messenger as will deliver this present note—to a trusted friend of mine, with instructions to forward it, and furthermore to have the contents printed and placarded on every street corner, *if you do not comport yourself, in the matter of the King, as behooves a man whom the King has paid so handsomely.* If, on the other hand, you render the services in this affair which you are well capable of doing, rest assured that they will not go unrecompensed. I have acquainted no other person with the contents of this letter: you need have no anxiety on that score.

Here was a rock cast in a calm pool with a vengeance. Danton had come back from Belgium very much against his will. The Convention's fiat meant that he would be once more up to the neck in the business of Louis XVI's trial, which he had tried to avoid by getting himself appointed to the military Commission on November 30. Now he was not only in danger of having to make good his promise to Lameth (who, we recall,

had visited him secretly during the autumn); a different and no
less grave peril faced him—blackmail by de Molleville.

That it *was* blackmail there can be no doubt; the former
Minister of Marine boasted about it afterward in his *Memoirs*.
But it was also bluff. Perhaps he had, at some point, seen a
receipt signed by Danton among Montmorin's papers; but he
did not possess either the receipt or the memorandum with which
he made such effective play when he wrote his letter on December 11, 1792. However, when Danton read it, on January 14,
1793, he had no inkling that the whole thing was a clever trick.
Montmorin was dead, killed in the Abbaye Prison during the
September massacres. As Minister of Justice, Danton rescued
Omer Talon and seven other persons, but he had made no
attempt to balk the murderers of their prey when it came to
Montmorin. He assumed that the dead man's papers had been
destroyed with him—and here was Bertrand de Molleville waving them under his nose!

How was he to extricate himself from this awkward position?
By intrigue, as always; and also by using one powerful trump
card—the absence of his name from the Iron Cupboard records
—to discredit de Molleville's letter if it did ever come into the
hands of the President of the Assembly.

The upshot of this affair is described by Dumouriez in his
Memoirs. Pitt did not deliver the money he had promised; and
since there were now no funds with which to bribe those who
wanted the King condemned, Danton made no effort to defend
him. Besides, he had already told Lameth: "If I lose all hope,
don't rely on me. In such a case, I freely admit that I shall vote
with those who condemn the King." Then, before he had openly
come out against Louis, (though he was not visibly for him,
either) Danton learned that de Molleville had put his threat
into execution. A letter had indeed reached the President of the
National Assembly. By a lucky chance, de Molleville's "trusted
friend" did not keep a copy and so had not been able to
"have the contents printed and placarded" all over Paris. It was
therefore from one man only, the President of the Assembly, that
this dangerous denunciation had to be retrieved. The President
was changed once a fortnight, and the Convention had nominated ten Deputies to that office since taking over. On January

14 the President was Vergniaud, the Girondist; but it was his predecessor, a nervous and colorless character called Defermon, who had actually received the ex-Minister's letter. Danton went and called on him. Dropping a discreet hint or two about his influence among the Montagnards, he declared that the letter was a monstrous fabrication. Lacroix, whose ascendancy over the Plain was well known, also visited Defermon, and spoke in support of Danton. At this, Defermon, alarmed at the prospect of being victimized by two out of the three parties, decided to destroy so compromising a document. Had he read it out in the Riding School, he might well have incurred the wrath of two thirds of the Assembly's membership.

De Molleville thought he was saving the King, whereas in fact he had destroyed him. "God protect me from my friends," Voltaire once prayed. "I can take care of my enemies." The exiled Count might have been inspired by this aphorism: what Danton now declared to Lacroix, in effect, was: "Threats mean nothing to me now. By trying to blackmail me into protecting the King, these friends of his have just signed his death warrant." Since he now had no intention of intervening in Louis's favor, he took advantage of his brief stopover in Paris to go and sample the atmosphere of the trial.

When Danton entered the Riding School there was no sign of the accused in the special dock that had been built below the benches. He found the Assembly (which purported to be functioning as an instrument of justice) discussing, of all things, a play. He had, in fact, walked in during a debate on freedom of speech in the theater. This odd topic had been provoked by a comedy entitled *L'Ami des Lois,* which presented politicians on-stage under pseudonyms, and the production of which had caused a sizable scandal. Danton took the floor. The old barn-stormer knew just how to produce the effect he was after: with censorious irony he began: "I will freely admit, citizens, that I came here under the impression that a tragedy was in progress—a tragedy which you have undertaken to perform with all Europe for an audience. Today, I anticipated, the tyrant's head would fall at your command beneath that keenest of axes, the law. And what do I find occupying your time? A wretched comedy!"

Now he was well away, the flow of his rhetoric unimpaired, emphasizing that Louis XVI's fate must be decided without a moment's delay. When Lanjuinais proposed that the Convention's verdict should depend on a clear two-thirds majority (a maneuver designed to save the King), Danton shouted him down and imperiously summoned his colleagues to come out in favor of an absolute majority. His eloquence carried the day, and the following morning, January 16, the Assembly in a state of feverish excitement began to vote.

Each Deputy in turn mounted the rostrum, explained the reasons for his decision, and then recorded his personal verdict. *Death; death; death*—the lips that framed this frightful word trembled with fright themselves, all the more because of the threats and catcalls from the packed public galleries. Each of these temporary judges was in the grip of the frightful fear, the contagious miasma which murder invariably seems to produce. The next session after the adjournment began at ten in the morning and went on till midnight; the accused was not present. When Danton ascended the rostrum in due course to express his own opinion, the words he uttered had the resonance and weight of cast bronze. "I am not numbered," he said, "among that common herd of statesmen who have yet to learn that there is no compounding with tyrants, who have yet to learn that the only place to strike a king is between head and shoulders, who have yet to learn that they will get nothing from Europe except by force of arms. I vote for the tyrant's death."

He had given his judgment without being present throughout the trial. He had not heard the Declaratory Act of Louis's Crimes, nor the formal charge which was subsumed under thirty-four heads. The questions put by the President, the replies of the accused, the speeches of the several advocates—all these momentous events had taken place while Danton was still in Belgium. Nevertheless he cast his vote, and not one person contested his entitlement to do so. A more appalling infringement of the Declaration of the Rights of Man it would be hard to imagine.

The balloting from the rostrum proceeded. Suddenly the

President announced that Lebrun, the Foreign Secretary, had just received a note from the Spanish Ambassador asking permission to address the Assembly. "What's *he* want to get mixed up in this for?" one Deputy shouted. But the news gave Danton a nasty jolt. Mention of Spain, and of Señor Ocariz, recalled the web of conspiracy woven in Liège and London—and also hinted at its possible unravelment in Paris. He sprang up at once, interrupting the Deputy who was then explaining his vote, and demanded to be heard. "You're not King yet, Danton," Louvet told him. "You enjoy no special privileges here."

This remark produced a vast uproar. In the end, however, Danton managed to get his point across. "I cannot find words," he roared, "to express my amazement at the audacity of a foreign power which sets out so shamelessly to influence the result of your deliberations. If everyone felt as I do, this House would at once vote for war with Spain. The Spanish do not recognize our Republic—yet they presume to dictate to it. They do not recognize it, I say; yet they presume to impose terms on its representatives, to play a part, with them, in determining the present verdict. I demand that we pass to the order of the day!"

By a unanimous vote the Convention rejected the Spanish diplomat's application, and the ballot continued.

All this time Dumouriez was waiting impatiently at the Hôtel de Saint-Marc, the Duke of Biron's town residence. Mrs. Elliott and Mme. de Buffon were with him. For once, Grace and Agnes found themselves in political agreement. Both hoped that Philippe Égalité would not vote for his cousin's death, and that Danton would come out in defense of the King. From time to time one of their messengers would return to give the anxious group the latest news from the Riding School. The session continued for hours. Each Deputy, after his explanatory speech, would end with a formal phrase—"I vote for death," "I vote for banishment," "I vote for confinement in chains," and so on. Dumouriez was discussing the monarch's chances with the two women and was just as much on edge as either of them. But the messages arriving from the Tuileries left little room for hope. Danton had betrayed the sacred cause; and

Orléans himself, carried away by the horrible—and contagious
—mood of the moment, had condemned the King.

Finally Dumouriez's last informant arrived, bringing the result of the ballot. Hearts sinking, the two women heard the
figures: 387 Deputies had voted for death, only 286 for detention or banishment. Agnes and Grace burst into tears, while
Dumouriez swore impotently. But the next day several Deputies
demanded a reprieve, and the whole issue was back in the
melting pot. The procession to the rostrum began all over again,
and now one single vote was to make a martyr of Louis XVI.

Nor was he the only martyr. A former member of the Royal
Bodyguard, a man called Pâris, went looking for Philippe-
Égalité in the arcades of the Palais-Royal, with the intention of
running him through. Having failed to find him, he did the
next best thing by splitting the skull of another "regicide," Le
Pelletier.

A wave of panic and terror swept through the capital. The
inhabitants saw assassins everywhere, and public opinion began
to have second thoughts about the rigorous justice meted out by
its representatives. Indeed, they came to be known as "blood-
drinkers." One name, Danton's, was on everyone's lips. Hostility
toward him reached such a pitch that on the evening of
January 21—the day the King was executed—he felt compelled
to declare from the rostrum: "I call you to witness—you,
Pétion, and you, Brissot; I call you all to witness, for at last I am
determined to make my true self known, to be recognized for
what I am; I call on all those who know me to say if I am a
blood-drinker!"

He was well away now, as usual, and went on talking for
another half hour. Personally, he said, he much preferred
Burgundy to blood. If he had ever chanced, in a purely figura-
tive sense, to "drink" the latter, it was always along with a large
number of his present listeners. Surely they were not going to
hold him responsible for the September massacres? Roland,
Clavière, Monge, and Servan had been Ministers then, just as
he was. Did they so much as raise their little finger to stop the
slaughter? Four days ago he had voted for the King's death.
But had the Girondists, who were attacking him now, taken a
different line? Then what was he being criticized for? His frank-

ness? Very well, then, since the subject had come up, he would
not mince his words. Little by little he demolished the public
images of Roland, who was still Minister of the Interior, and
Pache, who had taken over the War Department since Servan's
departure, assailing them in turn with highly cogent arguments.
He obtained the resignation of the first and the dismissal from
office of the second—who was replaced by Danton's own candidate, General Beurnonville.

This triumph allowed the wealthy Danton's enemies and
rivals to whisper that his object in toppling Pache was to let
Dumouriez have the Abbé d'Espagnac back again—and with
him all the contractors, such as Basire, Chabot, Delaunay
d'Angers, and Julien de Toulouse, who supplied that strange
priest with cardboard-soled boots, rotten meat, or weevil-riddled
lentils. (On all these items, needless to say, Danton would pre-
empt his own small commission.) Though the scandalmongers
could not substantiate these rumors, they nevertheless spread
them with great assiduity. They eventually reached Dumouriez,
who was furious. Since he had failed in his attempt to save
Louis XVI, he now returned to Brussels, forfeiting four days of
his leave.

To add the crowning touch to his victory over Roland and
Pache, Danton now pressed for the annexation of Belgium. In a
speech delivered on January 31 he recalled that the inhabitants
of Liège and Hainaut, when consulted in a kind of plebiscite,
had given a favorable response to this proposal; but he omitted
to point out that the rest of the country was solidly against it.
Indeed, he had the audacity to say: "It is not in my name alone,
but in the name of all Belgian patriots, of the whole Belgian
people, that I call also for the union of Belgium with France."
("Also" referred to the fact that the county of Nice had already
entered the French orbit.) "France's boundaries," Danton went
on, "have been marked out by Nature. We shall expand to
meet them on all sides—to the ocean, the Rhine, the Alps,
and the Pyrenees. Kings and emperors threaten us; but now
you have thrown down the gauntlet to them. That gauntlet is
the head of a king, and it heralds their own approaching
doom. . . . As for Belgium, the ordinary people, the small
property-owners are all in favor of union. . . . Once you pass

this decree, you can apply the laws of France to Belgium—and then priests, nobles, and aristocrats will be swept away, leaving a land of freedom behind them. Once this purge has taken place, we will have more men, more arms at our command. You will find among these Belgians Republicans of our own caliber, who will make their despots bite the dust. I am therefore in favor of the union of Belgium with France."

The report of this speech in *Le Moniteur* indicates that it was received with applause. Yet rumor had it that Danton—to the great indignation of his fellow Deputies who shouted down his closing words—did not in fact say "more arms" but "more *wealth*," and that the alteration of the text in Panckoucke's newspaper was achieved by a private deal with the shorthand reporter. *"More wealth"*: the effect of such a phrase on Danton's enemies can easily be imagined. It is possible that this slip prejudiced the success of his plea for annexation; on the other hand, Danton's setback may equally well have been occasioned by certain remarks of Bréard's. In his survey of the arguments favoring union, Danton had mentioned a petition by the citizens of Liège, requesting such a step. Bréard, who took the floor immediately afterward, challenged the sincerity, if not the very existence, of this petition. The Convention followed his advice and postponed a vote on annexation until fuller information was available. Meanwhile the Chamber's representative was requested to return to Belgium forthwith and enforce the decree of December 15, whatever the cost.

Danton set out that same evening. During the weeks he had spent fighting his political battles in Paris he had devoted very little time to his wife. He had been seen in the Jacobin and Cordelier Clubs, at the Riding School, and in restaurants, together with Desmoulins, Fabre, and Lacroix. Sometimes he even sought out the company of those notorious traffickers in military privation, Julien de Toulouse, Delaunay d'Angers, Basire, and Chabot—infamous creatures, who always had a bevy of pretty girls in tow.

Poor Gabrielle, now in the last, unwieldy stages of pregnancy, felt that her time was very near and that when it came her husband was bound to be somewhere else. Duty, duty, always duty. Good God, Gabrielle thought, if a good citizen has duties toward his nation, has he none toward his wife, too? Gabrielle was tormented with worry. She was afraid Danton might have some exotic mistress waiting for him in Belgium. Rumor had it that he was enjoying himself there in no uncertain fashion. Stories of this sort reached Gabrielle's ears daily, and she would weep in Louise Gély's arms.

But when Danton said good-by to her on January 31, she made an effort and held back her tears. It was evening, and the Convention's session had just ended. The oil lamps cast a flickering glow over this sad farewell scene, and Gabrielle's heart was filled with sudden ominous foreboding.

Ever since the death of Louis XVI and Danton's speech on the annexation of Belgium, public opinion in England had been clamoring for war with France. The King's execution made a very deep impression across the Channel; and if the threat against Belgium's independence became reality, there was a risk of Holland's security being jeopardized as well. Moreover, the Convention, in a decree promulgated on November 19 had promised to "help all nations desirous of recovering their liberty"; the English government could not but regard this French invasion of the Low Countries as a potential threat.

The diplomatic finesse of Talleyrand, Chauvelin, and Noël no longer served any useful purpose. By his refusal to defend the King, and his plea for the annexation of Belgium, Danton had destroyed the last faint hope of Great Britain remaining neutral. The Cabinet's new policy was clearly defined and admitted no compromise. Chauvelin was requested to leave England within eight days. As for Talleyrand, he was now no more than an ordinary impecunious *émigré:* his name—discovered in the Iron Cupboard files—figures from this period on the proscription lists of the Convention.

To replace them, Lebrun now sent Maret to London. Maret was an ex-lawyer turned journalist, the editor-in-chief of Panckoucke's *Moniteur.* His mission to London, however, proved a waste of time; even the British opposition was solidly aligned with the war party. The Convention, impatient with Lebrun's plodding, tenacious diplomacy, now decided to jump the gun and declare war on England rather than wait for Pitt to declare war on France. This disastrous decision took place on February 1, while Danton and Lacroix were traveling toward Brussels. The Rubicon had now been crossed, and the hostilities now beginning would reach their final conclusion only twenty-two years later, on the field of Waterloo.

The two French Commissioners, still blissfully ignorant of what lay in store for their country, did not hurry back to Belgium. Danton ordered the coachman to make a detour by way of Arcis-sur-Aube. He wanted to inspect his estates and look in on his mother and sisters. With Danton, personal and family interests were always put on the same level as those of the nation.

This flying visit lasted for twenty-four hours, and then he and his companion resumed their journey. At Vatry, a small town about nineteen miles from Arcis, they stopped to change horses. The postmaster recognized Danton and refused to serve him. An argument took place. The postmaster's wife, with typical feminine vindictiveness, screamed personal insults at him. Various peasants gathered around and took sides in the quarrel, some for Danton and Lacroix, others against them. Finally the two Deputies got back in their coach, still with the same exhausted horses; there was nothing to do but to keep on and get a fresh relay later.

They left Paris on January 31 and reached Brussels on the evening of February 3. As soon as they arrived, they went into conference in the Burgomaster's Hall with the thirty National Commissioners appointed by the Convention. Merlin de Douai, who was their unofficial president, had just heard about the declaration of war on England. He passed this news on to Danton, adding: "On the 29th of January Dumouriez gave orders for the invasion of Holland." These two events meant that the Commissioners were obliged to take action immediately. Map in hand, they parceled out the "republicanization" of Belgium between them. Danton, still firmly attached to his annexation project, urged them to "get it approved by the people." The votes they collected were, obviously, all favorable. Some of them, however, were obtained by coercion, or from non-French-speaking Flemish peasants; and the confiscation of estates from the Church and from aristocratic landowners meant that plots could be handed out to some of the Belgian *sans-*

culottes (leaving enough for certain French Commissioners, who made the most of their chances). The lucky ones were quite ready to vote for annexation.

Danton and Lacroix went back to their old bailiwicks, the provinces of Namur and Liège. This was a French-speaking region, where they could make themselves understood more easily, and where consequently they acquired a far from flattering reputation. General Miaczynski, a Pole in the service of France, who now commanded a brigade, complained one day about the personal material losses he had sustained during the campaign. "For heaven's sake," Danton said, "you're in enemy territory, aren't you? Just take whatever you need to compensate yourself!" Later, when this officer was put on trial for the part he played in Dumouriez's defection, he revealed that while Danton and Lacroix were in Liège they had set up a press to turn out counterfeit promissory notes. The man in charge of this operation, the General claimed, was a friend of Lacroix's, one Lapallière.

As for the wild private life that the two Commissioners are supposed to have led, there is too much evidence, all pointing in the same direction, for us to dismiss the charges against them altogether. Doubtless Danton's enemies exaggerated, but it would be a mistake if one presented him as a figure of monk-like chastity. He devoted at least as much time on this mission to beer, girls, and moneymaking as he did to his official duties.

In the midst of Danton's round of work and pleasure, tragic news reached him. Gabrielle had not had the strength to survive her fourth pregnancy, and she died during the night of February 10, after the birth of her third son. Danton was in the middle of a dinner party when he heard. He seemed half stunned. Only waiting long enough to inform Lacroix of what had happened, he set off for Paris—alone this time. Several times the coachman heard him sobbing.

He got home on the 16th, bowed down with grief. Slowly and heavily he trudged up the staircase. What point was there in hurrying now? When he entered his apartment he found it empty except for the two maids, Catherine Motin and Marie

Fougerot, and the latter's brother Jacques. Mme. Charpentier, it turned out, had taken the children.

Sometimes weeping, sometimes restraining their tears, Catherine and Marie told their master the story of Gabrielle's last hours. Louise Gély was talking to her when the pains began to come on, and she sent Catherine off to fetch Gabrielle's parents. M. and Mme. Charpentier had come to Paris in anticipation of Gabrielle's *accouchement,* and were staying with their son. They came immediately, and proved a great help to the midwife. But Gabrielle was in such pain, and so many basins were necessary, that they had to call in the *coincierge* as well. It was a frightful ordeal. Mme. Charpentier begged Louise to go back upstairs: this was no sight for a young girl. What with the exertion of her labor and a rapidly soaring temperature, Gabrielle had turned brick-red. The doctor who was in attendance could do nothing for her. The child was born, and its mother expired.

The clergy of the parish came for her next day. "Conforming" priests escorted her body to the church and thence to the cemetery. The whole family and numbers of friends followed her funeral procession. "Poor Madame," the maids sobbed as they told Danton about it, "poor Madame . . ." He heard them out, still unable to believe it was true, that he would never see Gabrielle again, never again hold her in his arms. His "prosaic charmer," whose voluptuous body gave him such refreshment after all his toils and escapades, was going to rot into nothing, was rotting already beneath six feet of earth. It passed all understanding. She had passed away only three weeks after Louis XVI's execution. It was as though her death were a terrible punishment for her husband. *I vote for death,* Danton had said.

He saw that seals had been placed on the drawers of the highboys, on every cupboard door, even on the rolltop cover of his desk. Marie, following his eyes, answered the unspoken question: "After the funeral," she said, "M. Charpentier came back here with a justice of the peace and the local magistrate's clerk. They put all these seals on to make sure nothing was moved in your absence. The magistrate, Citizen Thuillier, left me in charge. But he said that, according to the law, a woman wasn't an adequate caretaker, so I asked my brother to come." She indicated Jacques, who was present during this discussion.

She added that the magistrate had taken an inventory of all goods and chattels, even including the casks in the cellar; but that he had given M. Charpentier special permission to remove the cash in Danton's desk—fifty-two *louis d'or* and fifteen silver *livres*—"and keep them until you got back."

The grief-stricken widower walked slowly through every room in his apartment. He stood and gazed for a moment at Gabrielle's bed, overcome with emotion; he opened wardrobes and buried his face in the dead woman's clothes, breathing her well-remembered perfume.

The servants gave him several letters that had arrived before him. One of them was from Robespierre, and contained the following: "If, in the only kind of misfortune which can shake a spirit such as yours, the certain knowledge of possessing a tender and devoted friend can bring you any consolation, I hereby offer that consolation to you. I love you more than ever, and unto death. From this moment you and I are one. . . ." But the Incorruptible could not restrain the politician in him, as a further remark shows: "Let us ensure that the effects of our profound grief are felt by those tyrants from whom derive both our public and our private misfortunes." He concluded: "I should have come to see you had I not respected the first moments of your grievous affliction. Believe me, your friend," etc.—a friend who, only a year later, was to have Danton sent to the guillotine.

Next day Danton heard a most unpleasant piece of news. While he himself was still in Liège and as yet unaware of his wife's death, Collot d'Herbois—that actor turned Deputy—had been making political capital out of it. The news had reached the Riding School on February 11, about three or four hours after Gabrielle passed away. Two days before, the Girondists had pushed through a decree authorizing legal action against those responsible for the September massacres. Here was a fine opportunity for Collot d'Herbois. On the morning of February 11 he had this to say: "The Girondists have been responsible for the death of a citizen, a woman whose loss we all mourn. Let

us pay her the tribute of our tears; she is worthy of them. Yes, it
is Citizen Danton's wife of whom I speak! Her husband was
absent, and she lay confined to her bed, having just given birth
to a new citizen. It was at this moment that Roland and his
followers dealt her a mortal blow. . . . Danton was away in
Belgium: these cowardly creatures took advantage of his absence
to charge him with the responsibility for selecting the victims
to be murdered during September 2 and 3! When his poor wife
read this monstrous libel in the papers, she died of shock!"

The fact that she had died in childbirth was conveniently
ignored. The whole speech was an abominable travesty of the
facts, and Danton publicly dissociated himself from it. This did
not stop him thanking Collot when the latter, accompanied by
Robespierre, came to offer his condolences. After them all Danton's friends appeared: Desmoulins and his wife, the Roberts,
the Legendres, and many others.

That same day, February 17, Danton had to make arrangements for the future of his children. There were now three of
them. History has preserved no trace of the newly born infant,
and everything suggests that it lived only a short while. But it
was still alive when its father authorized Antoine Charpentier,
brother of the deceased, to "summon a meeting of relatives and
friends to appoint him [i.e. Danton] guardian of his *three*
children." This family council was held on the 22nd, presided
over by M. Thuillier, justice of the peace. It duly recognized
the widower as official guardian of his three children, with M.
Charpentier, his father-in-law, as deputy guardian. This latter
appointment was all the more necessary in that Danton had to
return to Belgium. It was also why he had granted Antoine a
power-of-attorney.

By the terms of this authorization Antoine was required to
"demand the removal, without inventory, of the seals set in place
after Mme. Danton's decease"; or, "if such removal without
inventory should be contested," to "call for any summary court
order that might be necessary, and proceed thereafter to make
an inventory of all goods and chattels," and then "to effect the
sale of the furniture."

The seals were lifted on the 25th, in the presence of the
person principally concerned, Danton himself, who was still in

Paris. Thuillier, a notary called Bévière, and a sheriff's officer drew up a descriptive inventory of all movables, chattels, and items of clothing. Their owner did not stay to oversee the cataloging of his library. The bookseller appointed by Thuillier would take several days to carry out a complete valuation, and Danton had to return to Belgium. He therefore left his brother-in-law to act in his name, and boarded a carriage for Brussels. This time he was accompanied by Robert, whom the Assembly had appointed a delegate to the Commission. Though a Deputy in the French National Convention, Robert was a Belgian, born at Liège, and delighted by the prospect of receiving "that parental embrace of which tyranny had for three long years deprived him."

The two friends crossed the border at Belleville on the morning of March 3. Danton found difficulty in restraining his emotions. For the first time he was leaving Paris with the absolute and ghastly certainty that he would never see Gabrielle again. What he did not know, as yet, was that the luck she brought her husband had been buried with her; that when Gabrielle died, it was as though his good angel had abandoned him.

CHAPTER XIV

The Revolutionary Tribunal

WHEN DANTON REACHED BELGIUM on March 5 he was confronted with a disastrous situation. The inhabitants, exasperated by the excesses of the National Commissioners, were in revolt against the French army. That very morning the bodies of some murdered soldiers had been found in a lonely part of the countryside. The Austrians, taking advantage of this reaction, had crossed the Roer and defeated Valence, one of Dumouriez's divisional commanders, at Aldenhoven. The Duke of Württemberg had recaptured Aix-la-Chapelle, while Miranda—another of Dumouriez's divisional commanders—found himself obliged to raise the siege of Maestricht, fall back on Liège, and then abandon Liège and retreat as far as Louvain. Dumouriez began to panic. From his headquarters in Brussels he sent out a constant stream of orders to his field commanders, but he could not inspire them with the will to win. Their hearts were no longer in the job.

Faced with a catastrophe of such magnitude, Danton had no option but to turn about and make straight for Paris. On March 8, only five days after his departure from the capital, he caused a sensation by reappearing in the Riding School. For the first time in six weeks he mounted the speakers' rostrum. Members gasped at his appearance. The double burden of grief he bore, as a widower and an anguished patriot, accentuated his ugliness. One had only to look at him to measure the extent both of his private distress and of the disaster that had befallen the nation.

At the beginning of his speech he spoke with a somber eloquence that sounded like a funeral knell; then, little by little, his tone quickened till, in one or two striking phrases, he recaptured the urgent beat of the tocsin. Referring to the abuses of the National Commissioners, he exclaimed: "When the house is on fire, I don't waste time attacking those who are determined to loot it; my first concern is to put out the flames." During his survey of possible measures to be taken, he had this to say: "The French character is so constituted that it can muster its full energy only in a crisis. That point has now been reached. The whole of France must be made to understand that there is not a moment to lose." After recalling the various blunders that had been made, by the Convention, by the government, by the people's delegates to the armed forces—in other words, by himself—he went on: "Let us hasten to repair our faults. Let the initial advantage gained by our enemies, like that which they won last year, be a signal for the reawakening of the nation."

He did not, however, include the generals in this fault-finding survey. They had been promised reinforcements to the tune of thirty thousand men. "Has even one solitary trooper appeared in Belgium?" Thanks be to heaven, France possessed a Dumouriez: but that was not enough. Barère interrupted at this point, shouting: "Dumouriez alone is worth an entire army!" Suddenly everyone wanted to speak. Danton could not prevent Robespierre supporting him, and at the same time demanding that "the sword of justice be held unremittingly over the head of all faithless generals." Were there in fact any such? The discussion of this point lasted for two days. Good generals had to be flattered and encouraged. Bad ones should be executed. The Incorruptible knew few in the former category. Like all sectarians, he was prone to generalize.

Danton at least did not share that glaring weakness. His powers of judgment were not paralyzed by the mere sight of a uniform. He had seen generals in action and valued them highly. Now he contrived to divert the storm against another category of Frenchmen, while at the same time regaining control of the debate in its legislative aspect. This he did by a proposal for taxing all wealthy citizens, who, instead of sinking their capital into the sustenance of the armed forces, were simply making a profit out of the crisis for their own benefit. This tax was to be applicable not only in Paris, "which does not enjoy a monopoly of patriotism," but also throughout the provinces. "Let your Commissioners set forth here and now, this very night; let them say to that craven class of citizen, the rich: 'Your money must pay for our exertions. The people have only their blood to give, but that they are lavishing on the cause. Come then, you miserable cowards, be equally lavish with your wealth!' "

Coming from Danton, such a curt demand did not lack ironic relish. But it stirred applause from all sides of the House, mingled with cries of "Bravo! He's right! Let the rich foot the bill!" When this ovation died down, Danton went on: "Think, citizens, of the splendid destiny that awaits you! You have a whole nation as your lever, and reason as your fulcrum—and you have not yet moved the world? What we need is resolution! . . . Death to our enemies! . . ."

His speech was now punctuated by rousing cheers. He had hit his most potent rhetorical vein again. After some decidedly risky allusions to the discussions before Valmy and to the September massacres, he had the audacity to declare: "I was in exactly the same position as I am now when the enemy was at the gates of Paris—though the circumstances then were far more difficult. I told our so-called patriots at the time: 'These discussions of ours are useless. You're all a bunch of traitors. Let's beat the enemy first, and argue afterward.' I told them: 'What do I care for my reputation? Let my name be tarnished, if only France remain free!' I let myself be branded as a blood-thirsty monster, gentlemen. Should we balk at drinking the blood of humanity's foes, if need be, to win liberty for Europe?"

The Assembly went wild with enthusiasm. Danton's eloquence had completely won them over again. There were no more divisions into Mountain, Plain, and Gironde; there was nothing but united admiration for Danton. They cheered him to the echo, and he took advantage of this to slip in an unexpected digression. For centuries the penalty to which insolvent debtors were liable had been confinement in a debtors' prison. Danton now made a plea on behalf of such persons. "You want all France to take up arms for our common defense," he said. "Yet there exists a certain class of men, unsullied by any crime, who are able-bodied and yet deprived of their liberty. I mean those unhappy persons imprisoned for debt. It shames our humanity and our philosophical pretensions that any man, merely by accepting money, can thus mortgage his person and his security. Principles are eternal, and no Frenchman can be robbed of his freedom except for heinous crimes against society. But property-owners have no cause for alarm. Doubtless certain individuals have gone too far; but the nation, now as always, is just and will respect the rights of ownership. Show respect for poverty, and poverty will show respect for wealth. . . . I ask the National Convention to proclaim that every citizen imprisoned for debt will be set at liberty!" "Motion passed by acclamation," the shorthand-writers noted.

Danton now returned to the most vital part of the debate. But he had been speaking for three hours already, and it had begun to get dark. The Convention had been sitting since early morning. A number of Deputies, overcome by weariness, began to get up and make for the exit. Gensonné, the President, wanted to adjourn the session. It was true that, so far, members had heard nothing but resounding rhetoric and, apart from the matter of imprisonment for debt, had passed no resolutions. What measures were to be taken for Dumouriez's relief remained undecided.

Danton, however, had no intention of letting the session break up. "I call upon all good citizens," he roared, "not to quit their post of duty!" Startled and cowed, the departing members stopped, hesitated, and finally slunk back to their seats. The tamer had mastered his wild animals. They heard him shout, from the middle of the ring: "The enemies of freedom are still brazen and unashamed! Though everywhere in retreat, they continue to stir up trouble wherever they can be found. You have the solution: snatch them away from the vengeance of the people, deal with them yourselves—"

"What about September?" shouted the Girondist Lanjuinais. Somewhat taken aback, Danton turned, flushing angrily, to face his interrupter. The words had been like some bloody clot cast full in his face. How would he answer them? In fact, he was relieved of the need to do so, since a loud chorus rose from

the Mountain, cries of "Order! Order!"—"Withdraw, Lanjuinais!"—"Apologize!" The President was quite defeated by
this uproar, and it took him ten minutes to bring the meeting to
some sort of order. When he had finally managed to do so,
Danton went on: "The people's safety calls for strong, indeed
ruthless, measures. I see no middle way between the normal
channels of justice and an extraordinary tribunal. Since one
speaker has dared to stand up before this Assembly and recall
those bloody days which all good citizens deplore, I also will
presume to make an assertion. If such a tribunal had existed
then, the people who have been so often, and so savagely,
reproached for the events of those days would never have stained
their memory with one drop of spilled blood."

"You carry on like a king!" one Girondist shouted.

"You talk like a coward!" Danton replied. The massed
applause of Mountain, Plain, and half the Gironde extinguished
this new flare-up before it had really got going. Danton shrugged
his shoulders. "Really, citizens!" he exclaimed. "At this moment
our position is so precarious that if Miranda were defeated—
and he well might be—then Dumouriez would find himself
surrounded and be forced to lay down his arms. How can you
think of dispersing until you have taken the far-reaching
measures needed to guarantee public safety? . . . It is important
that we take the judicial steps necessary to deal with counter-
revolutionaries. *They* are what makes this tribunal so necessary!
They are why it must be created as a reinforcement for that
highest of all tribunals, the vengeance of the people."

Cheers and catcalls ringing in his ears, Danton stepped down
from the rostrum and was literally carried off by the Montagnards. Marat, Robespierre, Collot d'Herbois, Fabre d'Églantine,
all pressed forward to congratulate him. At last Desmoulins
rescued him from this hysterical display of solidarity and took
him off home to dinner. Now was the time, as he sat between his
host and the smiling Lucile, for Danton to recall old memories
of Gabrielle. He still had to restrain his tears whenever he so
much as mentioned her name.

The debate was resumed next morning. The Mountain unanimously supported the creation of a Revolutionary Tribunal.

Among the Girondists, Vergniaud, Condorcet, Brissot, and some others were of similar opinion. On the other hand, Roland's bloc was violently opposed to the whole idea. Louvet, Guadet, Lanthenas, and above all Buzot—Manon Roland's would-be lover—all made impassioned speeches attacking it. Lanjuinais, as a good jurist, spoke out against "this violation of every principle in the Declaration of the Rights of Man"; while Larevellière-Lépeaux, a tiny hunchback dwarfed by Danton's vast bulk, denounced "those brigand-tyrants who, while themselves well fed, well housed, well clothed, and leading a life of pleasurable luxury, still hold forth such touching affection on the pitiable lot of the poor."

During the night agents of the Montagnards had energetically canvassed the City Hall and the various constituencies. Right from the beginning of the debate a large mob had been gathered outside the Riding School, in a decidedly angry mood, determined to make the Deputies vote as Danton wanted. Jean-Bon-Saint-André, acting as spokesman for his political friends, demanded "the establishment of a Revolutionary Tribunal to try disturbers of the public peace, a court whose judgments are final and cannot be referred to the Court of Appeal." Throughout this speech the threatening shouts of massed *sans-culottes* assembled in the Tuileries Gardens were quite audible. Other local partisans, learning that the government was opposed to the project, barricaded its members inside the Foreign Ministry to stop their speaking against it. Beurnonville, the Minister of War, managed to get through the cordon by jumping over a wall.

Next day, March 10, on a bitterly cold morning, the Convention at last bowed to the demands of Danton and those who supported him. Carried away by the speeches of Cambacérès, Robert Lindet, Duhem, Cambon, and finally of Danton himself ("Let *us* be ruthless, to relieve the people of the need to be!" he cried at one point), the Assembly decreed the creation of that horrific court of justice which was to become the chief instrument of the Terror. A year afterward, when Danton himself had fallen victim to it, he declared: "It was on just such a day that I brought the Revolutionary Tribunal into being. God and my fellow men forgive me, I never meant it to become the scourge of humanity it has. All I wanted was to forestall any recurrence of the September massacres."

Simply and solely by decision of the Convention, France had been at war with Great Britain and Holland since February 1. On the 7th she had declared war on Spain. At the very moment when the new Tribunal Extraordinary was being ratified by decree, the Assembly learned that Prussia, Austria, England, Portugal, Spain, Sardinia, the Two Sicilies, and the Papal States were signing a treaty of alliance. The news triggered off conspiracies in Paris, while in the provinces there was open insurrection.

After the first shock the Convention quickly recovered itself. If the enemy at home was to be crushed, the new tribunal must act swiftly and boldly. The existing police force was not adequate to the task of keeping this ogre supplied with meat. The Deputies therefore voted to extend the powers of the Committee of General Security, created a year previously but hitherto quite ineffectual. They made it responsible for tracking down suspects and delivering them to justice—i.e. justice as represented by Montané, the President of the Tribunal, Fouquier-Tinville, the Public Prosecutor, and, finally, Sanson, the executioner.

Vadier, Voulland, Amar, Lebas, Lacoste, and David, the artist, now became members of the Committee of General Security. Their first idea on entering office was to find some top-level victim. The person they decided to arrest was none other than Dumouriez himself—Dumouriez, the victor of Valmy and Jemmapes, the conqueror of Belgium, the General who, with a paltry force of thirteen thousand men and despite the defeats of his subordinate commanders on the Meuse, was now conducting a uniformly successful invasion of Holland.

Why, then, did they take this stern line with Dumouriez? Because of a strongly critical letter he had dispatched to the Convention on March 12. This letter denounced the exactions carried out by the National Commissioners at Anvers, who had confiscated all Church silver plate and carried it off to Lille. Dumouriez also gave a scathing account of the sack of the

Cathédrale Sainte-Gudule in Brussels, and described how Belgians accused of "noncooperation" had their property looted and were imprisoned on the flimsiest pretexts. He reported riots in Ghent, Bruges, Tournai, Ostend, Nieuport, and Furnes. He notified the Convention of the measures he had taken in consequence: the return of all offending Commissioners to France, the issue of three proclamations stigmatizing their conduct, and the closing of all political clubs that had sprung up in Belgium along the lines of those in Paris. Though he was Danton's friend, Dumouriez clearly had him in mind when he wrote: "You have been misinformed concerning the supposedly voluntary union of several regions in Belgium with France. *Your mistake was due to someone having told you a pack of lies.*" Calling upon the Assembly to rid him of these "troublesome intruders" (the National Commissioners), he concluded: "I await your decision with impatience. You will not, I know, allow your armies to be besmirched by crimes for which, in the end, they themselves must suffer."

The President dared not read this letter to the Assembly; instead, he passed it over to the General Defense Committee, which then proceeded to call in Danton. The Committee decided unanimously that, by overstepping his military duties and meddling in politics, Dumouriez had laid himself open to a charge of counterrevolutionary activities. The secret was leaked at some point, and by now the Committee of General Security not only knew of the letter's existence but had a fair idea of its contents. Anxious to display initiative, Committee members talked of having the General arrested and bringing him before the Revolutionary Tribunal. Echoes of this bombastic self-assertiveness made their way back to the Defense Committee, where Lacroix spoke up on Dumouriez's behalf. "Cut off my head if you must," he said, "but let the General keep his. France needs him." Danton offered to go and see Dumouriez in Brussels. "Let me take Lacroix with me," he said. "I promise you, I'll either make Dumouriez retract inside a week or bring him back to you bound hand and foot."

Such were the antecedents of Danton's last journey abroad. He set out from Paris on March 17, with his inseparable traveling companion once more at his side. Gabrielle had died on February 11, and her husband returned home on the 17th. Apart from that first week, when grief for his loss—not to mention all the legal business of settling his affairs—kept him out of circulation, Danton had, for a month now, tried to forget his sorrows by throwing himself wholeheartedly into the world of politics. As a result, he had certainly succeeded in relegating them to second place in his preoccupations. When he left town again he had not got over his loss, but at least he had recovered his balance and peace of mind.

This peace of mind, however, clearly did not extend to political matters, for Danton was well aware of alarming developments in the Vendée. To ensure the defense of the nation— now in conflict with more or less all Europe—the Convention had decreed the compulsory enlistment of 300,000 men, to be selected by lot. On March 10 the day when the names were to be drawn, the Vendée region—answering the call of its priests— rose in revolt.

Danton left Paris on the 17th, with Lacroix, and the two of them crossed the border twenty-four hours later. They reached Brussels on the 19th, having passed numerous deserters *en route,* but found that Dumouriez was out of town. Five National Commissioners informed them that the Commander-in-Chief had come back from Holland and was, that very day, fighting a battle against the Duke of Coburg's forces somewhere in the vicinity of Louvain. (The engagement in fact took place outside a village called Neerwinden.) But morale was so low, and desertions so frequent, that the French had no great hopes of winning. The seven delegates at once promulgated a decree announcing that all deserters and fugitives would be treated as traitors to their country.

Next day Danton and Lacroix boarded their carriage once more and set off in the direction of the battlefield. Their firm intention was to give Dumouriez a severe reprimand and then persuade him to send the Convention a letter withdrawing his earlier communication of March 12. But while they were still traveling along a road choked with peasant refugees, the battle of Neerwinden had been fought and lost. Neither Dumouriez's tactical skill nor the heroic conduct of General Valence (who was severely wounded during the action), nor the bravery of young Égalité and his men could halt the determined advance of the Austrian army. The catastrophe of Neerwinden sounded the death knell for France's occupation of Belgium.

Danton and Lacroix hurried from one divisional head-quarters to another, but could not find Dumouriez anywhere. At dawn on the 21st they ran into the former Duke of Chartres, whose regiments were bivouacking at the foot of Cumptich Ridge. (The Austrians, worn out after the previous day's battle, were snatching a short rest on the summit of the ridge itself.) Danton, recognizing the Duke of Orléans's son, repeated the question he had asked countless officers during the past twenty-four hours: "Where's Dumouriez?" "At Pellemberg," young Égalité told him, "with General Champmorain. He's regrouping his forces and trying to halt the retreat." He pointed toward the road they should take. "Come on then," Danton said, "let's go—" But Lacroix cut in: "Not just yet, I think. Before we leave, General, we should like to inspect your troops."

Égalité agreed to this request. He invited his visitors to leave their carriage and mount two horses which he provided for them. Anyone inspecting troops, he said, should do so on horse-back. It gave them more of a martial air and was less likely to antagonize the men. "All right, I agree about the horses," Danton told him. "But no special parades or guard of honor, please. We don't want to fatigue your men."

The young Duke galloped ahead of them to his bivouac. "Comrades!" he shouted. "Here are two delegates from the Convention who have come to see you. Fall in behind the colors!" Grumbling, the soldiers obeyed. Like all front-line troops, they had little time for politicians. The inspection was carried out at a brisk trot, without incident. But just before they were due to leave, Lacroix made a first-class gaffe. Pointing up at the line of glinting bayonets along Cumptich Ridge, he turned to the Duke and said: "What's that I see up there, General?" "Why," Égalité replied, "the Austrians, of course." At this Lacroix turned and, raising his voice so that the soldiers could hear him, exclaimed: "What? The Austrians? If they're that close, why the hell don't we attack them?"

If Lacroix had had any sense, he would have kept such ideas

to himself. His presumption drew insults and oaths from the rank and file. "Attack 'em yourself if you're so keen to, sonny— you can tell us all about it afterward. We've done our lot, thanks."

Apprehensive that his men might get really annoyed, Égalité wound up the inspection hurriedly, and the little party left amid catcalls. Danton approved of this young general. As they rode along side by side he suddenly said to him: "We must see Dumouriez as soon as possible. We've got to talk to him about that letter he wrote on March 12. His little campaign has had the most deplorable effects at home. He simply *must* back down."

But Égalité had not forgotten the counsel that Danton himself had given him during that interview in the Place Vendôme. "Oh, I know nothing at all about things like that," he said. "I've followed your advice—stick to military duties and keep clear of politics."

Five minutes later Danton and Lacroix dismounted, boarded their carriage again, and said good-by to the young Duke. They finally ran Dumouriez down near Tirlemont, in the thick of a rear-guard action to cover the retreat. Having other things to attend to just then, he arranged to meet them that evening in Louvain. The three men sat arguing till two o'clock in the morning. Despite his defeat at Neerwinden, Dumouriez flatly refused to climb down. The discussion, which had begun calmly enough, gradually became more heated. "Your Convention," Dumouriez told his visitors, "consists of three hundred fools who let two hundred knaves lead them by the nose! That kind of thing has *got* to stop, like it or not. Unless decent people come around to my way of thinking, France is done for!"

These ideas, as Danton rightly guessed, meant that Dumouriez now supported the re-establishment of the constitutional monarchy. But their long-standing friendship, the fact that both were Freemasons, and the many State secrets they shared made Dumouriez's visitor unwilling to accuse him, openly, of royalism. In Dumouriez's case, any such admission would automatically result in the death penalty. In the hope of saving him, Danton begged him to sit down there and then and write, if not a disavowal of his previous letter, at least a short note to the President of the Convention. "Ask him not to form any premature judgments concerning your letter of the 12th until you have had time to furnish him with a full explanation of it." Dumouriez agreed to do this and took down the note from Danton's own dictation. Danton gave a sigh of relief and pocketed this document. Would such a short and inadequate disclaimer suffice to clear Dumouriez in the Assembly's eyes? Danton had no great hope that it would; but he was anxious to play his one card as quickly as possible, however slim the chance of success. Above all, he could not risk some National Commissioner getting to the Riding School ahead of him. His mind was made up; he would leave right away. He shook hands with Dumouriez, left Lacroix to go on to Lille in another vehicle, and, boarding the carriage in which they had been traveling, set off for Paris alone. The trip was made at such breakneck speed that he arrived on March 23. At nine in the evening the official government carriage pulled up outside his front door.

It would have been natural for him to appear in the Riding School or at the General Defense Committee's conference room the following morning. But he did not; and this omission, on the face of it, is very hard to explain. It looks as though Danton had done some hard thinking on the way home. To defend Dumouriez would simply mean sharing his fate. For more than two days he never stirred outside his house. Besides, Gabrielle's ghost had begun to haunt him again; he wandered from room to room in an agony of grief, wiping his eyes and sighing deeply. Sometimes he would slump into a chair and sit there with his head in his hands. The maids watched him uneasily. "The master's thinking of doing away with himself, if you ask me," one of them said.

He did not even visit the Charpentiers to see his children. When he felt in need of consolation, he would go up to the apartment on the next floor. Marc-Antoine Gély and his wife felt sorry for him in his bereavement. Gély still held the job of usher in the Ministry of Marine, which Danton had obtained for him when the abolition of the Parliament lost him a similar position in the Law Courts. He therefore remained grateful to the ex-Minister; but he had no great liking for him, and Mme. Gély found him quite detestable. They were both devout Catholics who objected strongly to the Civil Constitution of the

Clergy, and they felt that Danton—with his more or less open anticlericalism and his contempt for religious observances—bore some share of the responsibility for the resultant strain on individual consciences.

But their daughter had been Gabrielle's intimate companion. Though Louise had been sent out by Mme. Charpentier on that last, fatal night, and thus had not been there at her dear friend's dying breath, at least she was present during Gabrielle's last hours. Danton's feelings toward this charming adolescent girl were so odd and complex that he could not analyze them. Gratitude for the care she had lavished on Gabrielle and the way she had looked after the children; fatherly affection on the part of this good-natured colossus toward a girl who was still little more than a child; and, lastly, the inevitable attraction which Louise's charms exercised on so unbridled a rake as Danton—all these elements were present in the emotional impulse which drove him to seek out her company. When he heard that caressing voice of hers, when he looked at her and divined what hidden delights lay beneath her dress, any idea of doing away with himself abruptly vanished.

This is why, after returning from Louvain on March 23, he delayed three days before submitting a report on his journey to the Defense Committee, though it was a matter of the utmost urgency. Lacroix, who knew him well, for once confused the effects of his latest passion with his habitual negligence. In a letter from Lille describing Dumouriez's retreat he wrote: "Do me the favor of shaking off your customary sloth . . . This is no time for idleness or indifference."

What aroused Danton from his torpor was the news of his own election to the Defense Committee. This took him there posthaste; but he was at something of a loss when it came to sticking up for Dumouriez, whom he admired as a soldier but disapproved of as a citizen. He stated his attitude more clearly at the Jacobin Club, during a speech on the difficulties he had had to face in Belgium. "More than once," he said, "I was tempted to have Dumouriez put under arrest. But, I told myself, if I take this radical step and then the enemy, having learned of his removal, proceeds to profit by it, I am bound to incur

severe criticism—perhaps even the suspicion of treachery. I ask
you, citizens, what would you have done in my place? This man
may have betrayed the people's cause, yet we found him in the
battle line, risking his own life at the head of his battalions.
Whatever his personal oddities, he still has military fire in his
belly. We were very undecided as to what course we should
take."

It was the Convention which finally resolved this ambiguous
situation. On April 1 it heard a report from three Commissioners—Proly, Péreyra, and Dubuisson—who had just got back
from Belgium. According to them, the Commander-in-Chief
made no secret of his intention to march on Paris, overthrow
the Republic, and restore the 1791 Constitution. Little Louis
XVII would be rescued from the Temple and set on the throne
—under a regency, of course, until he came of age. The Commissioners did not say *whose* regency, but all eyes turned
toward the back benches of the Mountain, where Philippe
Égalité sat, and the former ranking Prince of the Blood blushed
scarlet.

The Convention, which had been in an angry mood ever
since the setback at Neerwinden, now issued a summons to
Dumouriez bidding him appear at the Bar of the House to
explain his defeat. Furthermore, since he was thought to favor
young Égalité as Regent rather than Philippe d'Orléans himself
—a preference which the majority found equally reprehensible
—he was ordered to bring the youthful general with him. Suspecting the worst, they both refused to come.

To make them change their minds, the Convention wrote to
four other Commissioners—Bancal, Quinette, Lamarque, and
the inevitable Camus—with instructions to see Dumouriez right
away and either make him obey the voice of the people or else
bring him back to Paris by force, together with his subordinate
commander. This four-man delegation was further reinforced
by the Minister of War in person, General Beurnonville. Some
of them set out from Paris, the rest from Lille. They finally
converged on Saint-Amand, near Valenciennes, where Dumouriez's retreating forces now lay.

"Oh, so I must report to the Convention, must I?" Dumouriez
said. "In other words, they want me haled before this new

tribunal of theirs, the one that's been set up to secure convictions against all our most decent and honest citizens, eh? D'you think I'm out of my mind? My distinguished services, my victories will all go for nothing—no one's going to listen to me anyway. What you want, gentlemen, is my head, and that of the Duke of Chartres with it. I refuse to accompany you."

"In that case," Camus told him, "I hereby suspend you from your duties."

"That's enough of your damned impudence," said Dumouriez. "Guards! Arrest these men!" The four Commissioners and the Minister found themselves surrounded. Dumouriez said: "You know, I'm doing you a real favor, gentlemen. If you'd stayed in Paris, all your heads would have rolled sooner or later."

That same evening Dumouriez's hussars conducted their five captives to the Austrian outposts. The enemy received them, not as prisoners of war, but as political hostages. This brilliant *coup* was intended to prepare the way for Dumouriez's one-man restoration of the monarchy. He believed that the five hostages could be exchanged for the Queen and her children, thus saving their lives.

Now that he had chosen the path of rebellion, there was no turning back. In a manifesto addressed to "the citizen-administrators of the North," he recounted the handing over of these four Deputies and a Minister to the Austrians. "I shall march on Paris without delay," he went on, "and put a stop to the bloody anarchy which reigns there. I have hitherto defended freedom with all my heart; can I hold back at the very moment when it is most endangered? . . . I swear to you that I am far from aspiring to any kind of dictatorship, and I undertake to lay down all public office once I have saved my country."

But the army did not care for such outbursts of passion, and some of the troops mutinied against their commander. As Dumouriez was going through Condé, accompanied by the Duke of Chartres and his chief of staff, shots were fired at him. Dumouriez was now determined to restore discipline, and proceeded to take measures which achieved this end. His life, his freedom, and his honor were—or so he thought—all in jeopardy. He therefore packed up his personal baggage and slipped across

[9] Louise Gély and Antoine Danton ("L'Optique), by Boilly. (*Photo by Josse-Lalance*)

[10] Robespierre. Portrait by Boilly. (*Photo by Giraudon*)

[11] Camille Desmoulins. Portrait by Boze. (*Photo by Bulloz*)

[12] Hérault de Séchelles. (*Photo by Bulloz-Viollet*)

[13] Danton being led to the guillotine. Drawing by Wille. (*Photo by Josse-Lalance*)

the border with Louis-Philippe. An hour later they both surrendered to the enemy, thereby saving their heads; and so it came about that the Revolution, through its own excesses, lost two of its best servants.

The news of these tragic events had not yet reached Paris, but information filtering back from the front made it clear what was in the wind. A premature but strangely prophetic rumor concerning General Égalité's desertion spread rapidly through the Riding School. His fellow Deputies cast this act of treachery in poor Philippe's face. It was in vain that the ex-Duke replied, invoking the memory of Brutus: "If it were true, and I had my son here now, I would strangle him with my own hands!"

A few weeks earlier the Assembly had decreed the banishment of the Bourbons *en masse,* with the exception of the royal family incarcerated in the Temple and the "former Duke of Orléans, now an elected representative of the people." But if, as seemed likely, his son had defected, then the whole question was thrown wide open again. Philippe was horrified. He sat on the Mountain's back benches; yet it was the Mountain which now, not content with banishing him, demanded his arrest and delivery to the Revolutionary Tribunal.

However, a diversion now took place which gave him some respite. In the heat of the discussion, certain extremely serious charges were made against Danton by a group of Girondists. He had delayed for forty-eight hours before reporting his interview with Dumouriez to the Committee. He had failed to go straight to the Riding School and proclaim the General's dereliction of duty in public. He had concealed the existence of the letter Dumouriez wrote on March 12. He had misappropriated the 100,-000 *livres* which Lebrun had entrusted to him for the expenses of his original mission. Lastly, he had taken advantage of Dumouriez's dictatorship to oppress the Belgians and line his pockets at their expense.

Visibly shaken by this storm of criticism, Danton nearly choked with fury. Once or twice he shouted from the benches: "That's a lie, a damned lie!" But he kept himself more or less under control until Biroteau quoted a remark attributed to him and spread about (or so the speaker claimed) by Fabre d'Églantine: "After all, a king is the surest method of saving the Republic."

At this Danton strode to the rostrum. Several Deputies tried to bar his way, and he came to blows with them. "You're a scoundrel, sir!" he roared at Biroteau. "One day France will judge you! It was *you* who undertook the defense of the King, and now you're trying to blame us for your crimes!" He succeeded in reaching the platform. Then, turning to face the Girondists, he thundered: "You want to assassinate the true patriots—but the Mountain will fall upon you and crush you!"

Somehow he managed to make his tribute to the Mountain heard above the general uproar. Little by little, under the impact of that dominating personality, the interruptions died away. Then he sketched the state of affairs in Belgium, and the very necessary role which the Convention's delegates had to perform there. He added, however: "Your army Commissioners, though invested with your full confidence and wielding very considerable powers, lack means to enforce the execution of their commands. From our attire we might be mere secretaries to the Commission rather than Commissioners. There is no outward sign of our status." Why, he went on, some of the troops had mistaken him, Danton, for a general's clerk! If they were to impress the commanders and obtain respect from the rank and file, they must have some more martial uniform, half civil, half military. Lacking this, the Commissioners were seriously handicapped in their work on behalf of the Republic. If they had been unable to succeed, the blame lay with Dumouriez and with those who had flattered him after his victories, who asked him out to dine on his return to Paris. Were there any Montagnards among these sycophants? No indeed: they were Girondists to a man. Danton made an open reference to Alba-Lasource, and then passed on to a certain "sly old fox" whose name he did not mention, though he spoke of his young wife. Since every Girondist at once sprang to the defense of the ex-Minister (who happened to be absent from the Riding School that day), Danton decided to name him after all. The context is worth noting: "Roland wrote Dumouriez a note which the latter showed both to Lacroix and to myself," Danton alleged. "He said: 'You must join forces with us in order to crush one particular party in Paris, and above all one particular man—Danton.'"

This was a real bombshell. Deputies stamped, clapped their hands, and whistled. Fists were shaken across the benches. Scuffles broke out in the aisles. Ushers hastened to separate the combatants but found it a hard task. Finally, however, the President and his assistants restored order, and Danton continued. He referred to the Commission which his colleagues had appointed from among themselves to look into Belgian affairs. What had happened to this Commission? Why was it not already at work, busy compiling "a speedy report concerning those who have sabotaged public morale, attempted to incite the *départements* against the capital, and done all they could to save the King?"

"Daylight holds no fears for me," Danton concluded, hammering the desk with his fist. "I am entrenched within the citadel of reason and will sally forth behind the guns of truth. I will utterly crush my enemies; I will take the villains who have brought these charges against me and grind them into dust!"

Danton's speech was over; he stepped down from the rostrum to mingled cheers and jeers. But the whole thing had come as a godsend for Philippe Égalité. In all this confusion, and after a lengthy debate which settled nothing, he had been quite forgotten. Unfortunately, no sooner had Danton withdrawn, leaving his anthill audience dazed by what he had told them, than that sinister figure Marat stepped forward, head wrapped in his famous bandanna and the inevitable pistol stuck through his belt. The People's Friend began by bursting into laughter—a favorite trick of his when about to strike. Slowly, without any passion or hatred, he recalled a motion he had proposed several days previously. Its object was to abolish the immunity which representatives of the people at present enjoyed. Now, sarcastically, Marat brought his motion forward once more. He was clearly aiming at the Girondists, and perhaps also at one Montagnard, Philippe Égalité.

Biroteau, the Girondist whose attack had stung Danton into losing his temper, now hastened up the steps of the rostrum and made a speech supporting Marat. They were an unlikely pair of allies. But as a result of their joint exhortations, the

Assembly decided that "without regard to the immunity enjoyed by a representative of the nation," it would authorize "the prosecution of those of its own members against whom there rested a strong presumption of having conspired with the enemies of liberty, equality, and the Republican government."

This fatal enactment was approved by an almost unanimous vote. The Girondists supported it in the belief that it would help them to send Montagnards to the guillotine, while the Montagnards saw it as an instrument for disposing of the Girondists. Neither side realized that by endorsing the motion of Marat and Biroteau they had signed death warrants for a large proportion of their own membership.

Poor Égalité was one of the first who fell a victim to this decision. The news of Dumouriez's defection, together with that of the Duke of Chartres, burst on Paris like a bombshell; and the debate about the Orléans family was at once reopened. After Marat had planted his banderillos, Robespierre undertook the role of matador. "Citizens," he cried, "do you realize just who this king was whom Dumouriez wanted to impose on us? Doubtless the matter is of little moment to Republicans, who detest all monarchs with equal fervor . . . Nevertheless, the truth must be told. This general was dreaming of overthrowing the Convention and of offering the crown to some scion of our tyrants' family. Not to the little Capet child playing in the tower of the Temple, but to *His Grace* the Duke of Chartres, whose father, citizens, is sitting here among you!" Robespierre concluded: "I demand that all individual members of the Orléans family, known as Égalité, be brought before the Revolutionary Tribunal; and that this tribunal be further made responsible for instituting proceedings against all Dumouriez's other accomplices." Then, killing two birds with one stone, the Incorruptible proceeded to direct his righteous wrath against the Girondists. "Dare I name before this House such distinguished patriots as MM. Vergniaud, Guadet, Gensonné, Brissot, and others of their ilk? . . . In all matters concerning these illustrious Deputies, I rely upon the wisdom of the Convention."

Both Vergniaud and Guadet replied to Robespierre and obtained a provisional respite both for themselves and for their

Girondist friends. But they did not save the Duke of Orléans; they were only too happy to see this Montagnard crushed by the giants of the Mountain. Danton, too, who not long before had been the Duke's guest and accepted his hospitality, raised no voice on his behalf when Orléans was cast into prison—together with his youngest sons, Montpensier and Beaujolais, and his sister the Duchess of Bourbon, and his uncle the Prince de Conti. A decree was passed declaring their property forfeit to the State. But—with an odd display of personal solicitude—a coach, escorted by gendarmes, bore the whole family off to Marseilles, where the gates of Fort Saint-Jean closed behind them. In this distant retreat the Orléans family had nothing to fear from the Revolutionary Tribunal—at least, not for another seven months.

CHAPTER XV

Second Dictatorship and Second Marriage

THE ANARCHIC STATE of the executive was common knowledge in the armed forces, and played havoc with military morale. The era of Jemmapes gave place to that of Neerwinden. In the north, Belgium was lost. In the east, Custine pulled out and left Kléber to hold besieged Mayence as best he could. In the west, British squadrons were blockading the ports. In the south, Spanish troops were moving across the Pyrenees. The Empress of Russia had joined the general coalition. The insurrection in the Vendée had spread to Brittany and the borders of Normandy. Lyons was in revolt against the Republic. Throughout the country, food supplies were scarce and the cost of living was going up. To cope with this avalanche of disasters France had nothing but a puppet government, whose powers were continually being reduced still further by the Convention.

To rectify this situation meant, first of all, restoring law and order. For some while now Marat had been talking of a dictatorship. The pros and cons of this idea were thrashed out in a series of epic debates. Finally the Assembly, on the basis of a report to which Danton had contributed, voted for the establishment of such an authority, to be known as the Committee of Public Safety. This Committee consisted of nine members, elected by the Convention. Its deliberations were held in private, where public opinion could not influence them. Its authority overrode that of the Cabinet; indeed, its creation was a return to absolutism—not the absolutism of one ruler, as in the days of the monarchy, but of an oligarchic group. However, the group's mandate was limited; their colleagues reserved the right to prolong or terminate their tenure of office by monthly ballot.

At the first election Barère headed the list, with 360 votes. Danton was also elected, but only in fifth place, with 233. The other members of the Committee were his friend Lacroix, Robert Lindet, Cambon, Delmas, Bréard, Treilhard, and Guyton-Morveau the chemist, the doyen of the team.

The last-named had, in fact, just rescued Lacroix and Danton from a somewhat delicate situation. Toward the end of his fortnight's stint as President of the Convention, he had received some disturbing information from Béthune. Two covered wagons loaded with trunks from Belgium, which were addressed to Danton and Lacroix, had been stopped at a check point. It was discovered that no authorization had been obtained for their export, and that neither the convoying officer nor the drivers possessed passports. Since the former was promptly clapped into jail, he could not prevent the Béthune police from opening the trunks and examining their contents. If we are to believe the information that Guyton-Morveau had from Danton, all they had in them was "dirty linen." Danton added: "Do the administrators of the Pas-de-Calais suppose that Deputies travel like itinerant barbers, with all their possessions done up in a knapsack?"

Two wagonloads of trunks to transport dirty linen? The explanation sounds specious, to say the least. But the incident had no further repercussions: Guyton-Morveau sent the necessary passports and authorization to the convoying officer, and the police at once released him. The mysterious consignment of trunks reached Paris without further let or hindrance.

Was this the reason why Guyton-Morveau was elected President of the Committee? Or was it merely because he happened to be the oldest member? A little of each, no doubt. He had Bréard as his Vice-President, with Barère and Lindet as Joint Secretaries. Each of the nine members was made responsible for a ministerial department. Danton took over National Defense and, later, Foreign Affairs.

The oligarchs established their headquarters in the Tuileries, taking over part of the dead King's private quarters. Here, on the second floor of the Pavillon de Flore, now renamed the

Pavillon de l'Égalité, they could work undisturbed. From the very beginning, however, Danton's dominating personality imposed itself on the Committee as a whole. Just as he had ruled the whole Cabinet when he was Minister of Justice, so now he became a virtual dictator—so much so that the general public, instead of using the full, cumbersome title of Committee of Public Safety, simply referred to it as the Danton Committee. Since the Ministries continued to function, the Committee became a quasi-personified legal entity, with the rights and prerogatives normally held by an individual Head of State. For the second time in his life, the bourgeois from Arcis had replaced Louis XVI.

Unlike the Ministers, who resided in their various Ministries, the members of the Committee continued to live at home. The Pavillon de l'Égalité was not large enough to accommodate them and their families. Danton preferred it this way: in the rue des Cordeliers there was only one flight of stairs between him and Louise. Often he did not even need to go up to the floor above; when he got back from a meeting of the Committee he was quite likely to find her in his apartment. She was always slipping down to keep an eye on the children, who had now come back from their grandparents and were being looked after by the maids.

In Gabrielle's day Louise had been like a big sister to them; now she was acting as a substitute for their mother, and this imposed something of a dilemma on her young conscience. A man named Claude Dupin, some eight years her senior and Secretary General of the Seine *département,* had asked for her hand in marriage. This proposal pleased M. and Mme. Gély and was not unacceptable to their daughter. Yet she still hesitated to accept it. When Gabrielle was dying, she had made Louise promise to look after her children and her husband—a curious request to make of a fifteen-year-old girl and one which (short of openly telling her to marry Danton) was tantamount to demanding that she remain celibate for a more or less prolonged period.

Gabrielle was neither blind nor a fool; she had seen the expression of desire on Danton's face when he looked at Louise.

Tormented as she was by presentiments of death, by her husband's infidelities, by the uncertain future of her children, she began to sketch plans for Danton's remarriage to this charming adolescent girl. Quite obviously Danton wanted her; and Louise herself, despite his ugliness, was not insensible to his masculine drive and power. Moreover, she adored the children. By marrying Danton (a man some twenty years her senior) Louise would be fulfilling Gabrielle's private wishes, and not abandoning "her" little ones to some other less well-disposed stepmother. There could be no doubt that Danton, who loved family life and debauchery with equal fervor, would sooner or later marry again. This was why Louise refused the advances of Claude Dupin, though he loved her, and she by no means detested him; such a marriage would have cast doubt upon her affectionate regard for Gabrielle's memory. Louise felt that she must bide her time patiently, perhaps for a year or more, until Danton made up his mind.

While awaiting this day, which she both prayed for and feared, Louise—once more in accordance with the dead woman's wishes—undertook the upbringing of Danton's children. She often took them, with or without their father, to The Fountain of Love, that house in Sèvres where the Charpentier family now lived. (The one at Fontenay-sous-Bois had been sold and was now no more than a memory.) Though inconsolable for the death of their daughter, they were nevertheless very pleased to welcome Louise. They saw perfectly well that her affection for the children was mingled with some kind of matrimonial intrigue. Being broadminded and practical folk, they regarded this girl (who showed such consideration for them in their bereavement) as the future mother of their grandchildren rather than as a mere replacement for Gabrielle. Danton himself gave no hint that he had any such personal plans in mind, but his expression spoke for him. Besides, Louise's presence about the house had become increasingly indispensable. Overwhelmed by the vast amount of work which the Committee of Public Safety had to handle, France's new master could always be sure of finding domestic peace and harmony when he got home.

His burden of responsibility was heavy indeed. Everything had to be pulled into shape somehow, and time was all too short.

In the Vendée, rebel forces were executing endless batchs of Republicans by firing squad. Dumouriez, in Belgium, was probably briefing the Austrians on the weak points in the French defenses. Everywhere there were complaints of food shortages.

The old vague evasiveness of governmental communiqués was replaced by a new kind of language. A memorandum was circulated to every Minister, General, and Commissioner, ordering them—under pain of prosecution by the Revolutionary Tribunal —to submit a daily report to the Committee and initiate no action without the Committee's prior endorsement. "It is high time," the memorandum declared, "for people to realize how heavy a responsibility rests upon those whose mistakes, even when unintentional, cannot be excused. The National Convention requires the generals to obey the orders of the Committee of Public Safety. Each of them is answerable with his life for the execution of those orders." In this extract from the memorandum Danton's style is clearly recognizable.

As a first step, the Pavillon de l'Égalité turned over to the tribunal several former officers of Dumouriez's, who were charged with failing to prevent his act of treason. The jury acquitted Heugel, Lanoue, and Miranda, but condemned Miaczynski, Devaux, and Lescuyer. They were accompanied to the guillotine by an old woman tramp who had been heard shouting, "Long live the King!" when she was drunk.

So the Terror began. Would it save France? Would it once more preserve the Declaration of the Rights of Man? The motto embroidered on French military colors, "Victory or Death," was no mere symbolic phrase. Every defeated general was relieved of his head by Sanson, and the rest saw that there was no alternative, they simply *had* to win. And how, one may ask, did the Committee reward their success? By inserting a stereotyped formula in the *Bulletin des Lois:* "General So-and-So has not ceased to merit the trust of the Republic." Soldiers were rewarded with a Sword of Honor. Decorations were a thing of the past. Far be it from the Republic to ape the devices of the tyrants!

Such measures bred a new army. What was more to the point, soldiers were given an incentive to fight. They were struggling not only for the defense of equal rights, but also for the protection of their own plot of land. Any man who possesses property will defend it. In order to foster this sentiment, the Committee persuaded the Convention to impose the death penalty on "anyone who infringed the rights of property." Even Saint-Just supported this plea, declaring that "the property of patriots is sacred and inviolable."

Nevertheless, the Riding School still served as an arena for bitter partisan struggles. The conflict between Montagnards and Girondists grew steadily bitterer. At the time of Louis XVI's trial, the latter had suggested deciding his fate by means of a plebiscite among all qualified voters. The People's Friend, who had already criticized the Gironde for this "act of treason," returned to the charge in 1793. An address circulated to the Jacobins in the various *départements* called upon them to "wield the lightning of their petitions against those faithless delegates who attempted to save the tyrant." The Gironde got its revenge by persuading the Plain to join it in voting for Marat's arraignment. Between them they obtained a majority, and Marat found himself haled before the Revolutionary Tribunal. But the jury acquitted him, and a delirious crowd escorted him back to the Riding School, chaired shoulder high by his supporters. They invaded the Chamber, and an unseemly scuffle broke out in the aisles; violent blows were exchanged, and not a few sabers flashed out of their scabbards. For once, all Deputies stood up against this assault on the House's official dignity. By a well-nigh unanimous vote they decided that the Convention should be transferred to other premises. Since the Riding School was so vulnerable, their debates would henceforth be held in the theater of the Tuileries Palace. To reach its auditorium one had to negotiate endless staircases, corridors, and antechambers. The Assembly would be able to work in peace there—or so it believed. But converting the theater into a debating chamber took time, and the Assembly did not move there until May 10.

Meanwhile Montagnards and Girondists were polishing up their weapons for a decisive battle, and the Committee of Public Safety was forging the arms to secure victory both at home and abroad. As far as Danton was concerned, the enemy at home included the Girondists. At his instigation Camille Desmoulins published an inflammatory pamphlet with the title "Brissot Unveiled, or The History of the Brissotists." In this fearful tract

Desmoulins accused Brissot and the Girondists of every unpatri-
otic crime imaginable, and wound up with the demand that the
Convention should "spew them forth."

This produced a general outcry. The pamphlet was distributed in Paris by the Jacobins and spread about the provinces
by Montagnards acting as delegates to the armed forces; it
delighted the Left no less than it infuriated the Right. Danton,
dining with Desmoulins and his attractive wife, had a good
laugh over it.

He was leading a fantastically busy life now. Not content with
directing the Committee of Public Safety, he also sat on a
Commission charged with the task of drawing up the new Constitution. This body held its meetings in an office at the National
Assembly.

In the Pavillon de l'Égalité Danton also held conferences with
the arms manufacturers. Muskets, field guns, and munitions were
needed by the ton to combat both the foe abroad and the enemy
in their midst. In May he received Perregaux, the financier, and
the writer Beaumarchais. The former, who presumptuously styled
himself "Banker to the Committee of Public Safety," was conducting negotiations with Beaumarchais who, lured by the prospect of gain into the role of arms trafficker, had a stock of
53,000 muskets and bayonets stored in a Dutch warehouse. Fearing that the Netherlands government might seize them, he had
arranged for their fictitious sale to a London merchant resident
in the Low Countries, whose name was Lecointe. But when he
tried to get them back in order to sell them to the French army,
Beaumarchais was faced with a demand for compensation by
Lecointe, to the tune of 800,000 florins. Now he had come to
the Committee to secure Danton's endorsement for his raising
this sum by loan from Perregaux, and, further, to obtain the
vital permit without which his 922 crates of muskets could not
be freighted anywhere. On top of this, the author of *The Barber
of Seville* asked Danton for a personal passport: he had returned from abroad illegally in order to negotiate this sale with
the Committee. Since his name figured on the list of proscribed
persons, he risked suffering the far from enviable fate reserved
for *"émigrés* caught in possession of arms." He might possess

53,000 of the latter, but on the other hand, he had only one head to offer the executioner. He subsequently went into hiding and did not return to Paris, since as it turned out the arms were never delivered. Having been sworn to secrecy for reasons of State, Beaumarchais suddenly became scared of the rivalry between the Committee of General Security and the Committee of Public Safety. If the first had the convoy stopped and discovered what it was carrying, the second would be unable to defend Beaumarchais; the secret nature of the deal would effectively prevent it from doing so. Unfortunately for the Republic, the arms remained in Holland; and the owner, armed with Danton's passport, rejoined the *émigrés*.

This is a good example of the difficulties confronting the dictator. He and his colleagues did all they could to encourage the production of firearms, both in the arsenals and by private enterprise. France became one vast munitions factory. Individual citizens were requested to scrape the walls of their cellars to collect the saltpeter which was an essential ingredient for the manufacture of gunpowder. The Pavillon de l'Égalité was the scene of constant feverish activity, with an endless stream of messages going out to every part of the country.

So it was a great pleasure and relief for Danton when he returned to his two children, and Louise Gély, in the rue des Cordeliers. Louise might be young, but she was mature for her age and could hold her own in conversation with the great statesman. Tactfully she refrained from any reference to future plans. She had quick, bright eyes, a heart-shaped face, and fine chestnut hair. As she grew older she was becoming extraordinarily attractive—and so intelligent, too! She had refused Claude Dupin's proposal, which was a very hopeful sign.

But Danton had too many cares and responsibilities on his shoulders to become absorbed by the subtleties of a refined courtship. As though the determination to defeat France's enemies on the field of battle were not enough, he now entered upon negotiations with almost every country in Europe. And he was still dreaming of destroying the Girondists.

In fact, the day of their final defeat was close at hand. On May 10 the Convention moved its premises to the Tuileries Theater. The architects who had converted it had installed benches for the Deputies and galleries for the public. These galleries rested on a single enormous beam which withstood everything—the crowds, the shouted abuse, the fury, and the chaos. It bent but it never cracked, even in those famous days of June of 1793 when the Montagnards crushed the Gironde.

Both sides had supposed that this change of venue would enable them to legislate in peace. But party rivalry had already passed the point of no return. The Girondists were accused of "Federalism," a fearful crime against the "Republic one and indivisible." While Marat, Robespierre, and other Montagnards attacked them from the rostrum, Hébert's troops, together with 20,000 National Guardsmen under the leadership of their new commander, Hanriot, proceeded to besiege the Tuileries. Sweating with fright, the Deputies of the Plain joined the Montagnards in voting for the arrest of twenty-nine Deputies and two Ministers, accused of trying to "break up the country's unity and replace it with a federation of autonomous regions." All the leading Girondists found themselves in prison: Vergniaud, Brissot, Gensonné, Carra, Valazé, Lasource, Ducos, Sillery, and others. One or two managed to get away, however: Barbaroux, Pétion, and Guadet to Normandy, Lanjuinais to Brittany. Condorcet stayed in Paris but went into hiding in his mistress's apartment. Roland and Buzot joined each other at Rouen, but Manon—the former's wife, the latter's lover—was arrested in her house and thrown into the Abbaye Prison.

Even if Danton did not himself plan the downfall of these men—and of that one woman—he certainly gave Marat and Robespierre a free hand to do so. Doubtless Danton regretted the arrest of Lebrun, the Foreign Secretary, that valiant pacifist who had kept England neutral for nearly a year by posting Chauvelin, Talleyrand, Noël, and Maret to London. When it came to negotiating with the crowned heads of Europe and attempting to best them by diplomatic means, the Committee of Public Safety bowed to traditional usage and made the Foreign Secretary responsible for all this secret bargaining. Now at the time Danton was putting out some very delicate feelers: to England, a country he wanted to see pull out of the coalition; to Turkey, Sweden, Denmark, and Switzerland, in the hopes that they would not join it; and to Prussia, with whom he intended, if

possible, to conclude a separate peace. At this precise moment
Lebrun was caught up in the general purge of the Girondists.
Though he was not thrown into a prison cell—Danton managed
to secure this concession for him—he was placed under house
arrest, guarded by gendarmes, and forced to conduct his negotiations henceforth under the added handicap of this unconstitu-
tional detention.

On several occasions English spies saw him escorted like a
malefactor from his home to the Pavillon de l'Égalité, where he
and his masters worked together. All Europe soon heard of his
alarming predicament. France was made a laughingstock, and
the discussions collapsed. Poor Lebrun was the first victim.
Hauled out of his room by the gendarmes, he somehow managed
to escape and thus avoided joining the Girondists in prison. But
he was recaptured; and so this skilled diplomat paid for his
moderation, foresight, and love of peace under the knife of the
guillotine.

A few days after the arrest of the Girondists, Danton was
chatting with Robespierre and Marat in the private bar of a
café on the rue du Paon. "It was here," as Victor Hugo later
wrote in *Quatre-Vingt-Treize* ("Ninety-three"), "that there used
to meet, secretly and intermittently, men who were so powerful,
and so constantly under observation, that they shrank from talking together in public." From the whole discussion among the
three men—a classic display of skeleton-rattling in the family
cupboard—one need recall only one remark, supposedly spoken
by Marat toward the end of the exchange, and that because it
contains a suggestion which Danton in the end followed. *"Let
me give you one piece of advice, Danton. You're in love, you're
thinking of getting married again. Be a sensible fellow and
stop meddling in politics."*

Danton's matrimonial plans, it is true, were by now known to
everyone. Moreover, his energy and zest for battle had undergone
a marked decline. Even in the Pavillon de l'Égalité his colleagues
saw him less often. They sat every morning, from nine till midday, and again in the evening from seven o'clock onward. But
however urgent the problems to be dealt with, Danton never
turned up for the evening session. He preferred to spend the
time in Louise's company, either upstairs with her parents or in

his own apartment, where he would find her giving the children their supper when he got home.

A day came when he began to miss the morning sessions, too. Marat, denouncing this absenteeism, printed a somewhat daring allusion to the "Committee of Public Ruination." This sort of thing could not go on. Danton had two alternatives before him: he must either resign or rewed; either abandon his public career or else rediscover, in the emotional security of a second marriage, that peace of mind and sensuous satisfaction which would enable him to guide his country's destiny once more.

Less than four months after Gabrielle's death, he asked M. and Mme. Gély for Louise's hand. Though they had been expecting this proposal, the girl's parents nevertheless made difficulties. They disliked the idea of surrendering a fifteen-year-old child to this giant of thirty-four; especially they disliked the idea of doing so without a church ceremony. Marc-Antoine and his wife made great play with their own, and Louise's, piety and tried to fob Danton off by declaring that they could not possibly let their daughter marry a man who refused to go to Confession before his wedding. Furthermore, such Confession must not be made to a conformist priest. To their great surprise, Danton accepted these conditions. He agreed to everything—Confession, church wedding, and all—so long as it meant his getting this adorable ingénue.

The marriage contract was signed on June 12. Danton's previous contract, with Gabrielle, drawn up in 1787, provided for joint possession of property. This new one, on the contrary, established separate endowments for husband and wife. Danton made over to Louise a capital sum of 40,000 *livres*. Since Gély could not match this, Danton provided the *dot* himself; first, a sum of 10,000 *livres*, made over as a loan to his future father-in-law, interest-free and for life; and a second capital endowment of 30,000 *livres*, supposedly offered by an old aunt of Danton's, Mme. Lenoir, to her future niece-by-marriage. In this way Louise's fiancé avoided wounding her self-respect. He did not want anyone to be able to say that he had *bought* her.

This contract sheds a good deal of light on Danton's concern for his family. By marrying under the "separate property" dispensation (a very rare choice in his day) he was protecting the

future of Gabrielle's children. The 40,000 *livres* he made over
to Louise ensured her against the hazards of the Revolution. In
the law providing for the institution of the Extraordinary Tribunal there occurs the following stipulation: "The property of all
persons condemned to death shall be forfeit to the Republic."
Danton's marriage contract makes it very clear that, even then,
he foresaw the possibility of his falling a victim to the Tribunal
himself. There is one most unusual clause in it, making his wife
responsible (at the age of fifteen!) for the administration of all
his property. In the perspective of history this ingenious pretense can safely be ignored. Danton obviously went on managing
his affairs, though Louise signed the papers as her husband told
her. In the event of his arrest and trial, he would arrange for her
to freeze all surviving assets.

That just about covered the situation, and Danton must have
felt he could stop worrying. All that remained before he acquired
conjugal rights over Louise was his fulfillment of her parents'
conditions: to have his confession heard by a nonjuring priest,
and to obtain the nuptial blessing. Where was he to find such a
priest? As it turned out, Gély and his wife knew one, a former
incumbent of Saint-Sulpice named M. de Kéravénan. This heroic abbé had been imprisoned in Les Carmes in September
1792; by a stroke of luck he was in the lavatory when the
massacre began, and took warning from the shrieks and screams
of his fellow prisoners. Blessing his miraculous attack of constipa-
tion, he clambered up on the seat and managed to reach the
timber frame overhead. A section was loose because of repair
work, and he somehow squeezed through between the roof
beams, and waited there for twenty-four hours, till those dread-
ful cries had been replaced by a deathly silence. From then on
he had led a clandestine existence, sleeping in one place, eating
in another, moving on whenever his hiding place seemed liable
to discovery, yet always ready to fulfill his priestly duties if the
faithful called upon him.

Marc-Antoine Gély gave Danton his present address, and Danton sought him out in his garret. What, one wonders, would
people like Marat and Robespierre and Collot d'Herbois have
said had they seen their friend kneeling before a priest, or
witnessed his nuptial blessing—bestowed in so secret a place

that history has no record of it? Afterward Danton and his bride
went on to the City Hall, where a municipal official performed
the civil ceremony in private.

Danton's wedding night brought him great happiness; from
then on he seemed to recover all his old energies as a statesman.
He began to entertain again, and his friends found themselves
invited to dinner parties once more. While still dazzled by this
renewal of joy did he actually make the remark which Fouché
afterward, in 1797, attributed to him: "From now on all true
patriots should be able to eat ortolans?" In the *Mémoires de
Barras,* Rousselin de Saint-Albin afterward printed an alternative version, which conflicts with that given by Fouché. What
Danton said, according to his boyhood friend, was: "From
now on everyone [i.e. the French people] must have adequate
food and clothing."

There was only one way to attain such a goal, and that was
by ending the wars which drained away all the taxpayers'
money—and eradicating the traitors who made a fat living from
war itself, who hampered negotiations and demoralized the
troops. Danton began to appear on the rostrum again; both in
the Convention and at the Jacobin Club that thunderous voice
was raised anew. He lambasted the wretched Girondists, who
were still languishing in prison; as yet no one quite dared to hand
them over to Fouquier-Tinville's tender mercies. He also persuaded the Assembly to vote 4,000,000 *livres* into the secret
fund, this credit being earmarked to assist the Committee's
agents carry out work for peace in enemy countries.

Danton, in collaboration with Héraut de Séchelles, was also
drafting the text of the new Constitution. When the draft was
nearly complete he added one vital article. As a safeguard against
dictatorship, which he knew something about, this dictator laid
down that only the Legislature had the right to declare war. As
always, it was the problem of peace that haunted him to such
an extent that Robespierre and Marat began to regard him as
a "moderate"—a most heinous offense.

His rousing speeches before the Convention might lead one to
suppose that he was also working on the Committee; but in point
of fact he remained a constant absentee, especially at evening
sessions. Was he likely to leave Louise on her own then? Danton

had embarked on the great love affair of his life; never before
had he been so completely happy. Abundant revenues were coming in from his Arcis estates, and money flowed like water in the
rue des Cordeliers. The master of the house commissioned that
fashionable artist Boilly to paint the ravishing Mme. Danton's
portrait. She posed for him in her drawing room, together with
Antoine, the elder of her stepsons. The picture shows her standing at a table, showing Antoine the enlarged images produced
by a mounted lens. Its title is *L'Optique* ("The Optical Device"). In it Louise is portrayed as a *gamine*. Her tiny features
and wide-innocent eyes are poised above a dark bodice, cut
closely to the contours of her bust. But her long, light-colored
skirt, with its wide pleats falling right to the ground, completely
camouflages her hips and legs.

On Sunday the whole family went out to see M. and Mme.
Charpentier at Sèvres. They had understood, and forgiven, their
son-in-law's remarriage, and they welcomed Louise with every
kindness. On June 18 Danton was still there, enjoying the fresh
air of the countryside, when a grim piece of news reached him.
His secret agent in Brittany (the same Dr. Chévetel whom he
had rescued from execution during the September massacres)
had some while back attempted to show his gratitude by handing
over twenty-seven Bretons to the Committee of General Security.
This mixed bag of landowners and laborers, men and women,
had all been implicated in the plot organized by La Rouairie—
that aristocrat with whom Danton (using Chévetel as a go-between) had struck up a private alliance after the publication of
Brunswick's manifesto, so that he could still emerge on the right
side if the *émigrés* won the day. But the victory of Valmy
rendered this double game obsolete, and Chévetel had reverted
to treating La Rouairie as an opponent. He failed to organize
his capture, because the Marquis disobligingly died on him;
however, he did round up the Marquis's twenty-seven accomplices, bring them to Paris, and cast them into prison. Among
them were M. and Mme. de la Guyomarais, whose only crime
consisted of giving shelter to La Rouairie when he was dying
(in fact, he expired in their château). By denouncing this couple
the doctor had overstepped his master's instructions.

Danton did what he could to save the prisoners—not only M.

and Mme. de la Guyomarais, but their twenty-five companions
as well. He felt that it would be impolitic to bring them to trial
at a time when he was reopening negotiations with all the countries of Europe. The Committee of General Security, on the other
hand, wanted to execute them as a gesture of defiance to the
dictator. It took advantage of the newly-wed husband's exclusive preoccupation with his darling Louise to turn over M. and
Mme. de la Guyomarais, plus twelve of their fellow prisoners,
(including two women) to the bloodthirsty Public Prosecutor,
Fouquier-Tinville.

It was the news of this mass execution that reached Danton
on June 18, at his rural retreat near Sèvres. He was furious at
first but soon recovered his equanimity. Recriminations were
useless: a severed head could not be stuck on again. Chévetel
would get a good dressing-down, and that would be the end of
the matter.

The fresh country air of Sèvres, The Fountain of Love with
its parkland—all this would have made an idyllic Eden had the
honeymooners' more ardent moments not always been liable to
interruption by Gabrielle's two children and their grandparents.
To escape the noisy chatter of the young and the watchful eyes
of the old, Danton rented a pied-à-terre at Choisy-le-Roi (now
renamed Choisy-le-République) where the couple could enjoy
themselves undisturbed. Here Danton relaxed into delicious in-
dolence, slippers on his feet, his unwieldy body wrapped in a
dressing gown, and Louise perched on his knees en déshabillé.
Though she was submissive in a way that Gabrielle had never
been, this frail near-child had tamed the male in Danton. He
was often unfaithful to his first wife, but never once to his
second.

At Choisy, as at Sèvres, the walls muffled all rumors from
the outside world. The echoes of the Revolution scarcely penetrated to the two lovers. At the Tuileries Theater and the Pavillon de l'Égalité, where Danton now hardly ever appeared, he was
beginning to be known as "the sleepyhead." On June 23 Vadier
went further still. This Deputy for the Ariège region, who was
also a member of the Committee of General Security, protested
vigorously against "the sleeping partners" on the Committee of

Public Safety. Danton was still the member responsible for Foreign Affairs and National Defense. He had made a marvelous job of it, no doubt about that. But no doubt, either, that he seldom, if ever, put in an appearance there nowadays. No, he left his eight colleagues to cope with all the work, while he himself enjoyed the delights of the countryside and made love to his young wife.

It was at this point that a private joke, the implications of which were most alarming, began to circulate: a sinister kind of pun, a play on his beloved's first name. It was whispered that his hearty laughter, his wealth, his gluttonous appetites and his rare outbursts of eloquence on the rostrum were all "reserved for Louisette." Sometimes the name was given as "Louison." Now the guillotine, wrongly attributed to Dr. Guillotin because he recommended it in the Legislative Assembly, was actually the brain child of one Tobias Schmidt, a friend of Sanson's, and of a surgeon named Louis, who put the finishing touches to it. As a result, Paris wags began to refer to the instrument as the "Louisette" or "Louison." In June 1793 these two nicknames were still popular with the mob and had not yet been finally discarded in favor of the "guillotine."

So when Danton was told, by some visitors to Sèvres or Choisy, about the saying making the round of the Tuileries—that all he possessed was destined for "Louisette"—his blood ran momentarily cold. "By God," he exclaimed to Louise, "they're going to hear me now!" Then he took a horse and was gone.

On July 6 he mounted the speakers' rostrum: his bulk and ugliness and sheer power gave the man a terrifying yet bizarre appearance, like some kind of bogey. When his enormous voice rang out, even his most implacable enemies began to tremble. What was he going to discuss? As it turned out, the motion on the order paper, although this had been under debate since the previous day: but then he knew everything, understood everything, was up-to-date on all the latest developments. The former Duke of Biron, who commanded a Republican army in the Vendée, had written that two battalions from the Gironde region were threatening to desert and go back home. Levasseur, the General's official representative, asked, when he delivered this message, "that all who desert from the armed forces shall

be declared traitors to their country." Danton spoke out against
such a decree, which would make ordinary private soldiers liable
for arraignment before the Revolutionary Tribunal. He opposed
it, to begin with, because Biron's report, in his opinion, did not
present a sufficiently detailed case. But there was another reason
for Danton's attitude: when an animal tamer wants to restore
his authority in the ring, he has to give the beasts a taste of the
whip. "Are these battalions really so culpable?" he thundered.
"Before we accuse them, we should hunt down those malicious
and wicked persons who sow discord in our armies!" He denounced the fugitive Girondist Deputies, above all Buzot, and
that "craven Brissotism" of which the effects still persisted.
"Hitherto we have acted with prudence and restraint. Today let
us exercise that national authority with which we are invested,
and cast back, into the oblivion from which they arose, that
handful of seditious persons whose ephemeral reputation was
only established by error."

The Assembly applauded. While still in a state of great excitement, they suddenly learned that Catherine the Great had
banned the import of all French products throughout Russia,
until such a day as "legitimate government should be restored
in France." Furthermore, the Spanish General Ricardos (in imitation of Brunswick, but without any threats against the lives of
the inhabitants) had addressed a manifesto to the French people,
calling upon them to "overthrow the tyranny of an illegal and
usurping Assembly." Here were two rude rebuffs for Danton:
they made it only too plain that his negotiations, which had cost
the Treasury a cool 4,000,000 *livres,* had drawn a blank in both
the empire of the Russias and the Iberian peninsula.

The next day there came some highly disconcerting news from
Danton's protégé Westermann, who had just suffered a stunning
defeat in the Vendée. These three setbacks, taken together,
pushed the dictator's opponents into action. On July 10 Drouet,
the Deputy associated with the flight to Varennes took the floor
and in moving terms demanded that the law concerning the
Committee's renewal of tenure be now applied. The Assembly
granted his request and, all enthusiasm, held a fresh ballot on
the spot.

Danton was not re-elected. His first dictatorship had lasted fifty-nine days, his second ended after ninety-six. Defeated before he was even aware that his opponents had caught him off his guard, he accepted the blow philosophically. What good would it have done him to protest? Besides, this verdict gave him back his freedom. Now there was nothing to keep him away from Louise.

CHAPTER XVI

Robespierre in Power

IT WAS, IN FACT, Robespierre whose skillful string-pulling had brought about Danton's defeat. The Incorruptible had for long been highly critical, in private, of his friend's more dubious associates. There was Dr. Chévetel, widely regarded as a double agent; there was the Englishman Miles, sent out by Pitt (or so it was thought) to join the Jacobin Club and spy on his fellow members. There were Emmanuel and Junius Frey, two Austrian brothers who (in collaboration with Chabot, a former Capuchin monk and their future brother-in-law) speculated on the activities of the East India Company. There was Basire, a lawyer who had sacrificed his fortune to the Revolution but who nonetheless was accused of tampering with various orders concerning this company; there was Delaunay d'Angers—another friend of Danton's—who had the company compulsorily dissolved after selling all his own shares in it. There was Julien, once a Protestant clergyman, who was supposed to be in some way associated with the ex-Abbé d'Espagnac as an army contractor. There was Gusman, a Spanish banker of very questionable reputation; there was a Danish lawyer called Diedrichsen; there were, lastly, adventurers such as Proli, Comte, Dubuisson, and Desportes, who were, or so it was said, ready to turn their hand to anything.

These were the men whom Danton—if Robespierre was to believe half the rumors he heard—had employed as his negotiators, with the task of obtaining concessions from every country in Europe. But not one such concession had been extracted;

and this failure was directly attributable to the questionable characters of Danton's go-betweens. He had been seen with all of them at one time or another, dining in the most fashionable restaurants. There were, as Robespierre saw it, only two possible explanations. Either Danton was trafficking with these creatures (all of whom were more or less corrupt) to feather his own nest as well as theirs, or else he had given up hope of achieving victory by force of arms, and was now trying to patch up a peace at any price. This was why the Incorruptible, despite his personal and long-standing friendship with Danton, put Drouet up to make the intervention that brought about his downfall.

If Danton thought he would be free to seek consolation in Louise's arms, he was very much mistaken. Almost at once he had to hurry to the Jacobin Club and defend himself against a fresh charge. He was accused of recommending Admiral Dalbarade (who had been Minister of Marine since April 3) to appoint a man named Peyron as a port inspector. It turned out that Peyron was up to his neck in espionage activities. Danton, all patience exhausted, did not attempt to protect him. Instead he made a quibbling assertion to the effect that his recommendation was not to be treated as a guarantee. "I recommended employing Peyron, yes," he said. "But I also recommended setting other spies to keep an eye on him." To justify himself to his detractors, he pleaded the immense amount of work handled by the Committee; when he had been a member, he said, this had left him no time to refute those malicious persons who spread "endless lying stories" designed to blacken his reputation. But he no longer belonged to the Committee, thank God, and could now best help its newly elected members by supporting them in the Convention.

This new Committee, as a result of several additions, now had twelve members instead of nine. Among them three were especially prominent: Robespierre, Saint-Just, and Lazare Carnot—the prophet of the Revolution, the dark Byronic hero of the Montagnards, and the strategist who came to be known as the Organizer of Victory. The rest were almost all extreme "patriots," and Danton now had only two friends left on the Committee: Hérault-Séchelles and Thuriot. The former (who had dropped the hyphen between his names) came from an old

Norman family related to the Polignacs. In collaboration with Danton he had drafted the 1793 Constitution—the most democratic charter hitherto known in France, though it was never given practical application. Thuriot (formerly Thuriot de la Rozière) had taken part in the storming of the Bastille. These two converted aristocrats were now Danton's only "eyes" on the Committee over which only yesterday he had wielded supreme power: a terrible comedown.

The pattern of events which followed his resignation as Minister in 1792 now repeated itself. Large numbers of Deputies went out of their way to avoid him. *Vae victis!* Marat made sarcastic references to him in his broadsheet. Westermann, he said, should be guillotined; and he accused Danton and Lacroix of continuing to support this general "despite his having been an accessory to Dumouriez's treasonable defection." After this plain lie Marat added: "I flatter myself that they will not add the crowning touch to their shameless impudence by any attempt to save him from his just deserts." Marat plainly was a menace. But not for much longer. The very next day Charlotte Corday stabbed him in his bath. He died almost at once.

Danton gave a sigh of relief. But there were still the rest of them to be dealt with. For the past three days it had been openly said that he, Danton, had brought France to the brink of ruin; and since that morning another whispering campaign had begun, suggesting that he was secretly responsible for Marat's murder. Well, he knew a trick or two himself; what he must do now was to place himself at the head of this opposition, bay with the wolves—and then work on them, flip them over like so many pancakes, get public opinion on his side once more. The susceptibility of the Latin races to verbal persuasion was a never-failing stand-by. After speeches by Lacroix and Thuriot, calling for the arrest of Fauché (who was charged with aiding and abetting "the girl Corday"), Danton added his own indictment: "The people," he declared, "are all too restrained; the Convention is moderate to a fault." In Rome the consul would by now have announced the death of the malefactors. Thunderous applause.

This was no time for balance and restraint. At a time when men such as Robespierre and Saint-Just were doing their best to direct the actions of the "Great Committee," Danton had no option but to overbid them. His brazen lungs enabled him to shout louder than his colleagues, and he did not stint his advantage. In the end he rallied so many adherents that he found himself elected President of the Convention, though for a fortnight only, since the regulations did not allow a longer tenure. The date was July 25, two weeks after his downfall from power; he had made a swift and sensational comeback.

He took advantage of his success to announce that he would act as a "thorn in the flesh" of the Committee—"of all Committees." This was a clever way of hinting to the Robespierre Committee that sooner or later it would suffer the same inevitable fate as the one named after himself. Among other thorns implanted by the President during his brief term of office was the following: "I demand that every day some aristocrat, some enemy of the people, expiate his crimes on the guillotine!" It was as a result of this that on July 28 the Convention passed a motion authorizing the Committee of Public Safety to issue warrants for arrest. This was Danton's way of getting back at the Committee of General Security, hitherto the sole body to possess such a right and consequently a frequent stumbling block to the old Committee of Public Safety. Under the new dispensation it was Robespierre who controlled the police—a decision which Danton afterward bitterly regretted.

Almost at once, indeed, a minor incident occurred which put Danton in danger of becoming the edict's first victim. This nasty little affair began in an unsensational and somewhat insidious manner, at the opening of the biennial exhibition of painting and sculpture in the square Salon of the Louvre. The exhibition had been founded by Louis XIV, and still survived under the Revolution. (To satisfy democratic aspirations, artists who did not belong to the former Royal Academy were now permitted to exhibit their work side by side with that of members.) Since the Salon opened in August, it did not draw large crowds—a piece of luck for the President of the Convention. Somewhat to their surprise, visitors found one item described in the catalogue as "Bust of Citizeness Danton, exhumed seven days after burial: plaster cast molded from the body by Citizen Deseine, deaf mute." Its presence caused a buzz of speculation. Who could have been responsible for so macabre an exhibit? It was impos-

sible to see Danton's hand in the affair, even on the grounds
of besotted devotion. Much time had passed since the civic
authorities of Fontenay-sous-Bois, anxious to please Danton, had
named the thoroughfare in which the Charpentiers lived the
Avenue de la Belle-Gabrielle. Death, moreover, had destroyed all
her remaining beauty. Her cheeks were bloated, her features
distorted by suffering: eternal repose had not restored their
serenity; and the bosom outlined beneath that close-wound muslin shawl was opulent rather than delicate. The only feature
which recalled Gabrielle as she had been in life was her abundant wavy hair.

Deseine, the deaf-mute sculptor, had belonged to the now
defunct Royal Academy. Formerly a pensioner of the Prince de
Condé, he was responsible for the statues adorning the Château
de Chantilly. He had also executed a well-known bust of Louis
XVI and a portrait of d'Aguesseau as Chancellor. He remained
loyal to his onetime patrons and made no secret of his Royalist
opinions, which indeed he committed to paper—not in the public journals, but as formal letters of protest, to the Legislative
Assembly and, latterly, to the Convention, when these bodies
modified the regulations of the fine-art societies. Isolated from
the world by his deafness, Deseine was unaware of the storm
that raged all around him, and could not make his own voice
heard since it was literally nonexistent. It may well be that this
was his way of getting back at France's new masters, and that
by exhibiting so grisly a relic he hoped to expose Danton to public
obloquy. Both religious custom and the (as yet uncodified)
penal laws expressly forbade the practice of illicit exhumation;
no grave might be violated without a court order and sworn
witnesses. Deseine's deliberate exposure of this criminal act by
means of the art exhibition (and divulging the truth meant that
he himself was liable to be charged as an accessory) represented
a sacrifice of his personal security to his political convictions. He
may even have hoped that Danton would be removed from the
presidency and brought to trial. However, nothing so drastic
happened. The affair was hushed up, the bust removed from the
Salon, and the echoes of this minor scandal were soon lost amid
more pressing concerns. France had other things to worry about.

What really shook Paris was the arrest of Montané, President of the Revolutionary Tribunal. He had been removed by gendarmes while the tribunal was actually in session. Here was a scandal to eclipse that of the Salon. Fouquier-Tinville's case against the President was that he had tried to save Charlotte Corday from execution. Montané was imprisoned in La Force and replaced by Herman, a magistrate who, like Robespierre, came from Arras. Under him the Tribunal was never to know an idle moment. To keep it supplied with victims, the dictators in the Pavillon de l'Égalité reinforced the powers of the so-called *Cabinet Noir*. Set up by the tyrants to intercept and read private correspondence, abolished by the Constituent Assembly, and later revived by the Danton Committee, this back-room organization had since then operated under conditions of strict secrecy. The Incorruptible and his eleven colleagues proceeded to lift the veil from its activities. The *Cabinet Noir* was *officially* charged with the task of reading all mail entering or leaving Paris. Such was the origin of postal censorship, a device employed in every war from that time on.

As a safeguard against any danger of competition from the Committee of General Security, the Committee of Public Safety talked the Convention into voting them the right to renew the rival Committee's mandate at will and to nominate its members. Thus the entire police force now passed under Robespierre's control. On September 17, moreover, Merlin de Douai obtained the ratification of the terrible "Law concerning Suspect Persons." The least obnoxious of its articles stipulated that "those persons shall be regarded as suspect who, though they have done nothing against liberty, have also done nothing for it." Armed with instruments such as these, Robespierre now possessed more power than Danton had ever known.

Nevertheless the Incorruptible still defended Danton when the latter was under attack. One day Danton proposed that the Committee of Public Safety should be transformed into a Committee of Government. Though he had several times declared that he would never again serve on any committee himself, he found himself accused, by Hébert and his supporters, of aiming at a dictatorship. This produced an emphatic rejoinder from Robespierre, in a speech to the Jacobins: "How can they slander Danton, of all people—Danton, against whom no one has the

right to voice the least breath of criticism? Those who would
discredit such a man must first prove themselves more than a
match for him in energy, talent, and patriotic zeal." Then he
added: "I am not taking his side now in the hope of doing us
both a good turn; I only mention him by way of illustration."

However, Hébert continued his attacks in *Le Père Duchesne*.
According to him, Danton's displays of violence were a smoke-
screen concealing preparations for a general amnesty. He also
spread the rumor that his adversary (although now no more
than a plain Deputy) was reopening negotiations with Great
Britain and Prussia—despite Danton's thunderous assertions on
the rostrum. "There is only one way," he cried, "to make our
enemies understand and accept the Constitution—by cannon
fire! Now is the time to take our last and greatest oath—
let us swear to obliterate tyranny, or die, all of us, in the attempt!"

The crowd rose to him. "We swear it!" they shouted. After
such a speech it would be hard to maintain the charge that
Danton wanted "peace at any price." Yet he certainly spoke,
with constructive nostalgia, of the tasks peace would bring.
During the debate on public education he made a memorable
intervention: "After the glory of giving France her freedom, and
of vanquishing her enemies, there can be no greater achievement
than to establish, for future generations, an educational system
worthy of the freedom we have won. The people must be provided with national education. When you sow in the vast field
of the Republic, you should not count the cost of seed and
labor. *After bread, education is the people's greatest need.*"
(That final phrase was carved on the plinth of his statue in
1894.) According to Danton, the nobility feared general education because it would give the masses a taste for independence.
Then he drew a laugh from his audience by observing: "I speak
as a father myself—more so than the aristocrats who oppose
State schools, since they can never be sure of their children's
paternity!"

This talented versatility of his was something that always captivated an audience. Listening to Danton gave people genuine
pleasure. His colleagues would draft written speeches fifty or a
hundred pages long and take hours reading them, so that mem-

bers dozed off and the spectators up in the galleries began to fidget irritably. If Danton did nothing else, he woke everyone up. His trumpet sounded the charge, and the public brightened visibly. When word went around that he was about to make an intervention, crowds of people would hurry across to the Tuileries Theater.

Louise was now officially established as the great man's wife. On certain fixed days she was "at home" in the Cour du Commerce. A "domestic official" in knee breeches (the word "valet" had been dropped) helped the two "female domestic officials" to serve *petits fours*. (By way of a small economy, the same man also acted as coachman.) Gabrielle had played the clavichord, but Louise offered her guests the chance to enjoy a somewhat more striking talent. Her instrument was the guitar, and she sang to her own accompaniment. Danton went in for musically minded wives.

Like Gabrielle, too, Louise preferred to keep away from the Convention. Her marriage and the love she bore her husband had made no difference either to her religious beliefs or to her Royalist opinions. Like her parents, she detested the rabble-rousing atmosphere of the "national circus," and her appearances there were rare in the extreme. But being the wife of a man such as Danton had its drawbacks no less than its advantages. Through no fault of her own, Louise found herself the bone of contention during a public debate—not in the Assembly, but at that scarcely less influential (if unofficial) institution the Jacobin Club.

Nevertheless it was in the Convention that the incident really began, when Danton was still President. Garat, the Minister of the Interior, came within an ace of losing his head after that sinister ex-actor Collot d'Herbois had accused him of sowing dissension in the country. In fact, by the time Danton rose to defend the Minister, the warrant for his arrest had already been signed. But Danton's speech was so vigorous and effective that the Assembly disavowed Collot, and Garat was reinstated; however, sensing fresh trouble ahead, he finally resigned on August 20.

Two rival candidates entered the lists as his successor: Jules

Paré, Danton's boyhood friend and former chief clerk, and Hébert, the editor of *Le Père Duchesne* and Danton's successor as Deputy Public Prosecutor to the Commune. Naturally Danton backed Paré, who was duly elected Minister. This produced some angry invective in *Le Père Duchesne,* which described Danton and Paré as "thick as thieves—just as Danton was with Dumouriez." By this oblique reference to the Belgian mission, Hébert revived the old charges of fleecing and extortion. Delving still further into the past, he also accused Danton of having obtained compensation for his advocateship far in excess of the post's real value. Thanks to his various financial malversations, Hébert claimed, the former Minister had been able to settle 14,000,000 francs on his wife at the time of their marriage.

Danton, who detested writing but was unsurpassed as a speaker, did not reply to Hébert in print. Knowing that the latter would be present at the Jacobin Club on August 26, he appeared there himself to conduct his own defense. The 14,000,-000 francs Hébert had mentioned were in fact a mere 40,000 *livres.* And since when had it been considered reprehensible for a widower with a family to remarry so as to give his children a mother again? Since when had it been a crime for a husband to safeguard his wife's future? In any case, Danton's private life was his own affair. Descending from indignation to self-abasement, this independent character then admitted his dependence on the opposite sex. "I must have women," he declared tearfully, with a touch of farcical inspiration. But he had restricted himself to one, so there was no reason for people to persecute him like this. The 40,000 *livres* which his enemies were so skeptical about—though the figure could be checked from his marriage contract—had been earned by the sweat of his brow. "I am proud that I was born a *sans-culotte,*" he declared, "and that nature endowed me with sufficient physical strength to provide for my sustenance."

As he said this, he drew himself up, so that he looked even taller, threw out his chest, which added to his already formidable bulk, and rounded his big arms, as though the swelling muscles were visible through the stuff of his coat sleeves. Everyone burst out laughing. He had won again; he had got his audience where he wanted them. His speech was loudly applauded, and as he strode down from the rostrum he glanced contemptuously at Hébert. As always, he had managed to talk his way back into public favor.

Throughout September he was the idol of the Convention. To list all his many interventions would be a tedious task; let us restrict ourselves to one characteristic example, his plea that every citizen should be provided with a firearm for the defense of his country, and that the Treasury should earmark 100,000,000 francs for their manufacture. In this famous speech he proclaimed, with fulsome pomposity: "All homage to you, O sublime People! To your greatness you add the capacity for endurance; nothing can daunt you in the pursuit of liberty. To achieve that goal you have shed your blood, and accepted many privations. You must and shall win through! We shall march shoulder to shoulder with you! Your enemies will be confounded, freedom shall be yours!"

Newspapers reporting this speech asserted that at its close hats were thrown in the air, and the applause was so thunderous that it nearly brought the house down.

Prieur de la Côte-d'Or, a member of the Committee of Public Safety, afterward wrote in his *Mémoires sur Carnot:* "Billaud and Collot d'Herbois kept up a constant stream of criticism against everything we did. Finally we agreed that the only way to silence them was to make them members of the Committee." The Committee duly proposed this measure to the Convention, but received a shock when not only Billaud-Varennes and Collot d'Herbois were elected, but Danton and Granet, too. Both the latter refused to serve, however. Danton's words were: "I swear by the liberty of my country that I will never accept a place on the Committee!"

Coming from him, this might be thought a somewhat surprising oath. But in his heart of hearts he was fed up with the whole political game. These tub-thumping triumphs had begun to pall on him. Since his defeat he had not been able to spend a single undisturbed day with Louise. What was more, he felt ill, or perhaps just thoroughly exhausted: a sudden overwhelming sense of depression and fatigue, which he found it impossible to fight against. On September 12 or 13 he went to bed and slept for twenty-four hours.

When he woke, he did some serious thinking. Since Robespierre had taken over the reins of power in France, the Terror had been building up. The guillotine was now a permanent feature of the Place de la Révolution. The tribunal's original nervous scruples had been swept away by an increasingly prevalent fear of foreign intervention: this was a direct incitement to murder. Fouquier-Tinville, a willing slave of the Committee, was rounding up his notorious "batches of victims" for the guillotine; and Danton, in whose brain the whole process of "public safety" had originated, saw that the system was now being used not so much to defeat France's enemies as to crush France herself. The armies were more or less marking time; the only reason they were not in retreat before an advancing enemy was that the divided nations of Europe had failed to agree on any over-all strategy. On the other hand, the tools Danton himself had invented were now being used to forge the very Terror which he found so sickening. What could he do to stop it?

On the same day, September 14, he learned that the Convention had renewed the mandate of the Committee of General Security. All its members were now friends either of Robespierre (which could have been worse) or of Hébert (which was little short of disastrous). At this news Danton retired to bed with a fever. As he lay there various other items of information filtered through, one by one, each calculated to send his temperature up a little further. The police had raided Julien de Toulouse's house and found letters containing firm evidence of the Deputy's shady deals with d'Espagnac. Louis Robert had been caught in possession of eight barrels of rum, which he was hoarding in order to resell at an illegal profit. A search through the papers of Perrin, deputy Mayor of Troyes, showed that he had taken advantage of his position to make a profit of no less than 5,000,000 *livres* on the material he purchased and resold to the army. Perrin was tried on September 19: the Revolutionary Tribunal condemned him to six hours' exposure in the pillory, followed by twelve years in irons.

Finally the Committee of General Security decided to move

against Danton. Two of its members, Panis and David, came and questioned him in bed. When Danton had been the moving spirit behind the Committee, he employed the services of a man named Louis Comte. Comte was sent into Normandy to spy on the fugitive Girondists, and there found out—or so he afterward claimed—that Danton was in league with them; that in fact he was trying to arrange for the Duke of York to be brought over to France, with the object of selling him the throne. This charge was so nebulous that Danton heard no more about it officially; but it sent his temperature soaring, to the point where Louise, in considerable alarm, sent for several doctors. On October 13 the following note reached the President of the Convention: "Having, by the skill of my physicians, been saved from a most serious illness, I now—if I am to make my period of convalescence as short as possible—must go and breathe my own native country air. I therefore pray the Convention to authorize my departure for Arcis-sur-Aube. Needless to say, I shall hasten back to my post the moment I am strong enough to carry out my duties once more."

The leave of absence was somewhat grudgingly granted, and Danton, with his family, set off by post-chaise. Louise, the two children, a maid, the valet—all were delighted to be leaving town. The convalescent himself announced that he was sick to death of his fellow men. He knew that the Public Prosecutor's department, under Fouquier-Tinville, was—in its own fashion— preparing for the trial of the twenty-two Girondists imprisoned since June 2. He knew, too, that Marie-Antoinette, now transferred from the Temple to the Conciergerie Prison, was also awaiting her turn, and that the despicable Hébert was manufacturing a charge of incest against her. He knew that Philippe Égalité, who had been brought back from Marseilles on the 6th, no longer had any illusions about his fate. Danton had, furthermore, made it quite clear to Desmoulins that he would do his best to save all these prisoners—the Girondists, the Queen, the ex-Duke—from their virtually inevitable condemnation. Yet at the same time (as Garat, the former Minister, was to write in his *Memoirs*) he said he could read "his own death warrant in theirs." Then why did he withdraw to Arcis-sur-Aube? Why did this "triumphant athlete of democracy" (to quote Garat once more) give the impression that he was fleeing various terrible responsibilities? Because, we are told, "he needed to have a breathing space away from his fellow men."

While Danton was in his post-chaise, Marie-Antoinette appeared before Fouquier-Tinville. On October 16, the same day that the Danton *ménage* reached its destination, the Queen completed her own final journey—to the scaffold. From his friend Souberbielle, the surgeon—who had been a juryman on the tribunal—Danton learned that anaemia and neglect had left the poor woman half blind, so that she could barely find her way across the courtroom.

This hearing inaugurated a whole series of major political trials. The tribunal, presided over by Herman and later by Dumas, spent the next six months disembarrassing the Robespierre Committee of all those whose words or deeds seemed in any way prejudicial to national defense or the Republic's social achievements. This bloody sacrifice, in which the innocent victims outnumbered the guilty, was the price paid for the building of modern France.

The Committee conducted this campaign with highhanded self-assurance. Through the agency of its delegates to the armed forces—now decked out in uniforms which impressed the rank and file—it had General Houchard arrested in his own headquarters. Houchard had beaten the English at Dunkirk, Hondschoote, Furnes, and Menin; after all these victories his troops were so exhausted they could do no more. Treason! cried Robespierre's despotic minions. So the valiant Houchard was arrested and taken back to Paris, where Sanson relieved him of his head.

Jourdan, his replacement with the Army of the North, and Pichegru, Commander-in-Chief of the Rhine Army, each received the following laconic message: "The Committee orders you to win." They were well aware of the sinister implication behind this command. Jourdan proceeded to beat the Austrians at Wattignies; in the Vendée, Republican forces crushed the rebels at Cholet. The Robespierre Committee was triumphant on all fronts—a success which tended to lessen the popularity of those who had belonged to the late Danton Committee.

Danton, convalescing in his home town, soon learned of his successor's victories. He was naturally jealous of Robespierre's achievement and horrified by the sanguinary methods used to bring it about—so much so that he banned all newspapers in the house and formally prohibited their purchase. All he wanted to hear now was the prattling of children, Louise's amorous sighs, birds singing, and the sound of the local brook, the Pleuvard, which ran through their garden and irrigated it. One day he said to old Mme. Recordain: "Mother, I wonder if I'll ever be lucky enough to come and live here with you for good and have nothing to think about but planting my cabbages."

His old companion Béon, a former abbé, subsequently wrote of him that "he wanted something to take his mind off the stormy debates in the Assembly." So we find him boating, fishing, going out hunting (either alone or with a party), inspecting his estates, buying five new pieces of property, and drawing up agreements with Maître Finot for purchases to the total value of 6100 *livres.*

As part of its anticlerical drive the Convention had abolished the Christian era. The week was now replaced by the "decade." The new system of months began retroactively on September 22, 1792, the date of the Republic's proclamation. At the suggestion of Fabre d'Églantine, whose work as a Deputy had not destroyed his poetic talent, the new months bore such evocative names as Vendémiaire, Brumaire, Frimaire, and so on. This lyrical offshoot of a tragic situation did tend to complicate daily life, however, and people had to reckon up on their fingers to find out where they were. As a close friend of Fabre's, Danton went out of his way to employ the new dating system, and made his family do likewise.

So it was on 11 or 12 Brumaire in Year II, if we accept the evidence of Danton's sons, that he was strolling in his park with a certain M. Doulet, when up came another neighbor, waving a newspaper. "Good news!" he told them. "What news?" Danton asked. "Here, read it yourself—the Girondists have been condemned and executed!"

It was Danton's turn to raise his voice. "Do you call *that* good news, you wretch?" he cried, his eyes suddenly brimming with tears. "*Good news* that some Girondists are dead?" "Well, of course," the newcomer insisted. "They were factionaries, weren't they?" "*Factionaries,*" Danton said. "Aren't we all factionaries, every one of us? If the Girondists deserve to die, so do we all. And we shall; one after another, we shall suffer the same fate as they did."

This anecdote was recounted by Danton's sons when they had grown up. At the time of the actual incident the elder was not quite four, and the younger twenty-one months. Whether they were present or not, they could recall the conversation only by means of subsequent hearsay. If we admit its authenticity, the story at least suggests that their father's tears were shed as much in anticipation of his own fate as out of sorrow for the Girondists'. When he learned what had happened to them, he must have felt his own doom to be inevitable.

But there is at least one argument which makes it very hard to credit the more touching part of this reported conversation. That Danton regretted the fate of the Girondists seems true enough. In a part of the *Mémoires de Barras* composed by Rousselin de Saint-Albin, Danton's boyhood friend, it is asserted that at the time when the Girondists were hampering his governmental activities, Danton wanted nothing more drastic than their "elimination" from public affairs. Saint-Albin adds: "I have heard that he was disappointed—indeed, profoundly upset—when it was decided that the twenty-two Girondists should be dealt with by the Revolutionary Tribunal, i.e. sent to the scaffold."

Now this decision, the decree of committal for trial, took place on October 3. It was on the 14th that Danton left for Arcis-sur-Aube. If he was convinced, as his sons afterward claimed he was, that the execution of the Girondists would bring about his own, he would have either stayed in Paris to defend them or else fled the country as he did in 1791, after the clash on the Champ-de-Mars. The police could easily have brought him back to Paris from Arcis-sur-Aube. If he chose his home town rather than exile abroad, it was because it never occurred to him that the fate of the Girondists might influence his own. All his subsequent behavior confirms this. Basically, he was doing no more than adhere to his perennial strategy of always being somewhere else when it came to a fight. The storming of the Bastille, the

march on Versailles, Louis XVI's attempted escape to Saint-
Cloud, the massacre of the Champ-de-Mars, the attack on the
Tuileries—on every one of these occasions Danton was mysteriously absent. When the Girondists were about to be put on
trial, he removed himself once more.

The Girondists were not the only victims; another was Danton's old accomplice the Duke of Orléans. For seven months
Égalité remained in Fort Saint-Jean at Marseilles, believing himself forgotten; then he was brought back to Paris and arraigned
before the Tribunal. On 16 Brumaire he mounted the steps of
the scaffold. After him it was the turn of Mme. Roland; and
then Bailly, the onetime Mayor of Paris; and the maidens of
Verdun who had given flowers to Brunswick in 1792; and
various Deputies—Manuel, Girey-Dupré, Barnave, Duport-
Dutertre, Rabaut-Saint-Étienne, Kersain. The "nation's razor"
never had a day's rest—yet Danton, the only begetter of the
Revolutionary Tribunal, remained in Arcis-sur-Aube and shed
tears when the Girondists were put to death.

It sent a shiver through Louise to learn that Monsignor
Gobel, together with thirteen of his priests, had appeared before
the bar of the Convention and formally abjured his sacerdotal
calling. Head adorned with the red bonnet, Msgr. Gobel declared that he now recognized no creed save the Cult of Reason.
This new religion had been inaugurated three days earlier, when
the Goddess of Reason, impersonated by an actress wearing a
white tunic, was borne in a palanquin down the cathedral aisles
and all around the streets of Paris. This idolatrous notion had
been thought up by Hébert, and ran somewhat counter to
Robespierre's belief in the "Supreme Being." It also showed him
that "Père Duchesne" was an adversary to be eliminated.

Echoes of these bacchanalian junketings reached Danton in
his country retreat at Arcis. The trumpets he did not hear, for
he stopped his ears against them. In any case, he thought himself
well protected against any personal danger. One day, however,
he was forced to see just how perilous his position was. While he
was having a picnic lunch with his family and some old friends,
about three leagues from Arcis, he saw a horse and rider emerge
from the poplars. It was Mergez, his nephew. He vaulted out
of the saddle and rushed across to Danton.

"Uncle," he gasped, "I've just ridden straight here from Paris—can I speak to you in private?"

"You can say anything you like in front of these gentlemen. Now what's the matter?"

"Your friends—Citizens Fabre and Desmoulins—want you to come back now, as fast as you can. Robespierre and his followers are really out to get you—"

"You mean they want my head? They'd never dare—"

"Don't be too sure of that. Come back with me now, there's no time to lose."

Raising his great voice as though he were on the rostrum, Danton replied: "Go back and tell Robespierre that I'll be there in plenty of time to crush him, and his accomplices with him!"

But when Mergez was gone, Danton sat meditating over what he had said. The following day, November 18, he left Arcis. Traveling by a roundabout route, he finally reached the rue des Cordeliers on the evening of the 20th. As he, his wife, and his children descended from the post-chaise, he saw the letters carved in the stone at the street corner: *rue Marat*. Here was one change that had taken place during his thirty-six days' absence—but it was a modest one compared to those he found staring him in the face forty-eight hours later, at the Convention.

CHAPTER XVII

The Committee of Mercy

IN PUBLIC, Robespierre was carefully complimentary to the four men—Chaumette, Hébert, Pache, and Clootz—who had launched the Cult of Reason. But through his tools and supporters he put it about that in fact they all deserved to be guillotined for plotting against the régime and embezzling public funds. Hébert was alarmed by these rumors and on November 21 made a defense of himself and his followers at the Jacobin Club. Drawing a parallel with the *dantonistes,* "Père Duchesne" suddenly remarked: "There has been gossip about Danton, too—he'd emigrated, people said, run off to Switzerland with all the loot he'd squeezed out of the people. Well, I happened to meet him this morning, in the Tuileries. Since he's in Paris, he must really come and offer the Jacobins a *fraternal explanation* of his conduct. All good patriots are under an obligation to give the lie to any damaging stories in circulation concerning them."

This was a most curious volte-face. Before Danton's departure, Hébert had accused him, in his broadsheet, of making a fortune in Belgium by fleecing the inhabitants. Now, faced with the dangerous hostility of the Incorruptible, Père Duchesne had at last realized that Danton—now as much over a barrel as he was—represented a force with which he should, he must, form an alliance. A coalition of *hébertistes* and *dantonistes* could really block Robespierre's advance.

But Danton was not taken in by this hypocritical move. Though advised of Hébert's unexpected support, he scorned the suggestion that he should give the Jacobins any sort of "fraternal explanation." One did not compromise with a creature such as Père Duchesne—a journalist whose pen employed the most sordid terms in the whole lexicon of filth; a pamphleteer who, when describing the Queen's death, dared to head his article with the following words: "THE SUPREME JOY OF PÈRE DUCHESNE, having seen the head of the VETO female separated from her stupid f——ing whore's neck"; a Deputy Public Prosecutor to the Commune, a magistrate, whose horses and carriages and personal attire were an insult to the misery of the people, whom he both aroused and degraded by offering them such yellow journalism. A Danton could have no truck with this man—a man whom Desmoulins apostrophized thus: "Is there anything more disgusting or filthy than your broadsheets? Do you not realize, Hébert, that when tyrants wish to convince their slaves that France lies in the shadow of barbarism . . . do you not realize, you wretch, that it is extracts from these same broadsheets which they print in their gazettes—as though your indecencies were the nation's, as though a Paris sewer were the Seine!"

Though Danton was no prude himself, he could not embark on an alliance with such a paragon of obscenity. Hébert had even accused the Queen of having sexual relations with her son—a mere child at the time—which, he asserted, were even more reprehensible because they assumed the form of mutual masturbation. Robespierre, on the other hand, was in power and could not afford to ignore the influence which this guttersnipe possessed. However, he planned to crush Hébert with the help of Danton and his adherents—and then to strike down the *dantonistes* themselves, when they no longer had Hébert available as a potential ally. So it was that one morning the Incorruptible told Camille Desmoulins: "Only a journalist of your caliber has the ability to put down Père Duchesne."

This delicate machination was backed by another even more devious scheme. Though the Committee of Public Safety was responsible for nominating the members of the Committee of General Security, it still set spies to keep an eye on them; and the latter Committee, by way of returning the compliment, had its own agents watching members of the former. The stool

pigeons of both Committees were responsible to a certain Inspector Héron, whom each of the two organizations believed
devoted to their own cause. Héron in fact was a double agent,
with a foot in either camp. He had a large team of spies at his
disposal, recruited from all strata of society and extremely well
paid. Yet, oddly enough, the Deputy who presided over the
Committee of General Security, Guillaume Vadier, was a match
for Robespierre in virtue and integrity, and no less ruthless in
his methods. The Royalists called him "the Old Inquisitor."
He frequently employed Héron's underlings to shed a little light
on the financial double-dealing that went on among Danton's
supporters, who were all much given to speculation. As for
Danton himself, Vadier used to tell his friends: "We'll clean up
the rest of them first, and keep that great stuffed turbot till the
end."

Desmoulins, Fabre d'Églantine, Legendre, and Lacroix all
came to see Danton as soon as they heard he was back in town,
and warned him what was afoot. His only reply was: "Vadier?
I'll eat the fellow's brains—and then use his skull for a chamber
pot." This empty phrasemaking drew further very concrete
facts from Danton's visitors. The Committees had denounced the
political-*cum*-financial scandal of the East India Company
(*Compagnie des Indes*). Three Deputies—Chabot, Delaunay,
and Basire—had been expelled from the Convention and were
now in prison. Their accomplice, Julien de Toulouse, had managed to get away. D'Espagnac, Benoist, and Fabre d'Églantine
himself were compromised in the affair. Vadier's police had
left them at liberty, but were saying—as a smear on Danton—
that it was his friendship which protected them. Finally Lacroix,
looking very pale, told Danton that both of them had been
accused of trafficking with foreign powers during their missions
to Belgium.

When his informants had left, Danton did some very hard
thinking. To escape from the dangers threatening him he would
have to fight Robespierre, Vadier, and Hébert at one and the
same time—while simultaneously allying himself with each of
them against the other two. This Machiavellian strategy would
need to be repeated three times before all his antagonists were
disposed of—an epic if sordid conflict.

Like Robespierre and Vadier, Hébert, too, had a far from negligible force at his disposal. Formerly the Commune had possessed a Public Prosecutor and two Deputies—one of whom, in 1791, had been Danton himself. But since the Convention had come into office, there had been one Deputy only—Hébert. His word was law both in the City Hall and throughout the forty-eight urban boroughs: he only had to raise his hand for the *faubourgs* to march on the center. The circulation of his newssheet, *Le Père Duchesne,* reached 600,000 copies—an incredible figure for the period. Without the support of his "troops" (and the inflammatory editorials which worked them up to fever-pitch) Hanriot's National Guards would never have triumphed over the Girondists as they did six months earlier, when they laid siege to them in the Convention.

Despite the resources which such an adversary could command, Danton felt strong enough to take him on, and Robespierre and Vadier as well. This triple combat did not dismay him—always provided that it was fought out in the lists of the Tuileries Theater. Though he had no stomach for street battles, Danton showed real courage—indeed, temerity—in the political arena. Having made his mind up, he kissed Louise and set off at once for the Tuileries. It was the second day after his return from Arcis: Duodi 2 Frimaire, Year II, or Friday, November 22, 1793.

When he set foot in the Convention once more, he found it much changed. Of some 760 elected members, fewer than 400 were present. Twenty-two leading Girondists had been guillotined. About fifteen more had fled for their lives. Another 136 Deputies, accused—rightly or wrongly—of being Girondist fellow travelers, were either deprived of their seats or in prison. Some forty more had been placed under lock and key for miscellaneous reasons. Large numbers of Deputies were away on missions to the armed forces. Then there were those who were absent through sickness, on leave, or simply too scared to show their faces.

At the sight of this much-reduced Assembly, rendered uneasy by arbitrary measures, yet still composed of men with a real passion for legislation, Danton instantly sensed what tactics he had to employ. If he was going to win this battle he must make a great show of force—speak frequently, occupy the rostrum as often as possible, until he saw which way the wind was blowing.

When he arrived, a debate was just opening on the position of abdicating priests. Since the Bishop of Paris had abjured at the bar of the Convention, many other ecclesiastics had followed his example. What were they now living on? This was a problem that had to be settled; and Danton, speaking in support of those Deputies who asked that such unfrocked priests-turned-*sans-culottes* be granted pensions, made an impromptu intervention full of sound common sense. "The rule of priests is ended," he said, "but that of politics lies in your hands. You have to reconcile political claims with those of reason and sanity." There must be no intolerance, no persecution. "Do not protect any one cult to the detriment of the rest." But "if a priest is without any means of support, what do you expect him to do? He will either die, or go over to the rebels in the Vendée, or privately declare himself your irreconcilable enemy."

This logical conclusion was greeted with applause. It also dropped like a large stone into the pool labeled the Cult of Reason, so sedulously cultivated by Chaumette and Hébert. This project of theirs irked the deist in Robespierre. Moreover, by forbidding conformist priests—their nonjuring brethren had gone underground—to undertake any parochial ministry apart from actual church services, they were obstructing Robespierre's plan for making these clerics serve the Revolution, as priests of that Supreme Being whose vicegerent on earth would be the Incorruptible himself. Thus Danton, by attacking Hébert and Chaumette without naming them, simply and solely on the grounds of their paganism, won the calculated congratulations of Robespierre *qua* aspiring Pontiff. Upon which the entire Convention, in slavish obedience to its idol, proceeded to applaud the recipient of his compliments.

For several weeks Danton recovered, or thought he had recovered, his influence over the Assembly. One evening he recommended that an agent from the Committee should be sent to the chief town of every *département* (an idea which later inspired Napoleon to create the prefectorial system of administration). Another day he proposed reviving the ancient Olympic

Games in France. To Robespierre's satisfaction, he finally took up the cudgels on behalf of deism, and suggested a solemn celebration during which incense would be offered to the Supreme Being. "It has not been our purpose," he declared, "to eradicate superstition merely in order to establish the reign of atheism!" None of this, however, bore any immediate fruit; it remained mere talk, without substance.

On the other hand, he was to have more success when he tackled the subject of compulsory education. Many families refused to let their children attend school, preferring to see them employed in workshop or mill or on the farm. "A father," Danton declared, "has no more right to deprive his child of an education than a landowner has the right to let his fields lie fallow!"

Thus, amid chaos and conflict, the Convention was nevertheless building the modern world. Between bouts of murderous and nepotic in-fighting, it found time to pass innumerable laws which are still obeyed today. From its cruel yet timorous hands there emerged the primary schools and the *lycées,* the metric system, uniformity of weights and measures, the Central Astronomical Office, the National Debt Register, the Louvre Museum, the School of Arts and Crafts, the Academy of Music, the Military Academy of Artillery and Engineering, and the French Institute. It passed no less than eleven thousand decrees, some during Danton's lifetime, others after his death.

Yet the right to vote freely, as one's conscience dictated, had some formidable obstacles in its path. A crowded House might shout down the speaker's words, or bloodthirsty Deputies demand the guillotine for any lapse from perfection. There were endless pressure-groups to contend with—from all the towns in the provinces besides the Paris *quartiers* and urban boroughs. Members of the armed services were summoned before the Bar of the House to defend themselves against a series of more or less sordid charges. The clergy also appeared there, to renounce their vows and don the red bonnet, which they did with such a wealth of formal mumbo-jumbo that Danton finally lost patience with them and shouted: "We are not here to receive deputations and listen to a passel of abjuring priests! Always the same wearisome round to go through, the same old speeches dinned into

our ears! There is a limit to everything, and I put it to you that
that limit has been reached!"

Danton's protest shows signs of Louise's influence. Indeed, at
one point he repeated a phrase of his wife's verbatim: "I
demand," he thundered, "that there shall be no more *anti-
religious masquerades* within the body of this Convention!" An
angry buzz greeted his statement. For once Danton had gone too
far. In order to create a diversion, he moved on to another topic.
Since that morning reports of a conspiracy had been causing
much comment behind the scenes. Danton was worried by the
outcry which greeted this fabricated story, and he got himself
into still deeper waters by asking that the government, while
"resolutely repressing any plot," should nevertheless make a
clear distinction between "honest mistakes and deliberate
crimes." To support his contention he cited the example of
Henri IV (carefully remembering to describe him as a scoundrel), and reminded his listeners that this "tyrant," while treating real criminals with the utmost severity, was lenient in his
attitude to those who had been led astray.

Fayau, an obscure Deputy from the Vendée, rose at this point
and intervened to say: "Danton has—no doubt unintentionally
—let slip certain expressions which I find offensive. . . . At a
time when the people need to harden their hearts, Danton asks
them to show mercy!" *Mercy:* the criminal word flashed across
the benches of the House like a poisoned arrow. *"He didn't say
that!"* Danton's supporters protested, and Danton himself dealt
with the interruption thus: "I never once employed the word
'mercy'—nor did I suggest that any leniency should be showed
to real criminals! What I called for, as far as they are concerned,
was a vigorous revolutionary government!"

Naturally he made no further reference to "those who had
been led astray." Instead, as it was vital to turn the tide in his
favor, he accused "a nest of intriguers and genuine conspirators,
who hitherto have escaped the long arm of national justice."
At these words, the atmosphere relaxed. All the same, Danton
had sailed perilously close to the wind.

Yet the idea was in his mind, and had been there for some
time. The man who had restored public confidence when the

enemy was approaching Paris, who had inspired and built up
the new system of government and judicial administration, who
had declared that "a nation in the midst of a revolution is
nearer to vanquishing its neighbors than being vanquished by
them"—this coarse, muscular figure, whose final achievement
was the Terror, could now stand back and observe the outcome
of his labors. Everywhere the Republic was either victorious or
well on the road to victory. Thanks to Carnot, the conscription
of some 600,000 men had produced the most formidable army in
Europe. French troops fought to defend their rights or their
fields, whereas the soldiers of other nations were still mercenaries,
campaigning for pay. There was all the difference in the world
between them. The patriotic ardor of the French army proved
more than a match for the cash-based discipline of their opponents. This being so, why should heads continue to roll under
the guillotine?

One evening Danton and Desmoulins were on their way home
after a meeting of the Convention. As they strolled along beside
the Seine, the reflected rays of the setting sun stained the surface
of the water a bright crimson. The two friends happened to
meet Souberbielle (the surgeon summoned by decree to leave his
hospital and act as juror on the Revolutionary Tribunal), who
had just come from the Law Courts. Fifteen heads had rolled
that afternoon, and twenty-seven more were due to do so the
following morning. On hearing this news Danton said: "Look
at the Seine; it's flowing blood."

"It's true," the doctor remarked. "The sky's red. . . ." He
paused. "They asked for inflexible judges. What they want now
are obliging executioners. If we save some innocent head from
that chopping machine of theirs, they tax us with royalism.
But what can *I* do about it? I'm just an ordinary citizen. Ah,
if only I were Danton—"

"Danton is returning to the fray. He has slept too long."
Then the demagogue turned to Desmoulins and said: "There
has been too much blood spilled. Camille, take up your pen
again—appeal to them to be more merciful. I'll back you up.
You can see my hand, you know its strength—"

And Desmoulins promised. The literary skill of the one and

whole French people?' . . . These Deputies of whose names Legendre seems to be unaware are well known to the entire Convention. He has mentioned Danton—doubtless because he believes some special privilege attaches to his name. We want nothing more to do with privileges! Today we shall see whether the Convention is strong enough to smash this so-called idol—rotten long since—or whether in its fall it will crush Convention and French people together."

"Loud and prolonged applause," the *Moniteur* recorded. In some alarm at this ovation, Legendre heard Robespierre add, looking directly toward him: "'There are those who wish to make you fear that the whole people will fall victim to the Committees, and so perish! This is defiance of national justice! Does anyone tremble with fear as I speak? Then I say that person is guilty!'"

So much for Legendre. Terrified by this implicit threat and by the cheers which punctuated Robespierre's speech, the wretched butcher saw himself already in prison. He rose to his feet and, trembling, made the following explanation: "'If I advanced the motion which the previous speaker has attacked, it was solely because I have had no tangible proof that the prisoners are guilty—the kind of proof, I mean, which places concrete evidence before one's eyes. Apart from that, I have no intention of defending any individual person here."

The next speaker to mount the rostrum was Saint-Just, that paragon of all patriotic virtues, clutching a thick file of papers. In a silence made heavy by their stunned submission, Deputies of all ages heard the Revolution's *enfant terrible* read the title of his speech: "'A report on the conspiracy plotted these several years past, by divers criminal factions, to absorb the French Revolution into a change of dynasty; and charges against Danton, Lacroix, Camille Desmoulins, Philippeaux, Hérault-Séchelles, and Fabre d'Églantine, accused of complicity with the said factions, and of other personal offenses against liberty . . .'"

This exordium, in which every word was heavily loaded with evocative meaning, provided a fair summing-up of the discourse which followed. For two hours the servile Deputies sat and listened to Saint-Just. His report reeked of fanaticism, and in one prefatory remark openly admitted the fact: "'There is something he said, "four members of this Assembly were arrested during the night. I know that Danton is one of them; who the other three may be I cannot tell—if they are guilty, what do their names matter? But, citizens, I ask that the arrested Deputies be brought before the Bar of this House, and that you hear what they have to say for themselves; then you can absolve them or commit them for trial."

This proposal went even further than Danton could have hoped. If the Convention accepted it, he would have a better forum than the Tribunal in which to vindicate his own patriotism and to attack Robespierre. Was this pure coincidence, the demonstration of an empathy between Legendre and Danton? It seems unlikely. Legendre had been one of Louise's first visitors that morning. They lived very close, in the same street, almost opposite each other. Louise, having previously learned the truth from her husband, no doubt revealed to Legendre the reason for Danton's feigned apathy when Páris, Panis, and Robert Lindet came to warn him.

Meanwhile Legendre went on to acquaint the House with the reasons for his proposal. "Citizens, I swear to you, I believe Danton to be as innocent as I am. I do not intend to single out any particular member of the Committees of Public Safety and General Security; but I am entitled to express my fear that private enmities and passions may deprive Liberty of men who have rendered her the greatest service. It is fitting that I should say this of the man who, in 1792, aroused all France by the energetic measures which he initiated. . . . The enemy was then at the gates of Paris. Danton came, and his ideas saved our country. Since last night he has been in close confinement; no doubt it was feared that his answers would shatter the charges brought against him. I therefore ask that before you hear any report, the prisoners be brought here and heard in their own defense."

This proposal of Legendre's was instantly rebutted by Fayau, but nevertheless won a certain measure of approval. Various Deputies suggested putting it to the vote. But Robespierre now appeared, and the terror he inspired quickly reduced this caucus to meek submission. "I ask you," he cried, "should the interests of a few ambitious hypocrites take precedence over those of the

the oratorical genius of the other, so recently allied to create the Terror, joined forces that evening to plot its overthrow.

The first essential step was the elimination of Hébert's more fanatical supporters. A fresh opportunity to attack them occurred on 13 Frimaire, at the Jacobin Club—though as it turned out it was Danton himself who very nearly became the victim. That day (December 3) it was proposed that the Club should invite the Convention to make the rents of popular clubs a charge on the Treasury. Danton spoke against such a suggestion. In his view, its realization would have taken the people "beyond the limits of the Revolution." This was the first time he had publicly attacked the "ultra-revolutionists," and his audience reacted strongly. There were whistles and catcalls, followed by accusations of "aiding and abetting the traitors."

Robespierre, who was relying on Danton to purge Paris of *hébertistes,* had no option but to defend him vigorously. "Patriots and tyrants," he declared, "have one thing in common: their cause unites them all. Perhaps I am mistaken about Danton the man; but viewed in his family context he deserves unqualified praise. I have observed his political attitudes; a difference of opinion between us led me to study this aspect of him closely, and often with anger. He was, I know, too slow in suspecting Dumouriez, and he did not show himself implacable enough toward Brissot and his accomplices. But because he has not always seen eye to eye with me, must I conclude from this that he was betraying his country? Indeed not; he has always, to the best of my knowledge, served France with devoted zeal. If there is any person here present who has some criticism to make against Danton, let him do so now!"

No one dared take up this invitation; the prophet had spoken. Better still, Momoro—who had some while previously transferred his allegiance from Danton to Hébert—was heard remarking, in the hush: "Well, there's nothing to be said against Danton—that proves it." He went on to suggest that the President of the Club should give him "the brotherly accolade," i.e. a kiss of peace. This short-lived reconciliation took place amid applause.

The following day, December 5, there appeared the first

number of the *Vieux Cordelier*. Desmoulins, faithful to the pact concluded on that evening beside the Seine, had opened his campaign in favor of mercy. This inaugural issue was a very clever piece of work; it carefully avoided any call for leniency toward real or supposed opponents of the régime. On the contrary, the *Vieux Cordelier* went out of its way to sing Robespierre's praises. However, it did not neglect to bestow a like tribute upon "his rival in patriotic virtue, the permanent President of the Old Cordeliers." Before having this issue run off, Desmoulins made sure that Robespierre got, and read, a set of proofs.

Five days later, on December 10, the second number of this periodical appeared, again with the Incorruptible's *imprimatur*. This time the seal of approval covered an attack on Hébert and Anacharsis Clootz—a German baron who had plunged enthusiastically into the French Revolution and was now preaching paganism on behalf of Père Duchesne. The success of the *Vieux Cordelier*—it had a print order of fifty thousand copies —began to worry Robespierre. Desmoulins's views were very much in agreement with his own, but the journalist's eloquent pen seemed as though it might divert some of Robespierre's own popular acclaim.

When the third number was published, on December 15, the moving spirit behind the Committee of Public Safety held his breath. This time he had not read the proofs; if he had, he would have exploded with fury. Desmoulins had turned historian and satirist, with a sketch of Rome under the Caesars —its tyranny and excesses and victims. There could hardly have been a more pointed allusion to the *régime des suspects*.

Yet Robespierre made no move. He needed the *Vieux Cordelier* too badly, as a weapon with which to destroy *Le Père Duchesne*. Since Desmoulins waited ten days before publishing the fourth number, the Incorruptible took advantage of the delay to make it appear that he shared the views expressed in the third. While taking care to uphold "the sacred cause of justice," he announced the discussion of a measure which, by making all verdicts subject to confirmation and approval, would keep a check on "excesses committed in the name of patriotism."

This gave Desmoulins an admirable opening. In his fourth

number, published on December 25, he wrote: "Ah, my dear
Robespierre . . . the old companion of my school days, whose
eloquent speeches will be read by generations yet unborn, remember the lessons which history and philosophy teach us: that
love is stronger and more enduring than fear. . . . You have
come very close to this idea in the measure passed at your instance today, during the session held on Décadi 30 Primaire.
It is true that what has been proposed is rather a Committee
of *Justice*. Yet why should mercy be looked on as a crime
under the Republic?" Further on, crossing the Rubicon of
license, he wrote: "Release from prison those 200,000 citizens
you describe as 'suspects'; in the Declaration of Rights there is
no clause providing for imprisonment on suspicion. . . . You
are determined to exterminate all opposition by means of the
guillotine. Yet could any undertaking be more nonsensical?
You cannot destroy one opponent on the scaffold without making
ten more enemies from among his family and friends. Look at the
sort of people you put behind bars—women, old dotards, bile-
ridden egotists, the flotsam of the Revolution. Do you really
believe *they* constitute any danger? The only enemies still left in
your midst are those who are either too sick or too cowardly to
fight. All the brave and able-bodied ones have fled abroad, to die
at Lyons or in the Vendée. Those who remain do not deserve
your wrath. Believe me, freedom would be more firmly established, and Europe brought to her knees, if you had a
'Committee of Mercy.'"

This time the operative word had been stated openly. A
queue formed outside the premises of Desenne, the bookseller
who published the *Vieux Cordelier*. The price of the pamphlet
was two sous. Purchasers read it and then resold it at a profit.
As a result of this speculation the price soared to twenty francs.
First Paris, then all France was shaken by Desmoulins's audacity.
At last someone had dared to speak out against the Terror. The
appeal sped like an arrow to the heart of public opinion; such
courage took people's breath away.

God knows the courage was needed. "Camille is within a
hairsbreadth of the guillotine!" declared Nicolas, the bookseller,
during a speech before the Jacobin Club; and Père Duchesne
damned his adversary as a corrupt, villainous pro-aristocrat.

Danton, meanwhile, continued the struggle within the Convention itself. Any incident served as an excuse for criticizing the practices established by the Terror. When a crippled soldier was admitted before the Bar of the House to plead for public assistance, Danton roared: "Let him apply to the Minister of War, who has funds at his disposal for meeting this sacred obligation!" Couthon, one of Robespierre's disciples, asked that the remains of General Dampierre, who had been killed in Belgium, be removed from the Panthéon. In Couthon's view (he was not only a member of the Committee, but also paralyzed) the dead man had "falsely usurped the honors" reserved for patriots. He was an aristocrat at heart, ripe for defection at the time of his death. Danton boldly took up the cudgel on Dampierre's behalf. "Though he was unlucky enough to be born into the nobility, he nevertheless died serving the Republic!" His speech won the day, and Dampierre's ashes were allowed to rest undisturbed in the Panthéon.

Next day Souberbielle sent a note around to his friend, informing him that the Tribunal had just passed sentence of death on a wine seller for "hoarding." The crime of this "counterrevolutionary," it transpired, was laying in stocks of cheap red wine for his customers. Danton asked the Assembly to grant a stay of execution pending receipt of full information on the case. His eloquence triumphed; and as he was afraid that the reprieve might reach the Law Courts too late, he undertook to place it in Fouquier-Tinville's hands himself, with all possible speed.

On December 23, two days before the publication of the fourth number of the *Vieux Cordelier,* Danton came out in support of a Deputy named Philippeaux, who was under simultaneous attack from Hébert and the Committee. Philippeaux had been sent as an inspector to the Army of the West and came back disgusted with what he had seen there. It was not the troops he complained of, much less their valiant commanders —men such as Kléber and Marceau. His target was Ronsin, who "directed" field operations in the name of Bouchotte, the Minister of War, and of Vincent, his Permanent Under-Secretary. A former Quartermaster General in Belgium, Ronsin had risen from captain to general in a matter of four days. Now he was supported by a staff consisting of "Generals" Santerre (the brewer), Momoro (the printer), Rossignol (the goldsmith), and an actor named Grammont. This *hébertiste* and his friends were more interested in the spoils of war than in the war itself; they prolonged the second to avoid losing the first. This was why the Republic had so far failed to crush the rebels. Philippeaux first tried to get Ronsin and his henchmen dismissed, but Bouchotte and Vincent stood firm. He then published a pamphlet in which he described the negative result of his mission. This drew an immediate attack on him by Hébert and his clique. Danton, however, came out in defense of Philippeaux with such effect that Ronsin was first recalled and then placed under arrest, together with Vincent.

Hébert was furious. He now transferred the scene of the feud to the Jacobin Club, where he proceeded to make indiscriminate attacks on Philippeaux, Desmoulins, and, above all, Danton himself. The charges were always the same: Danton's venality, his prevarications, the way he had feathered his own nest in Belgium. It was on such an occasion that his victim declared, at the end of a stirring impromptu speech: "The enemy is at our gates, and yet we are still at one another's throats!"

This statement of Danton's was somewhat specious; the enemy was no longer at *all* the gates of France. The Republic's troops had triumphed on every front except the Vendée (where Ronsin's recall would greatly improve their chances of success) and in the north, where Carnot was even now mounting his full-scale spring offensive. But when he said, "We are still at one another's throats," Danton was not exaggerating. In the Place de la Révolution (one day to be renamed the Place de la Concorde—an ironic piece of mockery if ever there was one) the guillotine had already dispatched General Custine, Dervillé the Jesuit, Rosalie Dalbert the dancer, Custine's son, Marshal Luckner, Jean-Jacques Durand the Federalist, Baron de La Tude, General Rossi, General Marcé, Levigneur the journalist, Madame Du Barry, General Biron, and Bishop Lamourette, to name only the most celebrated of its victims. There had been countless others—nuns and priests, ordinary housewives, people who had blasphemed against the Republic in their cups, old women who had been heard regretting "the good old days" as they did their shopping, and those "suspects" whom the terrible law of September 17 had handed over to the mercies of jealous husbands, rejected lovers, business rivals, indeed all those for whom informing was merely a way to dispose of any obstructive embarrassment. Sanson was kept so hard at work that Danton observed, with grim wit: "If the Committees continue to prey on France in this manner, there will soon, as far as I can see, be only one man left on his feet—the executioner; and when he has no one left to guillotine, he'll end up by guillotining himself out of sheer desperation!"

Danton's luck continued to hold; once again, this time in the Philippeaux affair, his eloquence won the day. Though accused of being a "counterrevolutionary," a crime that carried the death penalty, Philippeaux still remained a free man. For the time being at least, the Jacobins made no move to force the Convention's hand and have him arrested.

Throughout this whole episode Robespierre—on the face of it an impartial spectator—had appeared to support Danton, whose help he needed if he was to crush Hébert and his followers. (Yet political expediency had already led him to make a tongue-in-cheek defense of Hébert, and he would do so again.) Privately, Robespierre had become jealous of his old friend's oratorical successes; Danton was now an adversary to be handled with tact and circumspection. A policy of mercy was something which the Incorruptible himself desired. His cruelty, far from being instinctive, simply formed part of his over-all strategy; its aim was to scare people. He was far too intelligent not to realize that lasting popular support could now be won by whoever delivered France from the nightmare of the Terror, and by no one else. Robespierre had earmarked this role for himself; but he was waiting for news of victory in the north before he moved. Danton, it seemed, intended to assume the liberator's mantle himself—at an earlier date and, above all, before Robespierre did so. Thus, Danton had to be destroyed.

In the corridors of the Convention the two men could be seen chatting together, apparently on the best of terms. They made a great show of protecting each other's interests and exchanging mutual advice: Danton unswervingly jovial, Robespierre forever pale and stiff with rectitude. Both publicly and in private,

Danton continued to proclaim that mercy, applied with proper discrimination, would save the country; that France no longer needed the Terror in order to vanquish her enemies. The news from Toulon bore out this assertion. The port had been captured by the English at the end of August but had recently fallen to the Republic once more. On December 22 its defenders, both British and Royalist, had withdrawn by sea. An unknown officer named Bonaparte had been promoted to general for his part in the victory. His superior, General Dugommier, had received the following categorical command, signed by four members—Barras, Saliceti, Robespierre, and Fréron: "The Committee orders you to reduce Toulon before December 31." There was a clear enough unspoken implication: "Otherwise, you're for the guillotine." Had such a threat also been necessary to coerce young Bonaparte? Danton asked. No, in his case patriotism had been enough. The inference was plain. "You can see very well that the Terror no longer serves any useful purpose!"

On December 31, however, Saint-Just returned to Paris from a mission to the army in Alsace. This twenty-six-year-old Adonis, the dark Byronic hero of the Mountain and the Committee, took a very different view. For him, to govern meant to fight, and to fight meant to kill; otherwise your opponent would kill you. When Saint-Just left Strasbourg he brought Schneider back with him. Schneider was the Revolutionary Tribunal's Public Prosecutor for the Eastern Provinces. In this capacity he had often agreed to save "traitors" in return for the favors of their wives or daughters. (Finally the brute married one of his wretched victims.) Saint-Just removed him from office, and the two of them returned to Paris together. Schneider was a choice victim for Fouquier-Tinville, who lost no time in sending his colleague to the guillotine.

Saint-Just took discipline seriously. For him, leniency was as bad as treason. He regarded the unforeseen humanitarianism of Danton and his supporters as part of a conspiracy—an exaggerated notion, beyond a doubt, but one with some convincing evidence behind it. For the past three months Danton had been obstructing the government's policy. He was the moving spirit behind an opposition group all the more formidable because of

the noble liberal principles it assumed. He had managed to
attract every type of malcontent: he had promised the monarchists an amnesty for the *émigrés,* and to the business lobby he
held out the abolition of price controls. He had guaranteed the
"suspects" a clearing of the prisons, while all anti-Republicans
looked forward to the restoration of the monarchy. He had
(Saint-Just asserted) hatched this plot during the most critical
period of the struggle against Europe, when enemy victories in
Alsace were reinforced by rebel successes in the Vendée and
Toulon had been established as a potentially dangerous English
bridgehead. Finally, there were his suspect connections with
various groups—the *affairistes* of the East India Company, the
army contractors, the middlemen who had come flocking in
from Belgium, Austria, Spain, Prussia, Switzerland, even from
England, with the sole object of bleeding France white. All this
convinced Saint-Just that Danton had to be eliminated.

Robespierre, however, put a curb on his lieutenant's vengeful
enthusiasm. First and foremost, the *hébertistes* had to be crushed
—with the indispensable aid of Danton and his supporters.
Saint-Just, convinced by this argument, returned to the border.
He was back again a fortnight later. The Convention, greatly
elated by the results of his missions, elected him President by
acclamation. Their enthusiasm left him even better armed for
the duel that lay ahead. As both President of the Parliamentary
Assembly and an influential member of the Committee of Public
Safety, this twenty-six-year-old oligarch was rapidly moving
toward a position of supreme power.

(One last touch to the portrait of the man who was to defeat
hébertistes and *dantonistes* alike: he would often dine while still
sitting at his worktable, off a hunk of bread and a few slices of
sausage. If the Tuileries clerks who witnessed Saint-Just's
frugality had looked in on Danton about the same time, they
would have found him enjoying a very different kind of meal.)

As far as Danton was concerned, the year had begun badly.
This was 1794, according to the superseded Gregorian system;
officially it was known as Nivôse Year II—Nivôse being the
fourth month in the *sans-culotte* calendar. But despite everything, the old nomenclature stuck in the mind more persistently

than the new. On January 4, 1794, then (Saint-Just had not yet returned to Paris), Fabre d'Églantine was implicated in an ugly scandal. The man who had invented such poetic names for the months in the Republican calendar now found himself charged with a different sort of literary activity—tampering with a document that had fallen into the hands of the police. It was clear that this friend of Danton's had known of, condoned, and perhaps even carried out the falsifications (previously attributed to Chabot, Julien, and Delaunay) in the winding-up order of the East India Company.

The situation was simple enough. Before the scandal blew up, shares in the company were worth about 2000 *livres* apiece. By a series of enactments designed to reduce the company's profits, the Deputies involved brought the market value of these shares down to 1500, 1000, and even less. The lowest quotation offered was 650 *livres*. At this point the Deputies bought up every share they could lay hands on, and got their friends Frey, Fabre d'Églantine, d'Espagnac, Desmoulins, and Danton to do the same. Then, by a new series of motions designed to strengthen the market, they pushed the price back up—2000, 3000, 4000, even 5000 *livres*. When the shares reached their peak, the speculators unloaded them at a vast profit, after which they began the whole process over again. They did it twice, three times. No wonder that they could provide dowries for their daughters. This was how the Freys' sister managed to put up no less than 400,000 *livres* when she married Chabot, the former Capucin.

When the Committee of General Security noticed that it was always the same people who profited by these transactions, they decided to dissolve the company. At this point the *affairistes* in the Convention approached the Board of Directors and said, in effect: "Let us have 500,000 francs, and we'll manage things in such a way that the company is made responsible for its own liquidation"—which meant prolonging its existence more or less indefinitely. The five conspirators (Delaunay, Julien, Basire, Chabot, and Fabre d'Églantine) split this sum, each receiving 100,000 francs. It was Delaunay himself who came before the Assembly with a bill for the company's suppression. But Cambon, that high-powered specialist in matters of finance, effectively blocked the attempt to make the company responsible for its own dissolution. The Convention voted accordingly, and the decree was sent to the printer. It was at this point that some person unknown (the choice afterward hesitated between Basire and Fabre) contrived to falsify the text by inserting, at a suitable point in the manuscript, the following seemingly innocent words: ". . . in accordance with the statutes and regulations of the company," a phrase which substituted the company for the government and thus made it responsible for its own liquidation. By this neat device the combine would be able to resume their share-pushing activities.

The police discovered this fraudulent insertion and arrested Chabot, Basire, and Delaunay while Danton was still at Arcis. Julien managed to get away. A close examination of the decree suggested that Fabre d'Églantine's poetic talents might equally well have been responsible for the falsification. However, since a reasonable margin of doubt existed, he was not imprisoned. This did not keep Robespierre from denouncing him as the guilty party in a speech to the Jacobins. Fabre made a feeble attempt at self-justification, but his lyre was sadly out of tune and drowned by the trumpet note of "Guillotine him!" from the benches—a view loudly echoed by the crowd at the back of the hall.

Everyone was waiting to see if Danton would come to his friend's rescue. After all, Fabre had been his Private Secretary in the old Ministry of Defense. But Danton seemed stunned by the suddenness of the affair, and managed nothing better than the following quibbling suggestion: "Let us leave some things to be dealt with by the *guillotine of public opinion!* Let us sacrifice our private differences and look only to the public good. Let us subordinate our personal enmities to the interests of the State." In this manner the problem was sidetracked, and the meeting broke up.

Next day there came reports of Fabre's imminent arrest, and the fifth issue of the *Vieux Cordelier* was published. Its timing was unfortunate, since Danton and all his followers were under a heavy cloud of suspicion. In describing Hébert as a "scoundrel" and "vilifier of the people" Desmoulins was still taking Robespierre's line. But he also attacked Barère and Collot d'Herbois, both members of the Committee of Public Safety; and this was a direct affront to Robespierre himself.

Robespierre upbraided Desmoulins for his lapse in another speech before the Jacobins. Though still treating him with tact and circumspection (the battle against Hébert remained Robespierre's first priority) he nevertheless tossed him one scornful aside: "You ought to realize that if you were not who you are, we could not possibly show you such leniency." He followed this with a proposal that the *Vieux Cordelier* should be seized and burned.

Suddenly Danton roused himself. "Citizens!" he cried. "Let all your decisions be made calmly, and in accordance with the dictates of justice! When you pass judgment on Desmoulins, take care lest you strike a deadly blow at the freedom of the press!"

The debate was resumed two days later. Several Jacobins demanded Desmoulins's expulsion. Robespierre rose to declare: "Whether the Jacobins expel Desmoulins or not is a matter of complete indifference to me. He is only an individual." Lucile was badly shaken by the turn events had taken. On January 12 she wrote to Fréron, who was still on a mission in the Midi: "Come back, Fréron, please come back quickly. . . ." She went on to describe the danger threatening them all. Then, referring to Danton by the nickname they had given him during their holidays in the country, she added: "They no longer listen to Marius; he is losing his nerve, becoming weak. D'Églantine has been arrested and imprisoned in the Luxembourg: they are preparing some very grave charges against him. . . ."

The Luxembourg Palace had, in fact, been doing duty as a prison ever since the Count of Provence went into exile. On January 12 the same day as Fabre's incarceration, Danton attempted to defend him before the Convention. The criminal act attributed to his friend he described as "the scratchings of some unknown hand." With prophetic foresight Billaud-Varennes exclaimed: "Woe to him who has sat beside Fabre d'Églantine and is still taken in by him!"—an unpleasant way of putting the finger on Danton and threatening him with similar sanctions.

Robespierre's approach was more subtly skillful than that of Billaud, and he kept any stray impulses he might have had well under control. His policy still needed Danton's group behind it. He successfully prevented the Club from expelling Desmoulins, and in the Convention he satisfied Danton by not pressing for a bill of attainder against Fabre d'Églantine. Meanwhile he and Saint-Just were preparing the way for Hébert's condemnation. The fellow lived in great style. What was the source of his wealth? Where could they claim he got it from? From abroad, Robespierre thought. The ignorant rabble who followed Hébert with such blind devotion would be unlikely to think of the profit he extracted from *Le Père Duchesne,* with its circulation of 600,000. No, from abroad; much better.

Robespierre cleverly brought in Desmoulins to fight the opening round. If anyone lost his popularity at this point, it would be Camille rather than himself; and Desmoulins—only too glad to find himself back in the good books of an adversary whom he reckoned on eliminating when Hébert and his clique were out of the way—walked blindly into the trap that had been set for him.

The *Vieux Cordelier* served as his mouthpiece; in it he accused Hébert of collusion with the enemy. Hébert struck back from the City Hall by calling out his followers under arms. Convinced that he could repeat the rabble-rousing tactics which had got the better of the Girondists, Père Duchesne now called on the whole body of his supporters to rush the Tuileries. But General Hanriot, Commander-in-Chief of the National Guard, this time chose the Convention rather than the Commune. Furthermore, Hébert did not know that Saint-Just—still, as the Assembly believed, in favor of Desmoulins—was at that very moment mounting the rostrum to deliver his final blow and finish the battle. By denouncing a "foreign-backed conspiracy," a plot which would "bring about famine and fresh restrictions," the "Antinoüs of the Montagnards" managed to secure a bill of attainder against Hébert and his supporters. Before the latter could launch their gang of cutthroats into action, agents of the Committee of General Security arrested them, on the night of March 13. On hearing that their idols had "received money from the enemy," the rabble, with characteristic fickleness, cheered the news of their imprisonment—just as they would have acclaimed their triumph had it not been for Robespierre's subtle maneuver.

Danton distrusted this sudden approbation by the masses, who, now as always, remained the dupes of their leaders. He was afraid their mood might swing around again, in an explosion of anger that would send Père Duchesne's partisans storming through the prisons. If they wished to avenge him, surely their obvious course was to begin the September massacres all over again?

This idea sent Danton hurrying around to La Force. The prison *concierge,* Mme. Lebau, was an old friend of his; indeed, she owed her position to the former Minister of Justice. He asked her if it were not in La Force that Citizen Beugnot was imprisoned. This former Attorney General for the Aube region had saved Danton's life in 1791. When the latter reached Arcis after the battle on the Champ-de-Mars, Beugnot warned him that he was liable to be arrested at any moment. Hence his flight to England.

Such a good turn was not to be forgotten, even when one's benefactor belonged to a different political group. Knowing that Beugnot was detained as a "suspect," his fellow countryman wanted to save him from being massacred. The *concierge* suggested bringing the prisoner down to her lodge. Beugnot himself afterward wrote in his *Memoirs:* "Danton refused to see me, but nevertheless told her: 'Get this into your head, and don't forget it: if—which is quite possible—there is another attack on this place, or any kind of major outbreak, have Beugnot brought down here, and shut him in your kitchen. Then, as soon as the coast is clear, let him go free.'"

Mme. Lebau did not, in fact, have occasion to carry out these instructions. Paris remained calm. Nevertheless Danton deserves credit for his action. By doing what he did he risked his neck— if only because it was unlikely that such a gossip as the *concierge* would be able to hold her tongue; and his heroism was all the greater because the Committee of Public Safety, having finally disposed of the *hébertistes,* was now concentrating all its forces against Danton and his followers. It had just expelled the one friend he could still count on in the Pavillon de l'Égalité, Hérault-Séchelle, who had been imprisoned on nebulous charges of intrigue. On March 17 Saint-Just asked the Convention to ratify this arrest, accusing Hérault-Séchelle of "complicity with

the enemies of the Republic." By "enemies" the virtuous President of the Assembly meant the speculators of the East India
Company—that is, in the last resort, Danton himself. The battle
was warming up.

A mild diversion was provided by the trial of Hébert and his
accomplices—a splendid dish for Fouquier-Tinville, who gob-
bled them up at one fell swoop. There were no less than thirteen
death sentences.

With *hébertism* eliminated and the Cult of Reason abolished,
Robespierre and Saint-Just felt the time had come to deal with
Danton. Various third parties, perceiving the danger, tried to
mediate between them. Not mutual friends, since the Terror had
suppressed all common bonds of friendship, but a group of
Deputies argued that if Danton went to the scaffold, all those
who disapproved of Robespierre would follow him there sooner
or later. One Deputy named Laignelot, a friend of Barras's, was
chosen by the latter for the role of peacemaker and persuaded
Danton to accompany him to the house of M. Duplay, the joiner
in the rue Saint-Honoré with whom the Incorruptible lodged.

So Danton entered Robespierre's apartment with the air of one
seeking a favor, and found the great man putting the final
touches to his toilet. He had a smock on over his green-striped
coat and was powdering his hair. His visitor was less punctili-
ously attired; he wore an open-necked shirt exposing his throat—
the famous *col Danton* that he had brought into fashion.

"Well," Robespierre said to them, "what is it you want of
me?"

"To make peace with you," Danton said, "for the sake of
liberty, and for no other reason. It is under attack from our
enemies. They are slandering us and deceiving the people." He
used the familiar second person singular when he addressed
Robespierre.

"What are you trying to say?" Robespierre himself carefully
avoided any familiarity. "You can put what interpretation on
my speeches you please, I couldn't care less. *I'm* not the person
responsible for the errors committed during a certain mission to
Belgium! Your friend Lacroix—"

"You talk like the aristocrats!" Danton broke in. "Such people defame the Revolution by slandering its founders; and are we not, you and I, its founders-in-chief?"

Robespierre began to get annoyed; he found the discussion irksome. Laignelot realized that the two men were beyond any reconciliation on his part. He tried to change the subject, but failed, and finally found himself out in the street with a furious Danton, who was cursing him, Robespierre, and Barras simultaneously and with equal fervor.

A second meeting was arranged somewhere just outside Paris —not a mere formal interview but a dinner party which took place in the house of Humbert, the Comptroller of the Foreign Office. Danton was taken there by Villain Daubigny, who had arranged the whole thing. The guests included Legendre, Panis, and Déforgues. Robespierre, that near-teetotaler, was persuaded to drink champagne. He felt uneasy: he was beginning to get drunk, and did not know what might come of it. After long and difficult discussions he consented to embrace Danton—but it was the kiss of Judas, on both sides. Their fellow guests believed them reconciled, but the two antagonists knew how false such optimism was.

Nevertheless, since their gesture had at least proclaimed a truce, Danton decided to leave town for Sèvres. He was stifling in Paris; he needed fresh country air to purify his lungs and mind alike. He reached his destination on 2 Germinal, together with his wife and children, and his nephew, M. Menuel's son. M. and Mme. Charpentier were delighted, and spent much time romping with their grandchildren. It was March 22, the first real day of spring, and The Fountain of Love was bathed in bright sunshine, warm and invigorating.

But two days later the weather—both physical and political —took a turn for the worse. Danton huddled drowsily by the chimneypiece, feet stretched out to the log fire. A peal on the front-door bell roused him from his torpor. The visitor was his friend Thibaudeau, Deputy for the Vienne region.

"Your lackadaisical attitude astonishes me," Thibaudeau told him. "I simply can't understand why you're being so apathetic. Don't you realize that Robespierre is planning to destroy you?"

"If I believed he was even thinking of such a thing I'd eat him alive—"

Words and fine phrases, as always. Even sprawled in an armchair, Danton imagined himself on the rostrum. When Legendre
came to reinforce Thibaudeau's plea, he roared: "Better, a hundred times better, to suffer the guillotine than to inflict it on
others!" And to Rousselin de Saint-Albin he said, four days
later: "My head's still sitting on my shoulders, isn't it? Why on
earth would they want to destroy me?" Finally, when Desmoulins,
Lecointre, Lacroix, and Courtois all talked to him of emigration,
he made one of the remarks that has achieved immortality: "Can
a man take his country with him on the soles of his shoes?"

In 1791, after the affray on the Champ-de-Mars, he had
thought otherwise. At the time of his flight to England he believed himself done for. But now, in March 1794, he had greater
confidence in his own eloquence. So it was that, on 9 Germinal,
he decided to return to Paris and throw his weight into the
struggle. The old lion had enjoyed his woodland peace for no
more than a week. Why did he refuse to seek refuge abroad?

He had only five more days to live.

CHAPTER XVIII

Famous Last Words

ROBESPIERRE'S BEHAVIOR SUGGESTS that all he wanted was Danton's political elimination. If Danton, exhausted by partisan struggles and (as he was often fond of saying) "sick of his fellow men," had retired to plant cabbages in Arcis-sur-Aube, doubtless Robespierre would have spared his life. But Billaud-Varennes and Vadier were implacably set on having him executed. Billaud —that "foursquare Republican and choleric patriot," as Desmoulins called him—regarded Danton's "moderatism" as a plot against the régime and his dealings with the *affairistes* as part of an intrigue to undermine the nation's finances. As for Vadier —the other Incorruptible—this impotent old ex-rake, this Republican puritan would never forgive the virility of which Danton made such abundant demonstration. He envied him his size, his strength, his eloquence. He was jealous of his successes with women—not least his possession, at thirty-four, of a wife who had barely reached adolescence. Later, after his downfall, Vadier declared: "Little Louise was our most useful assistant during this crisis. It was her fresh complexion and melting eyes that disarmed the circus strong man for us."

Disarmed Danton seemed to be indeed, in sober earnest, after his return from Sèvres. Though he reached Paris on the evening of 9 Germinal, he did not do what he should have done, which was to hurry to the Jacobin Club without a moment's delay and make his voice heard there. All next day he spent in dressing gown and slippers, drowsing in front of the fire, only leaving his armchair from time to time to throw on more logs. Louise

would come in occasionally and the lovers would exchange a kiss.
When Danton's two children went scampering through with
their cousin, he called them over and dandled them on his
knee. It is hard to understand this persistent mood of apathy and
inaction. Why did he not go straight to the Convention? Had he
forgotten that the Committees were bent on destroying him?
Was he unaware that Vouland, Amar, Couthon, Collot d'Herbois, and Barère were all behind Billaud-Varennes and Vadier,
and that Robespierre had authorized the terrible Saint-Just to
draw up the indictment against him?

On the evening of March 30 the street bell rang once more.
A servant showed in Fabricius Pâris, the copying clerk who was
now both a member of the jury and Clerk of the Court to the
Revolutionary Tribunal—a post he had secured through Danton's offices. Every day he went over from the Law Courts to the
Tuileries, to collect the Committee of Public Safety's latest orders
and deliver them to Fouquier-Tinville. That evening, however,
the chamber in which France's masters conducted their deliberations had been locked. Intrigued, he hurried through the other
rooms of the Pavillon de l'Égalité (he knew the layout of the
building very well), and found a keyhole through which he
could see Saint-Just, who had a series of papers in his hand
and was reading their contents aloud to the members of both
Committees. Fabricius Pâris then applied his ear to the keyhole,
and what he heard boded ill for his patron. The very next day, it
transpired, Saint-Just intended to ask the Convention to approve Danton's arrest and trial.

Danton's only response to this revelation was a shrug of the
shoulders. "They would never dare," he said. But Pâris had
failed to discover one vital piece of evidence, the draft decree
still preserved in the Musée des Archives: "The Committees of
Public Safety and of General Security hereby decree that Danton, Lacroix (of the Eure-et-Loire *département*), Camille Desmoulins, and Philippeaux, all members of the National Convention, shall be arrested and taken to the Luxembourg Prison, there
to be kept in solitary and secret confinement. And they do command the Mayor of Paris to execute this present decree immediately on receipt thereof." The document was signed, in that
order, by Billaud-Varennes, Vadier, Carnot, Le Bas, Louis, Col-

lot d'Herbois, Saint-Just, Jagot, C. A. Prieur, Couthon, Dubarran, Voulland, Moyse Bayle, Amar, Élie Lacoste, Robespierre, and Lavicomterie.

Not all these despots could match Saint-Just and Vadier for implacability, or Billaud-Varennes and Collot d'Herbois for bloodthirstiness, or Le Bas and Robespierre for ambition. If men as estimable as Carnot, Louis, Prieur, and Lacoste (who could meet the Incorruptible on his own ground) were prepared to sign what virtually amounted to a death warrant, they must have believed Danton guilty of the charges against him.

Only two Committee members refused to append their names at the foot of the document: the aged Rühl, of the Committee of General Security, and Robert Lindet, of the Committee of Public Safety. The former was a onetime Presbyterian minister who owed what fame he possessed to the so-called Massacre of the Sacred Ampulla at Rheims. The Ampulla was the vessel that held the holy oil, and Rühl had smashed it before an enthusiastic crowd. Lindet, who had been elected to the Robespierre Committee several months before, could not forget his earlier membership of the same Committee under Danton.

Both of them deputed Panis (a former member of the Commune of August 10) to go without delay and attempt to rouse Danton from his lethargy. Panis reached the rue Marat between midnight and one o'clock. Louise opened the door to him; the servants were all asleep. Somewhat alarmed, she took the visitor to her husband. Panis found him sitting by the fireside in his dressing gown, sunk deep in his own thoughts. To the somewhat vague report of Fabricius Pâris he added one concrete and indisputable fact: the warrant for Danton's arrest had been issued. Danton got up and poked at the fire. "I can't believe it," he said.

Robert Lindet appeared in person to confirm the truth of Panis's statement. There was no longer room for doubt; the arrest had been planned for that very night. "You've still got time to get away," Danton's friend urged him. But Danton made evasive replies, and after a while Lindet took himself off, aghast at the lack of interest which his old comrade showed in saving his own skin. Was he still hoping against hope that all would be well?

In fact, the lion was sharpening his claws. It was no longer defense that was called for, but attack—a frontal assault on Robespierre, Billaud, Vadier, the whole clique. Danton had not forgotten how Marat had been arraigned by the Girondists, haled before Fouquier-Tinville, acquitted by the Tribunal, and carried back in triumph to the Convention. This near-victory for Brissot and his group had been turned to utter defeat, a defeat which dug the grave of the Girondist movement. If Marat, who was no great speaker, could thus triumph over a pusillanimous jury, then Danton, with his brazen voice, could not fail to do likewise. He would deliver a slashing indictment of the Terror, and its agents, from the dock. The public in the galleries, always easily impressed, would be behind him. So would at least two jurors, Souberbielle and Fabricius Pâris, and they would carry the rest with them. And was not Fouquier-Tinville Desmoulins's cousin? Was it not Danton who, at Camille's request, had obtained for him his position? Then how could he possibly demand the death penalty for either of them? No, all the cards were stacked favorably. Let them arrest him and put him on trial. He asked nothing better. He would triumph as Marat had triumphed, and Robespierre, together with his clique, would suffer the fate of the Girondists.

At this point he heard the tramp of numerous footsteps in the silent street outside, the clink of sabers, the sound of muffled voices. Louise opened the window and peered out. She turned pale. "They're here," she whispered.

"Don't worry, my dear. I'll soon be back."

Three minutes later the apartment was invaded. Gendarmes stationed themselves at every window to prevent any attempt at escape or suicide. They found Danton in his room, quite unruffled, putting on his clothes. Louise was half swooning. A municipal bailiff presented Danton with the warrant. "All right, I'll come with you," he said. Yet he must have been a little distressed, since he almost forgot to kiss his wife and did not say good-by to the children.

Dawn was breaking. When Danton reached the palace-turned-prison, he found Desmoulins, Philippeaux, and Lacroix there already. Once the formalities of committal were over, warders hustled the four men into an entrance hall. The other prisoners—those who enjoyed relative freedom of movement—were astonished to see the founders of the Republic appear among them: Desmoulins, whose speeches at the Palais-Royal had launched the mass attack on the Bastille; and Danton, the giant who had overthrown the monarch on that never-to-be-forgotten August 10.

"Gentlemen," Danton said to the prisoners who gathered around him, "I was reckoning on being able to get you all out of here—but now, unfortunately, I find myself incarcerated with you. When men make stupid mistakes, one must learn to treat them lightly. If common sense does not prevail very soon, this is nothing to what you will see."

Among his audience Danton recognized one old friend, Hérault-Séchelles, a member of the Committee of Public Safety who had been removed from office by his colleagues a few days before to ensure that he did not speak up in Danton's defense. The two men embraced each other.

From this moment on, the hurried preparation of the case, and the trial itself, might well be entitled "An Anthology of Famous Historical Sayings." Most of these were delivered by Danton himself and his fellow prisoners. It is fashionable in certain quarters (just as it is thought a *sine qua non* of good taste) to deny these telling retorts, witty sallies, and sententious aphorisms any shred of authenticity. Sometimes the critics are right, but very often they are quite wrong. In the case which particularly concerns us I shall try, at each stage of its development, to separate truth from falsehood, the possible from the probable.

For instance, when Louis Blanc credits Danton with saying, to the prisoners crowded around him, "They're sending me to the scaffold, and I tell you, my friends, I shall go cheerfully," one may well suspect that this particular *mot* belongs to the realm of legend. A man who has decided to make a fight of it in court and wipe the floor with his enemies, does not produce that kind of disillusioned remark. Other evidence points in the same direction. When Lacroix exclaimed: "Oh, if only I had known that they intended to arrest me!" Danton's comment contained an implicit admission: "I did know," he said. "I was warned in advance." A man such as Danton, fond of good living and pretty women, a devoted father, a wealthy hedonist determined to squeeze existence like an orange—this is not the kind of person who goes "cheerfully" to the scaffold.

Much the same applies to another "historical saying," reported by a police officer named Sénart, and of such doubtful ascription that it is set sometimes in the Luxembourg, sometimes in the Conciergerie. "What matter if I die now? I have played a crucial part in the Revolution. I have spent my money well. I have wined and wenched as a man should. It is time for a long sleep." Once again the authenticity of the saying is at least open to doubt, since Danton intended to, and actually did, turn the dock into a prosecutor's stand.

Meanwhile the warrant specified that all four prisoners were to be held in secret and solitary confinement, and their jailers adhered to these conditions. Danton was separated from his three companions and shut in a room overlooking the Luxembourg Gardens. But as the others were given adjoining rooms, they could still communicate with one another merely by raising their voices. Desmoulins, to his great surprise, even managed to squint through a tiny hole in the wall and see Fabre d'Églantine in the adjacent cell.

Meanwhile the police were going through Danton's apartment (and those of the other three) with a fine-toothed comb. Louise, tearful and furious, watched them ransack the whole place—her husband's desk, bookcases, and cupboards—stacking up files and documents which they took away with them. Out of all these papers there was one letter, unwisely preserved, which was to make the poor girl a widow at sixteen.

That morning all Paris heard the incredible news: the hero of the Bastille and the hero of August 10 both in prison! Incredulous Deputies hurried to their homes, hoping to scotch the rumors. But the sight of Lucile and Louise in tears quickly disillusioned them.

In the Convention, various contradictory reports were circulating and causing much alarm. Legendre was on the rostrum. In a voice full of emotion, which he made no attempt to conceal, the butcher of the rue Marat pleaded for his friend: "Citizens,"

terrible about the sacred love one bears one's country; so exclusive is it that it sacrifices all else, without fear or favor, without pity or personal consideration, to the public interest." With a kind of wild intoxication the speaker mingled truth and falsehood, the absurd and the plausible. Danton a Republican? Rubbish; he had been hand in glove with Dumouriez to restore the King. Ever since the fall of the Bastille, he and his friends "had followed the trail of every enemy faction, just as snakes will follow the line of a stream bed." If they had served liberty for the past five years, they had only done so in the manner of "the tiger stalking his prey." Liberty for them was a source of plunder, the Revolution meant nothing to them except a handy way of lining their pockets. To crown his other acts of infamy, Danton was now attacking the militant policy of the Grand Committee —a policy implemented in order to save France. Saint-Just's final words were: "The days of crime are ended: woe to those who support such a cause!"

It hardly needs saying that this threat brought over the still-hesitant voters—not that there were many of them after such a speech. *By unanimous decree*—Legendre, defeated, added his voice to the rest—the Convention approved the indictment. Robespierre was heard to observe, to a group of intimates: "I must say, Danton has some pretty cowardly friends." The Incorruptible did not, however, number himself among them— though it was he who had written to Danton, after the death of Gabrielle: "I love you more than ever, and unto death. From this moment you and I are one. . . ."

That evening Saint-Just gave another reading of his report, this time before the Jacobin Club. The twenty-six-year-old autocrat wanted to attack Legendre on his home ground, for Legendre had for some time now been President of the Club. Once again Saint-Just spoke for two hours, and those members of his audience who happened to be Deputies thus heard the indictment twice over. An unusual expenditure of energy and patience, one might suppose, simply to kill five men.

Couthon made a similar speech, attacking Danton, Lacroix, and Desmoulins. He also took Legendre to task with some vehemence for his attempted defense of Danton in the Convention.

The President of the Jacobins nervously protested his good intentions. Ever since he had known Danton, he said, he had "always regarded him as a blameless patriot." His attempt to defend him had been a mistake, and he admitted it. He underscored his capitulation with the abject words: "I shall abide by the decision of the Revolutionary Tribunal."

The following day, 12 Germinal, Louise and Lucile went to Duplay's house and begged the joiner to let them see Robespierre. Robespierre was informed of their presence but refused to meet them. (He had, one recalls, been a witness at Camille's wedding.) Tearfully they took their leave and went on to knock at a good many other doors; but always they were met by the same blank and terrified refusal. No Deputy or magistrate, not even an influential Montagnard, would compromise himself by dealing with these widows-to-be. Finally they retired to weep on the bosoms of their respective mothers. After this they dried their eyes and went for a walk through the Luxembourg Gardens with Mme. Hérault-Séchelles. Kept at a distance from the Palace by the barrier erected around the new prison, they raised anxious, tear-filled eyes toward its upper stories—and were overjoyed by the sight of Hérault and Camille at the windows of their cells.

But they did not see Danton, since at that moment Fouquier-Tinville and Judge Denizot were in the process of interrogating him—if one can call it an interrogation. They asked him one question only: "Have you conspired against the French people by attempting to restore the monarchy, and to destroy national representation and Republican government?"

Danton shrugged his shoulders.

"Have you a defense counsel?" Denizot asked him.

"I can defend myself, thank you."

Despite this disclaimer he was saddled with Maître Fleutrie, an impecunious lawyer who had been bought by the judiciary, and who had a well-established reputation for getting his clients convicted. But Danton remained indifferent; his main object was not so much to defend himself as to attack his accusers. The same applied to Lacroix. Both men were determined to have their case heard by those who wielded the real power. While they were in the Clerk of the Court's office they exchanged a quick word on the subject. Lacroix said: "We must refuse to answer any questions except before both Committees in joint session." To which Danton replied: "Yes, and to make sure we get our way, we must first do our best to arouse the people."

During the night of 12 Germinal, two horse cabs escorted by mounted gendarmes carried Danton, Lacroix, Desmoulins, Hérault-Séchelles, and Fabre d'Églantine to the Conciergerie, the prison attached to the Law Courts. From the moment of their arrival in this antechamber to the scaffold, they once more began to deliver historical *mots,* to be preserved in the hall of fame for posterity. Honoré Riouffe, a native of Rouen who became a Préfect under the Empire, was incarcerated in the Conciergerie at the time of Danton's admission. In an account published afterward he recorded several of these *mots,* some of which are mutually incompatible. For example, Danton is said to have exclaimed, through the bars of his cell: "What an appalling mess I'm leaving everything in!" This remark clearly indicates that he thought his fate a foregone conclusion. But he could have escaped had he wanted to, and his declaration that he knew he was to be arrested gives the lie to the saying quoted above.

Riouffe records another historical *mot,* a highly vulgar one, and for that reason frequently abbreviated by Danton's biographers. It was the bowdlerized version which Paul Gaulot printed in the nineteenth century, in his *Récits des Grands Jours de l'Histoire:* "If I left my legs to Couthon, the Committee of Public Safety might stagger on a bit longer." (Couthon, we remember, was paralyzed from the waist down.) In actual fact, Danton delivered a neat left-and-right. What he really said was: "If I left my testicles to Robespierre and my legs to Couthon . . . ," etc.

"If I left"—there we have the kind of expression used by a prisoner who feels his case is hopeless. But when he said of his judges: "We shall see what kind of a figure they cut when they appear before us," this reversal of roles makes it clear that Danton saw himself as prosecutor rather than as the prisoner in the dock. And prosecutor he incontestably was when, only twenty-four hours after his committal to the Conciergerie, he appeared before the Tribunal.

The hearing opened on the morning of 13 Germinal, at ten o'clock according to some eyewitnesses, at eleven according to others. This small detail, as we shall see later, is not without some importance. Herman presided over the proceedings, assisted by his deputy, Dumas, and a panel of four judges. Fouquier-Tinville and his two assistants, Liendon and Lescot-Fleuriot, occupied the Public Prosecutor's bench. The Committee had imposed the two last-named figures on Fouquier-Tinville because they were not sure of him. No one could forget that he owed his position to Danton and Desmoulins. The Minister of Justice (as Danton was in 1792) had, on Camille's recommendation, agreed to find a place for this "esteemed cousin" to alleviate his distress.

Furthermore, the Committee had another card in reserve—warrants for the arrest of Fouquier-Tinville and Herman. These warrants were signed and needed only to be passed on to the police. Both magistrates were warned of this move; it was no more than they expected. When, after several hearings, it became clear that they were determined to secure convictions, a message was sent around to General Hanriot (while the trial was still in progress) enjoining him "on no account to arrest either the President or the Public Prosecutor." The Committee left nothing to chance.

With such a threat hanging over his own head, it is not surprising that Fouquier-Tinville was so rigorous in his selection of jurors. This was why the trial, which should have begun at eight in the morning, was held up until ten or eleven. Naturally Fouquier expelled from the jury the Clerk of the Court, Fabricius Pâris, whose friendship with Danton was common knowledge. On the other hand, he kept Dr. Souberbielle, whom he regarded as "solid," and six others who, together with Souberbielle, formed a seven-man jury. Yet Article VII of the decree which brought the Tribunal into being stipulated a jury of twelve. Not that such a violation of the law mattered to Fouquier-Tinville. He had to obtain the death sentence in any case. Apart from Dr. Souberbielle, the jury consisted of the following: Renaudin, a violinmaker; Desboisseaux, a cobbler; Ganney, a wigmaker; Trinchard, a joiner; Lumière the musician; and the former Marquis Leroy de Montflobert, now known as "Leroy-

Dix-Août" in honor of August 10. These were the men on whom Robespierre's lackey relied to send his presumptively guilty victims to the scaffold.

Herman, as President, ordered the accused to be brought in. A door opened, and Danton appeared under police escort; he resembled some furious bull, optimistically determined to gore the Tribunal on the horns of his rhetoric and win over the crowds in the public galleries. As he approached the bench reserved for the accused, Fabricius Pâris—a juror no longer, but still Clerk of the Court—was seen to rise from his seat, moist-eyed, and hurry across to his friend. The two men embraced.

After Danton came Desmoulins, Fabre d'Églantine, Lacroix, Hérault-Séchelles, Philippeaux, Basire, Delaunay d'Angers, Emmanuel and Junius Frey, Chabot (their brother-in-law), the Abbé d'Espagnac, Gusman the Spanish banker, and the Danish lawyer Diedrichsen—a mixed bag, including atheists, Catholics, a priest, two Jews, an ex-Capuchin monk, and a Protestant.

What was the reason for assembling so heterogeneous a group of prisoners, fourteen men of such diverse origins and religious faith, and with such a variety of charges against them? Why this "medley"? The word was Vadier's; the idea originated with Fouquier-Tinville. The Public Prosecutor specialized in this kind of human magma. Politicians such as Danton, Desmoulins, Lacroix, Hérault-Séchelles, and Philippeaux, accused of conspiracy against the Republic, found themselves bracketed with forgers and swindlers (Fabre d'Églantine, Basire, Delaunay, and Chabot), speculators (the two Austrian bankers and the Spanish financier), and *affairistes* (d'Espagnac the contractor and the Danish lawyer). This was a clever way of making people believe that Danton and his friends had been involved in the other defendants' various shady practices, and thus discrediting them both in the eyes of the jury and, more important, with the crowd that had begun to gather around the Law Courts during the past three hours.

In front of the accused sat the lawyers assigned to defend them: La Fleutrie for Danton, Pantin for Chabot and the Freys, Chauveau-Lagarde for Hérault-Séchelles, Desmoulins, and Philippeaux. The others were without legal representation—not that this put them at much of a disadvantage, since La Fleutrie,

Pantin, and Chauveau-Lagarde knew nothing whatsoever about the cases they had taken on. Some had come into their hands the previous day, the others that same morning.

Having concluded our description of the *dramatis personae,* let us move on to the play. For what now took place was a kind of comedy, a hideous burlesque, with the Law Courts as its setting, and a plethora of famous last words to amuse the groundlings.

The first act of the farce took place on 13 Germinal. When the President called the names of the accused, the star performer replied: "Georges-Jacques Danton, thirty-four years old, born at Arcis, profession lawyer, Deputy to the Convention. Place of residence? Very soon my body will lie in oblivion and my name be recorded in the Panthéon of history. The people will revere my head even when the guillotine has severed it from my shoulders!"

It looks as though he had given up any hope of repeating Marat's triumph.

When Desmoulins's turn came he produced yet another *mot historique:* "I am thirty-three years old—the age at which Jesus, the *sans-culotte,* died!" The poor fellow made himself out a year younger than he was, so as not to spoil his punch line. After all, the theater does take liberties with history. Asked the same question, the former Count Hérault de Séchelles, remembering that he had lately been a distinguished member of the legal fraternity, replied: "My name is Jean-Marie, one of little renown among the saints; I once sat on the Bench in this Chamber, and parliamentary lawyers had little cause to love me."

One after another, the fourteen accused persons gave their name, age, profession, and domicile. This formality concluded, the President had the seven members of the jury sworn in: a fine oath, which enjoined them to "administer justice impartially." Camille Desmoulins objected to the inclusion of Renaudin, the violinmaker, who was a personal enemy of his; they had come to blows one day in the Jacobin Club. The Tribunal, as one might expect, overruled his objection. Then the Clerk of the Court began to read out the lengthy indictment.

During this part of the proceedings Danton observed several

members of the two Committees slip in behind the President's dais. He recognized Amar, Voulland, and Couthon in his wheel-chair. Then, interrupting Fabricius Pâris, he rose to his feet and thundered: "I demand permission to write to the Convention and have a Commission appointed to hear my denunciation, and that of Desmoulins, against dictatorial practices in the Committees of Public Safety and Security—"

The uproar these words produced—loud protests from the Court, equally loud applause from the crowd—was of such dimensions that Danton's final remarks were inaudible. Herman panicked and declared the Court adjourned. The prisoners were escorted back to their cells in the Conciergerie, down on the ground floor of the Law Courts.

"The bastards wouldn't let me finish," Danton complained. "Never mind, I'll make mincemeat of the judges tomorrow." Magnanimously he added: "After that, I'll throw myself on their mercy."

The second hearing—and second act of the drama—took place on 14 Germinal. To the great surprise of everybody concerned—the accused, the jurors themselves, and the public, who had packed the galleries even more thickly than the day before—the number of prisoners ushered into the dock had risen from fourteen to sixteen. Who were the two newcomers? The crowd recognized one of them, at least: it was General Westermann, deputy commander to Danton during the *coup* of August 10 and among those responsible for bringing down the monarchy. The other was Lhuillier, the former Attorney General. There is some doubt as to whether Fouquier-Tinville even knew what crime the latter was supposed to have committed. The wretched man occupied a bed in a cell. There were far too many prisoners. In order to make more room, some had to be either beheaded or released.

Furthermore, the presence of these two newcomers increased the effect of the "medley." Westermann and Lhuillier became linked in people's minds with Danton and Philippeaux, just as the latter were already assimilated to Chabot, d'Espagnac, or Delaunay. Confronted by this amalgam of "conspirators" and "Royalists," profiteers and forgers (not to mention a victim of

the Vendée campaign, one of the "Victory or Death" group),
the Paris proletariat lumped them all together—and therefore
failed to come to Danton's rescue.

Westermann began protesting almost as soon as he was in the
dock. He demanded to be interrogated.

"A useless formality," the President told him.

"We are all," Danton remarked, "here by way of a formality."
This observation drew laughter from his fellow prisoners.

"I must call you to order," Herman exclaimed.

Danton said: "If I am out of order, you have forgotten all
decency. We have the right to be heard in this place! I was
responsible for creating this Tribunal, I know its rules of procedure better than anyone!"

In the midst of the uproar set off by this exchange, Herman
could be heard desperately ringing his hand bell. Danton was
still speaking, but his words were lost in the general hubbub.
Somehow, nevertheless, another question was asked—and answered by another historical *mot*.

"Didn't you hear my bell?"

"A man fighting for his life pays no attention to bells. He
just shouts."

Suddenly Danton spotted Cambon in the courtroom. The financial expert had been cited as a witness (for the prosecution,
it goes without saying).

"Cambon," he called out, "do you really believe we're conspirators?"

Cambon grinned despite himself. This drew another *mot
historique:* "Look, he's laughing! He doesn't believe it! Monsieur Clerk of the Court, put it in the record that he laughed!"
Everyone present—judges, jury, police, spectators—collapsed
with mirth themselves at this, and there was loud applause from
the galleries.

But a statement by Westermann soon restored the proceedings
to the plane of tragedy. An assessor had just read out the charge
against him—not before the Court, but in an adjacent room,
so as not to delay the trial. As soon as the General had been
escorted back to his place in the dock, he addressed the President.
"I demand," he said, gesturing toward the public gallery, "I
demand permission to strip myself naked before the people and

let them see my scars. I have received seven wounds, all of them in front. Only once have I been stabbed in the back—by this indictment!"

Westermann's eloquence had its effect. The hubbub died away, which gave Herman a chance to pass on to the affairs of the East India Company. His main object in so doing was to postpone Danton's defense, about which he felt decidedly apprehensive. Despite strenuous objections from the accused, he managed to impose this order of events on them. Cambon was called to the witness box and gave a full account of the share-pushing venture. He had no difficulty in convincing his audience that the speculators had indeed committed the crime with which they were charged.

At last came the moment everyone had been waiting for. In a weighty, sententious voice the President declared: "Danton, the Convention accuses you of showing undue favor to Dumouriez; of failing to reveal his true nature and intentions; and of aiding and abetting his schemes to destroy freedom, such as that of marching on Paris under arms in order to crush the Republican government and restore the monarchy."

Danton shrugged. Just as he was about to begin his reply, however, Fabricius Pâris—the friend of the accused whom Fouquier-Tinville had removed from the jury—got up and, in his official capacity as Clerk of the Court, began to read out Saint-Just's enormous report. For the first time Danton himself heard the cutting phrases composed by his most implacable adversary. His respect for the etiquette of justice kept him from moving or interrupting, but there was an angry glint in his eye. He listened attentively, taking no notes, relying on his memory. At last Pâris, almost weeping, came to the end of the laborious task imposed on him, and Herman finally gave Danton permission to speak— "for as long as you like," he added, magnanimously.

The President could afford to be generous: he had observed the effect which Saint-Just's indictment produced in the galleries. Stunned by the possibility, if not the certitude, that Danton was about as guilty as a man could be, the crowd sat in silence, ready to turn on their idol. But as soon as he began to speak they changed their minds.

"My voice has made itself heard time and again on the peo-

ple's behalf," Danton told them, "supporting and defending their
interests. It should have little difficulty now in refuting mere
slander. Would my cowardly persecutors dare to attack me to
my face? I doubt it. Let them but show themselves, and soon
enough I will cover them with the ignominy and opprobrium
which are their fitting lot in life. . . . I insist that the Convention appoint Commissioners to investigate my exposure of dictatorial practices. Yes, I, Danton, will strip the mask from this
shameless and naked dictatorship! I, Danton—"

At this point Herman interrupted him. "Audacity," he said,
"is a characteristic of guilt. Innocence keeps a cool head."

"If you will let me—"

"Self-defense is a legitimate privilege. But it must contain itself
within limits. The defendant must show proper respect for everything and everybody—even his accusers."

"*Individual* audacity is, doubtless, reprehensible," Danton
thundered, "but *national* audacity, which I have used time and
again to serve the public weal, is a different, and quite legitimate,
human characteristic. Besides, when I find myself faced with so
grievous and unjust an accusation, how am I to control the
anger and resentment which boil up in me? And is a revolutionary extremist such as myself the kind of person from whom
you expect a frigid, unemotional defense?"

Indeed, his speech was more of a fiery diatribe. The charge
of conspiracy he swept aside with the joking remark: "Me a conspirator? I'm too busy kissing my wife every night!" Complaints
of his venality he rebutted with another historical aphorism: "*I
sell my allegiance? Why, there is no price high enough for a man
of my caliber!*" He went on to demand that the prosecution
furnish "proof, or part proof, or any evidence whatsoever" of his
supposed corruption. If he had been bought by Mirabeau or the
Duke of Orléans or the Court, then let his accusers provide
chapter and verse to prove it. "Bring these creatures before me,
and I will hurl them back into the obscurity from which they
never should have emerged! Vile imposters, stand forth, and let
me strip off the mask you wear to protect yourselves against
public obloquy!"

His voice was drowned in applause, and he had to stop. From
this point until the adjournment Herman had no effective con-

trol over the proceedings. Danton, by his fiery eloquence, had usurped the President's position and held the floor uninterrupted throughout. His skillful blend of wit and seriousness captivated the spectators. He recalled his past triumphs before the Jacobins and the Cordeliers, as a Minister, in the Riding School. He evoked the trust which his fellow Deputies had placed in him. With nice irony he concluded: "How odd that the Convention remained so blind to my faults until now! And how truly miraculous this sudden collective delusion concerning me!"

As he paused for a moment to draw breath, Herman cut in: "Your irony is no answer to the charge that you used patriotism as a mask, behind which you gave secret support to the monarchy!"

With still heavier irony Danton sneered: "Ah yes, indeed, I remember. Now how did I promote the restoration of the monarchy and safeguard the tyrant's attempted flight? As I recall it, by doing everything in my power to prevent his trip to Saint-Cloud, by hedging him about with a forest of pikes and bayonets. If that is to prove oneself a dedicated Royalist, then I must plead guilty to the charge!"

This statement drew laughter and applause from the gallery. With a flash of pride he exclaimed: "You are the people, and when I have presented my case it is you who will judge me! My voice should not be heard by you alone, but by all France!" The applause redoubled.

The word that Danton was gaining the upper hand over his opponents rapidly spread throughout the Law Courts, from mouth to mouth, down corridor and staircase, until at last it penetrated the Conciergerie. Full of anxious hope, the prisoners waited, sure that Danton's victory, if he achieved it, would secure their own release.

He came within a hairsbreadth of success. The whole Tribunal, President, judges, jury, Public Prosecutor, everyone, seemed overwhelmed by his onslaught. Herman passed a note to Fouquier-Tinville which read: "In half an hour I shall adjourn the hearing." Meanwhile Danton himself was beginning to tire. He had been speaking for over an hour, and his voice had lost its strength. Despite everything, he feared for his life, and the terror he felt made a drain on his reserves of energy. As he paused to

recover his breath, one juror called out: "Could you enlighten
us as to why Dumouriez failed to pursue the Prussians during
their retreat?"

Danton sidestepped this allusion to the mystery of Valmy by
saying: "I was only concerned with the war in its political as-
pects. Military operations as such were a closed book to me."
Herman stepped in and took over from the juror, but was no
more successful in pinning Danton down to an explanation. Exhausted by the strain of defending himself, but resolute in his
determination not to reveal the truth, Danton pulled out a
handkerchief and mopped his forehead. With a certain sly
duplicity, Herman suggested adjourning till the next day, so that
he could "continue his apologia in greater calm and tranquillity."

Danton accepted, and this was his undoing. Before he sat
down, he asked the Court not to forget to summon his witnesses for the next hearing. He then supplied a list of them. His
fellow prisoners supported such a move. Herman raised various
objections. This gave rise to an argument, which soon degenerated into noisy chaos. Some of those present thought they
heard Danton exclaim, amid the uproar: "If they refuse me my
witnesses, there's no point in my defending myself any longer."

The first scene of the third act took place that same evening,
14 Germinal, in the Pavillon de l'Égalité. Robespierre, Couthon,
and Saint-Just—that famous triumvirate—were at work with
their colleagues, when one of Fouquier-Tinville's messengers delivered the following hastily scribbled note by Herman: "We
have had an extremely stormy session from the moment it
started. The accused are insisting, in the most violent manner,
on having witnesses examined for the defense. They have listed
the following Deputies: Simon, Courtois, Laignelot, Fréron,
Panis, Lindet, Calon, Merlin [the member for Douai], Gossuin,
Legendre, Robin, Goupilleau, Lecointre [the member for Ver-
sailles], Brival, and Merlin [the member for Thionville]. They
are calling the public to witness what they term the refusal of
their just claims. Despite the firm stand taken by the President
and the entire Tribunal, their reiterated demands are holding
up the case. Furthermore, they openly declare that until their

witnesses are heard, and a decree passed to that effect, they will persist in such interruptions. We therefore appeal to you for an authoritative ruling on what our response to this request should be, since the law does not offer us any legitimate excuse for refusing it."

To unearth such an excuse, however, was not beyond the Machiavellis on the Committee—thanks to a couple of informers, named Amans and Laflotte, then imprisoned in the Luxembourg. Laflotte came to the Tuileries and told Robespierre of a plot he had discovered. The report of Danton's forensic triumph had penetrated the Luxembourg. Two prisoners, a Deputy named Simon and General Dillon, at once conceived the idea of organizing a mass revolt. Simon was on Danton's list of defense witnesses. Dillon, a close friend of Desmoulins's, was supposed—mistakenly—to be Lucile's lover. Lucile, we remember, took a silly pleasure in passing herself off as a loose woman—a curious way of keeping the flame of passion and jealousy alight in a husband whom she adored. Laflotte, who knew all about Lucile's weakness for boasting of imaginary lovers, claimed that she was going to send Dillon a thousand *écus,* to bribe enough men to follow him. Once the warders of the Luxembourg had been overpowered, Dillon intended to launch this assault force against the Revolutionary Tribunal.

The second scene of the third act took place that same evening, 14 Germinal, in the former Tuileries Theater, now the Chamber of the Convention. Flickering torchlight shone over an assembly of ghosts. One of these phantoms stood on the rostrum, a sheaf of papers in his hand. Saint-Just, beyond a doubt now the "strong man" of the Committee, was making a simultaneous attack on the "shameless conduct" of Danton and his group, and the "plot hatched by the Desmoulins woman." He did not read out Fouquier-Tinville's letter, preferring to interpret it, very freely, in his own words. "The Public Prosecutor," he declared, "has notified us that this revolt by the guilty parties means that the course of justice will remain in abeyance until the Convention takes steps to deal with the situation. You have just escaped the greatest danger ever to threaten the cause of liberty. But all the plotters are now unmasked; and this revolt of the criminals, at the very feet of justice, reveals the secret guilt that burdens their consciences. Their despair and anger, everything about them makes it plain that the bonhomie they previously assumed was the most hypocritical trick ever played upon the Revolution."

Announcing Lucile's arrest, Saint-Just added: "She had accepted money for the purpose of stirring up a movement, the object of which was to assassinate patriots and members of the Tribunal." As a result he demanded the right, "in the interests of national justice, to *remove from Court,* on the spot," any accused person who raised his voice against the judges' decisions. The Chamber was thoroughly cowed, sweating with fright from every pore. Saint-Just got what he wanted. His purpose was, quite simply, to let Herman muzzle his prisoners; it gave him full authority to remove them from the Court and try them in their absence.

The fourth act, and third session, of the trial, took place at eight in the morning on 15 Germinal (April 4). The atmosphere was already fairly stormy when the court usher cried: "Citizens! The Tribunal!" The prisoners were brought in, and the interrogation of the Frey brothers began. Danton at once protested. Yesterday he had been assured that he would be allowed to conclude his defense speech today. While he was arguing with Herman, an usher whispered a few words in Fouquier-Tinville's ear and the latter went out by the private door. Here, in the lobby, he found Voulland and Amar, both of the Committee for General Security, who had just arrived from the Tuileries.

"Here's the thing you asked for," one of them said, handing him a document. It was the decree passed the previous night. Fouquier-Tinville sighed with relief. "My God," he said, "we certainly needed it." He returned to the courtroom and asked the President for leave to speak. Facing the dock, he said, with smooth hypocrisy: "I shall now read out the Convention's reply to the petition of the accused."

The prisoners smiled and relaxed. At last the Assembly had agreed to hear them. Would it be indirectly, through a Committee, or, better still, in Tuileries Theater itself? But what was this? What was Fouquier-Tinville saying? In a sudden and absolute

silence the Public Prosecutor read out the decree authorizing
the removal of defendants from the Court. This was tantamount
to a death warrant. Everyone, judges, jury, accused, spectators,
stared in open-eyed amazement. The decree stated, specifically,
that any defendant who might have offended the Court could be
expelled from the Chamber.

At this point Danton rose, a terrifying figure. He said: "I
have never insulted the Tribunal in any way whatsoever. I call
the people to witness that this is so. The decree you have read
is nothing but a devilish machination to destroy us. I call on
the judges and members of the jury, I ask the public to declare,
on oath, whether we have staged any revolt! You want to condemn us without hearing us! I refuse. I shall be Danton still, till
my death. And tomorrow I shall sleep in glory."

Herman's only answer was to adjourn the proceedings.
Speechless with anger, the prisoners were escorted back to the
Conciergerie.

What was to be the final hearing (Herman and Fouquier-
Tinville had decided this the night before) took place on
16 Germinal, Year II, which those with a nostalgic hanker-
ing for the Gregorian calendar still persisted in calling April 5,
1794. As soon as the Tribunal assembled, the President told
Danton and Lacroix: "I have a large number of witnesses available to testify against both of you. Their evidence is generally
incriminating." However, he went on, magnanimously; "I do
not intend to call them." Then he added: "The accused will be
judged solely on documentary evidence," a most alarming remark.

The accused protested. Objections were voiced from the dock.
What did this mean? Were there to be no witnesses at all, for the
prosecution no less than the defense? Danton, the man in command, silenced his companions. The absence of witnesses he was
prepared to tolerate. But he reminded the President of the as-
surances he had obtained two days previously. On the grounds
of exhaustion, he had been granted the right—by the President
himself—to continue his defense speech during a subsequent session.

But Herman took a different view. He turned to the jury

and said: "Have you all the information you need?" After de-
liberating for five minutes in a nearby room, the jury came back
with an affirmative response. The President then announced that
the hearing was closed.

"*Closed?*" Danton roared. "What do you mean, closed? It
hasn't opened yet! You haven't read the statements or called any
witnesses—"

"I insist on speaking!" cried Desmoulins. "Are you going to
pass judgment on me without hearing my defense?" He had a
written speech in his hand. When Herman refused him permission to read it out, he crumpled it into a ball and hurled it at
the President in a fit of temper. His fellow prisoners were making
similar angry demonstrations. Fouquier-Tinville took advantage
of their behavior to brandish the decree at Herman and shout:
"I demand that the accused be removed from the Court!"

The President agreed, and the courtroom thereupon became
the scene of a heartrending spectacle. Fabre d'Églantine was
cursing. Hérault-Séchelles shook his fist at the Bench, Danton
hurled scornful abuse at them. Camille Desmoulins was cling-
ing desperately to his bench and struggling with three policemen,
who finally wrenched him free and bore him off, still gesticulating wildly. Blows were exchanged on all sides between court
officials and prisoners in the dock. Before he finally vanished,
Danton shouted: "My name is linked with every revolutionary
institution! The Committees, the Tribunal, the armed forces—
I was the man who made them what they are! Now, it seems,
I am to die for them. Is this the record of a moderate or a conspirator?"

While the sixteen unfortunate prisoners were descending the
staircase to the Conciergerie, the seven jurors retired to consider
their verdict. Yet, extraordinary as it may seem, those bloodthirsty creatures still hesitated. The jury room was on the top
floor of the building, next to the refreshment room. As the seven
men came through the latter, David was sitting there over a
drink. Hearing one of them express some doubt as to Danton's
guilt, the painter exclaimed: "What do you mean, not guilty?
Has he not already been condemned at the bar of public opinion? What are you waiting for? Only cowards could behave in
such a manner!"

Yet the discussion lasted a very long time. In order to speed it up, Herman and Fouquier-Tinville went along to add the weight of their cynicism to the proceedings. One of the jurors began to moan about the difficulty he found in making up his mind. At this point Souberbielle is supposed to have asked him: "Which of the two, Robespierre or Danton, is more essential to the Republic?" Now Souberbielle was an old friend of Danton's: it is hard to tell whether he had gone over to the other side or genuinely hoped that his fellow juror would opt for Danton. But the juror replied: "The more essential of the two is Robespierre." "In that case," Souberbielle said, with an effort, "we must send Danton to the guillotine."

At this point two members of the Committee of General Security, Amar and Vadier, arrived and joined the deliberations behind closed doors. Ten minutes later there was a clatter of footsteps descending the stairs. As a clerk reported afterward, "the jurors came down from the refreshment room looking quite frenetic and no longer bothering to conceal their bloodthirsty delight. Trinchard, the joiner, was waving his arms about and saying, 'The scoundrels are done for now!' while David and the rest kept repeating, 'At last we've got them where we want them!'"

What in fact had happened was that the emissaries from the Committee of General Security had produced a letter found in Danton's desk during the search carried out on 11 Germinal. Did it prove his guilt? The jurors certainly thought so; and the Tribunal convicted them on the mere sight of this document—which was not, however, made available to the defense.

Later it was thought that the letter must have been a forgery, or some old note sketching a plan for Marie-Antoinette's escape—Danton had certainly wanted to save her. But in the dossier of the case (still on view today in the National Archives) there is included a letter, impounded from Danton's apartment on 11 Germinal, which all the evidence tends to identify as the one that sent him to the scaffold. It came from the Foreign Office in London and was addressed to M. Perregaux, that Swiss banker whom we have met once already, bringing Beaumarchais and Danton together when the dramatist had a stock of firearms to dispose of. At this period Perregaux styled himself "banker to

the Committee of Public Safety." Why a note addressed to the
financier in the rue du Mont-Blanc should end up in Danton's
desk is no more baffling than the general tenor of the note itself:

> Whitehall, Friday the 13th
>
> The latest lot of information you sent us is very satis-
> factory and has given 12 really heartfelt gratification. We
> want you to continue your efforts, and ask that you advance
> 3000 *livres* to M.C.D., 12,000 to W.T., and 100 to De M.
> for the vital services they have rendered us in fanning the
> flames and pushing the Jacobins into such exaggerated dem-
> onstrations of fury. We hope that, thanks to your efforts
> and those of other persons whom we are sending you soon,
> the old 7 will soon be re-established—or at least that the
> present O will last for some years yet. Staley brought us your
> last dispatch safely. We have decided to accept C.D.'s de-
> mands. Would you kindly advance him 18,000 *livres,* and
> be good enough to help him discover the channels through
> which the money can be distributed with most chance of
> success. We have much heavy pressure of work here at the
> Ministry today, and in the circumstances I am obliged to
> sign this letter myself on behalf of S——e.

Though this communication is dated Friday the 13th, it indicates neither the month nor the year. It proves that Perregaux
was working as a link man between the Intelligence Service
(S——e) and those Frenchmen whose task was to aggravate the
Revolution's troubles and mistakes, in the hope of turning public opinion against the new régime. What names are concealed
behind the various numbers and initials—12, M.C.D., C.D.,
W.T., De M., "the old 7," and "the present O"? At first glance,
the initials C.D. and M.C.D. suggest Camille Desmoulins—
the former simply omitting the polite form of address—while
W.T. would be Westermann, and O, Orléans. But this is no
more than pure guesswork.

Still, Perregaux must have entrusted this letter to Danton,
since it was found in the latter's possession. Therefore it concerned him directly. At the time of the search, April 1, Perregaux was resting in Switzerland. His wife had died on January
22, and he had retired, grief-stricken, to his native land. He was
not to return until after the events of 9 Thermidor, and the
police could not therefore interrogate him. Also, he was secretly

playing a double game. The Committee had asked him to take advantage of his trip into neutral Switzerland to buy arms there. Thus for reasons of State, in this case the secret obligations of national defense, the Tribunal was unable to allow the Foreign Office letter any publicity.

Nevertheless it certainly enlightened the jury about the activities of Danton's group. They acquitted Lhuillier, but condemned the remaining fifteen defendants to death. The President did not dare recall them to hear the sentence read out. Both Herman and Fouquier-Tinville were afraid that their cries might spark off a mass public rising.

The comedy was over. The drama was about to begin.

As they waited in the outer office of the Conciergerie, the fifteen condemned men no longer nursed any illusions about their fate. Through the wooden grille that divided the room they could see Sanson and his assistants. It was 16 Germinal (April 6), and pale spring sunshine flooded the Cour du Mai, where a crowd had assembled around the three tumbrels. Little light penetrated the room where Saint-Just's victims sat waiting for the end. When Judge Ducray came to read them the sentence of the Court, Danton interrupted him with the following apostrophe: "I don't give a —— for your judgment; I don't want to hear it. It is posterity that will judge us both—blazoning my name in the Panthéon, and abandoning yours to public obloquy!"

Ducray, quite unperturbed, continued to read the sentence. Danton, more garrulous than ever, kept on talking at the same time, so that his companions heard only fragments of the verdict.

Then, one after the other, they each had to sit on the stool which so many illustrious victims had occupied before them, and undergo the ordeal known as the *toilette du condamné*. On this stool, its edges rounded and worn by much use, Marie-Antoinette had spread her tattered skirts, stained here and there with traces of the hemorrhages she had suffered. On this stool Mme. Du Barry, screaming and gesticulating, rested the buttocks that a king's hand had lately caressed. On this stool Mme. Roland displayed her courage, and Charlotte Corday her unshakable faith in the righteousness of her crime. Danton and his companions now underwent the same experience as these four women (so different in their lives, united only by the manner of their death), the same as the Girondists, who sang the "Marseillaise" as they mounted the scaffold, the same as the sniveling and cowardly Hébert: they were one with all the martyrs and heroes of liberty. Sanson's assistant tore their shirts open at the collar, bound their hands behind them, and cut off all the hair that grew over their necks. In this way, with the chill steel of the scissors, they had a kind of foretaste of the guillotine. Each victim would punctuate the operation with curses, boasts, or groans, according to his character.

Finally the master executioner gave the fateful order to move off. The fifteen condemned men were escorted out into the courtyard and hoisted up into the three tumbrels on ladders. As they jolted along over the Paris cobbles, the famous last words began to blazon themselves on the scroll of legend once more. There was Desmoulins's "Lucile my darling, my little son —what will become of you both?" He was also responsible for a *mot* by Hérault-Séchelles, who, seeing that Desmoulins was more shaken by sobs than by the jolting cart said: "Let us at least try to die with dignity." Fabre d'Églantine told Danton: "I shall die without finishing my verse play, *The Maltese Orange*." To which Danton replied: "Verses, indeed! A week from now you'll have made millions of them!"

That laugh of Danton's—huge, forced, nervous, a kind of dominating hilarity—drowned all the rest: Desmoulins's pleas for mercy, Basire's protestations, Westermann's barrack-room oaths; the Latin prayers of d'Espagnac, recalling his days in the priesthood; the Hebrew litanies intoned by the Frey brothers, who dredged them up from their distant childhood and had no idea what they meant; the harrowing screams of Chabot, the ex-Capuchin, who had managed to take arsenic in the Conciergerie (he fainted after a while and was hoisted on to the scaffold in a coma)—through the buzz of the throng and his companions' mingled cries Danton's laugh rang like a fanfare, a clash of cymbals.

All along the route—Pont-au-Change, Quai de la Mégisserie, rue de la Monnaie, rue Honoré, rue Nationale—vast crowds watched as tumbrels, mounted police, executioners, and condemned men moved past in slow procession. Many witnesses afterward testified that it was like the funeral of liberty. There was little noise from the spectators, no cries of approval or protestation. In the packed windows sorrow and fear met and mingled.

As they passed the Café du Parnasse, the scene of his first love affair, Danton's face saddened, and the executioner heard him murmur: "Gabrielle—" Farther, much farther on, near the end of the interminable rue Honoré, they came to the house owned by Duplay, the Incorruptible's landlord. This evoked a new, and oracular, *mot historique:* "Robespierre, you will follow me!" But the rest of the prophecy—"Your house will be razed to the ground, and men will sow salt were it stood!"—is less accurate: in fact, the building still survives.

One man who secretly followed the procession, according to tradition, was Père de Kéravenen, the priest who absolved Danton the night before his marriage and gave the union his secret blessing. At Louise's request, he walked along in the crowd, wearing red bonnet and carmagnole and silently reciting the prayers for the dying.

About half past five the cortege reached the Place de la Révolution. Here the crowds seemed more nervous. The so-called *lécheuses de la guillotine,* those terrible viragoes who were paid by the Committee of General Security to sit applauding around the scaffold, infected the close-packed mob with their own frenzy. Normally, after every decapitation, the crowd shouted, "Long live the Republic!" When he saw these Furies, and the men pressing all about them, Danton threw off another memorable remark: "Stupid clods! They'll shout 'Long live the Republic!' when the Republic no longer has a head!"

There were fifteen necks to be sliced through; the knife had to be got into position fifteen times. The whole operation took two minutes, making half an hour in all—but a century for each of the fifteen waiting his turn at the foot of the scaffold.

Since the execution of the Girondists, Fouquier-Tinville had been responsible for deciding the order of execution, which he then passed on to Sanson. That day's list began with Hérault-Séchelles and kept Danton till last of all. Since their hands were tied behind their backs, the two men tried to touch each other's cheeks with their lips. One of the executioner's underlings separated them, so roughly that Danton exclaimed: "Fool! Do you think you can stop our heads from kissing in the basket?" This particular *mot historique* is of somewhat doubtful authenticity, since the "basket," so amply described by generations of historians, was in fact a leather bag.

So for half an hour the fallen demagogue stood and watched while his fourteen companions were beheaded. Each of them, before he died, slipped a little (as did his executioners) in the slowly coagulating pool of blood which now lay on the planking of the scaffold. Then he would be stretched out on the block of the guillotine, and Sanson would cry, "Next!" Danton observed every move of his friends' beheading without a flicker of weakness: it was as though he were inoculating himself against panic. When his own turn came at last, the executioners heard him murmur: "I shall never see you again, my darling—" Then, steeling himself, he whispered: "Come, Danton: no weakness!"—and tossed posterity his last *mot historique:* "Sanson, you will display my head to the people; it is worth your trouble!"

Parisians who live near the Parc Monceau perhaps do not realize that they sleep every night in company with the ghosts of Danton, Desmoulins, Fabre d'Églantine, and their friends. On this site, in 1794, stood the little cemetery of Les Errancis; and it was here, on the evening of April 6, that their bloody heads and truncated bodies were buried—to be joined, a week later, by the similarly decapitated remains of Msgr. Gobel, General Dillon, Lucile Desmoulins, and—tragic juxtaposition—the widow of Père Duchesne, whom Danton and Desmoulins had helped Robespierre to strike down a few days before their own downfall.

Time finally extinguished the last echoes of this multiple tragedy. Paris spread out until it embraced the Plaine Monceau, which, despoiled of its fields and meadows and cemetery, became one of the capital's smartest districts. Architects raised large apartment blocks on the site where the bones of the Republic's founders, dissolved by the quicklime which was scattered over them, formed a noble humus with the earth in which they lay. So the bodies of Danton and his friends were buried, to be followed four months later, in the same place, by those of Robespierre, Saint-Just, Couthon, and their accomplices. All bear stark witness to the bloody fate that befalls all revolutionaries, ever the victims of the revolutions they have made.

And what became of Louise, Danton's child wife, left a widow at sixteen? It will suffice to glance back at the Prologue to recall the future that lay in store for the charming and delectable creature, now so suddenly prostrate with grief, who had been Danton's final love.